Introduction

Congratulations for finding this book and _ _ _
copy. I will begin this introduction with the following
disclaimer that this book is a warning but also a message of
love to a dying world. Please bear this in mind as you study
its pages, because I consider most humans to be loving and
kind with dreams of their own for their future and may be
unaware of other events taking place around them that will
eventually have an impact on earth's inhabitants. This book
is not designed as an attack on anyone's belief systems, it is
an effort to share vital information that may well surprise
the reader, but more importantly it is to establish the
evidence which should enable one to make an informed
choice. You may be wondering about the title of this book,
what is the connection between Covid-19, Climate Change
and The Great Reset? Who are the players that may be
using Covid-19 and climate change to bring about The
Great Reset and why? How long have the players been
working at their plan? What's next if "The Great Reset"
occurs? What you need to be aware of is that on many
occasions what you see in the media is quite often not what
it seems. Ask yourself the question, is there more to what
you already know? How deep below the surface have you
dug to check if what you have been told or seen is what it
actually is? Does what I have seen or read make logical
sense? I must warn that some of the content of this book
could be traumatic to read. I also believe that most of us
humans have the best of intentions and do not go out of our
way to get deceived. When you discover truth, what will
you do with it? Embrace it and live by it or ignore it?

If only one person understands from this book what is
really going on in the world, then my many years of
research and observation will have been well worth the
effort.

You may have found this book through searching because of its title, or parts of its title, or it has been recommended to you by a friend, work colleague, or relative.

By whatever means you arrived here, do continue to read on. You are about to embark on an amazing and perhaps surprising journey.

You will unearth the truth about, Climate change the Vatican and an Impending and stupendous global financial collapse and reset that most of earth's inhabitants are blissfully unaware of. Yes, many of us may have experienced the "Global Financial Crisis - GFC" of the 80's, many of us will have not even been born yet, but are we aware of the Impending global financial collapse, why it is inevitable and who is behind it? You will be astonished. You will need to complete the reading and study of the contents of this book to understand.

You will be brought through various stages of history, through various historical and contemporary writers and through the pages of the world's best-selling book of all time. The very first book ever printed in Europe on the Guttenberg Press.

You will find within these pages secrets to two great mysteries, The Mystery of Godliness and The Mystery of Iniquity. They have been on a collision course for Millennia and are about to arrive at their ultimate showdown. This showdown will affect everyone on planet earth when it happens. The rumblings of it are all around us right now. There will be a winner. Which side do you want to be on? Which side will you be on? The truth will help you decide.

Quoting from a famous deceased Jesuit writer, Malachi

Martin:

"Willing or not, ready or not, we are all involved in an all-out, no-holds-barred, global competition. Most of us are not competitors, however. We are the stakes. For the competition is about who will establish the first one-world system of government that has ever existed in the society of nations. It is about who will hold and wield the dual power and authority and control over each of us as individuals and over all of us together as a community; over the entire six billion people expected by demographers to inhabit the earth by early in the third millennium.

The competition is all-out because, now that it has started, there is no way it can be reversed or called off. No holds are barred because, once the competition has been decided, the world and all that's in it-our way of life as individuals and as citizens of the nations; our families and our jobs; our trade and commerce and money; our educational systems and our religions and our cultures; even the badges of our national identity, which most of us have always taken for granted – all will have been powerfully and radically altered forever. No one can be exempted from its effects. No sector of our lives will remain untouched." Keys of this blood pg. 15

The beginning of the third millennium being referred to by Malachi Martin is the year 2000, in 2020 we are 20 years on from Malachi Martin's confirmation of his account of what is in progress.

The very first printed book in Europe, the Holy Bible, will be describing what has been happening over the past few millennia in the spiritual realm and how those events have affected and are affecting the literal world. Many may ask, is there a Spiritual Realm. There most certainly is. Where

3

do "ghosts" come from? How real are séances and the many other activities that are directly linked to the spiritual realm? Witches and wizards, sound familiar? The information shared is a solemn warning to our world about what is about to happen within a very short space of time with blinding force. All of earth's inhabitants need to know and understand the real issues that will affect us all. What you are about to read may be confronting to your established belief systems, but please bear with me as you examine **all** of its pages.

Consider this logically. As the world is not the way it was meant to be, then something must have gone wrong. What went wrong and how will we know? Our current state of affairs began with deception and therefore will continue in deception, but in the end the truth will vanquish the error. We are in a war in the spiritual realm, a spiritual realm that is having a direct influence in our literal realm. How will we determine how that spiritual realm has and is manifesting itself? Where is it hidden and how do we escape?

I will paraphrase the words of Jesus found in the last book of the Bible; yes, the book that contains the information on the two mysteries. Revelation (the Revealing - This in itself should spark your curiosity). The same Jesus that history proves was here (BC, AD?), the same Jesus who died and resurrected, the same Jesus that promised he would return to take those that believe in Him to where He is and the same Jesus that in His word told us what to expect before He returns. This revealing is to guide us, to let us know we are on the right track. Jesus wants to restore this planet and its inhabitants to His original plan, but to do that He needs to remove the disease of disobedience and rebellion from His universe that is rampant on this planet. When Jesus created human beings, He wanted beings that He could

4

communicate with on an intelligent and rational level, this meant freedom of choice and inherent in that is the danger of doing differently to what is in our best interest and this is where a fallen angel came in.

"The Revelation of Jesus Christ, which God gave unto him, to show unto his servants **things which must shortly come to pass**; *(emphasis mine)* and he sent and signified [it] by his angel unto his servant John:

Who bare record of the word of God, and of the testimony of Jesus Christ, and of all things that he saw. Blessed [is] he that readeth, and they that hear the words of this prophecy, and keep those things which are written therein: for the time [is] at hand." Revelation 1:1-3

Revelation and other Bible books describe events that "must shortly come to pass" – <u>That will happen, **not might happen, but will happen**</u>.

We are living in very solemn, dangerous and confusing times. Society is seemingly falling apart in every sphere. What is going on in our world? Our generation is heavily pregnant with thoughts and fears of the end of the world and we are reminded of this often through movies released in cinemas and other media. Earthquakes, storms, floods, extreme heat and cold weather events are becoming more violent and pronounced. Crime, mass shootings in schools and shopping centres etc, terrorism, wars, famines, diseases like never before. Mankind seems to be running helter-skelter to develop A.I. robotics, slaughter-bot drones, etc. where will this all lead?

Entering the scene in this great drama is Covid-19 that has led to the greatest financial, domestic and international upheaval the world has ever seen. Where will it all end? I will dedicate a whole chapter to this question.

Were these developments shown to the prophets of old to occur at the end of time?

Here is an example written in the 7th century BC by a writer/prophet named Nahum: "The chariots shall rage in the streets, they shall jostle one against another in the broad ways: they shall seem like torches, they shall run like the lightnings." Motor vehicles in our day would seem to run like lightning and seem like torches, and rage in the streets, *(especially when we hear the sound of the big V8's, or tearing round the racing tracks)* and jostle one against the other in the time period the writer saw them.

Mass animal deaths of all types of creatures both on land and sea confirm something is horribly wrong with planet earth. The constant bombardment of our senses from proponents of 'Anthropogenic' *(human induced climate change, a newly invented word?)* climate change via the mass media, all forebodings of the "end" of the world. Movies abound spreading the idea that we humans are the ones who are in control and who can prevent the downward spiral to disaster. But can we, really?

We are witnessing increasing demands from the public for legislation to be enacted to combat 'climate change' but what is the real truth behind 'climate change'? You may have begun reading this book because you picked it for yourself or from a recommendation or gift from a friend, family member, neighbour or work colleague. Keep reading. There was indeed a planet wide climate change event several thousand years ago that is touched on very briefly in Appendix 7 and events are shaping up to more climate change events as we approach the doomsday scenarios that many are alluding to.

Your persuasion may be that evolution is true and God is not real; or allah, buddha, confucius, bahá'í, darwinism, hinduism, paganism, humanism etc is where you should put your confidence and even the teachings of some 'professed' Christians. I say 'professed' with some caution because I understand from God's word that He says, "And other sheep I have, which are not of this fold: Them also I must bring, and they shall hear my voice: and there shall be one fold, and one shepherd." John 10:16.

In this period before the final test, we will be judged according to what we know, but the time will come when the decision process will be in the entire global public domain. Judgment day is real, unlike the various movies that have hit the box office. So why not make the time to explore, and ask yourself this question, 'how much do I stand to lose if my established beliefs, even 'Christian' ones, have been slightly off track, or if God really exists and my denial is unfounded?

The book known as the Holy Bible that has been around for millennia, is it a work of fiction or of fact?

What if it is the Creator's manual to mankind? And if so, what information has been buried in it's pages? His Code of Conduct?

Could it be that the bible is the greatest repository of the history of this planet?

Could it have in it's pages an explanation of current events?

Could it even describe in detail what the outcome of mankind's future is?

Some of my readers may be sceptical, but the bible does indeed tell us about the future, the outcome is already written, it makes sense to know that outcome doesn't it? Continue with me on this journey of discovery. You will be glad you did. I will lay out the evidence for you to follow, all I ask is your patience and an open mind and a willingness to explore. What do you have to lose?

"We have also a more sure word of prophecy; whereunto ye do well that ye take heed, as unto a light that shineth in a dark place, until the day dawn, and the day star arise in your hearts:

"Powerful Hurricane Irma registers as multiple earthquakes. The massive tempest continues marching across the Caribbean, tripping seismometers along the way."

"But these things have I told you, that when the time shall come, ye may remember that I told you of them....." John 16:4

Knowing this first, that no prophecy of the scripture is of any private interpretation. For the prophecy came not in old time by the will of man: but holy men of God spake [as they were] moved by the Holy Ghost." 2 Peter 1:19-21.

"Now I tell you before it come, that, when it is come to pass, ye may believe that I am [he]." John 13:19

"Behold, the former things are come to pass, and new things do I declare: before they spring forth I tell you of them." Isaiah 42:9.

The holy bible described many centuries ago the events and conditions that we are now experiencing.

"Therefore shall the land mourn, and every one that dwelleth therein shall languish, with the beasts of the field, and with the fowls of heaven; yea, the fishes of the sea also shall be taken away." Hosea 4:3. This is a warning of the mass and apparently, sudden unexplainable deaths of all forms of creatures we are witnessing across the globe both on land and from the oceans.

Weather analysts describe Hurricane Maria as setting a key record for hurricane rapid intensification in the Atlantic. They could not find anywhere in the records where any other tropical cyclone grew from a tropical depression to a category 5 in two and a half days. Even further the 2017 hurricane season was described as unprecedented because when one category 5 forms in the Atlantic it is described as a notable event, but two in the same year until 2017, unthinkable.

Residents of Dominica, a caribbean Island that had never experienced a category 5 hurricane described the ferocity and noise as the sound of multiple angry demons and wild animals raging.

Monetary losses from Maria alone is estimated at $90 Billion. Katrina in 2005 was $160 Billion and over the decade between 2008 and 2018 in the USA alone, hurricane disasters have amounted to $402 billion dollars. This does not include fires, earthquakes and other storms. What about other countries? How many more of these mega disasters can the world's economy sustain?

How about 2019? America experienced a record breaking arctic weather event, Australia suffered record-breaking heat and flooding events. The flinders river in Queensland swelled to over 70 kilometres wide following unprecedented rainfall in early February. Argentina suffered an unprecedented rain event where over 6 million acres of Soya Beans were destroyed. Beira city in Mozambique was 90% damaged or destroyed with entire villages swept away as a result of Cyclone Idai in March. Again in 2019, 500,000 hectares of crops damaged, 1.85 million people affected in Mozambique, 250,000 in Zimbabwe and 870,000 in Malawi. During March 2019, USA, Extreme flooding hits the Midwest with over $1.6 Billion damages to crops. A June heatwave being described as "Hell on earth" swept large parts of Europe with some spots reaching over 45C. The list goes on and on.

An eyewall shrouded in electricity

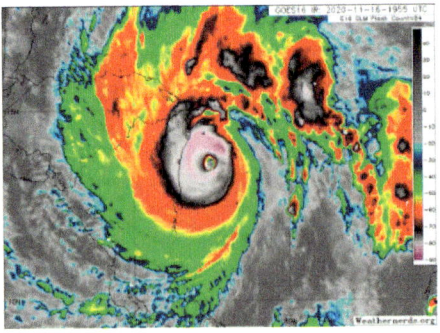

Lightning flashes about Iota's eye Monday afternoon. (Weathernerds.org)

Iota's furious eyewall was crackling with electricity Monday afternoon, a rarity in tropical storms and hurricanes. Usually, the updrafts and sideways spiral of air is insufficient to induce charge separation, which gives rise to lightning. But not with Iota. When a hurricane produces frequent lightning in its eyewall, you know it's a top-tier storm.

(Hurrican Iota striking Central America on the 16th November, 2020)

In 2020 the Atlantic witnessed it's busiest Hurricane season since records began, 30 named storms. The USA and Australia have experienced their worst fire seasons ever. Disasters of all types are increasing across the globe. The Pacific Ocean Cyclone season opened with a Category 5 Cyclone Yasa, Devastating Fiji. A category 5 so early in the season? December 2021 ended with the deadliest tornado event in US history. Will it get any better?

Dear readers, these events are not **global warming or climate change** as many of our eco scientists or media moguls and uninformed climate change activists are describing. *(One of the most vocal of groups calling themselves 'Extinction Rebellion' chanting "What do we want? Climate Justice, when do we want it? Now")* They are **global warnings** and I will explain exactly what is going on later in this book, you will understand the big picture. Here are a few examples of what was written about the current state of our planet.

"The earth mourneth and fadeth away, the world languisheth and fadeth away, the haughty people of the earth do languish. Because they have transgressed the laws, changed the ordinance, broken the everlasting covenant." Isaiah 24:4-5.

What is the covenant with humanity that has been broken? The answer is in the pages of this book.

"Lift up your eyes to the heavens, and look upon the earth beneath: for the heavens shall vanish away like smoke, and the earth shall wax old like a garment, and they that dwell therein shall die in like manner: but my salvation shall be

for ever, and my righteousness shall not be abolished."
Isaiah 51:6.

"And there shall be signs in the sun, and in the moon, and in the stars; and upon the earth distress of nations, with perplexity; the sea and the waves roaring; Men's hearts failing them for fear, and for looking after those things which are coming on the earth: for the powers of heaven shall be shaken." Luke 21:25-26.

My appeal to you as you read this book is that you not only read it but study it. We are now living in a society that seems only intent on, not offending anyone, being politically correct, live as we please, but at what price? If our only reference point of existence is evolution then we have only one place to turn to, ourselves, but if we were to allow ourselves the opportunity to consider another basis for our existence then we will be able to open our minds to a different reality.

Are we willing to pay the price of not knowing the truth, or of missing out on a huge inheritance that was made available aeons ago that will eclipse the lifestyle of the richest billionaires that have ever lived?

What is the purpose of life if it is only that we are born, become aware of our existence, grow into adults, begin our own families, some of us live extremely comfortable lives, some okay and a vast quantity just get by and still more exist in abject poverty, then die? Death was never part of the original plan. Consider the vastness of the universe, we were meant to enjoy it. That would need a lifespan of eternity wouldn't it? What went wrong?

Every cell in our bodies, muscles and tissues, even the bones we were born with will have been replaced several times over within our lifetimes, yet we still age. Why is that?

What is there after death? If all there is to life is that we eventually all die and become only memories, what was the point of our existence? To live for eternity we need something that is not on planet earth, we lost access to it, but we can regain that access.

It is said by many that there is life after death and that there are many paths to attaining that life, on the other hand we are told that there is only one way to life and that this was spoken by a being, who came from heaven, the son of God? Born in a manger (regularly celebrated at Christmas time), grew to manhood, ministered to thousands, was crucified, then resurrected, (regularly celebrated at Easter) returned to heaven, who said whilst He was here and recorded in His book, the bible, written for us, "I am the way, the truth, and the life: no man cometh unto the Father, but by me" John 14:6. He also makes it very plain in the books of Genesis 1 & 2 that He created us and all that we see, even the vast expanses of the universe. Why do we only have one version of our existence, evolution, promulgated all around our educational institutions? Have you ever paused and asked yourself, is there another view of our existence apart from evolution, the big bang etc.?

This profound and emphatic "I Am the way..." statement claims that there is only one 'pathway,' one truth. Isn't this statement worth exploring?

Jesus also told us many other things that would happen after He returned to Heaven according to scripture (Jesus is real, check Appendix 1, even the calendar shouts out the fact that Jesus was here on earth, BC and AD?), in fact there are over 300 prophecies about Him and His time

13

spent on earth, that were fulfilled only in Him, but we will be focusing on significant events about to happen in our time as found in Daniel 11.

Reading this book will take you on a very interesting and exciting journey, unearthing centuries, in fact millennia of secrets, intrigue, plots, scheming and amazing revelations. Bear the following verses in mind as we begin our journey of discovery.

"John to the seven churches which are in Asia: Grace [be] unto you, and peace, from him which is, and which was, and which is to come; and from the seven Spirits which are before his throne;

And from Jesus Christ, [who is] the faithful witness, [and] the first begotten of the dead, and the prince of the kings of the earth. Unto him that loved us, and washed us from our sins in his own blood,

And hath made us kings and priests unto God and his Father; to him [be] glory and dominion for ever and ever. Amen.

Behold, he cometh with clouds; and every eye shall see him, and they [also] which pierced him: and all kindreds of the earth shall wail because of him. Even so, Amen." Revelation 1:4-7.

What I am aiming to do with this book is to educate you about some of the things that have happened in the great history of humanity on planet earth. Things that are going on behind the scenes that you may or may not be aware of and things that are yet to happen that could cut you off from your inheritance through wrong choices. If you are sceptical about certain points, check them out for yourself to establish whether there are any grounds for what I have shared.

As we are so close to the last of the prophecies of Daniel 11 being fulfilled and because there have been many developments in society, our governments and religious organisations, the focus of this book is going to be on the last verse of Daniel 11 as follows:

"And he shall plant the tabernacles of his palace between the seas in the glorious holy mountain; yet he shall come to his end, and none shall help him." Does this verse indicate that a particular power will come to its end at Jerusalem?

We will examine the relationship if any that the following portions of scripture have with the last verse of Daniel 11, namely Revelation 13:13-14, 17:5 and II Thessalonians 2:4, 7-10.

"And he doeth great wonders, so that he maketh fire come down from heaven on the earth in the sight of men, And deceiveth them that dwell on the earth by [the means of] those miracles which he had power to do in the sight of the beast; saying to them that dwell on the earth, that they should make an image to the beast, which had the wound by a sword, and did live." Who is it that will bring fire down from heaven and why?

"And upon her forehead [was] a name written, MYSTERY, BABYLON THE GREAT, THE MOTHER OF HARLOTS AND ABOMINATIONS OF THE EARTH." Who opposeth and exalteth himself above all that is called God, or that is worshipped; so that he as God sitteth in the temple of God, showing himself that he is God." Revelation 17:5

"For the mystery of iniquity doth already work: only he who now letteth [will let], until he be taken out of the way. And then shall that Wicked be revealed, whom the Lord shall consume with the spirit of his mouth, and shall destroy with the brightness of his coming: [Even him], whose coming is after the working of Satan with all power and signs and lying wonders. And with all deceivableness of unrighteousness in them that perish; because they received not the love of the truth, that they might be saved"

For many of us the word Mystery seems quite self-explanatory. Something intriguing, hidden. We will understand how the word Mystery applies to a religious system that has its origins in antiquity, from Babel through to Ancient Babylon and beyond; and how the vast majority of this world may be inadvertently following that same system under many guises, therefore the term "Mystery."

According to Webster's third new international dictionary the term "Iniquity" is "absence of or deviation from just dealing: wrongful conduct: wickedness.

"Reveal" to make (something secret or hidden) publicly known: reveal indicates a making known or setting forth sometimes comparable to unveiling; it may apply to supernatural or inspired revelation, to simple disclosure or to indication by signs, symptoms, or similar evidence." Therefore the whole matter will be made known.

The Apostle Paul in II Thessalonians 2:7-9 makes it plain that there is something strange afoot. He called it "The Mystery of Iniquity," and he goes on to say that it would be "revealed."

We see from the above, that this hidden secret, absent of just dealing, will be revealed for what it truly is and what it stands for.

The Biblical perspective indicates who, and what is this "Mystery of Iniquity" Paul continues, "after the working of Satan, with all power and signs and lying wonders, and with all deceivableness of unrighteousness."

We must pause for a moment to assess the word "after" because clarifying the context will greatly assist in understanding the phrase "after the working of Satan."

'After' can have different meanings, for example coming up later, behind etc., or with similar behaviour. The original Hebrew word is 'Kata' and has the following meaning: "according to, toward, along." So we can understand that this mystery is working along with, according to the working of Satan, or working toward Satan.

What I am setting out to do is to trace the "working of Satan" from millennia gone by on this earth to our present age, into the future and the ramifications for all on planet earth before Jesus returns. My research has meant that it is has been necessary to quote from numerous sources to piece together a jigsaw of information to create a picture of upcoming events. I have given credit, where possible, to all authors or sources of the past and present. Many articles have had to be included for educational purposes.

What is education?

Descriptions include: Teaching, instruction, training, preparation, guidance, enlightenment, edification, development, improvement. All of these I hope will be

17

achieved when you have completed your review of this book.

You are being taken on a journey from antiquity to its ultimate climax in a spiritual battle where it is likely that we will see a supernatural event in literal Jerusalem that will then convince Spiritual Jerusalem, (which is the world), to accept a New Economic and Religious Order. It is highly likely that this system will follow an inevitable global financial collapse. Is this collapse accidental or deliberate? Hopefully by the end of this book you will be able to come to answer the question for yourself. You will get to understand that there has been a battle for our souls over the past millennia.

Jesus warned us very plainly in Matthew 24:15 "When ye therefore shall see the abomination of desolation, spoken of by Daniel the prophet, stand in the holy place, (whoso readeth, let him understand :)"

What is it that we must understand? With the help of the pages of holy writ along with pages of history that will be shared in this book I hope you, dear reader, will understand.
"And he said unto them, unto you it is given to know the mystery of the kingdom of God: but unto them that are without, all [these] things are done in parables:" Mark 4:11.

Those that are in the know behind the scenes, though they may be few, are fully aware of their plans, whilst the majority of the human race they hope to keep in darkness, until it is too late. This book, I hope, will make a big difference in enlightening its readers.

One final point in this work is that I have chosen to quote from the King James Version of scripture because many modern translations delete passages or alter the meanings of key portions of scripture that have a direct bearing on events yet to take place. If you have an incorrect reference point, then arriving at an incorrect destination is highly inevitable. May you be blessed by reading this book and because the contents are so important you need to recommend it to your family, friends and work colleagues. By the time you have read this book events will no doubt have moved ahead.

Louis King

"…..thine heart [is] lifted up, and thou hast said, I [am] a God, I sit [in] the seat of God, in the midst of the seas;…." Ezekiel 28:2.

"The great masses of the people will more easily fall victims to a big lie than to a small one." Adolf Hitler.

"A lie told often enough becomes the truth." Vladimir Lenin.

"What is truth?" Pontius Pilate.

"When you have eliminated the impossible, whatever remains, however improbable, must be the truth." – Sir Arthur Conan Doyle.

"Howbeit when he, the Spirit of truth, is come, he will guide you into all truth: for he shall not speak of himself; but whatsoever he shall hear, [that] shall he speak: and he will show you things to come." John 16:13.

"Now I tell you before it come, that, when it is come to pass, ye may believe...." John 13:19.

"And arms shall stand on his part, and they shall pollute the sanctuary of strength, and shall take away the daily…., and they shall place the abomination that maketh desolate." Daniel 11:31.

Covid-19 and the Great Reset

In this chapter I will be sharing information that you will need to consider, deeply consider and ask yourself, is what I am seeing what it is, or is there something more sinister going on? There are various schools of thought, the reality is that people are dying, I am not denying that fact. What will be the outcome? Is Covid-19 merely a new flu virus? What comparisons do we see in the following tables? The symptoms info below is from the CDC.

Flu Symptoms	People with COVID-19 have had a wide range of symptoms reported –
Influenza (flu) can cause mild to severe illness, and at times can lead to death. Flu is different from a cold. Flu usually comes on suddenly. People who have flu often feel some or all of these symptoms:	ranging from mild symptoms to severe illness. Symptoms may appear 2-14 **days after exposure to the virus**. People with these symptoms may have COVID-19:
<ul><li>Fever* or feeling feverish/chills</li><li>Cough</li><li>Sore throat</li><li>Runny or stuffy nose</li><li>Muscle or body aches</li><li>Headaches</li><li>Fatigue (tiredness)</li><li>Some people may have vomiting and diarrhea, though this is more common in children than adults.</li></ul>	<ul><li>Fever or chills</li><li>Cough</li><li>Sore throat</li><li>Congestion or runny nose</li><li>Muscle or body aches</li><li>Headache</li><li>Fatigue</li><li>Nausea or vomiting</li><li>Diarrhea</li><li>Shortness of breath or difficulty breathing</li><li>Loss of taste or smell</li></ul>
*It's important to note that not everyone with flu will have a fever.	This list does not include all possible symptoms. CDC will continue to update this list as we learn more about COVID-19.

The greatest tragedy of all this is that local and global economies are dying. Millions may lose their homes, thousands of businesses are and will cease trading * and even more millions could face starvation paving the way for a "great solution" to be presented to the masses. Is that the plan?

Covid-19 is reported as making its appearance in Wuhan, China, late 2019, since then as most of us know, it has gone global. What has been the results?

The numbers below is what we have been told by global authorities.

Last updated: October 30, 2020, 17:19 GMT

Graphs - Countries - Death Rate - Symptoms - Incubation - Transmission - News

Coronavirus Cases:
45,652,853

view by country

Deaths:
1,190,212

Recovered:
33,093,901

Let's do the maths, 45 million have allegedly contracted the virus, 33 million have so far recovered? Close to 1.2 million have allegedly died? Therefore (2.6%)? Since November 2019. I use the word allegedly because that is what the official media are reporting, other data and facts indicate otherwise. Understand this, any other media that does not fit the 'official media' narrative is being censored and deleted from all social platforms including YouTube.

We will examine a set of statistics as produced by the British Government. Take very careful not that once you are diagnosed with Covid-19 and that you die within 28 days of that diagnosis of any other cause (being run over by a bus?) your death will also be listed as a Covid-19 death. Is this honesty? Absolutely not. People may be dying 'because of' Covid due to restrictions of other healthcare services, but not of Covid?

Coronavirus in the UK

Total deaths

41,403

Total confirmed cases

322,280

Latest daily figure

6 new deaths

14-day trend

⬇ since 6 Aug

Latest daily figure

1,182 new cases

14-day trend

⬆ since 6 Aug

Figures revised to only include deaths within 28 days of a positive test result
Source: Gov.uk dashboard, 20 August 2020

BBC NEWS

Deaths in United Kingdom ▾

Deaths within 28 days of positive test by date reported   ◉ By nation   ○ UK total

Number of deaths of people who had had a positive test result for COVID-19 and died within 28 days of the first positive test. Data from the four nations are not directly comparable as methodologies and inclusion criteria vary

Daily   Cumulative   Data   About

■ Wales ■ Scotland ■ Northern Ireland ■ England

23

What are the other causes of death as of 30/10/2020?

10,801,614	Communicable disease deaths this year	[+]
407,033	Seasonal flu deaths this year	[+]
6,324,560	Deaths of children under 5 this year	[+]
35,415,501	Abortions this year	[+]
257,181	Deaths of mothers during birth this year	[+]
42,215,118	HIV/AIDS infected people	[+]
1,398,751	Deaths caused by HIV/AIDS this year	[+]
6,833,674	Deaths caused by cancer this year	[+]
816,157	Deaths caused by malaria this year	[+]
11,195,786,724	Cigarettes smoked today	[+]
4,159,514	Deaths caused by smoking this year	[+]
2,081,069	Deaths caused by alcohol this year	[+]
892,262	Suicides this year	[+]
$ 332,866,066,997	Money spent on illegal drugs this year	[+]
1,123,200	Road traffic accident fatalities this year	[+]

In the above list we can see 4 areas that have exceeded the covid-19 deaths, yet none of those have been called a pandemic and subsequently had lockdowns mandated across the globe. The top four at the time of writing?

Abortions - 35,415,501, Cancer - 6,833,674, Smoking - 4,159,514, Alcohol - 2,081,069. Interestingly the authorities have allowed off licenses, pubs and bars to remain open, but most houses of worship must remain closed? What is that all about? Why aren't our Ministers clamouring for houses of worship to remain open? Clearly the governments of our world should be locking down liquor and tobacco businesses and abortion clinics and products that are carcinogenic. Is there another agenda behind the devastating lockdowns?

Following is an example of censorship by the media of any evidence that provides information that does not fit the official narrative. An interview between Professor Norman Fenton, Professor of Risk Information management from Queen Mary, University of London and Maajid Nawaz on LBC radio on the 4th December 2021, discussing the systematic Mis-Categorisation of Covid Mortality based on Vaccine Status. Professor Fenton clearly shows that the data confirms a spike in all cause deaths within 14 days of both first and second dose jab recipients, classified as "unvaccinated" – the phrase "unvaccinated" is used implying that the jab is not effective until after 14 days?

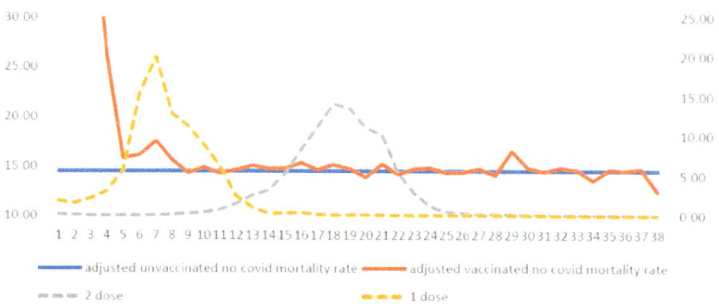

Figure 16: Adjusted non-Covid mortality rate in unvaccinated and unvaccinated versus % vaccinated for age group 60-69 (weeks 1-38, 2021)

This is again a clear example of gross dishonesty of the official narrative to then tell the public that the high death rates are amongst the unjabbed, when it is the jabbed that are dying as a direct consequence of being jabbed. The

25

interview was published on YouTube, here is the original link
https://www.youtube.com/watch?v=Jxkb2yhdLiA&t=9s
but when you click on that link this is the outcome (at the time of writing)

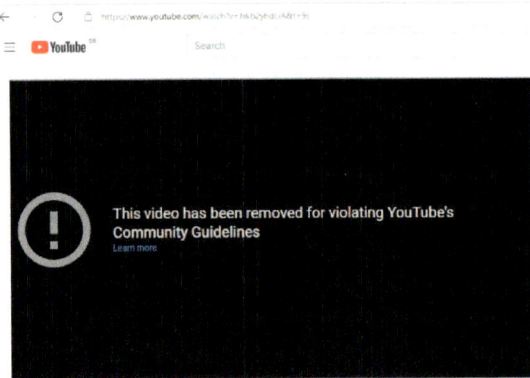

See Appendix 8 to download the full researchgate document.

What does Pope Francis have to say about Covid-19?

ROME — Pope Francis told a Spanish journalist Sunday that nature never forgives and the coronavirus pandemic is nature's cry for humans to take better care of creation. Asked by a Spanish journalist via Skype whether the COVID-19 pandemic is nature's way of taking "revenge" on humanity, the pontiff suggested that nature is calling for attention.

Pope Francis: Coronavirus Pandemic Is Nature 'Throwing a Tantrum'
https://www.newsbreak.com/news/1532776499590/pope-francis-coronavirus-pandemic-is-nature-throwing-a-tantrum

Take a good look around you and assess what you are seeing. How much of our liberties are being eroded and what are they planning? Their plans may not eventuate to their specific dates or strategies, information being shared is to provide an indication of their intentions. At some stage though, the biblical prophecies indicating a global plan will eventuate. A 'Global' health care crisis is a perfect opportunity to take control of all of us.

You may be astonished about the following news coming out of Canada, check it out for yourself. If it does not happen, then great. If it does, at least you have been warned.

CANADA GOING TYRANNICAL! 2nd "Total" Lockdown; ISOLATION CAMPS for "Refusers"

14 October 2020

Hal Turner Radio Show

"I received this from an elected member of the Canadian Government who is aghast at the Prime Minister's Office (PMO) plans for our neighbors to the north . . .This is a nightmare unfolding!

"I want to provide you some very important information. I'm a committee member within the Liberal Party of Canada. I sit within several committee groups but the information I am providing is originating from the Strategic Planning committee (which is steered by the PMO).

I need to start off by saying that I'm not happy doing this but I have to. As a Canadian and more importantly as a parent who wants a better future not only for my children but for other children as well.

The other reason I am doing this is because roughly 30% of the committee members are not pleased with the direction this will take Canada, but our opinions have been ignored and they plan on moving forward toward their goals.

They have also made it very clear that nothing will stop the planned outcomes.

The road map and aim was set out by the PMO and is as follows:

- Phase in secondary lock down restrictions on a rolling basis, starting with major metropolitan areas first and expanding outward. Expected by November 2020.

Daily new cases of COVID-19 will surge beyond capacity of testing, including increases in COVID related deaths following the same growth curves. Expected by end of November 2020.

- Complete and total secondary lock down (much stricter than the first and second rolling phase restrictions). Expected by end of December 2020 - early January 2021.

Reform and expansion of the unemployment program to be transitioned into the universal basic income program. Expected by Q1 2021.

- Projected COVID-19 mutation and/or co-infection with secondary virus (referred to as COVID-21) leading to a third wave with much higher mortality rate and higher rate of infection. Expected by February 2021.

- Daily new cases of COVID-21 hospitalizations and COVID-19 and COVID-21 related deaths will exceed medical care facilities capacity. Expected Q1 - Q2 2021.

- Enhanced lock down restrictions (referred to as Third Lock Down) will be implemented. Full travel restrictions will be imposed (including inter-province and inter-city). Expected Q2 2021.

- Transitioning of individuals into the universal basic income program. Expected mid Q2 2021.

- Projected supply chain break downs, inventory shortages, large economic instability. Expected late Q2 2021.

- Deployment of military personnel into major metropolitan areas as well as all major roadways to establish travel checkpoints. Restrict travel and movement. Provide logistical support to the area. Expected by Q3 2021.

What we were told was that in order to offset what was essentially an economic collapse on an international scale, that the federal government was going to offer Canadians a total debt relief.

This is how it works: the federal government will offer to eliminate all personal debts (mortgages, loans, credit cards, etc.) which all funding will be provided to Canada by the IMF under what will become known as the World Debt Reset program.

In exchange for acceptance of this total debt forgiveness the individual would forfeit ownership of any and all property and assets forever.

The individual would also have to agree to partake in the COVID-19 and COVID-21 vaccination schedule, which would provide the individual with unrestricted travel and unrestricted living even under a full lock down (through the use of photo identification referred to as Canada's HealthPass).

Committee members asked who would become the owner of the forfeited property and assets in that scenario and what would happen to lenders or financial institutions, we were simply told "the World Debt Reset program will handle all of the details".

Several committee members also questioned what would happen to individuals if they refused to participate in the World Debt Reset program, or the HealthPass, or the vaccination schedule, and the answer we got was very troubling. Essentially we were told it was our duty to make sure we came up with a plan to ensure that would never happen. We were told it was in the individual's best interest to participate.

When several committee members pushed relentlessly to get an answer we were told that those who refused would first live under the lock down restrictions indefinitely.

And that over a short period of time as more Canadians transitioned into the debt forgiveness program, the ones who refused to participate would be deemed a public safety risk and would be relocated into isolation facilities. Once in those facilities they would be given two options, participate in the debt forgiveness program and be released, or stay indefinitely in the isolation facility under the classification of a serious public health risk and have all their assets seized.

So as you can imagine after hearing all of this it turned into quite the heated discussion and escalated beyond anything I've ever witnessed before.

In the end it was implied by the PMO that the whole agenda will move forward no matter who agrees with it or not. That it won't just be Canada but in fact all nations will have similar roadmaps and agendas. That we need to take advantage of the situations before us to promote change on a grander scale for the betterment of everyone. The members who were opposed and ones who brought up key issues that would arise from such a thing were completely ignored. Our opinions and concerns were ignored. We were simply told to just do it.

This email communication to me from a VERIFIED member of the Canadian Parliament very much fits with something that came out on October 8, via televised proceedings in Parliament. Here a Member of Parliament asks if "the people of Ontario should prepare for Internment camps?" He was told "yes" but in a vague and ambiguous way:" Hal Turner Radio Show.

One more letter, entitled "Letter to POTUS" (President Of The United States) double tongued from a Catholic Cardinal, Carlo Maria Vigano, but nevertheless confirms what this Canadian MP has exposed and been relayed by Hal Turner. Bear in mind page 3 of his letter where he mentions *"kathèkon"* (Implying Trump) it is an example of the forked tongue of the Mystery of Iniquity we will begin to explore in the next chapter. The activities highlighted in the letter is in reality being orchestrated by the Catholic Church itself with its cohorts, including Jesuits. Here is the letter.

OPEN LETTER

TO THE PRESIDENT OF THE UNITED STATES OF AMERICA
DONALD J. TRUMP

Sunday, October 25, 2020
Solemnity of Christ the King

Mister President,

Allow me to address you at this hour in which the fate of the whole world is being threatened by a global conspiracy against God and humanity. I write to you as an Archbishop, as a Successor of the Apostles, as the former Apostolic Nuncio to the United States of America. I am writing to you in the midst of the silence of both civil and religious authorities. May you accept these words of mine as the "voice of one crying out in the desert" (John 1:23).

As I said when I wrote my letter to you in June, this historical moment sees the forces of Evil aligned in a battle without quarter against the forces of Good; forces of Evil that appear powerful and organized as they oppose the children of Light, who are disoriented and disorganized, abandoned by their temporal and spiritual leaders.

Daily we sense the attacks multiplying of those who want to destroy the very basis of society: the natural family, respect for human life, love of country, freedom of education and business. We see heads of nations and religious leaders pandering to this suicide of Western culture and its Christian soul, while the fundamental rights of citizens and believers are denied in the name of a health emergency that is revealing itself more and more fully as instrumental to the establishment of an inhuman faceless tyranny.

A global plan called the **_Great Reset_** is underway. Its architect is a global élite that wants to subdue all of humanity, imposing coercive measures with which to drastically limit individual freedoms and those of entire populations. In several nations this plan has already been approved and financed; in others it is still in an early stage. Behind the world leaders who are the accomplices and executors of this infernal project, there are unscrupulous characters who finance the World Economic Forum and Event 201, promoting their agenda.

The purpose of the Great Reset is the imposition of a health dictatorship aiming at the imposition of liberticidal measures, hidden behind tempting promises of ensuring a universal income and cancelling individual debt. The price of these concessions from the International Monetary Fund will be the renunciation of private property and adherence to a program of vaccination against Covid-19 and Covid-21 promoted by Bill Gates with the collaboration of the main pharmaceutical groups. Beyond the enormous economic interests that motivate the promoters of the Great Reset, the imposition of the vaccination will be accompanied by the requirement of a health passport and a digital ID, with the consequent contact tracing of the population of the entire world. Those who do not accept these measures will be confined in detention camps or placed under house arrest, and all their assets will be confiscated.

Mr. President, I imagine that you are already aware that in some countries the Great Reset will be activated between the end of this year and the first trimester of 2021. For this purpose, further lockdowns are planned, which will be officially justified by a supposed second and third wave of the pandemic. You are well aware of the means that have been deployed to sow panic and legitimize draconian limitations on individual liberties, artfully provoking a world-wide economic crisis. In the intentions of its architects, this crisis will serve to make the recourse of nations to the Great Reset irreversible, thereby giving the final blow to a world whose existence and very memory they want to completely cancel. But this world, Mr. President, includes people, affections, institutions, faith, culture, traditions, and ideals: people and values that do not act like automatons, who do not obey like machines, because they are endowed with a soul and a heart, because they are tied together by a spiritual bond that draws its strength from above, from that God that our adversaries want to challenge, just as Lucifer did at the beginning of time with his "non serviam."

Many people – as we well know – are annoyed by this reference to the clash between Good and Evil and the use of "apocalyptic" overtones, which according to them exasperates spirits and sharpens divisions. It is not surprising that the enemy is angered at being discovered

34

just when he believes he has reached the citadel he seeks to conquer undisturbed. What is surprising, however, is that there is no one to sound the alarm. The reaction of the deep state to those who denounce its plan is broken and incoherent, but understandable. Just when the complicity of the mainstream media had succeeded in making the transition to the New World Order almost painless and unnoticed, all sorts of deceptions, scandals and crimes are coming to light.

Until a few months ago, it was easy to smear as "conspiracy theorists" those who denounced these terrible plans, which we now see being carried out down to the smallest detail. No one, up until last February, would ever have thought that, in all of our cities, citizens would be arrested simply for wanting to walk down the street, to breathe, to want to keep their business open, to want to go to church on Sunday. Yet now it is happening all over the world, even in picture-postcard Italy that many Americans consider to be a small enchanted country, with its ancient monuments, its churches, its charming cities, its characteristic villages. And while the politicians are barricaded inside their palaces promulgating decrees like Persian satraps, businesses are failing, shops are closing, and people are prevented from living, traveling, working, and praying. The disastrous psychological consequences of this operation are already being seen, beginning with the suicides of desperate entrepreneurs and of our children, segregated from friends and classmates, told to follow their classes while sitting at home alone in front of a computer.

In Sacred Scripture, Saint Paul speaks to us of "the one who opposes" the manifestation of the mystery of iniquity, the kathèkon (2 Thessalonians 2:6-7). In the religious sphere, this obstacle to evil is the Church, and in particular the papacy; in the political sphere, it is those who impede the establishment of the New World Order.

As is now clear, the one who occupies the Chair of Peter has betrayed his role from the very beginning in order to defend and promote the globalist ideology, supporting the agenda of the deep church, who chose him from its ranks.

Mr. President, you have clearly stated that you want to defend the nation – One Nation under God, fundamental liberties, and non-negotiable values that are denied and fought against today. It is you, dear President, who are "the one who opposes" the deep state, the final assault of the children of darkness.

For this reason, it is necessary that all people of good will be persuaded of the epochal importance of the imminent election: not so much for the sake of this or that political program, but because of the general inspiration of your action that best embodies – in this particular historical context – that world, our world, which they want to cancel by means of the lockdown. Your adversary is also our adversary: it is the Enemy of the human race, He who is "a murderer from the beginning" (John 8:44).

Around you are gathered with faith and courage those who consider you the final garrison against the world dictatorship. The alternative is to vote for a person who is manipulated by the deep state, gravely compromised by scandals and corruption, who will do to the United States what Jorge Mario Bergoglio is doing to the Church, Prime Minister Conte to Italy, President Macron to France, Prime Minster Sanchez to Spain, and so on. The blackmailable nature of Joe Biden – just like that of the prelates of the Vatican's "magic circle" – will expose him to be used unscrupulously, allowing illegitimate powers to interfere in both domestic politics as well as international balances. It is obvious that those who manipulate him already have someone worse than him ready, with whom they will replace him as soon as the opportunity arises.

And yet, in the midst of this bleak picture, this apparently unstoppable advance of the "Invisible Enemy," an element of hope emerges. The adversary does not know how to love, and it does not understand that it is not enough to assure a universal income or to cancel mortgages in order to subjugate the masses and convince them to be branded like cattle. This people, which for too long has endured the abuses of a hateful and tyrannical power, is rediscovering that it has a soul; it is understanding that it is not willing to exchange its freedom for the homogenization and cancellation of its identity; it is beginning to understand the value of familial and social ties, of the bonds of faith and culture that unite honest people. This Great Reset is destined to fail because those who planned it do not understand that there are still people ready to take to the streets to defend their rights, to protect their loved ones, to give a future to their children and grandchildren. The levelling inhumanity of the globalist project will shatter miserably in the face of the firm and courageous opposition of the children of Light. The enemy has Satan on its side, He who only knows how to hate. But on our side, we have the Lord Almighty, the God of armies arrayed for battle, and the Most Holy Virgin, who will crush the head of the ancient Serpent. "If God is for us, who can be against us?" (Rom 8:31).

Mr. President, you are well aware that, in this crucial hour, the United States of America is considered the defending wall against which the war declared by the advocates of globalism has been unleashed. Place your trust in the Lord, strengthened by the words of the Apostle Paul: "I can do all things in Him who strengthens me" (Phil 4:13). To be an instrument of Divine Providence is a great responsibility, for which you will certainly receive all the graces of state that you need, since they are being fervently implored for you by the many people who support you with their prayers.

With this heavenly hope and the assurance of my prayer for you, for the First Lady, and for your collaborators, with all my heart I send you my blessing.

God bless the United States of America!

+ Carlo Maria Viganò
Tit. Archbishop of Ulpiana
Former Apostolic Nuncio to the United States of America

Viganò Corrects Himself: Not Trump - But Church - Holds Back Evil

For this present rise of the New World Order which is the City of the Devil, God placed the Church and particularly the Pope, as kathèkon, Archbishop Viganò said at the October 24 RemnantNewspaper's "Catholic Identity Conference."

The kathèkon is the one who opposes the mystery of iniquity (2 Thess 2:6-7). In an October 1 interview, Viganò had claimed that Trump, who is a nondenominational Christian, was this kathèkon.

Now, it seems to Viganò that the end times are approaching because the mystery of iniquity is spreading throughout the world and the kathèkon's opposition grows weaker. He recalls the biblical warning that the kathèkon will cease to exist when the Antichrist fully appears.

What is the truth about the matter? To answer the question I need to take you way back in history right back to where the biggest climate change event in history took place with the author of a religious system that still exists today after many thousands of years. What we are witnessing is the final stages surrounding the most intriguing series of events that are heading for a great climax and there will only be one winner.

Ω

 * Whilst millions have been suffering financial and other hardships what do we see happening? The rich are getting richer.

Synopsis - The billionaires of the world amassed fortunes in excess of $10 trillion this year"

39

"Amid all the doom and gloom, the world's richest businessmen and women continued to quietly go about doing what they do best: Get richer.

According to a study by consulting firm PwC and Swiss bank UBC, billionaires of the world — over 2,000 of them — cumulatively amassed fortunes in excess of $10 trillion this year.

One of the biggest lockdown success stories has been Eric Yuan, founder of Zoom. Ironically enough, he didn't even intend for it to be used by the general public at large. The company's bread and butter, the BBC wrote, are paid subscriptions by corporates. However, as the company's usage soared by 1,900 per cent, Yuan has added several [billion] dollars to his account."
https://bit.ly/39fmhni The Economic Times - Panache

"Billionaires see fortunes rise by 27% during the pandemic
By Simon Read Business reporter

Published 7 October 2020

Billionaires have seen their fortunes hit record highs during the pandemic, with top executives from technology and industry earning the most.
The world's richest saw their wealth climb 27.5% to $10.2trn (£7.9trn) from April to July this year, according to a report from Swiss bank UBS.

That was up from the previous peak of $8.9trn at the end of 2017 and largely due to rising global share prices.

UBS said billionaires had done "extremely well" in the Covid crisis. It also said the number of billionaires had hit a new high of 2,189, up from 2,158 in 2017.

It comes as a World Bank report on Wednesday showed **extreme poverty is set to rise this year for the first time in more than two decades** due to the pandemic.

No doubt the numbers will have changed by the time you read this book.

Rising demand

Among the billionaires, the biggest winners this year have been industrialists, whose wealth rose a staggering 44% in the three months to July.

"Industrials benefited disproportionately as markets priced in a significant economic recovery [after lockdowns around the world]," UBS said.

- China's new richest person is a bottled water tycoon
- Inventor Sir James Dyson tops UK Rich List

Tech billionaires have also had a good pandemic, seeing their wealth soar 41%. UBS said this was "due to the corona-induced demand for their goods and services" and social distancing accelerating "digital businesses [and] compressing several years' evolution into a few months".

Healthcare billionaires also benefited as the crisis put drug makers and medical device companies in the spotlight. https://bbc.in/38v2TDu

The Mystery of Iniquity

As earlier quoted "The earth mourneth and fadeth away, the haughty people... do languish. The earth also is defiled under the inhabitants thereof; because they have transgressed the laws, changed the ordinance, broken the everlasting covenant." This indicates that there is a problem with the planet in that certain laws of existence have been compromised. What laws? To understand what has been compromised we need to get as close as we can in the written records to the beginning of mankind. I will begin by examining various aspects of history related to the inception of the mystery religion. Paul states "For the mystery of iniquity doth already work: only he who now letteth [will let], until he be taken out of the way." 2 Thessalonians 2:7.

Who is this he?

Take careful note that the "mystery of iniquity" **was already working**. We need to examine the two main words in the above quote, "mystery" and "iniquity" the following are print screens from e-sword's concordance of the meaning of the words in their original language.

2Th 2:7 For^{G1063} the^{G3588} mystery^{G3466} of iniquity^{G458} doth already^{G2235} work: ^{G1754} only^{G3440} he who now letteth^{G2722 G737} will let, until^{G2193} he be taken^{G1096} out of^{G1537} the way.^{G3319}

G3466

μυστήριον
mustērion
moos-tay'-ree-on

From a derivative of μύω muō (to *shut* the mouth); a *secret* or ▢mystery▢ (through the idea of *silence* imposed by *initiation* into religious rites): - mystery.

Paul is here referring to a secret or mystery through the idea of silence imposed by initiation into religious rites, rites that were directly linked to iniquity.

ἀνομία
anomia
an-om-ee'-ah
From G459; *illegality*, that is, *violation of law* or (generally) *wickedness:* - iniquity, X transgress (-ion of) the law, unrighteousness.

What would spring to mind immediately with the word iniquity according to the dictionary would be vice, evil, sinfulness, immorality etc., however, the original version of the scriptures has Paul being more specific in describing "iniquity" as the violation/transgression of the law as follows:

Here then are two questions, what secret initiation by religious rites that existed in Paul's time that wickedly transgressed the law? This then demands the second question - what law? – The answers will become clear as we progress through the pages of this book.

Paul emphasises in II Thessalonians, "after the working of Satan, with all power and signs and lying wonders, and with all deceivableness of unrighteousness..."

That the Mystery of Iniquity commenced before our first parents were created, is evidenced by the fact that the "tree of the knowledge of good and evil" Genesis 2:17 was placed in the centre of the garden of Eden not merely as a test of obedience to God, but acknowledging also that evil had entered into God's universe. Seeing that the God of Heaven would not wish any harm on His creation, it can only be said that there was an instigator of evil to contend with.

Revelation 12:7-9 confirms that Satan was ejected from Heaven, however, it is not the purpose of this chapter to go into detail with this particular aspect, but rather to trace the commencement of the problems we as a race have been faced with since the fall of our first parents.

How did our first parents get deceived?

"Now the serpent was more subtle than any beast of the field which the LORD God had made. And he said unto the woman, Yea, hath God said, Ye shall not eat of every tree of the garden? And the woman said unto the serpent, We may eat of the fruit of the trees of the garden: But of the fruit of the tree which [is] in the midst of the garden, God hath said, Ye shall not eat of it, neither shall ye touch it, lest ye die. And the serpent said unto the woman, Ye shall not surely die: For God doth know that in the day ye eat thereof, then your eyes shall be opened, and ye shall be as gods, knowing good and evil. And when the woman saw that the tree [was] good for food, and that it [was] pleasant to the eyes, and a tree to be desired to make [one] wise, she took of the fruit thereof, and did eat, and gave also unto her husband with her; and he did eat. And the eyes of them both were opened, and they knew that they [were] naked; and they sewed fig leaves together, and made themselves aprons." Genesis 3:1-7

Adam and Eve in their unfallen state would have known how wise serpents were, but to actually hear one speak, was totally new and unexpected, and would have attracted the attention of anyone. And it is also for the fact that serpents were considered wise, why Satan chose such a medium to introduce his first deception. Any of us faced with similar circumstances, may have been fascinated with this apparent increase in abilities of this smartest of beasts of the field.

Jesus in Matthew 10:16 reminds His disciples of this. "Behold, I send you forth as sheep in the midst of wolves: be ye therefore wise as serpents, and harmless as doves."

We all know for a fact that snakes cannot hold verbal conversations with humans, it is true that animals have various means of communicating, but not as complex as is unique to the Human Race. Who then was speaking through the serpent, hiding behind the serpent in camouflage of his true identity to carry out his malicious designs? Satan himself. God communicated openly with Adam and Eve and did not need any disguises or possession of the body of another creature.

In his disguise of the snake, Satan cloaks his deception, beginning with the truth. "Yea, hath God said, ye shall not eat of every tree of the garden?"

This statement is made in such a way that it requires an answer. Eve proceeds thus "We may eat of the fruit of the trees of the garden; but of the fruit of tree which [is] in the midst of the garden, God hath said, ye shall not eat of it, neither shall ye touch it, lest ye die."

Satan having now gained her confidence comes with an outright lie, in verse 4, which would sow the first seed of doubt or curiosity in her mind about God, just as he still does in millions of human minds today.

"And the serpent said unto the woman, ye shall not surely die:"

This statement would have immediately brought questions to her mind but Satan pre-empted those questions, like any skilled tactician would by continuing with this further statement in verse 5, which we regret to say in this instance was the truth, but seeing that its' purpose was deception it amounted to a lie.

"For God doth know that in the day ye eat thereof, your eyes shall be opened, and ye shall be as gods, knowing good and evil."

Until that event, they only knew good. Evil (sin) only known by God and his angels, and Satan and his angels. Good was obedience to God's instructions, evil? = disobedience of God's instructions.

Paul declares in Romans 3:20. "... for by the law is the knowledge of sin," and in 5:12 "Wherefore, as by one man sin entered into the world, and death by sin;..."

Eve was now faced with a dilemma, she will not surely die, she will become more advanced than she was then, in that she would become like "gods." Unfortunately, she had no idea what that knowledge would bring. We, her descendants, are left with the legacy of that ill-fated decision.

There in the garden, alone from the company of her husband, Satan deceived her. She took of the fruit, ate it, and brought some to her husband, and he ate it also, verse 6. So dear readers was the first ever deception which befell the human race, needless to say, Satan's deceptions have become ever so subtle over time, some of them we hold as tradition without realising. He will continue to deceive until he will be completely unmasked, but it is important that we become aware of his devices, that we may escape them, and run to the loving arms of our creator and redeemer, Jesus Christ.

Unfortunately many will be deceived, why? Because they do not want to know the truth. 2 Thessalonians 2:10. "And with all deceivableness of unrighteousness in them that perish; because they received not the love of the truth, that they might be saved."

Therefore if we do love the truth we will not be deceived; since truth is of God, His divinely revealed words will lead us to Him, the truth.

From Eve and Adam's fall it was downhill from there. Genesis chapter 3 verses 22 to 24, we lost access to the regenerative Tree of Life.

Chapter 4 verses 1-8 describe the circumstances of the first death, by murder, a direct result of sin entering our Planet.

Chapters 6-8 cover the circumstances resulting in the great flood of Noah's day, when God repented of making man because of the extent of sin in the earth. (Verses 5&6 of chapter 6, describes humanity's condition and how God was very disappointed. "And God saw that the wickedness of man [was] great in the earth, and [that] every imagination of the thoughts of his heart [was] only evil continually. And it repented the LORD that he had made man on the earth, and it grieved Him at His heart.") Can you picture that? Every thought of man was only evil, all the time. Are you surprised to read that God experiences grief in His heart? Are we almost at the same point again where man's thoughts are evil continually?

What we are going to explore now is that soon after the flood the mystery would be set up by some of the descendants of Noah who again turned away from God, and this happened whilst Noah was still alive and the memory of the great global flood was still fresh in their minds.

Coming back to our earlier questions. To unravel a mystery we need to do some sleuthing. What are the clues?

Another of the apostles, John the Revelator in Revelation 17:5 links the word MYSTERY with BABYLON.
"And upon her forehead [was] a name written, MYSTERY, BABYLON THE GREAT, THE MOTHER OF HARLOTS AND ABOMINATIONS OF THE EARTH."

Are both these apostles referring to the same MYSTERY? We will begin with Babylon. What are the origins of the word Babylon? Notice the upper case emphasis John places on the majority of the verse. The contents of this verse must be VERY IMPORTANT.

Clue, right back to just after Noah's flood –

"And the whole earth was of one language, and of one speech.
And it came to pass, as they journeyed from the east, that they found a plain in the land of Shinar; and they dwelt there.
And they said one to another, Go to, let us make brick, and burn them thoroughly.
And they had brick for stone, and slime (bitumen [concordance H2564]) had they for mortar.
 And they said, Go to, let us build us a city and a tower, whose top [may reach] unto heaven; and let us make us a name, lest we be scattered abroad upon the face of the whole earth.
And the LORD came down to see the city and the tower, which the children of men builded.
And the LORD said, Behold, the people [is] one, and they have all one language; and this they begin to do: and now

48

nothing will be restrained from them, which they have imagined to do.

Go to, let us go down, and there confound their language, that they may not understand one another's speech.

So the LORD scattered them abroad from thence upon the face of all the earth: and they left off to build the city.

Therefore is the name of it called Babel; because the LORD did there confound the language of all the earth: and from thence did the LORD scatter them abroad upon the face of all the earth." Genesis 11:1-9.

Gen 11:9 Therefore [H5921 H3651] is the name[H8034] of it called[H7121] Babel; [H894]

Again from e-sword concordance we find that the word Babel (confusion) is linked with Babylon. Genesis 11:9 confirms that was where and when God confounded the sole language and from there those who could understand each other would have dispersed into new groupings based on understanding each new language. The important point is that Babel is identified with Babylon (confusion).

H894

כָּבֶל

bâbel

baw-bel'

From H1101; *confusion*; *Babel* (that is, Babylon), including Babylonia and the Babylonian empire: - Babel, Babylon.

Who set in motion the building of the tower and city?

"And Cush begat Nimrod: he began to be a mighty one in the earth. He was a mighty hunter before the LORD: wherefore it is said, Even as Nimrod the mighty hunter before the LORD. And the beginning of his kingdom was Babel, and Erech, and Accad, and Calneh, in the land of Shinar." Genesis 10: 8 to 10.

Where was the land of Shinar in those days? Historians will confirm that the land of Shinar is the region where modern Iraq is located.

Here it is confirmed that Nimrod is the one leading all of these developments in disobedience to God. The building of the tower is a direct display of disbelief in and rebellion against God.

God promised that He would never again destroy the earth with a flood by setting the rainbow in the clouds.

"And God spake unto Noah, and to his sons with him, saying, ...I establish my covenant with you, and with your seed after you; ....neither shall all flesh be cut off any more by the waters of a flood; neither shall there anymore be a flood to destroy the earth. And God said, This is the covenant which I make between me and you and every living creature that is with you, for perpetual generations: I do set my bow in the cloud, and it shall be for a token of a covenant between me and the earth. And it shall come to pass, when I bring a cloud over the earth, that the bow shall be seen in the cloud: And I will remember my covenant, which is between me and you and every living creature of all flesh; and the waters shall no more become a flood to destroy all flesh..." Genesis 9:8-15.

God saw it necessary to make a promise with Noah and his sons, that he would not totally destroy the earth with a flood again by placing a rainbow in the clouds. Nimrod and his follower builders of Babylon decided to build a tower that would "reach unto heaven," they obviously did not believe the promise made by God. Since they did not believe God, they had by then already apostatised.
What else did Nimrod do in his apostasy against God? He set up a false religion steeped in idolatry and secret

religious rites. A day of worship contrary to God's commands, worshipping Satan instead, that exists until today.

On examining the history of Ancient Babylon, its' religion, and the tower, commonly known as the tower of babel, the MYSTERY will be understood. We will establish how Nimrod was the leader of the mystery religion of Babel, and how the tower was central to that false religion. The nations of the earth, after having their languages confused, and then scattered over the earth, would have carried with them to their new homelands, the false Babel (Babylonian) systems of worship.

"The first city in the world after the flood (from whence the commencement of the world itself was often dated) that had towers and encompassing walls was Babylon." The two Babylons by Alexander Hislop p30.

"Primitive bricks were sun-dried, but the brick kiln was invented at an early date; bricks used in the Middle Eastern temples and ziggurats built in the 3rd Millennium BC were kiln-fired. Sun-dried bricks proved effective only in climates having low humidity and rainfall, and even then they required safeguards against dissolution. From Babylon and other such centres the ancient craft of brick making appears to have spread westward to Egypt and the Mediterranean, and eastward to India and China. The romans acquired this knowledge and improved the durability of both bricks and mortar.... Roman techniques... were passed on to the Byzantines who.... influenced the Selzig and Ottoman Turks... Inspired by the Italian example (and perhaps also by the east through the crusades), brickwork then began to appear elsewhere and came to dominate the architecture of Northern Germany, Denmark, the low countries, and parts of England." Enc. Brit. 2:510:1a.

These references confirm the biblical record of the first city, and the first instance of brick-burning (baking). History books are replete with numerous occurrences that confirm the authenticity of the scriptures, the above, of the earliest developments of modern life. Just as we find brick-buildings all around us, a legacy of ancient Babylon, so we have been handed down the Ancient Babylonian religion in its' various forms.

Among other titles of which Nimrod was worshipped was that of "Ala-Mahozine," the "god of fortifications" and "Phoroneous" the "emancipator" or "deliverer." The reasons will be understood from the following extract from The two Babylons by Alexander Hislop pp 50-52.

"The amazing extent of the worship of this man (Nimrod), indicates something very extraordinary in his character; and there is ample reason to believe, that in his own day he was an object of high popularity. Though by setting up as king, Nimrod invaded the patriarchal system, and abridged the liberties of mankind, yet he was held by many to have conferred benefits upon them that amply indemnified them for the loss of their liberties, and covered him with glory and renown.

By the time that he appeared, the wild beasts of the forest multiplying more rapidly than the human race, must have committed great depredations on the scattered and straggling populations of the earth, and must have inspired great terror into the minds of men. The danger arising to the lives of men from such a source as this, when population is scanty, is implied in the reason given by God himself for not driving out the doomed Canaanites before Israel at once, though the measure of their iniquity was full. (Exodus 23:29-30): "1 will not drive them out from before thee in one year, lest the land become desolate, and the beast of the field multiply against thee. By little and little I will drive them out from before thee, until thou be increased."

The exploits of Nimrod, therefore, in hunting down the wild beasts of the field, and ridding the world of monsters, must have gained for him the character of a pre-eminent benefactor of his race. By this means, not less than by the bands he trained, was his power acquired, when he first began to be mighty upon the earth; and in the same way, no doubt, was that power consolidated. Then, over and above, as the first great city-builder after the flood, by gathering men together in masses, and surrounding them with walls, he did still more to enable them to pass their days in security, free from the alarms to which they had been exposed in their scattered life, when no one could tell but that at any moment he might be called to engage in deadly conflict with prowling beasts, in defence of his own life and of those who were dear to him.

Within the battlements of a fortified city no such danger from savage animals was to be dreaded; and for the security afforded in this way, men no doubt looked upon themselves as greatly indebted to Nimrod. No wonder, therefore, that the name of "the mighty hunter," who was at the same time the prototype of "the god of fortifications," should have become a name of renown.

Had Nimrod gained renown only thus, it had been well. But not content with delivering men from the fear of wild beasts, he set to work also to emancipate them from that fear of the Lord which is the beginning of wisdom, and in which alone true happiness can be found. For this very

53

thing, he seems to have gained, as one of the titles by which men delighted to honour him, that of the "Emancipator," or "Deliverer." The other of "Phoroneus."

The era of Phoroneus is exactly the era of Nimrod. He lived about the time when men had used one speech, when the confusion of tongues began, and when mankind was scattered abroad. He is said to have been the first that gathered mankind into communities, the first of mortals that reigned, and the first that offered idolatrous sacrifices. This character can agree with none but that of Nimrod.

Now the name given to him in connection with his "gathering men together," and offering idolatrous sacrifice, is very significant. Phoroneus, in one of its meanings, and that one of the most natural, signifies the "Apostate." That name had very likely been given him by the uninfected portion of the sons of Noah. But that name had also another meaning, that is, "to set free;" and therefore his own adherents adopted it, and glorified the great "Apostate" from the primeval faith though he was the first that abridged the liberties of mankind, as the grand "Emancipator!" and hence, in one form or other, this title was handed down to his deified successors as a title of honour.

All tradition from the earliest times bears testimony to the apostasy of Nimrod, and to his success in leading men away from the patriarchal faith, and delivering their minds from that awe of God and fear of the judgments of heaven that must have rested on them while yet the memory of the flood was recent. And according to all the principles of depraved human nature, this too, no doubt, was one grand element in his fame; for men will readily rally round anyone who can give the least appearance of plausibility to any doctrine which will teach that they can be assured of happiness and heaven at last, though their hearts and natures are unchanged, and though they live without God in the world."

From the information supplied, we can see, that Nimrod being the instigator, by his various means, turned men away from the true God, and under the title of "Baal-Aberin;. "Lord of the mighty ones," he became deified, and so other kings who followed in his rule, would become the deified leaders of the kingdom, covering both civil and religious matters; if therefore they were no longer serving the primeval God of Noah, the true God, who then were they serving except Satan. As the scriptures made a specific point of mentioning that they were building the tower to reach unto heaven, a symbol of their defiance of God, it must also have been central to their worship of Satan.

That this was the case we will examine historical records of the purpose of its construction. In the Britannica Vol. 1. 770:3b there is a description of Babylon and the Tower of Babel.

"Nebuchadnezzar's' Babylon was the largest city in the world, (during that era) covering 2,500 acres (1,000 hectares). The Euphrates which has since shifted its course, flowed through it, the older part of the city being on the east bank. There the central figure was Esagila, the great temple of Marduk, with its associated Ziggurat (a tower built in several stages) Etemenanki. The latter, popularly known as the tower of Babel, had a base 100 yds on a side, and its seven stages, the uppermost a temple in blue glaze, reached to a height of 300 feet (91 metres).

(You may be thinking, wait a minute, 300 feet is not very high. The answer is found in Genesis 11:4 "And they said, Go to, let us build us a city and a tower, whose top [may reach] unto heaven; and let us make us a name,...." [may reach] indicates might reach or planned to reach, and that they were wanting to "make a name" for themselves in disobedience to God. Verse 8 also states "....and they left off to build the city...." Which confirms they did not complete what they set out to achieve. Another example of reaching to heaven is found in Deuteronomy 1:28 "Whither shall we go up? Our brethren have discouraged our heart, saying, the people [is] greater and taller than we; the cities [are] great and walled up to heaven; and moreover we have seen the sons of the Anakims there." The walls did not actually reach up to heaven, they were so high they appeared as if to heaven. Even in our modern times, when we are amongst inner city office blocks and some residential towers, we can stand at the bottom of them, looking up they appear as reaching up to heaven.

Who was Marduk that had a temple "Esagila"? And also a temple on top of the tower of Babel?

"Marduk, in Mesopotamian religion, the chief god of the city of Babylon and the national god of Babylonia: as such he was eventually called simply, Bel, or Lord. Originally he seems to have been a god of thunderstorms. A poem known as Enuma Elish and dating from the reign of Nebuchednezzar 1 (1124-03 BC), relates Marduks' rise to such pre-eminence that he was the god of 50 names, each one, that of a deity or of a divine attribute. After conquering the monster of primeval chaos, Tiamat, he became "Lord of the gods of heaven and earth." All nature, including man, owed its existence to him; the destiny of kingdoms and subjects was in his hands.

Marduks' chief temples at Babylon were the Esagila and the Ettemenanki, a Ziggurat with a shrine of Marduk on the top. In Esagila the poem "Enuma Elish" was recited every year at the New Year festival.

Marduks' star was Jupiter, and his sacred animals were horses, dogs, and especially the so-called dragon with forked tongue, representations of which adorn his city's' walls. On the oldest monuments Marduk is represented holding a triangular spade or hoe, interpreted as an emblem of fertility and vegetation. He is also pictured walking, or in his war chariot. Typically, his tunic is adorned with stars; in his hand is a sceptre, and he carries a bow, spear, net, or thunderbolt. Kings of Assyria and Persia also honoured Marduk and Zarpanit on inscriptions and rebuilt many of their temples." Britannica vol. 7:831:1a.

"The dwellers on the plain of Shinar established their kingdom for self-exaltation, not for the glory of God. Had they succeeded, a mighty power would have borne sway, banishing righteousness and inaugurating a new religion. The world would have been demoralized. . . . But God never leaves the world without witnesses for Him. At this time there were men who humbled themselves before God and cried unto Him. "O God," they pleaded, "interpose between Thy cause, and the plans and methods of men." When the tower had been partially completed, a portion of it was occupied as a dwelling place for the builders; other apartments, splendidly furnished and adorned, were devoted to their idols. . . ." Conflict and Courage p.43 E. G. White

"They left off to build. The tower that was to rise to heaven was never completed. However, it is evident from the bible and from history that the local population subsequently completed the work of building the city." SDA Bible Commentary, Vol. 1, p. 286.

We will be examining the construction and usage of those temples later, which may be obvious, however, an examination of what transpired in them is also important in understanding the mystery. We will at this time deal with Marduks' creation epic, "Enuma Elish," which parallels some aspects of the creation as related in Genesis, leaving the only conclusion that Marduk represents Satan himself. This "Enuma Elish had to be recited every new year in the temple. The poem has been termed a myth, myths usually tell of unbelievable things in a deliberate manner, so that a myth can mean both an untrue story, and a story containing religious truth. With these points in mind, coupled with the facts that Babylon, the tower and the mystery religion were very real, we must take Marduks' poem as a serious threat to the truth, and blasphemy against God.

"..Enuma Elish, which may be dated to the later part of the 1st dynasty (c.1894-1595 BC). Babylon: archenemy then was the sealand, which controlled Nippur and the country south of it - the ancestral country of Sumerian civilisation. This lends political point to the battle of Marduk (thunder and lightning deity), the god of Babylon, with the sea, Tiamat..." it also tells "how in the beginning there was nothing but Apsu, the sweet waters underground, and Tiamat, the sea, mingling their waters together." Enc.Brit. 24:81:lb.

Genesis 1:2,"And darkness was upon the face of the deep."

Exodus 20:4, "Thou shalt not make unto thee any graven image, or any likeness of anything that is in heaven above, or that is in the earth beneath, or that is in the water under the earth."

"The gods stood for energy and activity, and thus differed markedly from Apsu and Tiamat, who stood for rest and inertia." The story unfolds until a battle ensues between the gods. Marduk the young god proved willing to fight the other gods, but demanded absolute authority. He was to be supreme. (The scriptural account of Satan's ambitions is to be found in Isaiah 14:13-14. "I will ascend into heaven, I will exalt my throne above the stars of God... I will be like The Most High.")

"In the ensuing encounter with Tiamat's forces, Kingu and his forces lost heart when they saw Marduk, only Tiamat stood her ground... Marduk angrily denounced her and her older generation... Marduk loosed the winds against her, pierced her heart with an arrow, and killed her. Kingu and the god who had sided with her he took captive.

Having thus won a lasting victory for his suzerain, king Anshar, he gave thought to what he might do further. Cleaving the carcass of Tiamat, he raised half of her to form heaven, ordered the constellations, the calendar, the movements of sun and moon, and, keeping control of atmospheric phenomena for himself, made the earth out of the other half of her, arranging its mountains and rivers."

In Genesis 1:6, God created the heavens, separating the waters, verse 9, He caused the dry land to appear, calling it earth, verses 14-18, He created the sun, moon and stars. Why has Satan had to duplicate the creation story? He does this because he requires homage which is due only to God, and he does not have any original achievements, except disobedience. Notice also how the story relates removal of the older generation?

"Having organised the various administrative tasks, he put their supervision in Ea's hands: to Anu he gave the tablets of fate he had taken from Kingu."

Does this sound a lot like the tables of stone handed to Moses by God, our eternal, living, Creator, on the mountain? [And the LORD said unto Moses, Come up to me into the mount, and be there: and I will give thee tables of stone, and a law, and commandments which I have written; that thou mayest teach them Exodus 24:12] we continue –

"His prisoners he paraded in triumphal procession before his fathers he then bathed, dressed and seated himself on his throne, with the spear "security and obedience," named from his mandate at his side. The old fear and urgent need for protection was gone, but in its' stead had come a promise held out by Marduk's organisational powers; so when the gods reaffirmed their allegiance to him as king they used a new formula: "benefits and obedience." From then on Marduk would take care of their sanctuaries and they, in turn, would obey him.

Marduk then announced his intention of building a city for himself, Babylon, with room for the gods when they come there for assembly; and his fathers suggested that they move there themselves to be with him and help in the administration of the world he had created."

From this it is clear that Satan's seat was in Babylon, and that his angels would also dwell with him there giving him adoration alongside with apostate humanity. It can be observed also how he wanted his true creators to be under him, as in the legend, his fathers came down to earth to help him in his administration.

"Next, he pardoned the gods who had sided with Tiamat and had been captured, charging them with the building tasks. Grateful for their lives, they prostrated themselves before him, hailed him as king, and promised to do the building. Pleased with their willingness, Marduk magnanimously wanted to relieve them even from this chore and planned to create man to do the toil for them."

Here again is further evidence that man should give him (Satan) homage as their creator.

"At the advice of his father Ea, he had them indict Kingu as instigator of the rebellion, Kingu was duly sentenced and executed, and from his blood Ea created man."

Other references state that Kingu's blood was mixed with soil. This would then render man part-human, part-divine, therefore when we die the fleshly body rots away, and since our divine part cannot die a natural death, we would then of course be subject to reincarnation etc. Sounds familiar?

"Then Marduk divided the gods into a celestial and a terrestrial group, assigned them their tasks in the cosmos and allotted them their stipends. Thus freed from all burdens, the gods wanted to show gratitude to Marduk and as a token they took of their own free will, for one last time, spade in hand to build Babylon and Marduk's temple Esagila. In the new temple the gods then assembled, distributed the celestial and terrestrial offices, the "great gods" went into session and permanently appointed the "seven gods of destinies" or better "of the decrees," who would formulate in final form the decrees enacted by the assembly."

Seven gods who decree –

Four primary: Anu, Enlil, Enki, Ninhursag.

Three sky gods: Inanna/Ishtar, Nanna/Sin, Utu/Shamash.

There in the new temple; (although it was in reality built by man, but because the myth reached its height in later generations, it was possible that they would accept that account as genuine); Satan seated himself.

"And after the gods had prostrated themselves before him they bound themselves by oath - touching their throats with oil and water - and formally gave him kingship, appointing him permanently lord of the gods of heaven and earth."

Does this remind you of Isiah 14 "I will be like the most high"?

"After this they solemnly named his 50 names expressive of his power and achievements. The myth ends with a plea that it be handed on from father to son and told to future rulers, that they may heed Marduk..."

This too sounds familiar to another set of verses found in the holy bible, Deuteronomy 6:5-8.

"And thou shalt love the LORD thy God with all thine heart, and with all thy soul, and with all thy might. And these words, which I command thee this day, shall be in thine heart: And thou shalt teach them diligently unto thy children, and shalt talk of them when thou sittest in thine house, and when thou walkest by the way, and when thou liest down, and when thou risest up. And thou shalt bind them for a sign upon thine hand, and they shall be as frontlets between thine eyes."

"Mesopotamian worshippers might worship in open-air sanctuaries, chapels in private houses, or small separate chapels located in the residential quarters of town; but the sacred place par excellence was the temple. Archaeology has traced the temple back to the earliest periods of settlement, ... the temple was the god's house or dwelling. In its more elaborate form, such a temple would be built on a series of irregular artificial platforms, one on top of the other; by the 3rd dynasty of Ur, near the end of the 3rd millennium, these became squared off to form a ziggurat. On the lowest of these platforms a heavy wall - first oval, later rectangular - enclosed storerooms, the temple kitchen, workshops, and other such rooms. On the highest level, approached by a stairway, were the god's living quarters... The god's place was on a podium in a niche, at the short wall farthest from the entrance..."

"The function of the temple, as of all other sacred places in Mesopotamia, was primarily to ensure the god's presence and to provide a place where he could be approached. The providing of housing, food, and service for the god achieved the first of those purposes. His presence was also assured by a suitable embodiment - the cult statue, and, for certain rites, the body of the ruler."

Notice that for certain rites the presence of a statue was required, but others required the actual body of the ruler, through whom the god would present itself? Therefore when that person or ruler was worshipped, the god himself was really the one being worshipped.

In Exodus 20:3-4, God expressly said that we should have no other gods before Him, therefore bowing to a statue or even a human being is in reality an act of homage to Satan because you will not be worshipping the true God.

"In view of the magnitude of such an establishment provided for the gods and the extent of lands belonging to them and cultivated for them - partly with temple personnel, partly by members of the community holding temple land in some form of tenure or another - it was

63

unavoidable that temples should vie in economic importance with similar large private estates or with estates belonging to the crown..." Enc. Brit. 24:82:2b-85:1c.

Observe that the temples were the places of worship par excellence, and that they vied in economic importance.

"Esagila, most important temple complex in Ancient Babylon dedicated to the god Marduk, the tutelary deity of that city. The temple area was located south of the huge Ziggurrat, Etemenanki; (meaning "House of the foundation of heaven and earth" [the current temple – more on this later - also boasts access to heaven and hell]) it measured 660 feet (200 metres) on its longest side and its three vast courtyards were surrounded by intricate chambers. The whole complex reflects centuries of building and rebuilding by the Babylonian kings, especially Nebuchadrezzar 2nd (reigned 604-562 BC). The tremendous wealth of Esagila was recorded by the Greek historian Herodotus, who is believed to have visited Babylon in the 5th century BC. Babylon was excavated in 1899 - 1917 by the Deutsche Orient Gesellschaft; few objects of value, however, were found in Esagila, which had been thoroughly plundered in antiquity." Enc.Brit.4:553:la.

Equally, the current version of the temple that has continued the mystery religion into our modern age, is by far, the wealthiest organisation on earth, eclipsing even the wealth of entire nations. This mystery religion has been accumulating wealth for millennia. Read the description given by John the Revelator.

"And I heard another voice from heaven, saying, Come out of her, my people, that ye be not partakers of her sins, and that ye receive not of her plagues. For her sins have reached unto heaven, and God hath remembered her iniquities.

Reward her even as she rewarded you, and double unto her double according to her works: in the cup which she hath filled fill to her double.

How much she hath glorified herself, and lived deliciously, so much torment and sorrow give her: for she saith in her heart, I sit a queen, and am no widow, and shall see no sorrow.

Therefore shall her plagues come in one day, death, and mourning, and famine; and she shall be utterly burned with fire: for strong [is] the Lord God who judgeth her.

And the kings of the earth, who have committed fornication and lived deliciously with her, shall bewail her, and lament for her, when they shall see the smoke of her burning, Standing afar off for the fear of her torment, saying, alas, alas that great city Babylon, that mighty city! for in one hour is thy judgment come.

And the merchants of the earth shall weep and mourn over her; for no man buyeth their merchandise any more:

The merchandise of gold, and silver, and precious stones, and of pearls, and fine linen, and purple, and silk, and scarlet, and all thyine wood, and all manner vessels of ivory, and all manner vessels of most precious wood, and of brass, and iron, and marble, and cinnamon, and odours, and ointments, and frankincense, and wine, and oil, and fine flour, and wheat, and beasts, and sheep, and horses, and chariots, and slaves, and souls of men.

And the fruits that thy soul lusted after are departed from thee, and all things which were dainty and goodly are departed from thee, and thou shalt find them no more at all.

The merchants of these things, which were made rich by her, shall stand afar off for the fear of her torment, weeping and wailing,

And saying, alas, alas, that great city, that was clothed in fine linen, and purple, and scarlet, and decked with gold, and precious stones, and pearls!

For in one hour so great riches is come to nought. And every shipmaster, and all the company in ships, and sailors, and as many as trade by sea, stood afar off,
And cried when they saw the smoke of her burning, saying, What [city is] like unto this great city!
And they cast dust on their heads, and cried, weeping and wailing, saying, Alas, alas, that great city, wherein were made rich all that had ships in the sea by reason of her costliness! for in one hour is she made desolate." Revelation 18:4-19.

This temple could not have acquired the enormous wealth that it has to this day without the cooperation of Kings and Queens, merchants and business people, bankers and corporations, billions of duped members and daughter churches. Take courage though, God recognises that He has honest souls in the mystery religion, He says, ".... come out of her my people."

"In the Ancient Mesopotamian view, gods and humans shared one world. The gods lived among men on their great estates (the temples), ruled, upheld law and order for men, and fought their wars. In general, knowing and carrying out the will of the gods was not a matter for doubt: they wanted the practice of their cult performed faultlessly, work on their estates done willingly and well,... on occasion, however, man might well be uncertain: did a god want his temple rebuilt or did he not? In all such cases, and others like them, the Mesopotamian sought direct answers from the gods through divination, and conversely the gods might take the initiative and convey specific wishes through dreams, signs, or portents" Enc. Brit. 24:82.

For the purposes of clarification, Mesopotamia is the same region as Ancient Babylonia.

Divination can be practised in various ways. Webster's defines it as follows.

"The art or practice that seeks to foresee or foretell future events or discover hidden knowledge usually by means of Augury or by making use of a physical condition of the diviner in which supernatural powers are assumed to cooperate (as in the case of a spiritualistic or crystal gazer) also an instance of this practise."

So there we have it, the temples were built specifically as the dwelling place, and place of worship of the gods, "Marduk" being the chief god of Babylon, who would present himself, as earlier discovered, or on more important occasions, he would present himself in the rulers body, therefore actually entering and taking possession of his body. From the outside therefore, those who were unaware would think they were honouring the person. Whereas those who knew, would welcome the presence of their false god. In the Two Babylons by Hislop, we find further reference to these supernatural powers or manifestations, for in order to become possessed by demons, you must depart from the true God.

"Under the title of "Zoroaster" given him after his death, by his wife "Semiramis," in order to keep her position as Priestess of the Mysteries; everything was so contrived as to wind up the minds of the novices to the highest pitch of excitement, that, after having surrendered themselves implicitly to the priests, they might be prepared to receive anything. After the candidates for initiation had passed through the confessional, and sworn the required oaths "strange and amazing objects," says Wilkinson," presented themselves. Sometimes the place they were in seemed to shake around them; sometimes it appeared bright and resplendent with light and radiant fire, and then again covered with black darkness, sometimes thunder and lightning, sometimes frightful noises and bellowings, sometimes terrible apparitions astonished the trembling spectators. Then, at last, the great god, the central object of their worship, Osiris, Tammuz, Nimrod, or Adonis was revealed to them in the way most fitted to soothe their feelings and engage their blind affections."

Even today the mystery religion still carries on the work of the confessional, and just as the Babylonian priests took it upon themselves to be the only interpreters of religion, in order to hide the mystery, so in the recent past, the modern Babylonian church (or should we say the same Babylonian church) has and will again insist on being the only true interpreters of scripture. As the initiated would see an apparition of the version of their god, in reality, it was none other than the manifestation of the devil himself.

Hislop continues "An account of such a manifestation is thus given by an ancient pagan, cautiously indeed, but yet in such a way as shows the nature of the magic secret by which such an apparent miracle was accomplished: "In a manifestation which one must not reveal... there is seen on a wall of the temple a mass of light, which appears at first at a very great distance. It is transformed, while unfolding itself, into a visage evidently divine and supernatural, of an aspect severe, but with a touch of sweetness." Two Babylons P. 67-68.

2 Corinthians 11:14, "And no marvel; for Satan himself is transformed into an angel of light."

What else happened with the ancient mystery religion?

"Shamash-Eribu, was conquered by Xerxes' son-in-law, and violent repression ensued: Babylon's fortresses were torn down, its temples pillaged, and the statue of Marduk destroyed; this latter act had great political significance: Xerxes was no longer able to take the hand of (receive the patronage of) the Babylonian god. Whereas Darius had treated Egypt and Babylonia as kingdoms personally united to the Persian Empire (though administered as satrapies), Xerxes acted with a new intransigence. Having rejected the fiction of personal union, he then abandoned the titles of king of Babylonia and king of Egypt, making himself simply "king of the Persians and the Medes."

It was probably the revolt of Babylon, although some authors say it was troubles in Bactria, to which Xerxes alluded in an inscription that proclaimed:

And among those countries (in rebellion) there was one where, previously, daevas had been worshipped, afterward, through Ahura Mazda's favour, I destroyed this sanctuary of daevas and proclaimed, "Let daevas not be worshipped!" there, where daevas had been worshipped before, I worshipped Ahura Mazda. Xerxes thus declared himself the adversary of the daevas, the ancient pre-zoroastrian gods, and doubtlessly identified the Babylonian gods with these fallen gods of the aryan religion." Enc. Brit. 12 797:3a.

Webster's explain daeva as follows: "Daeva or Deva, akin to sanskrit Deva-god - more at deity, Zoroastrianism: a maleficient supernatural being: an evil spirit: Demon."

The temples and statue of Marduk having been destroyed, the scriptures speak of the mystery continuing until it was to be revealed immediately prior to Christ's Second Advent. Where did the mystery religion go?

We will go first to Rev. 2:12-13, then refer to history books etc, for confirmation.

"And to the angel of the church in Pergamos write; these things saith he which hath the sharp sword" (Jesus Christ) "with two edges; I know thy works, and where thou dwellest, even where Satan's seat is: and thou holdest fast my name, and thou hast not denied my faith, even in those days wherein Antipas was slain among you, where Satan dwelleth"

By now the correctness of biblical history cannot be in any doubt. Where was Pergamos? And what was so significant about Pergamos that Christ would state that Satan's seat was there? As already established, temples were constructed as dwelling places for the gods, the most important temple in whatever city was dedicated to the chief god, the chief of the false gods being Satan.

"Pergamos means "height" or "elevation. "The city stood on an elevation of 1,000 feet and was built by the Aeolian Greeks about 1150 BC. The elevation was a natural defense, and the city considered impregnable. Kings sometimes deposited their treasure there for safekeeping. Lysimachus placed his fortune of $10,000,000 in this city. It was "a royal city." It was made capital of the province of Asia when Attalus 3rd, the last of the Attalid kings, bequeathed his kingdom to Rome in 133 BC.

The proconsuls who ruled there were vested with the symbol of authority the broad, double-edged sword. The supreme court of the province was also located there. Life or death awaited the prisoners who came to this court... Pergamos was the headquarters of Satan's religion... When the Persians overthrew Babylon, they gave the inhabitants of the city their freedom. But the Babylonian priests later led a revolt and were driven from the city." The defeated Chaldeans fled to Asia Minor, and fixed their central college at Pergamos, and took the palladium of Babylon, the cubic stone, with them. Here independent of state control, they carried on the rites of their religion." William B. Barker, Lares and Penates, pp232, 233.

Pergamos, therefore, became the "seat" of the Satanic system of the Babylonian "mysteries.".... Pergamos was for some time the headquarters of this mystery cult. But when the king of Pergamos bequeathed his kingdom to the Romans, this whole cult was transferred to Rome. Pergamos thus became a link between Ancient Babylon and Rome. It seemed natural then for the deification of the emperors to begin in this city.

"Pergamos was a city of temples, the most important of which was the temple of Zeus... A famous school of medicine was also located there, the emblem of which was the serpent or the caduceus twined around a pole." Unfolding the Revelation by Roy Allan Anderson pp22-25. We also find confirmation of the expulsion of the Chaldean priesthood from Babylon to Pergamos, in Hislop's Two Babylons pp240-241, and how Julius Caesar by taking on the title "Pontifex Maximus," and becoming Emperor, the supreme civil ruler of the Romans, head of state and of the Roman Religion, laid claim to the divine dignity of Attalus and his kingdom bequeathed to Rome. The connection with the transfer of the mystery religion can also be made through the principal gods of those cities.

"Marduk's star was Jupiter. Jupiter, or Iuppiter was the chief Roman god equivalent to the Greek Zeus, originally a sky-god with the attributes of thunder and the thunderbolt. Zeus became for the Greeks, their principal god by his defeat of his father Cronus (whom see). Of the sons of

71

Cronus, Hades took the lower world, Poseidon the sea, and Zeus the heavens and upper regions of the earth including mountaintops. His sanctions were thunder and lightning.... he could also assume a role of awesome majesty. Jupiter is sometimes given additional names (e.g., Jupiter Optimus Maximus). All of these gods had as parts of their attributes the thunderbolt and lightning. Marduk was frequently appealed to in incantations for healing the sick, Aesculapius, the serpent god, also worshipped as the originator of good and evil, and as the divine healer, was appealed to for the healing of the sick in the temple of Zeus at Pergamos."

"Pergamum, originally a mountain fortress, became in the long run an important continental power through the careful manoeuvring of its rulers, Philaterus and later his nephew Eumenes (ruled 263-241). Attalus 1 (ruled 241-197) took advantage of the growing weakness of the seleucid kingdom to further expand his influence. He broke the power of the Galatians in two battles before 230, adopted the title of king, and for several years (238-223) ruled over the entire seleucid territory north of the Taurus mountains.... Disturbed by the new expansionism of the seleucids; Egypt, Rhodes and Pergamum appealed to Rome for help in 200 ... A new and final stage of Roman involvement was reached when Attalus 3rd(138-133), the last in the line of the Attalids, bequeathed the kingdom of Pergamum to Rome."

What are some of the aspects of Nimrods' religion that was taken to the world with the scattering? And what key aspect of Nimrod's religion that are in use today? We will go to Enc.Brit.28:911:2b.

Ziggurats: This type of structure can be found in many parts of the world. The majority were constructed in

Ancient Mesopotamia, however, similar structures were built by the Incas, Aztecs, Hindus, Buddhists etc. Hindu and Buddhist temples are not only centres of worship, but major tourist attractions.

Places of worship and sacrifice:

"Throughout man's history, there is evidence that he worshipped at natural sites as well as at sites constructed for ritualistic purposes. In the protohistory and perhaps the prehistory of most ancient civilizations, people venerated trees, stones, bodies of water, and other natural objects, which gradually became the objects of established cults and which often were included, in some form, as aspects of later official ritual.

Initially, the objects of this frequently occurring process were sacred trees considered to be the habitats of spirits or gods, such as in Vedic, Brahmanic, and Buddhist India or pre-Islamic Arabia; sacred stones, such as fragments of meteorites, menhirs (upright stones), and rocks—such as the celebrated Ka'bah, the black stone of Mecca; flowing waters, natural lakes, and sacred and purifying rivers, such as the Ganges; crossroads and junctions, such as the tirtha (river fords and, by extension, sacred spots) in India; and other such objects or places of nature. According to Hesiod, an 8th-century-BC Greek writer, such objects of nature were venerated in the popular piety of the rustic people of Greece in his times.

The association on the same site of four natural elements (mountain, tree, stone, and water) is supposed to constitute a sacred whole (a quarternity of perfection), a sacred landscape or "geography" similar to the world of the gods. Such sites, in many civilizations, were the initial points of departure for pilgrimages or for the establishment of places of worship. In some instances the natural sacred places were gradually adapted for religious use (e.g., the oracle at Delphi, in Greece), but in others the earlier natural sites were artificially recreated by using man-made symbolic equivalents. An artificial or natural hill, such as a barrow, mound, or acropolis (elevated citadel), often served as a base for the temple, but in many instances the temple itself has been an architectural representation of the mountain, as were the bamot ("high places," usually constructed with stones) of the ancient Hebrews, the ziggurats (tower temples) of the ancient Babylonians, and the pyramidal temples of Cambodia, Java, and pre-Columbian Mexico. ...

Stone transformed into an altar, has been either to support or seat the image or symbol of the deity, or to receive sacrifices, burnt offerings, plant offerings, or aromatic perfumes. ... The whole assemblage of actual or symbolic mountains, trees, stone, water is usually arranged architecturally within an enclosed space. An example of this arrangement is the typical Christian church, with its raised chancel (the mountain), the cross or crucifix (the tree), the altar (usually stone, but sometimes wood), and the baptismal font or tank (water)....
The most sacred furnishings of temples are those most closely related to altars, such as the Jewish ark of the Law, or aron ha-qodesh, in the synagogues, which is made in the image of Moses' ark of the Covenant, and the tabernacle (the receptacle containing the consecrated bread and wine) of the Roman Catholic and Eastern Orthodox Churches. ....
The tabernacle, made of wood, metal or stone, is a locked chest" Enc. Brit: 869:2b-870:1a, 1e.

Representational objects:

"In many religions, the god or divine order is represented among men by objects, which may be regarded simply as the god's material form on earth or may be totally identified with the god and endowed with his powers. In pre-Hellenistic Egypt the god was believed to be present in his statue, and elsewhere the statue frequently was believed to contain the god.

Figures. Statues of human or animal figures are the most explicit of the objects representing the divine order. In most iconic (image-using) religions the gods are generally anthro-pomorphic, half man, half animal (as in Egypt and India) or often entirely animal. In most cases the statues conform to an ideal physical type that is symbolic and conventional. The formulation of the ideal is governed by precise aesthetic and iconometric (ritual image proportion) rules, as well as by iconographic (image-representation) requirements, as in Egypt, Greece, and India. All such standards and requirements guarantee conformity to the divine model and, therefore, the effective presence of the god in his statue. Typical in this regard are the sculptured animals of the Hindu pantheon, such as elephants, lions, horses, bulls, and birds, which erected at sacred places in India and other Hindu-influenced countries serve as ever-ready sacred mounts (vahana) for the journeys of the corresponding gods.

The masks representing beneficent and maleficent sacred or holy forces in religious dances particularly in Buddhist monasteries of Nepal, Tibet, and Japan and in the majority of primitive societies constitute another category of sacred representational objects. They are usually worshipped just as statues are worshipped. Certain customs incorporating representational figures have been widespread since prehistoric times and appear to be more related to magic than to religion. One example of this type of practice is a custom observed in primitive or prehistoric societies the incorporation of a skull in an anthropomorphic statue in order to emphasize its divine, sacred, or magical character.

To some extent, a similar use of a skull, human bones, a mummified corpse, or a skeleton appears in Christian churches in the veneration of relics." Enc. Brit: 872:1: a-d.

What is the theme of the above and of Nimrod's religion? Disobedience to the Creator God and a demand for worshipping created things.

"For the invisible things of him from the creation of the world are clearly seen, being understood by the things that are made, [even] his eternal power and Godhead; so that they are without excuse:
Because that, when they knew God, they glorified [him] not as God, neither were thankful; but became vain in their imaginations, and their foolish heart was darkened.
Professing themselves to be wise, they became fools, and changed the glory of the uncorruptible God into an image made like to corruptible man, and to birds, and four-footed beasts, and creeping things.
Wherefore God also gave them up to uncleanness through the lusts of their own hearts, to dishonour their own bodies between themselves: Who changed the truth of God into a lie, and worshipped and served the creature more than the Creator, who is blessed for ever. Amen." Romans 1:20-25.
Genesis states "In the beginning God created the heaven and the earth. And God saw every thing that he had made, and, behold, [it was] very good. And the evening and the morning were the sixth day. Thus the heavens and the earth were finished, and all the host of them." Genesis 1:1, 31, 2:1.

"Thou shalt have no other gods before me. Thou shalt not make unto thee any graven image, or any likeness [of any thing] that [is] in heaven above, or that [is] in the earth beneath, or that [is] in the water under the earth: Thou shalt not bow down thyself to them, nor serve them: …" Exodus 20:3-5

There are volumes and volumes of information of all the pagan practises that have stemmed from Babel/Babylon, however, the mystery having been sufficiently traced, especially after the great flood from Babylon through to Pergamos and Rome, our next task is to define in what form it is in now.

"And I stood upon the sands of the sea, and saw a beast rise up out of the sea, having seven heads and ten horns, and upon his horns ten crowns, and upon his heads the name of blasphemy. And the beast which I saw was like unto a leopard, and his feet were as the feet of a bear, and his mouth as the mouth of a lion: and the dragon gave him his power, and his seat, and great authority." Revelation 13:1-2.

Another clue - This power brought to light in these verses, receives the seat, power, and authority of Satan.
"And there came one of the seven angels which had the seven vials, and talked with me, saying unto me, Come hither; I will show unto thee the judgment of the great whore that sitteth upon many waters:
With whom the kings of the earth have committed fornication, and the inhabitants of the earth have been made drunk with the wine of her fornication.
So he carried me away in the spirit into the wilderness: and I saw a woman sit upon a scarlet coloured beast, full of names of blasphemy, having seven heads and ten horns.
And the woman was arrayed in purple and scarlet colour, and decked with gold and precious stones and pearls, having a golden cup in her hand full of abominations and filthiness of her fornication:

And upon her forehead [was] a name written, MYSTERY, BABYLON THE GREAT, THE MOTHER OF HARLOTS AND ABOMINATIONS OF THE EARTH.

And I saw the woman drunken with the blood of the saints, and with the blood of the martyrs of Jesus: and when I saw her, I wondered with great admiration.

And the angel said unto me, Wherefore didst thou marvel? I will tell thee the mystery of the woman, and of the beast that carrieth her, which hath the seven heads and ten horns.

The beast that thou sawest was, and is not; and shall ascend out of the bottomless pit, and go into perdition: and they that dwell on the earth shall wonder, whose names were not written in the book of life from the foundation of the world, when they behold the beast that was, and is not, and yet is.

And here [is] the mind which hath wisdom. The seven heads are seven mountains, on which the woman sitteth." Rev. 17:1-9.

In chapters 3 & 4 we will confirm the current location and form of this MYSTERY. If we had to beware of the blatant idol worshipping religions we would have nothing to worry about, but because God does not put warnings in His holy word for no reason we need to sit up, investigate, listen and act on our findings. As it is very clear that idol worshipping is to false god's we need to look elsewhere for the Mystery Religion, Yes?

Remember Revelation means revealing. There are some dire warnings to be found in the book of Revelations about the MYSTERY.

"And he causeth all, both small and great, rich and poor, free and bond, to receive a mark in their right hand, or in their foreheads: And that no man might buy or sell, save he that had the mark, or the name of the beast, or the number of his name." Rev.13:16-17.

Is Jesus telling us in these verses that there will be a time when we will be forced under pain of 'economic sanctions' to receive the mark, name or number of this system?

What else does Jesus share about this?

And there followed another angel, saying, Babylon is fallen, is fallen, that great city, because she made all nations drink of the wine of the wrath of her fornication.

And the third angel followed them, saying with a loud voice, If any man worship the beast and his image, and receive [his] mark in his forehead, or in his hand,

The same shall drink of the wine of the wrath of God, which is poured out without mixture into the cup of his indignation; and he shall be tormented with fire and brimstone in the presence of the holy angels, and in the presence of the Lamb:" Rev. 14:8-10.

Based on these two last sets of verses we must definitely research this because there are dire warnings associated with knowingly being part of and remaining in the MYSTERY system.

"And there appeared another wonder in heaven; and behold a great red dragon, having seven heads and ten horns, and seven crowns upon his heads. And his tail drew the third part of the stars of heaven, and did cast them to the earth: ...." Rev.12:3-4, the same dragon that camouflaged himself as a serpent right there in the beginning of our human race in the garden of Eden.

Further investigations will show that the third part of the stars drawn from heaven are the angels that were deceived. The lines used to deceive the previously 'holy angels' must have been more sophisticated than what was used on Eve because she was freshly created and had no background knowledge of the dragon whereas the angels were companions and fellow-created beings with the being that became a 'dragon'.

Remember God says in John 3:16-18 "For God so loved the world, that He gave His only begotten son that whosoever believeth in Him should not perish, but have everlasting life. For God sent not his Son into the world to condemn the world; but that the world through him might be saved.
He that believeth on him is not condemned: but he that believeth not is condemned already, because he hath not believed in the name of the only begotten Son of God"

If we believe in the Son Jesus Christ we will not want to worship any image or seek salvation from any other form of worship, ideology or source.

But why do we choose to follow beliefs and practises that are against our creator? Because we may not know or we may want to do our own thing like Cain did in the beginning. There is only one pathway to God.

"And in process of time it came to pass, that Cain brought of the fruit of the ground an offering unto the LORD.
And Abel, he also brought of the firstlings of his flock and of the fat thereof.
And the LORD had respect unto Abel and to his offering:
But unto Cain and to his offering he had not respect.

And Cain was very wroth, and his countenance fell.
And the LORD said unto Cain, Why art thou wroth? and why is thy countenance fallen?
If thou doest well, shalt thou not be accepted? and if thou doest not well, sin lieth at the door….." Genesis 4:3-7.

Cain gives us an example of wanting to worship how we want or worship in defiance. In the next chapter we will trace the nation that cradled, cradles and gave rise to the MYSTERY RELIGION right through into modern times. In the Capital city of the nation is an independent walled City State. Appendix 6.

From Pagan to Ecclesiastical Rome

In this chapter we will explore the amazing transformation of Pagan Rome to Papal or Ecclesiastical Rome, and how Papal Rome have for many centuries claimed to be the Christian and only true church, through which all inhabitants of earth, have any hope of salvation. This development was given to the Prophet Daniel in vision centuries before they occurred. The prophecies describe a nation, Pagan Rome that would overrun and subdue all nations that existed before it and would be characterised by its dominant metal, Iron. Out of Pagan Rome a new spiritual power would emerge.

"After this I saw in the night visions, and behold a fourth beast, dreadful and terrible, and strong exceedingly and it had great iron teeth: it devoured and break in pieces, and stamped the residue with the feet of it: and it was diverse from all the beasts that were before it; and it had ten horns. I considered the horns, and, behold, there came up among them another little horn, before whom there were three of the first horns plucked up by the roots: and, behold, in this horn were eyes like the eyes of man, and a mouth speaking great things...." Daniel 7: 7-8.

"... and the dragon gave him his power, and his seat, and great authority." Revelation 13:2.

Julius Caesar, being pagan, was the first Roman Emperor to take on the title "Pontifex Maximus" in the year 63BC. What are the origins and significance of those titles or positions?
"This counterfeit religion was built on the claim that it made a bridge between Heaven and Earth. The ruling Monarch became the head of the system. He had many

titles, one of which, "Pontifex Maximus," is significant. Pont means a bridge; Factio, I make; and Maximus, greatest. Put together, it simply means the greatest bridge builder. In Genesis 11:1–5, we have the story of the Ancient Babel builders. They wanted to have a tower whose top might reach unto Heaven, or "be in the heavens," as other translators read the passage. This occurred shortly after the great flood in the days of Noah. Tremendous physical changes took place in our world at that time. In Genesis 8:22 we read of "cold and heat." These changes of temperature so real in our lives nowadays seem to have been unknown before the deluge.

Notice also from Genesis 1:7, that there was water above the sky (firmament) as we now know it, and waters under the sky. Therefore when the sun's rays struck the waters which were above the firmament, the effect would have been even temperatures around the globe, therefore explaining the reasons why tropical vegetation and tropical animals have been found all around the globe even in the frozen icecaps.

The waters that were above the firmament came down to earth during the great flood, see Gen; 7:11, when "the windows of heaven were opened," thus removing that global temperature control, allowing the Ice-caps to form.

Prior to the flood it never rained as it does in our day, resulting in such disasters and soil erosion that current environmentalists seem so concerned about. Gen. 2:6 confirms that the earth was watered by mist. "But there went up a mist from the earth, and watered the whole face of the ground."

Today's environmentalists can be compared to the ancient Babel builders who did not accept the "primeval account" of the great flood with the great antediluvian apostasy against God which brought the catastrophe in the first place. They must also ignore the scriptural account of the causes of the great calamities and disasters which are befalling this world, although deforestation is credited to assisting along with CFC's etc., in the greenhouse effect, these are again the results of mans' greed. The 'greenhouse effect' I believe is another deception of Satan to detract people's attention from the true causes of the problems? Humanity's growing rejection of their living creator, God. Exactly how Satan has rejected God's rulership in his life and is leading us humans to do the same thing.

I must point out that I am not against protecting what has been given to humanity to look after. Genesis 2:15 "And the LORD God took the man, and put him into the garden of Eden to dress it and to keep it." and God is not happy that many of us are destroying it for gain. "...., and thy wrath is come....., and that thou shouldest give reward unto thy servants the prophets, and to the saints, and shouldest destroy them which destroy the earth" Revelation 11:18.

How many acres of tropical or other rainforests are being destroyed all over the globe, every year, for a meat industry that is killing us all through cancer and the hormones and steroids being fed to the animals?]

"The inhabitants of that time were not ignorant of the world in which they lived. But what caused the flood? That was the question in their minds. And would there be another flood? God had assured Noah and his family that the world would never again be destroyed by a flood, but these scientific and religious philosophers were not content with the divine promise, they wanted to build a tower - an observatory - high enough to reach above the dense atmosphere and thus enable them through scientific investigation to discover a natural cause for the flood and possibly assure themselves that nothing like that could ever happen again. The whole movement was apostate and grew out of unbelief of God's promise. The Mystery Cult of Babylon sprang from this, and in one form or another this apostate religion has plagued the people of God ever since." Unfolding the Revelation by Roy Allan Anderson pp 23 – 24.

Remember that the tower and its associated temple was also built for worshipping the false god.

"For some time after the kingdom of Pergamos was merged in the Roman dominions, there was no one who could set himself openly to lay claim to all the dignity inherent in the old title of the kings of Pergamos. The original powers of the roman pontiffs seem to have been by that time abridged, but when Julius Caesar, who had previously been elected Pontifex Maximus, became also, as Emperor, the supreme civil ruler of the Romans, then, as head of the Roman state, and head of the Roman religion, all the powers and functions of the true legitimate Babylonian Pontiff were supremely vested in him, and he found himself in a position to assert these powers. Then he seems to have laid claim to the divine dignity of Attalus, as well as the kingdom that Attalus had bequeathed to the Romans, as centring in himself; for his well-known watchword, "Venus Genetrix," which meant that Venus was the mother of the Julian race, appears to have been intended to make him "the son" of the great goddess, even as the "Bull-Horned" Attalus had been regarded. Then, on certain occasions, in the exercise of his high pontifical office, he appeared of course in all the pomp of the Babylonian costume, as Belshazzar himself might have done, in robes of scarlet, with the crosier of Nimrod in his hand, wearing the mitre of

Dagon and bearing the keys of Janus and Cybele." Two Babylons pg 241.

As mentioned before, Julius Caesar became "Pontifex Maximus" in the year 63: Rome then being Pagan Rome. It will be interesting to compare this with the papal account of the time period in which the papal church was supposed to have received the keys of salvation through Peter. It is vital to note also that the mystery religion has counterfeited or even adapted the truths of Christianity, to suit its purposes. However, by the grace of God, His true children will not be deceived. The significance of these keys in the Roman church today we will discuss later in this work. The next person of significance we need to introduce at this stage who also bore the title "Pontifex Maximus" is the Emperor Constantine. He comes upon the scene as a "Christian?" after decades if not centuries of persecution of the Christians by the pagans, which began under Emperor Nero (55-68 AD).

"Christianity unique in its' Universal clarity and unique also in its demand for a noble effort of faith in Jesus' blend of divinity and humanity, was the religion that prevailed in the Roman world. It satisfied the Roman Emperor Constantine's impulsive need for divine support, and from AD 312 onward, by a complex and gradual process, it became the official religion of the empire.

For a time, coins, and monuments continued to link Christian doctrines with the worship of the sun, to which Constantine had been addicted previously. But even when this phase came to an end, Roman Paganism continued to exert other, permanent Influences, great and small. The emperors passed on to the popes, the title of chief priest Pontifex Maximus... The ecclesiastical calendar retains numerous remnants of pre-Christian festivals - notably

Christmas, which blends elements including both the feast of the Saturnalia and the birthday of Mithra." Enc. Brit. 18:922:1b.

"Constantine's 'conversion' to Christianity had a far-reaching effect. Like his father, he had originally been a votary of the Sun in the Vosges Mountains of Gaul, where he had his first vision - a pagan one. During his campaign against Maxentius, he had a second vision - a lighted cross in the sky - and he had painted on his men's shields a figure that was perhaps Christ's monogram (although he probably had Christ confused with the sun in his manifestation as summa divinitas ("the highest divinity"). After his victory he declared himself Christian. His conversion remains somewhat mysterious and his contemporaries Lactantius and Eusebius of Caesarea - are scarcely enlightening and even rather contradictory on the subject.... He was progressive and greatly influenced by the capable bishops who surrounded him from the very beginning." Enc. Brit. 20:353:2b.

"Constantine's adherence to Christianity was closely associated with his rise to power. He fought the battle of Milvian Bridge in the name of the Christian God" (supposedly), "having received instructions in a dream to paint the Christian monogram, the Pax Christus, (⚹) on his troops 'shields.

This is the account given by the Christian apologist Lactantius; a somewhat different version, offered by Eusebius tells of a vision seen by Constantine during the campaign against Maxentius, in which the Christian sign appeared in the sky with the legend "In this sign conquer." Despite the Emperor's own authority for the account, given late in life to Eusebius, it is in general more problematic than the other; but a religious experience on the march from

Gaul is suggested also by a pagan orator, who, in a speech of 310 referred to a vision of Apollo received by Constantine at a shrine in Gaul." Enc. Brit. 16:687:2b.

"The most famous of monograms, known as the sacred monogram, is formed by the conjunction of the first two Greek letters of ΧΡΙΣΤΟΣ, meaning Christ, usually taking the form (✼)" Enc. Brit. 263:2a.

That symbol is also known as the "Pax Christus" or "The Peace of Christ."

This "Pax Christus" according to Hislop, Must have served as an encourage-ment to the Christian soldiers to fight in the name of Christ as the 'P' over the

'X' were meant to identify Christ, whereas the pagans regarded the 'X' as a sign for their god "Ham" (otherwise known as "Horus" one of the names initialized in the Eucharist I.H.S. Isis, Horus, Seb). Here again one of Satan's clever manipulations using a symbol purporting to be of Jesus Christ, to deceive.

"Constantine, foreseeing the ultimate triumph of Christianity, became its champion. As Emperor, he was already invested with the power and honours of Paganism. These he did not renounce, but, instead brought them over into Christianity. He therefore became the bridge uniting paganism with Christianity. Half a century later, AD 375, the Christian Emperor Gratian refused the vestments and the pagan title "Pontifex Maximus." But the bishop of

Rome, seeing an opportunity to exalt his dignity, assumed the title and vestments of "Pontifex Maximus." This was the historic title of the high priest of paganism. These titles and vestments perpetuated paganism in the church, but always under the guise of Christianity." Unfolding the Revelation by Roy Allan Anderson pg 124.

So we see how through all those manoeuvres that Pagan Rome began to become Papal Rome. The term "began" is used because even then Papal Rome had not yet begun to wield its full power; that was to come later. How much later?

I must warn my readers that from this point on the connection will begin to be made between the Ancient Mystery Religion, Rome and The Papal system.

We have demonstrated the fulfilment of Revelation 13:2, where the dragon transferred his seat from Pergamos to Rome. The prophecy of Revelation 13:1-10 confirms that the Papacy receives the dragons' seat, power and great authority. Verses 5-7 describes the actions of the Papacy as follows - "And there was given unto him a mouth speaking great things and blasphemies; and power was given unto him to continue forty and two months. And he opened his mouth in blasphemy against God, to blaspheme his name, and his tabernacle, and them that dwell in heaven. And it was given unto him to make war with the saints, and to overcome them: and power was given him over all kindreds, and tongues, and nations."

The aspects of Papal action outlined in these verses which we will discuss first, is concerning the time period over which the Papacy would make war with the saints overcoming them, and the power given to him over all the then known nations and tongues, etc. This time period and actions is also described by the Prophet Daniel in chapter 7 verses 7-8, 23-25.

"After this I saw in the night visions, and behold a fourth beast, dreadful and terrible, and strong exceedingly and it had great iron teeth: it devoured and break in pieces, and stamped the residue with the feet of it: and it was diverse from all the beasts that were before it; and it had ten horns. I considered the horns, and, behold, there came up among them another little horn, before whom there were three of the first horns plucked up by the roots: and, behold, in this horn were eyes like the eyes of man, and a mouth speaking great things.... Thus he said, the fourth beast shall be the fourth kingdom upon earth, which shall be diverse from all kingdoms, and shall devour the whole earth, and shall tread it down, and break it in pieces. And the ten horns out of this kingdom are ten kings that shall arise: and another shall arise after them; and he shall be diverse from the first, and he shall subdue three kings. And he shall speak great words against the most high, and shall wear out the saints of the Most High, and think to change times and laws and they shall be given into his hand until a time and times and the dividing of time."

Notice that the "little horn" power would uproot three kings in its rise to power according to prophecy, and that he was to continue at the height of his power for a time, times, and dividing of time; forty and two months according to Daniel, and Revelation respectively. On examination it will be found that the forty-two months and the time, times and the dividing of time, relate to the same time period; the three kings are three kingdoms that would be obliterated from the face of the earth, actually ceasing to exist. On the destruction of these three kingdoms, the beginning of the time of total papal supremacy, and its temporary loss of power at the end of the prophetic time period will be proven to have been exactly fulfilled. We will now proceed to the scriptures for explanation of these time periods. As is usual, scriptural understanding requires some digging. In the book of Numbers 13-14 we find related the experience of the Israelites wanderings in the Wilderness for forty years. Their wanderings were the results of their murmurings and disbelief of the information about the Promised Land relayed to them by the 12 men sent to search out the land; these men spent forty days spying the land; therefore in verse 34 of chapter 14, the Lord said the following:

"After the number of days in which ye searched the land even forty days, each day for a year, shall ye bear iniquities, even forty years, and ye shall know my breach of promise."

Also in Ezekiel 4:5-6, we find days relating to years. "For I have laid upon thee the years of their iniquity, according to the number of the days, three hundred and ninety days: so shalt thou bear the iniquity of the house of Israel. And when thou hast accomplished them, lie again on thy right side, and thou shalt bear the iniquity of the house of Judah forty days: I have appointed thee each day for a year."

Therefore, each day is representative of a year. The Jewish month was based on 30 days, therefore 42 months x 30 days would equal 1260 days then translate to 1260 years. (According to Wikipedia this method of calculation was not unique to the Jews *The 360-day calendar is a method of measuring durations used in financial markets, in computer models, in ancient literature, and in prophetic literary genres.")* Therefore the Papacy would have 1260 years of supremacy over all nations kindreds and tongues that it came into contact with. But in order to do so, the Papacy had to destroy three kingdoms, as the scriptures state, "plucked up by the roots, "once a plant, etc., is pulled out by its roots, it will inevitably die, if not replanted within a limited time period. The scriptures give no such confirmation that any replanting or transplanting took place. The destruction of these three kingdoms would herald the commencement of the 1260 year period, indicated in prophecy.

"It is a matter of both interest and importance, to inquire into the causes which resulted in the development of this arrogant power. The first pastors or bishops of Rome enjoyed a respect proportionate to the rank of the city in which they resided. For the first few centuries of the Christian era, Rome was the largest, richest, and most powerful city in the world. It was the seat of Empire, The capital of nations. "All the inhabitants of the earth belong to her," said Julian; and Claudian declared her to be "The fountain of Laws." "If Rome is the queen of cities, why should not her pastor be the king of bishops?" was the reasoning these Roman Pastors put forth." Why should not the Roman Church be the mother of Christendom? Why should not all nations be her children, and her authority their sovereign law, It was easy," says D'Aubigne, from whom we quote these words, "for the ambitious heart of man to reason thus." Ambitious Rome did so.

The bishops in different parts of the Roman Empire felt a pleasure yielding to the Bishop of Rome some of that honour which that city received from the nations of the earth. There was originally no dependence implied in the honour thus paid. "But," continues D'Aubigne usurped power increases like an avalanche. Admonitions at first simply fraternal, soon became absolute commands in the mouth of the pontiff. The western bishops favoured this encroachment of the Roman pastors, either from jealousy of the eastern bishops, or because they preferred submitting to the supremacy of a pope rather than to the dominion of a temporal power." Such were the influences clustering around the bishop of Rome, and thus was everything tending toward his speedy elevation to the spiritual dominance of Christendom.

Challenge of Arianism. - But the fourth century was destined to witness an obstacle thrown across the path of this ambitious dream. The prophecy had declared that the power represented by the little horn would "subdue three kings." In the rise and development of Arianism early in the fourth century and the challenge it presented to papal supremacy, we find the causes leading to the plucking up of three of the kingdoms of Western Rome by the papal power.

Arius, parish priest of the ancient and influential church of Alexandria, promulgated his doctrine to the world, occasioning so fierce a controversy in the Christian church that a general council was called at Nicea, by the Emperor Constantine in AD 325, to consider and rule upon its teaching. Arius maintained "that the Son was totally and essentially distinct from the Father, that he was the first and noblest of those beings whom the father had created out of nothing, the instrument by whose subordinate operation the Almighty Father formed the universe, and therefore inferior to the Father. Hereupon Arius was banished to Illyria, and his followers were compelled to give their assent to the creed composed on that occasion.

The controversy itself, however, was not to be disposed of in this summary manner. For ages it continued to agitate the Christian World, the Arians everywhere becoming the bitter enemies of the pope and of the Roman Catholic Church. It was evident that the spread of Arianism would check the onward march of Catholicism, and that the possession of Italy and its renowned Capital by a people of Arian persuasion, would be fatal to the supremacy of a Catholic bishop....

The position is here confidently taken that the three powers, or horns plucked up by the roots, were the Heruli, the Vandals, and the Ostrogoths; and this position rests upon reliable historical data. Odoacer, the leader of the Heruli, was the first of the Barbarians who reigned over the Romans. He took the throne of Italy, AD 476. Of his religious belief Gibbon says: "Like the rest of the barbarians he had been instructed in the Arian heresy; but he revered the monastic and episcopal characters, and the silence of the Catholics attests the toleration which, they enjoyed."

The same author says: "The Ostrogoths, the Burgundians, the Suevi, and the vandals, who had listened to the eloquence of the Latin clergy, preferred the more intelligible lessons of their domestic teachers; and Arianism was adopted as the national faith of the warlike converts who were seated on the ruins of the western empire. This irreconcilable difference of religion was a perpetual source of jealousy and hatred; and the reproach of Barbaria was embittered by the more odious epiphet, of heretic. The heroes of the north, who had submitted with some reluctance to believe that all their ancestors were in hell, were astonished and exasperated to learn that they themselves had only changed the mode of their eternal condemnation."

The Arian doctrine had a marked influence on the church at that time, as will be observed in the following paragraphs: "The whole of the vast Gothic population which descended on the Roman Empire, so far as it was Christian at all, held to the faith of the Alexandrian heretic,...

Rank states: "But she (the church) fell, as was inevitable into many embarrassments, and found herself in an entirely altered condition. A pagan people took possession of Britain; while the Lombards, long attached to Arianism, and as neighbours most dangerous and hostile, established a powerful sovereignty before the very gates of Rome. The Roman bishops meanwhile, beset on all sides, exerted themselves, with all the prudence and pertinacity which have remained their particular attributes, to regain the mastery at least in their patriarchal diocese."

Machiavelli says: "Nearly all the wars which the Northern Barbarians carried on in Italy, it may be here remarked, were organised by the pontiffs, and the hordes with which the country was inundated, were generally called in by them..."

While the Catholics were feeling the restraining power of an Arian king in Italy, they were suffering a violent persecution from the Vandals in Africa, Elliott says, "The Vandal kings were not only Arians, but persecutors of the Catholics; in Sardinia and Corsica, under the roman episcopate, we may presume, as well as in Africa."

Such was the position of affairs, when in AD 533, Justinian entered upon his vandal and gothic wars. Wishing to obtain the influence of the pope and the Catholic party, he issued the memorable decree which was to constitute the pope the head of all the churches, and from the carrying out of which AD 538, the period of papal supremacy is to be dated. And whoever will read the history of the African campaign, 533-534, and the Italian campaign, 534-538, will notice that the Catholics everywhere hailed as deliverers the army of Belisarius, the general of Justinian.

But no decree of this nature could be carried into effect until the Arian horns which stood in its way were overthrown. A turn came, however, in the tide of affairs, for in the military campaign in Africa and Italy the victorious legions of Belisarius dealt a crushing blow to Arianism, so much so that its final supporters were vanquished. Procopius relates that the African war was undertaken by Justinian for the relief of the Christians (Catholics) in that quarter, and that when he expressed his intentions in this respect, the prefect of the palace came very near dissuading him from his purpose. But a dream appeared to him in which he was bidden "not to shrink from the execution of his design; for by assisting the Christians he would overthrow the power of the vandals."

Mosheim declares: "It is true, the Greeks who had received the decrees of the council of Nice (that is, from the Catholics), persecuted and oppressed the Arians wherever their influence and authority could reach; but the Niceneans, in their turn, were not less rigorously treated by their adversaries (the Arians), particularly in Africa and Italy, where they felt, in a very severe manner, the weight of the Arian power, and the bitterness of their resentment. The triumphs of Arianism were, however, transitory; and its prosperous days were entirely eclipsed when the vandals were driven out of Africa, and the goths out of Italy by the arms of Justinian."

From the historical testimony above cited, we think it clearly established that the three horns plucked up were the powers named: the Heruli, AD 493, the Vandals, in 534, and the Ostrogoths finally in 553, though affective opposition by the latter ceased when they were driven from Rome by Belisarius in 538,..."

According to the Enc.Brit:5: 893:3a, the Heruli vanished from history in the mid-6th century. 8:1038:1b, the Ostrogoths became extinct following a war which began in 535 under Justinian although the wars lasted 20 yrs. Ibid 12:262:2a, "the Vandals as a name has remained synonymous for wilful desecration or destruction,.... were ardent Arian Christians, and their persecutions of the Catholic church in Africa were at times fierce... In 533 the romans under Belisarius invaded Africa.... in one campaigning season the vandal kingdom was destroyed. Rome again ruled the area and restored the churches to the Catholics. The vandals played no further role in history."

As demonstrated by history, the three powers were not uprooted at once, at the same time, but rather gradually, as depicted by the prophecy.

From the decree of Justinian in 538 to the time of the captivity of Pope Pius VI by the French General Berthier in 1798, fulfils exactly the prophetic time period of 1260 years.

During that time period other prophecies in connection with the papacy were to be fulfilled, namely, thinking to change times and laws, speaking blasphemies, and making war with the saints and overcoming them. As for the latter, it could only mean the persecutions and wars fought against the true followers of Christ, who were condemned as heretics by the papacy for no other reason than that they insisted on a "thus saith the Lord." Some of the records of this are to be found in Fox's Book of Martyrs, he states that the papacy "under the guise of Christianity, committed more enormities than ever disgraced the annals of paganism. Disregarding the maxims and the spirit of the Gospel, the papal Church, arming herself with the power of the sword, vexed the Church of God and wasted it for several centuries, a period most appropriately termed in history, the "dark ages," the kings of the earth, gave their power to the "beast," and submitted to be trodden on by the miserable vermin that often filled the papal chair, as in the case of Henry, emperor of Germany.

The storm of papal persecution first burst upon the Waldenses in France." As for the catalogue of monstrous acts carried out against the bodies of the victims, they are far too horrible and extensive to enumerate in this work; perhaps a copy of the said book can be obtained for personal examination, suffice to say that one or two examples may be referred to later, as the chapter of papal persecution has not quite ended, because Satan will raise the papal monster yet again to be unleashed against the entire world, with the aid of the world's super-power nation, in his final struggle before the second coming of Christ. If anyone who reads or has read Fox's book of Martyrs shudders at the thought of such scenes occurring again, do not be surprised, as our bodies have been made to warn us, through its nervous system of any physical damage which could be taking place and it is this fact that Satan is aware of why he uses such vile acts to attempt to turn us away from the love and true Gospel of Christ. I say attempt because he cannot dissuade a true Christian from following Christ. He may be able to harm our bodies, but not our souls. John the Revelator states:

"Woe to the inhabiters of the earth and of the sea! For the devil is come down unto you, having great wrath, because he knoweth that he hath but a short time." Rev. 12:12. In verse 17 we read of the people who his final war is against "And the dragon was wroth with the woman (true church), and went to make war with the remnant of her seed (followers), which keep the commandments of God, and have the testimony of Jesus." These two factors define the final and true church. (That remnant church exists today and its members will be mercilessly hunted, but not all will perish. More on this later.)

Under what authority did the roman church lay claim to absolute authority on earth? As noted earlier in this chapter Julius Caesar laid claim to the divine dignity of Attalus, the last king of Pergamos, took on the title "Pontifex Maximus" was also Emperor, and in the course of his duties on certain occasions, in the exercise of his pontifical office, appeared in all the pomp of the Babylonian costume, with the crosier of Nimrod in his hand, wearing the mitre of Dagon, and bearing the keys of Janus and Cybele, all of these still being used to this very day. However, the keys are the most potent of symbols of the roman church's authority. At this stage I feel it pertinent to explore the history of the entrance of the keys into the roman church and the reasons of its usage. Remember that this religion has its roots in ancient Babylon.

"That the key was one of the symbols used in the Mysteries, the reader will find on consulting Taylors' note on Orphic hymn to Pluto, where that divinity is spoken of as "keeper of the keys." Now the Pontifex, as "Hierophant," was "arrayed in the habit and adorned with the symbols of the great creator of the world, of whom in these mysteries he was supposed to be the substitute." (Maurices Antiquities, Vol. 3 p356).

The primeval or creative god was mystically represented as Androgyne, as combining in his own person both sexes (Ibid vol. 5 pg 953), being therefore Janus and Cybele at the same time. In opening up the mysteries, therefore, of this mysterious divinity, it was natural that the Pontifex should bear the key of both of these divinities."

Who was this Primeval Creative god, represented as Androgyne?

"Creation by World Parents"

"The world is created as the progeny of a primordial mother and father. The mother and father are symbols of Earth and Sky respectively. In myths of this kind, the world parents generally appear at a later stage of the creation process; chaos in some way exists before the coming into being of the world parents. In the Babylonian myth Enuma Elish, it is stated.

When on high the heaven had not been named

Firm ground below had not been called by name, Naught but primordial Apsu, their begetter, (and) Mummu-Tiamat, she who bore them all,

Their waters comingling as a single body; . . .

even though the world parents are depicted and described as in sexual embrace, no activity is taking place. They appear as quiescent and inert.... The union of male and female in sexual embrace is another symbol of completeness and totality. In the African myth from the Dogon..., sexual union is a sign of androgyny (being both male and female), and androgyny, in turn, a sign of perfection." Enc. Brit. 17:369:2b.

According to these articles, perfection is to be androgyne. The keys of Janus and Cybele meaning exactly that. On further examination; according to websters "An-dro-gyne" also Androgyn from latin Androgynus, from Greek Andrognos, 1:Hermaphrodite

2 - an effeminate man "Hermaphrodite": Homosexual, Bisexual.

Does it come as any surprise then that there is so much Homosexuality and Bisexuality in the world today; the modern version of the mystery religion is rampant with homosexuality and child homosexual rape and abuse by it's priests. Homosexuality was also rampant in the time of the Romans, especially during the reign of the infamous Caligula. That this was the case, the Apostle Paul in his epistle to the Romans in chapter 1:14-28, states the following:

"I am debtor both to the Greeks, and to the Barbarians; both to the wise and the unwise. So, as much as in me is, I am ready to preach the gospel to you that are at Rome also. For I am not ashamed of the gospel of Christ: for it is the power of God unto salvation to every one that believeth; to the Jew first, and also to the Greek. For therein is the righteousness of God revealed from faith to faith: as it is written, The just shall live by faith. For the wrath of God is revealed from Heaven against all ungodliness and unrighteousness of men, who hold the truth in unrighteousness; Because that which may be known of God is manifest in them; for God hath shewed it unto them. For the Invisible things of him from the creation of the world are clearly seen, being understood by the things that are made, even his eternal power and Godhead; so that they are without excuse; ... Professing themselves to be wise, they became fools."

How could they become fools if they were supposed to be wise? Only because their wisdom was not of God. What then happened to them because they refused to acknowledge the true God? "And changed the glory of the uncorruptible God into an image made like to corruptible man, and to birds and four–footed beasts and creeping things."

Here, Paul was talking about the various gods they were worshipping in their various forms. "Wherefore God also gave them up to uncleanness through the lusts of their own hearts, to dishonor their own bodies between themselves: who changed the truth of God into a lie, and worshipped and served the creature more than the Creator, who is blessed forever. Amen."

Worshipping Satan or deified humans more than God.

"For this cause God gave them up to vile affections: for even their women did change the natural use into that which is against nature: And likewise also the men, leaving the natural use of the woman, burned in their lust one toward another; men with men working that which is unseemly, and receiving in themselves that recompense of their error which was meet. And even as they did not like to retain God in their knowledge, God gave them over to a reprobate mind, to do those things which are not convenient;"

Those actions Paul has mentioned are clearly the results of all who believe in Satans' lies and the deception of androdygynous perfection, and refusing to accept the truth, God had to leave them (give up on them) to their own devices. This besides other things is what the keys of Janus and Cybele represent, and those keys have been blasphemously called the keys of St. Peter or "The Petrine Keys."

The keys of Janus & Cybele now popularly known as the Petrine Keys

"The Pope now pretends to the supremacy in the church as the successor of Peter, to whom it is alleged that our Lord exclusively committed the keys of the kingdom of Heaven. But here is the important fact that, till the Pope was invested with the title, which for a thousand years had had attached to it the power of the keys of Janus and Cybele, no such claim to pre-eminence, or anything approaching to it, was ever publicly made on his part, on the ground of his being the possessor of the keys bestowed on Peter. Very early, indeed, did the bishops of Rome show a proud and ambitious spirit; but, for the first three centuries, their claim for superior honour was founded simply on the dignity of their see, as being that of the imperial city, the capital of the Roman world.

When, however, the seat of empire was removed to the east, and Constantinople threatened to eclipse Rome, some new ground for maintaining the dignity of the Bishop of Rome must be sought. That new ground was found when, about 378, the Pope fell heir to the keys that were the symbols of two well-known Pagan divinities at Rome. Janus bore a key, and Cybele bore a key; and these are the two keys that the Pope emblazons on his arms as the ensigns of his spiritual authority. How the Pope came to be regarded as wielding the power of these keys will appear in the sequel; but that he did, in the popular apprehension, become entitled to that power at the period referred to is certain.

Now, when he had come, in the estimation of the pagans, to occupy the place of the representatives of Janus and Cybele, and therefore to be entitled to bear their keys, the Pope saw that if he could only get it believed among the Christians that Peter alone had the power of the keys and that he was Peter's successor, then the sight of these keys would keep up the delusion, and thus, though the temporal dignity of Rome as a city should decay, his own dignity as the bishop of Rome would be more firmly established than ever. On this policy it is evident he acted.

Some time was allowed to pass away, and then, when the secret working of the Mystery of iniquity had prepared the way for it, for the first time did the Pope publicly assert his pre-eminence, as founded on the keys given to Peter.
About 378 was he raised to the position which gave him, in pagan estimation, the power of the keys referred to. In 431, and not before, did he publicly lay claim to the possession of Peter's keys. This, surely, is a striking coincidence.

Does the reader ask how was it possible that men could give credit to such a baseless assumption? The words of scripture, in regard to this very subject, give a very solemn but satisfactory answer. (2 Thess.2 10-11) "because they received not the love of the truth, that they might be saved.... For this cause God shall send them strong delusion that they should believe a lie."

Few lies could be more gross; but, in course of time it came to be widely believed; and now, as the statue of Jupiter is worshipped at Rome as the veritable image of Peter, so the keys of Janus and Cybele have for ages been devoutly believed to represent the keys of the same apostle." *(Notice that Jupiter is still worshipped in Rome under the guise of St. Peter.)* "While nothing but judicial infatuation can account for the credibility of the Christians in regarding the keys as emblems of an exclusive power given by Christ to the Pope through Peter it is not difficult to see how the pagans would rally round the Pope all the more readily when they heard him found his power on the possession of Peter's keys.

The keys that the Pope bore were the keys of a "Peter" well known to the Pagans initiated in the Chaldean Mysteries. That Peter the apostle was ever Bishop of Rome has been proved again and again to be an arrant fable. That he ever even set foot in Rome is at the best highly doubtful. His visit to that city rests on no better authority than that of a writer at the end of the second century or the beginning of the third-viz., the author of the work called the Clementines, who gravely tells us that on the occasion of his visit, finding Simon Magus there, the Apostle challenged him to give proof of his miraculous or magical powers, whereupon the sorcerer flew up into the air, and Peter brought him down in such haste that his leg was broken.

All historians of repute have at once rejected this story of the Apostolic encounter with the magician as being destitute of all contemporary evidence; but as the visit of Peter to Rome rests on the same authority, it must stand or fall along with it, or, at least, it must be admitted to be extremely doubtful. But, while this is the case with Peter the Christian, it can be shown to be by no means doubtful that before the Christian era, and downwards, there was a "Peter" at Rome, who occupied the highest place in the Pagan priesthood.

The priest who explained the Mysteries to the initiated was sometimes called by a Greek term, the Hierophant; but in primitive Chaldee, the real language of the Mysteries, his title, as pronounced without the points, was "Peter" i.e., "the interpreter." As the revealer of that which was hidden, nothing was more natural than that, while opening up the esoteric doctrine of the Mysteries, he should be decorated with the keys of the two divinities whose Mysteries he unfolded. Thus we may know how the keys of Janus and Cybele would come to be known as the keys of Peter, the "interpreter" of the Mysteries.

Yea, we have the strongest evidence that, in countries far removed from one another, and far distant from Rome, these keys were known by initiated Pagans nor merely as the "Keys of Peter," but as the keys of a Peter identified with Rome. In the Eleusinian Mysteries at Athens, when the candidates for initiation were instructed in the secret doctrine of Paganism, the explanation of that doctrine was read to them out of a book called by ordinary writers, the "Book Petroma;" that is, as we are told, a book formed of stone. But this is evidently just a play upon words, according to the usual spirit of Paganism, intended to amuse the vulgar.

The nature of the case, and the history of the Mysteries, alike show that this book could be none other than the "Book Pet-Roma;" that is, the "Book of the Grand interpreter," in other words, of Hermes Trismegistus, the great "Interpreter of the gods."

In Egypt, from which Athens derived its religion, the books of Hermes were regarded as the divine fountain of all true Knowledge or the Mysteries. In Egypt, therefore Hermes was looked up to in this very character of Grand Interpreter, or "Peter - Roma." In Athens, Hermes as is well known, occupied precisely the same place and of course in the sacred language must have been known by the same title. The priest, therefore, that in the name of Hermes explained the Mysteries... must have been decked not only with the keys of Peter, but with the keys of "Peter-Roma." Here then, the famous "Book of stone" begins to appear in a new light and not only so but to shed new light on one of the darkest and most puzzling passages of Papal History.

It has always been a matter of amazement to candid historical inquirers how it could ever have come to pass that the name of Peter should be associated with Rome in the way in which it is found in the fourth century downwards – how so many in different countries had been led to believe that Peter, who was an "Apostle of the circumcision," had apostatised from his divine commission, and become bishop of a gentile church, and that he should be the spiritual ruler in Rome, when no satisfactory evidence could be found for his ever having been in Rome at all.

But the book of "Peter-Roma," accounts for what otherwise is entirely inexplicable. The existence of such a title was too valuable to be overlooked by the Papacy; and according to its usual policy, it was sure if it had the opportunity, to turn it to the account of its own aggrandisement and that opportunity it had. When the Pope came, as he did, into intimate connection with the Pagan priesthood; when they came at last, as we shall see they did, under his control, what more natural than to seek not only to reconcile Paganism and Christianity, but to make it appear that the Pagan "Peter-Roma," with his keys, meant "Peter of Rome," and that that "Peter of Rome" was the very apostle to whom the Lord Jesus Christ gave the "Keys of the kingdom of Heaven"? Hence, from the mere jingle of words, persons and things essentially different were confounded; and Paganism and Christianity jumbled together, that the towering ambition of a wicked priest might be gratified; and so, to the blinded Christians of the apostasy, the Pope was the representative of Peter the apostle, while to the initiated Pagans he was only the representative of Peter, the interpreter of their well-known Mysteries. Thus was the Pope the express counterpart of "Janus, the double-faced...."

'The reader will now be prepared to understand how it is that the Popes Grand Council of State, which assists him in the government of the church, comes to be called the College of Cardinals. The term Cardinal is derived from Cardo, a hinge. Janus, whose key the Pope bears, was the god of doors and hinges, and was called Patulcius, and Clusius "the opener and the shutter." This had a blasphemous meaning, for he was worshipped at Rome as the grand mediator. Whatever important business was in hand, whatever deity was to be invoked, an invocation first must be addressed to Janus, who was recognised as the "god of gods," in whose mysterious divinity the characters of father and son were combined, and without that no prayer could be heard - the "door of heaven" could not be opened. It was this same god whose worship prevailed so exceedingly in Asia Minor at the time when our Lord sent by his servant John, the seven Apocalyptic messages to the churches established in that region and therefore in one of those messages we find him tacitly rebuking the profane ascription of his [the pope's] own peculiar dignity to that divinity, and asserting his exclusive claim to the prerogative usually attributed to His rival. Thus Rev. 3:7. "And to the angel of the church in Philadelphia write: These things saith He that is holy, He that is true, He that hath the key of David, He that openeth, and no man shutteth; and shutteth and no man openeth."

Now, to this Janus, as mediator, worshipped in Asia Minor and equally, from very early times, in Rome, belonged the government of the world; and "all power in heaven, in earth, and the sea" according to Pagan ideas was vested in him. In this character he was said to have "jus vertendi cardinis"- the "power of turning the hinge"- of opening the doors of heaven, or of opening or shutting the gates of peace or war upon the earth. The Pope therefore, when he set up as the High-Priest of Janus, assumed also as the "Jus vertendi cardinis," "the power of turning the hinge,"- of opening and shutting in the blasphemous pagan sense. Slowly and cautiously at first was this power asserted; but the foundation being laid, steadily, century after century, was the grand superstructure of priestly power erected upon it. The pagans, who saw what strides under Papal directions, Christianity, as professed in Rome, was making towards Paganism, were more than content to recognise the Pope as possessing this power; they gladly encouraged him to rise, step by step, to the full height of the blasphemous pretensions befitting the representative of Janus - pretensions which, as all men know, are now, by the unanimous consent of Western Apostate Christendom, recognised as inherent in the office of the Bishop of Rome.

To enable the Pope, however, to rise to the plenitude of power which he now asserts, the co-operation of others was needed. When his power increased, when his dominion extended and especially after he became a temporal sovereign, the key of Janus became too heavy for his single hand - he needed some to share with him the power of the "hinge." Hence his privy councillors, his high functionaries of state, who were associated with him in the government of the Church and the world, got the now well-known title of "Cardinals"- the priests of the "hinge." This title had been previously borne by the high Officials of the Roman Emperor, who, as "Pontifex Maximus," had been himself the representative of Janus, and who delegated his powers to servants of his own. Even in the reign of Theodosius, the Christian Emperor of Rome, the title of Cardinal was borne by his Prime Minister. But now both the name and the power implied in the name have long since disappeared from all civil functionaries of temporal sovereigns and those only who aid the Pope in wielding the key of Janus – in opening and shutting – are known by the title of Cardinals, or priests of the "hinge." Two Babylons pp 206 - 211.

The above image compares an aerial view of St. Peter's square and the basilica, laid out as a keyhole, with the obelisk in its centre. (Compare keyhole image) Even the architecture gives credence to its claim of being the access to the gates of heaven and hell? Notice also the pagan sundial, the largest in the world.

But how could those deceptions enter the Christian church since most authors view the Roman Church as having its roots in Christianity?

"Little by little, at first in stealth and silence, and then more openly as it increased in strength and gained control of the minds of men, "the mystery of iniquity" carried forward its deceptive work. Almost imperceptibly the customs of heathenism found their way into the Christian church. The spirit of compromise and conformity was restrained for a time by the fierce persecutions which the church endured under paganism. But as persecution ceased, and Christianity entered the courts and palaces of kings, she laid aside the humble simplicity of Christ and his apostles for the pomp and pride of pagan priests and rulers; and in place of the requirements of God she substituted human theories and traditions. The nominal conversion of Constantine in the early part of the fourth century, caused great rejoicing; and the world, cloaked with a form of righteousness, walked into the church. Now the work of corruption rapidly progressed. Paganism, while appearing to be vanquished, became the conqueror. Her spirit controlled the church. Her doctrines, ceremonies, and superstitions were incorporated into the faith and worship of the professed followers of Christ." The Great Controversy, E G White pp 49-50.

Does the Papacy still insist in our modern times that the Petrine Keys (The keys of Janus and Cybele) give them absolute authority on earth? Let's examine the following statement:

"Because it was only to Simon Peter, the chief of his Apostles, and to Simon Peter's lawful successors in the Holy See, that Jesus confided the Keys of his moral authority, the Roman Catholic Church has always claimed -

111

and, under John Paul II, claims today - to be the ultimate arbiter of what is morally good and what is morally bad in human actions. Those Keys, sanctified and strengthened in the blood of Jesus himself, are the symbol and the substance of John Paul's insistence upon a moral assessment of the world he travels and monitors so closely." The keys of this blood, Malachi Martin p 157.

(It has been established that Simon Peter was never in Rome so unfortunately this assertion of him being the first Pope is a fable.)

As has been established so far, Satan is using the Papacy and the Catholic Church to establish his own ends. John the Revelator has identified that organisation as "MYSTERY, BABYLON THE GREAT, THE MOTHER OF HARLOTS AND ABOMINATIONS OF THE EARTH." Notice how this description has been capitalised, there is not another portion of scripture that this has been done to, except where Jesus states in Exodus 3:14 "I AM THAT I AM" Such an emphasis in the case of the papal church must be to emphasise the great importance of the statement, similar to emphasising in an email or text message.

The "Petrine Keys" having been identified as nothing else but the sign of the absolute authority of Satan, under a pagan symbol (and the dragon [Satan] gave him [the papacy] his [Satan's] power and his [Satan's] seat and great authority. What then could the papacy be using to so absolutely deceive the nations of earth into believing that the Roman church is the true church of Christ, except that she uses the true Gospel to cloak her fallacies. In the following chapter we will bring to light some of the most important of the practises that God describes as abominations.

Another clue – this power will be established on seven mountains (hills). We quoted from Revelation 17:9 in the previous chapter "And here [is] the mind which hath wisdom. The seven heads are seven mountains, on which the woman sitteth."

"The Archbasilica of St. John Lateran is the oldest and most important of the four Major Papal Basilicas in the Catholic Church. And, it is this because it is the seat, or cathedra, of the Pope, the Bishop of Rome.

St. John Lateran basilica stands on the site of an ancient palace on the Caelian Hill (one of the famous seven hills) of Rome which formerly belonged to the family of the Laterani. This palace was part of the dowry of Fausta, the wife of the Emperor Constantine; and Constantine gave it to the Church when he converted a portion of the Laterani palace to serve as the papal residence. The original dedication in 324 A.D. was to the Redeemer (S. Salvator–see the words [Christo Salvatore] in the picture above); but after destruction by an earthquake in 896 A.D., the church was rebuilt by Pope Sergius III (904–11), who dedicated it to St. John the Baptist."

113

It became, and still is the Ecclesiastical seat of the Bishop of Rome. In it is a throne called the 'Cathedra' which is a seat, a chair with arms.

"The Revelation of Jesus Christ, which God gave unto him, to show unto his servants things which must shortly come to pass; and he sent and signified [it] by his angel unto his servant John: Who bare record of the word of God, and of the testimony of Jesus Christ, and of all things that he saw." Revelation 1:1-2.

Notice the sequence – Jesus' revelation, given to Him by God, to show His servants (those that choose to love Him) things that are definitely going to happen, sent by His angel to John who records everything that he sees and hears.

Rev 1:1 The Revelation[G602] of Jesus[G2424] Christ,

Revelation means to reveal and as we are on the subject of the MYSTERY we are assured that the MYSTERY will be revealed for all those that want to know the truth.

G602

ἀποκάλυψις

apokalupsis

ap-ok-al'-oop-sis

From G601; *disclosure:* - appearing, coming, lighten, manifestation, be revealed, revelation.

"And after these things I saw another angel come down from heaven, having great power; and the earth was lightened with his glory. And he cried mightily with a strong voice saying, Babylon the great is fallen, is fallen, and is become the habitation of devils, and the hold of every foul spirit, and a cage of every unclean and hateful bird. And I heard another voice from heaven, saying, come out of her, my people, that ye be not partakers of her sins, and that ye receive not of her plagues." Rev. 18:2-4.

Inscription on Saint John Lateran Archbasilica: "The Mother and Head of all Churches, in the City and of the World"

"MYSTERY, BABYLON THE GREAT"

"..MYSTERY, BABYLON THE GREAT, THE MOTHER OF HARLOTS AND ABOMINATIONS OF THE EARTH."

It has already been pointed out that the above verse is in upper case? Many of us are aware if we capitalise words in text messages, emails etc. then we are shouting? Rev: 17:5 is 'SHOUTING' at us, therefore, EXTREMELY IMPORTANT.

How do we avoid receiving the plagues of this fallen church and what has this fallen church done and will continue to do? Remember the papal claim as per the inscription on St. John Lateran Basilica in Rome?

"The mother and head of all churches, in the city and of the world"

The points to be considered in the Roman church becoming what she is today are so numerous, that the problem could be, what aspects do you begin with? It would be easy to say begin at the beginning. What you will discover is that it is the same Mystery Religion from the time of Nimrod that is cloaked as 'Christian'. What better way is there to deceive than to pretend to be a Christian church. We will also be touching on other current manifestations of this MYSTERY Religion in this chapter.

"Beware of false prophets, which come to you in sheep's clothing, but inwardly they are ravening wolves." Matthew 7:15.

"For I know this, that after my departing shall grievous wolves enter in among you, not sparing the flock." Acts 20:29.

The exposure of some of the Roman church's many pagan rites, will also expose other religions or organisations that carry out similar practises, or deviations from the original Gospel as outlined in scripture as daughter harlots, rendering the term "MOTHER OF HARLOTS" quite appropriate. A mother would not be a mother without offspring and similarly, daughters would not exist without a mother; this is in itself a significant clue that things are not what they seem to be, not only in the Catholic Church but across Christendom and churches generally around the world.

In this chapter we will be focusing on the Eucharistic Practises/Tabernacles, Mary Worship, Seeking to change times and Laws and other organisations and their leaders that support the mysteries. What will be discovered is that some of them publicly declare their connection to the MYSTERIES but the real danger for the humanity is that a church that professes to be Christian is actually Pagan and the cradle of the MYSTERY, therefore perfectly described by scripture as MYSTERY, BABYLON THE GREAT, THE MOTHER OF HARLOTS AND ABOMINATIONS OF THE EARTH.

A harlot implies unfaithfulness, selling one's body to whoever. In a religious sense it would imply harlotting with all types of ideas that are not true. In the case of a married couple, the moment you became physically involved with another person apart from the one you were avowed to, you become an adulterer. A harlot specifically sells herself to all and sundry and therefore in a religious sense selling herself to all and sundry religious ideas and practises. This is a very dangerous organisation to be associated with and this why Jesus tells us without any equivocation that this false church of Satan will eventually be destroyed.

As outlined in the previous chapter, the Petrine Keys having been identified as none other than the keys of Janus and Cybele an androgyne god; Marduk the patron god of Babylon being the earliest example and being the god of 50 names. One of his names being Bel, otherwise known as Baal, Moloch, etc. worshipped under all these titles as the sun god, the first creative god, as Marduk, was known. The Eucharist is a symbol of the sun god and the vast majority of Catholics are unaware of this. Before you can receive the Eucharist you need to confess your sins to a priest in order to receive pardon. What does Jesus have to say about this as described by John in Revelation 13:5-6?

"And there was given unto him a mouth speaking great things and blasphemies and he opened his mouth in blasphemy against God, to blaspheme His name, and His tabernacle, and them that dwell in heaven." This verse indicates clearly that the system represented here blasphemes God, and his tabernacle etc. how does this happen?

In the Gospels we find two indications of what constitutes blasphemy. In John 10:33 we read that the Jews falsely charged Jesus with blasphemy because, said they, "Thou, being a man, makest thyself God." This in the case of the Saviour was untrue, because He is the Son of God. He was "Immanuel, God with us. "But for man to assume the prerogatives of God and to take the titles of deity this is blasphemy.

Again, in Luke 5:21 we see the Pharisees trying to catch Jesus in His words, "Who is this which speaketh blasphemies?" said they, "Who can forgive sins, but God alone?" Jesus could pardon transgressions, because He is the divine Saviour. But for man, mortal man, to claim such authority is definitely blasphemy. Blasphemy, is to declare the ability to forgive sins, if you are not God.

We ask if the power represented by this symbol has fulfilled this prophecy? Observe what the pope and papal priests say about their power to forgive sins:

"The priest holds the place of the Saviour himself, when, by saying, "Ego te absolvo" (I thee absolve), he absolves from sin... To pardon a simple sin requires all the Omnipotence of God... But what only God can do by his Omnipotence, the priest can also do by saying "Ego te absolvo a peccatis tuis." (I absolve you from your sins) .. Innocent III has written: "Indeed, it is not too much to say that in the sublimity of their offices that the priests are so many gods."

Note still further the blasphemous utterances of this power: "But our wonder should be far greater when we find that in obedience to the words of his priests – Hoc Est Corpus Meum (This is my body) - God himself descends on the altar, that He comes wherever they call Him, and as often as they call Him, and places Himself in their hands, even though they should be His enemies. And after having come, He remains, entirely at their disposal; they move Him as they please, from one place to another; they may, if they wish, shut Him up in the tabernacle, or expose Him on the altar, or carry Him outside the church; they may, if they choose, eat His flesh, and give Him for the food of others."

"Oh, how very great is their power," says St. Laurence Justinian, speaking of priests. "A word falls from their lips and the body of Christ is there substantially formed from the matter of bread, and the Incarnate Word descended from Heaven, is found really present on the table of the altar!"

"Thus the priest may, in a certain manner, be called the creator of his creator ... The power of the priest, says St. Bernardine of Sienne, is the power of the divine person; for the transubstantiation of the bread requires as much power as the creation of the world."

This beast power blasphemes the temple in heaven by turning the attention of his subjects to his own throne and palace instead of to the tabernacle of God; by diverting their attention from the sacrifice of the Son of God, to the sacrifice of the mass. He blasphemes them that dwell in heaven by assuming to exercise the power of forgiving sins, and so turns away the minds of men from the mediatorial work of Christ and His heavenly assistants in the sanctuary above.

The Roman church insists that you make a confession of your sins to the priest, before and to qualify you to take part in the sacrifice of the mass and receive the bread or wafer, that is called the host, the host after it has been consecrated, then becomes the rounded eucharist, (it's miraculous transformation by the priest into the body of Christ), before you can be absolved of your sins.

There are several fundamental problems with the mass as conducted by the Roman Catholic priests.

Christ did say "this is my body," He also said "this do in remembrance of me," This did not mean that it was His actual body. If that was the case, He would have been cannibalising his own flesh; He meant that the last supper was to remember His personal sacrifice, through death, for the sins of humanity.

Christ broke the bread and gave his disciples, and they all ate. The Eucharist, by contrast, must be taken in its completely rounded form. (its rounded form is to do with sun-worship).

The Eucharist is worshipped as the actual divine presence of Christ. The Lord states in the scriptures that we should not worship the likeness of anything that is in heaven or earth, except God himself. Worshipping the Eucharist would therefore become idolatry. The Lord left us His instructions so that we would not be deceived into worshipping false gods.

A general confession of all sins is insisted upon by the priesthood before receiving the Eucharist in order to be absolved (forgiven) of your sins. The Lord requires us to request forgiveness of sins only through Him. "Our father which art in heaven... forgive us our trespasses," the only exception is when someone has personally wronged you, you can forgive them either if they approach you, or if you forgive them as Christ requests us to by His Gospel, "as we forgive them that trespass against us." There is nowhere to be found in scripture that we have to make any general confession to any other human being or priest in order to receive forgiveness of our sins, and any sins we commit is ultimately against God not against the mortal priests of the Roman Catholic Church. Jesus Himself said in John 14:6 "…, I am the way, the truth, and the life: no man cometh unto the Father, but by me." Plain as ABC, there is no priest between Jesus and the Father.

The Eucharist is offered up to Mary to be blessed, and then given back to be consumed, therefore attempting to make her the mediator between the priest and Christ. We have no account of Mary ever going to heaven, or of her being the mediator from scripture; where then are such origins? Mary is dead and buried like all other dead human beings, and as Mary is dead, who is the Eucharist being offered up to or being blessed by? An apparition? Furthermore as apparitions are not real but manifestations of demons, then the Eucharist is actually being blessed by and to demons and ultimately to Satan. The bible does describe the Vatican as "…..the habitation of devils, and the hold of every foul spirit, and a cage of every unclean and hateful bird." This is a terrible description and we must run away as far as possible into the loving arms of Jesus and ask Him to help us find His true church.

Jesus after his resurrection, went to the Father in Heaven and is now mediating on our behalf in the Heavenly sanctuary. While the Israelites were in the wilderness, the priests officiated in the sanctuary that was modelled after the Heavenly. This idea of the confessional has been handed down directly as part of the initiations into the Ancient Babylonian Mysteries, and has nothing whatsoever to do with the forgiveness of sins, except for leading penitents into greater and more diabolical sins than they could have personally imagined.

I remember my late father telling me that when he came out of his first confessional as a young man that his mind was far more corrupted than when he went in because of the lewd questioning of the priest. There are numerous accounts of the corrupting influences of the priest found in a book entitled "The Priest, the woman and the confessional" Truly disturbing reading and no doubt there are other books.

The Enc. Brit. 24:705:2b indicates that the Mysteries commenced with fasting etc., further it states "In all the mystery religions the candidates swore an oath of secrecy; ... before initiation, a confession of sins was expected."

"It is impossible to assign an exact date for "Auricular confession" - the confessing of faults by an individual penitent to a priest – but it must have arisen in the early middle-ages with the disappearance of the penitential system. This is the penitential rite that has endured into modern times. It was rejected by most of the reformers on the ground that God alone can forgive sins.

The Roman Catholic Church claims that the absolution of the priest is an act of forgiveness; to receive it the penitent must confess all serious (mortal) sins and manifest genuine "contrition" sorrow for sins, and a reasonably firm purpose of amendment. No quality or Quantity of sin is too great for sacramental absolution." Enc. Brit. 26:955: lb.

"There are some Christians who are awake to what is going on, but there are many Christians today who believe everything is just fine. Everybody loves everybody else. The Christians, Mormons, Jews, Jehovah Witnesses, Moslems are all serving the same God, but in different ways. If I asked "Can you partake of the Lord's supper with Catholics?" they'd say, "Why not?" Let's find out if there is a difference between the Lord's supper and the mass. Before I go on, let me explain that the bread, or wafer, used in the mass is called the host. When the host has been consecrated and offered as a sacrifice in the mass, it then becomes the Eucharist. I am going to try and put into everyday language what is one of the great motivating forces behind the Roman Catholic Institution.

It is the Eucharist. I call it the little Jesus Cookie... The Roman Catholic Institution in their Canon Laws state: "If any one shall deny that the body and blood, together with the soul and divinity of our Lord Jesus Christ, and therefore entire Christ, are truly, really, and substantially contained in the Sacrament of the Most Holy Eucharist; and shall say that he is only in it as a sign, or in a figure, let him be accursed." (Accursed means to be damned, under a curse.) "If anyone shall say that Christ, the only begotten Son of God, is not to be adored in the Holy Sacrament of the Eucharist .... and that he is not to be publicly set before the people to be adored, and that his adorers are Idolaters, let him be accursed."

That's when, beloved, the priest walks out holding up the cookie in the monstrance, which looks like a sunburst, and people come up and kiss it and adore it and if any protestant would say, "Hey, that's Idolatry," that protestant is to be accursed. Now, to sum this up, the Roman Catholic Institution teaches that you must believe that the bread, or host consecrated in the mass actually becomes Jesus Christ and is to be worshipped as God Almighty. This is why, back in 1554, a priest carrying the Eucharist could stand before a family of Christians in Scotland, tied to posts with dried brush up to their waists, he'd hold that piece of bread before them and ask if what he held in his hand was actually the body, blood and deity of Jesus Christ. When they said "No, it is only a symbol," the priest's assistant placed his flaming torch into the brush and set those Bible-believers on fire. As the victims screamed in agony, the priest held up his crucifix and said," All this is for the greater glory of God."

It holds firm, just as strong today, as it did in the time of the middle ages, that anyone who ridicules it, or says that it only represents Christ, is damned. The Vatican II council "(fall of 1962 and December 1965)" re-affirmed this. Pope John XXIII said, "I do accept entirely all that has been decided and declared at the Council of Trent." That Canon

Law is still in effect today, beloved." Smokescreens by J.T.Chick pp 7-ll.

In 2017 the Catholic Church still teaches that Christ is physically present in the Eucharist. "(Vatican Radio) Pope Francis has reminded the faithful that the Eucharist is a wonderful event during which Jesus Christ, our life, becomes present." Pope Francis 8th November 2017 speaking to a crowd gathered in St. Peter's Square.

The Eucharist which is received as the final indication of a penitents' forgiveness of his/her sins, after the auricular confession, is one of the most diabolical of blasphemous inventions of Satan through which he receives homage; however, as is known, it is impossible to receive the Eucharist without first confessing; this confession, is the tool that Satan uses to doubly damn souls to hell, if such a term can be used; it is degrading, suggestive, monstrous. The following extracts from a book written by an ex-priest of Rome will give some indication, if not already experienced, of the devastation caused by the auricular confession.

"There are two women who ought to be constant objects of the compassion of the Disciples of Christ, and for whom daily prayers ought to be offered at the mercy-seat—the Brahmin woman, who, deceived by her priests, burns herself on the corpse of her husband to appease the wrath of her wooden gods; *[it is rumoured to be continuing even in our modern times of 2018]* and the Roman Catholic woman, who, not less deceived by her priests, suffers a torture far more cruel and ignominious in the confessional-box to appease the wrath of her wafer-god."

"For I do not exaggerate when I say, that for many noble-hearted, well-educated, high-minded women, to be forced to unveil their hearts before the eyes of a man, to open to him all the most secret recesses of their souls, all the most sacred mysteries of their single or married life, to allow him to put to them questions which the most depraved woman would never consent to hear from her vilest seducer, is often more horrible and intolerable than to be tied on burning coals.

More than once, I have seen women fainting in the confessional-box, who told me afterwards, that the necessity of speaking to an unmarried man on certain things, on which the most common laws of decency ought to have for ever sealed their lips, had almost killed them! Not hundreds, but thousands of times, I have heard from the lips of dying girls, as well as of married women, the awful words; "I am forever lost! All my past confessions and communions have been so many sacrileges! Shame has sealed my lips and damned my soul!"

How many times I remained as one petrified, by the side of a corpse, when the last words having hardly escaped the lips of my female penitents, who had been snatched out of my reach by the merciless hand of death, before I could give her pardon through the deceitful sacramental absolution I then believed, as the dead sinner herself had believed, that she could not be forgiven except by that absolution.

For there are not only thousands but millions of Roman Catholic girls and women whose keen sense of modesty and womanly dignity are above all the sophisms and diabolical machinations of the priests. They never can be persuaded to answer "Yes" to certain questions of their confessors. They would prefer to be thrown into the flames, and burnt to ashes with the Brahmin widows, rather than allow the eyes of a man to pry into the sacred sanctuary of their souls.

Though sometimes guilty before God, and under the impression that their sins will never be forgiven if not confessed, the laws of decency are stronger in their hearts than the laws of their cruel and perfidious church. No consideration, not even the fear of eternal damnation, can persuade them to declare to a sinful man, sins which God alone has the right to know, for he alone can blot them out with the blood of his Son, shed on the cross.

But what a wretched life must that be of those exceptional noble souls, which Rome keeps in the dark dungeons of her superstition? They read in all their books, and hear from all their pulpits, that if they conceal a single sin from their confessors, they are forever lost! But, being absolutely unable to trample under their feet the laws of self-respect and decency, which God himself has impressed in their souls, they live in constant dread of eternal damnation. No human words can tell their desolation and distress, when at the feet of their confessors, they find themselves under the horrible necessity of speaking of things, on which they would prefer to suffer the most cruel death rather than to open their lips, or to be forever damned if they do not degrade themselves forever in their own eyes, by speaking on matters which a respectable woman will never reveal to her own mother, much less to a man!

I have known only too many of these noble-hearted women, who, when alone with God, in a real agony of desolation and with burning tears, had asked Him to grant them what they considered the greatest favour, which was, to lose so much of their self-respect as to be enabled to speak of those unmentionable things, just as their confessors wanted them to speak; and, hoping that their petition had been granted, they went again to the confessional-box, determined to unveil their shame before the eyes of that inexorable man. But when the moment had come for the self-immolation, their courage failed, their knees trembled, their lips became pale as death, cold sweat poured from all their pores! The voice of modesty and womanly self-respect was speaking louder than the voice of their false religion.

They had to go out of the confessional-box unpardoned - nay, with the burden of a new sacrilege on their conscience. Oh! How heavy is the yoke of Rome - how bitter is human life - how cheerless is the mystery of the cross to those deluded and perishing souls! How gladly they would rush into the blazing piles with the Brahmin women, if they could hope to see the end of their unspeakable miseries through the momentary tortures which would open to them the gates of a better life!

I do hereby publicly challenge the whole Roman Catholic priesthood to deny that the greater part of their female penitents remain a certain period of time – some longer, some shorter - under that most distressing state of mind. Not a single Roman Catholic priest will dare to deny what I say on this matter; for they know that it would be easy for me to overwhelm them with such a crowd of testimonies that their grand imposture would be forever unmasked....

How many times have I wept as a child when some noble-hearted and intelligent young girl, or some respectable married woman, yielding to the sophisms with which I or some other confessor, had persuaded them to give up their self-respect, and their womanly dignity, to speak with me on matters on which a decent woman would never say a word with a man. They have told me of their invincible repugnance, their horror of such questions and answers, and they have asked me to have pity on them. Yes! I have often wept bitterly on my degradation, when a priest of Rome!

I have realised all the strength, the grandeur, and the holiness of their motives for being silent on these defiling matters, and I could not but admire them. It seemed at times that they were speaking the language of angels of light; that I ought to fall at their feet, and ask their pardon for having spoken to them of questions on which a man of honour ought never to converse with a woman whom he respects.

But Alas! I had soon to reproach myself, and regret those short instances of my wavering faith in the infallible voice of my church; I had soon to silence the voice of my conscience, which was telling me, Is it not a shame that you, an unmarried man, to dare to speak on these matters with a woman? Do not you blush to put such questions to a young girl? Where is your self-respect? Where is your fear of God? Do you not promote the ruin of that girl by forcing her to speak on such matters?

I was compelled by all the popes, the moral theologians, and the councils of Rome, to believe that this warning voice of my merciful God was the voice of Satan; I had to believe in spite of my own conscience and intelligence, that it was good, nay, necessary, to put those polluting, damning questions. My infallible church was mercilessly forcing me to oblige those poor, trembling, weeping, desolate girls and women, to swim with me and all her priests in those waters of Sodom and Gomorrah, under the pretext that their self-will be broken down, their fear of sin and humility increased, and that they would be purified by our absolutions.

With what supreme distress, disgust, and surprise, we see, today, a great part of the whole Episcopal Church of England struck by a plague which seems incurable, under the name of Puseyism, or Ritualism, and bringing again - more or less openly – in many places the diabolical and filthy auricular confession among the Protestants of England, Australia and America. The Episcopal Church is doomed to perish in that dark and stinking pool of Popery - auricular confession, if she does not find a prompt remedy to stop the plague brought by the disguised Jesuits, who are at work everywhere, to poison and enslave her too unsuspecting daughters and sons....

Christian nations! If you could know what will become of the virtue of your fair daughters if you allow secret or public slaves of Rome under the name of ritualists to restore the auricular confession, with what a storm of holy indignation would you defeat their plans." The Priest, the woman, and the confessional pp 13-15, 17, 39.

For a fuller account of the tragedies brought about by the confessional, it is recommended that the whole book is read.

How widespread was the problem? – Pope Pius IV about the year 1560, requested all penitents who were seduced by their priests to denounce those priests that they may be dealt with. It was found that the number of priests who were guilty, rendered it impossible to punish them all, so the inquest was abandoned, and the guilty confessors remained unpunished. Ibid p.43.

Does the Roman Church still consider confession of sins to priests important?

130

"Pope John Paul II... on Tuesday told Roman Catholics to seek forgiveness through the church and not directly from God. In a major document on the need for confession of sin, the pontiff laid down guidelines for the world's nearly 800 million Roman Catholics on the purpose of confessing sins to priests. The requirements for confessing sin through priests is one of the fundamental principles of Roman Catholicism." The Associated Press. December 11th, 1984.

All of this is done in the name of the mass. Since the Lord Jesus Christ would not have such evil practises carried out in His name; Logic leaves us to consider that the only other power that could have organised such a debasing practise is Satan himself. That the round wafer - Eucharist - represents Satan, we will now set out to prove.

"We find the women of Judah represented as simply "burning incense, pouring out drink-offerings, and baking cakes to the queen of heaven" (Jeremiah 44:19). The cakes were "the un-bloody sacrifice" she required. That "un-bloody sacrifice" her votaries not only offered, but when admitted to the higher mysteries, they partook of, swearing anew fidelity to her. In the fourth century, when the queen of heaven, under the name of Mary, was beginning to be worshipped in the Christian church, this "un-bloody sacrifice also was brought in. Epiphanius states, the practise of offering and eating it began among the women of Arabia; and at that time it was well known to have been adopted from the pagans. The very shape of the un-bloody sacrifice of Rome may indicate whence it came. It is a small thin, round wafer; and on its roundness the church of Rome lays so much stress, to use the pithy language of John Knox in regard to the wafer - god, "If, in making, the roundness of the ring be broken, then must another of his fellow cakes receive that honour to be made a god, and the crazed or cracked miserable cake, that once was in hope to be made a god, must be given to a baby to play withal."

What could have induced the Papacy to insist so much on the "roundness" of its "un-bloody sacrifice"? Clearly not any reference to the divine institution of the supper of the Lord; for in all the accounts that are given of it, no reference whatever is made to the form of the bread which our Lord took, when he blessed and brake it, and gave it to his disciples, saying, "Take, eat; this is my body: this do in remembrance of me." As little can it be taken from any regard to injunctions about the Jewish Paschal bread; for no injunctions on that subject are given in the books of Moses.

The importance, however, which Rome attaches to the roundness of the wafer, must have a reason; and that reason will be found, if we look at the altars of Egypt. "The thin, round cake," says Wilkinson, "occurs on all altars." Almost every jot or tittle in the Egyptian worship had a symbolical meaning. The round disk, so frequent in the sacred emblems of Egypt, symbolised the sun. Now, when, Osiris, the sun-divinity, became incarnate, and was born, it was not merely that he should give his life as a sacrifice for men, but that he should also be the life and nourishment of the souls of men.

It is universally admitted that Isis was the original of the Greek and Roman Ceres. But Ceres, be it observed, was worshipped not simply as the discoverer of corn; she was worshipped as "the Mother of corn." The child she brought forth was He-Siri, "The Seed," or, as he was most frequently called in Assyria, "Bar, "which signifies at once "the son" and the "corn." The uninitiated might reverence ceres for the gift of material corn to nourish their bodies, but the initiated adored her for a higher gift - for food to nourish their souls - for giving them that bread of God that

Cometh down from heaven - for the life of the world, of which, "if a man eat, he shall never die." Does anyone imagine that it is a mere New Testament doctrine, that Christ is the "Bread of Life"?

There never was, there never could be, spiritual life in any soul, since the world began, at least since the expulsion from Eden, that was not nourished and supported by a continual feeding by faith on the Son of God, "in whom it hath pleased the Father that all fullness should dwell" (Colossians 1:19) "that out of his fullness we might receive, and grace for grace" (John 1:16). Paul tells us that the manna of which the Israelites ate in the wilderness was to them a type and lively symbol of "the Bread of Life;" (1 Corinthians 10:3), "They did all eat the same spiritual meat" i.e., food that was intended not only to support their natural lives, but to point to him who was the life of their souls.

Now, Clement of Alexandria, to whom we are largely indebted for all the discoveries that in modern times have been made in Egypt, expressly assures us that, "in their hidden character, the enigmas of the Egyptians were very similar to those of the Jews." That the initiated pagans actually believed that the "corn" which ceres bestowed on the world was not the "corn" of this earth, but the divine "Son through whom alone spiritual and eternal life could be enjoyed, we have clear and decisive proof. The Druids were devoted worshippers of Ceres, and as such they were celebrated in their mystic poems as "bearers of the ears of corn."

Now, the following is the account which the Druids give of their great divinity, under the form of "Corn." That divinity was represented as having, in the first instance, incurred, for some reason or other, the displeasure of Ceres, and as fleeing in terror from her. In his terror, "he took the form of a bird, and mounted into the air. That element afforded him no refuge; for the lady, in the form of a sparrow-hawk, was gaining upon him. Shuddering with dread, he perceived a heap of clean wheat upon a floor, dropped into the midst of it, and assumed the form of a single grain. Ceridwin (i.e. the British Ceres) took the form of a black high-crested hen, descended into the wheat scratched him out, distinguished, and swallowed him. And as the history relates, she was pregnant of him nine months, and when delivered of him, she found him such a lovely babe, that she had no resolution to put him to death."

Here it is evident that the grain of corn, is expressly identified with "the lovely babe"; from which it is still further evident that Ceres, who, to the profane vulgar was known only as the mother of "Bar," "the corn," was known to the initiated as the mother of "Bar," "the son." And now, the reader will be prepared to understand the full significance of the representation in the celestial sphere of "the virgin with the ear of wheat in her hand." That ear of wheat in the virgin's hand is just another symbol for the child in the arms of the virgin mother.

Now, this son, who was symbolised as "corn" was the sun-divinity incarnate, according to the sacred oracle of the great goddess of Egypt: "No mortal hath lifted my veil. The fruit which I have brought forth is the Sun." What more natural then, if this incarnate divinity is symbolised as the "bread of God" than that he should be represented as a "round wafer," to identify him with the sun?"

Notice how this pagan legend exactly mimics the virgin birth of Jesus Christ, the Son of God, by the Virgin Mary. Mary was with child before she knew any man - not even her husband - (No mortal hath lifted my veil). "Behold a

Virgin shall be with child." Matthew 1: 23. Notice also that this sun-divinity was to be a sacrifice for men and also the life and nourishment of the souls of men?

"Is this a mere fancy? Let the reader peruse the following extract from Hurd, in which he describes the embellishments of the Romish altar, on which the sacraments or consecrated wafer is deposited, and then he will be able to judge; - "A plate of silver, in the form of a Sun, is fixed opposite to the sacrament on the altar; which, with the light of the tapers, makes a most brilliant appearance."

What has that "brilliant" "sun" to do there, on the altar, over against the "Sacrament," or round wafer? In Egypt, the disk of the Sun was represented in the temples, and the sovereign and his wife and children were represented as adoring it. Near the small town of Babain, in upper Egypt, there still exists in a grotto, a representation of a sacrifice to the sun, where two priests are seen worshipping the sun's image.

In the great temple of Babylon, the golden image of the sun was exhibited for the worship of the Babylonians.

In the temple of Cuzco, in Peru, the disk of the sun was fixed up in flaming gold upon the wall that all who entered might bow down before it.

The Paeonians of Thrace were sun-worshippers; and in their worship they adored an image of the sun in the form of a disk at the top of a long pole.

In the worship of Baal, as practised by the idolatrous Israelites in the days of their apostasy, the worship of the sun's image was equally observed; and it is striking to find that, the image of the sun, which apostate Israel worshipped, was erected above the altar. When the good king Josiah set about the work of reformation, we read that his servants in carrying out the work, proceeded thus (2: Chronicles 34:4). "And they break" "down the altars of Baalim in his presence, and the images (margin, sun-images) that were on high above them, he cut down." We will pause from this extract to highlight other popular names under which this deity, represented as the sun, was worshipped.

"The worship of Baal was popular in Egypt from the later New Kingdom c. 1400 to its end (1085 BC), and, through the influence of the Aramaeans, who borrowed the Babylonian pronunciation Bel, he ultimately became known as the Greek Belos, identified with Zeus. Baal was also worshipped by various communities as a local god. The Old Testament speaks frequently of the Baal of a given place or refers to Baalim in the plural, suggesting the evidence of local deities, or lords, of various locales. It is not known to what extent that the Canaanites considered those various Baalim identical, but the Baal of Ugarit does not seem to have confined his activities to one city, and doubtless other communities agreed in giving him cosmic scope." Enc. Brit: 1:762:2e.

"The worship of Bel and Astarte was very early introduced into Britain, along with the Druids, the priests of the groves." Some have imagined that the Druidical worship was first introduced by the Phoenicians, who, centuries before the Christian era, traded to the tin-mines of Cornwall. But the unequivocal traces of that worship are found in regions of the British Islands where the Phoenicians never penetrated, and has everywhere left indelible marks of the strong hold which it must have had on the early British mind. From Bel, the 1st of May is still called Beltane *(May day)* in the Almanac; and we have customs still lingering at this day among us, which prove how exactly the worship of Bel or Moloch (for both titles belonged to the same god) had been observed even in the northern parts of this island...."Two Babylons pg. 103.

Remember that Marduk was also known as Bel. We find above that this Bel was also worshipped as Baal. Does the picture begin to come clearer? As established also, Marduk is representative of Satan himself. The scriptures now also makes the connection plain. The chief of these Baals - Baalzebub - known also in the New Testament as "Beelzebub, let us read; "But when the Pharisees heard it, they said, this fellow doth not cast out devils, but by Beelzebub the prince of the devils." Matt. 12:24.

"But some of them said. He casteth out devils through Beelzebub the chief of the devils." Luke 11:15.

The chief of the Baals is none other than Satan himself.

We now continue with the earlier extract:-

"Benjamin of Tudela, the great Jewish traveller, gives a striking account of Sun-Worship even in comparatively modern times, as subsisting among the cushites of the east, from which we find that the image of the sun was even in his day, worshipped on the altar. "There is a temple," says he, "of the posterity of chus" (or cush), "addicted to the contemplation of the stars. They worship the Sun as a god, and the whole country, for half a mile round their town, is filled with great altars dedicated to him. By the dawn of morn they get up and run out of town, to wait the rising of the sun, to whom, on every altar, there is a consecrated image, not in the likeness of a man, but of the Solar orb, framed by Magic art. These orbs as soon as the sun rises,

137

take fire, and resound with a great noise, while everybody there, men and women, hold censers in their hands, and all burn incense to the sun."

From all this, it is manifest that the image of the sun above, or on the altar, was one of the recognised symbols of those who worshipped Baal or the Sun. And here, in a so-called Christian church, a brilliant plate of silver, "in the form of a Sun," is so placed on the altar, that everyone who adores at that altar must bow down in lowly reverence before that image of the "Sun."

Whence, I ask, could that have come, but from the ancient sun-worship, or the worship of Baal? And when the wafer is so placed that the silver "Sun" is fronting the "round wafer," whose "roundness" is so important an element in the Romish Mystery, what can be the meaning of it, but just to show to those who have the eyes to see, that the "Wafer" itself is only another symbol of Baal, or the Sun. If the sun-divinity was worshipped in Egypt as "the seed," or in Babylon as the "corn", precisely so is the wafer adored in Rome."

In the time of the Babylonians, it was easy for Satan to deceive the Babylonians with his version of the creation story etc; But as is obvious that he is an excellent bible scholar, knowing that in the future - between Babylon and our time that the tower and Babylon would be destroyed, he had to, right from there, begin to instil into the minds of the pagan, or Mystery religion followers another symbol which was, and would be always present for all to see, that being the Sun.

Everyone knows that if the Sun was to stop shedding its rays of light and warmth, every living thing, both plant and animal would perish on the earth and in the sea. What better then, than a symbol of his false claims to deity, the Sun.

"Bread-corn of the elect, have mercy upon us, is one of the appointed prayers of the Roman litany, addressed to the wafer, in the celebration of the mass. And one at least of the imperative requirements as to the way in which that wafer is to be partaken of, is the very same as was enforced in the old worship of the Babylonian divinity. Those who partake of it are required to partake absolutely fasting.... Considering that our Lord Jesus Christ instituted the Holy Communion immediately after his disciples had partaken of the Paschal Feast, such a strict requirement of fasting might seem very unaccountable. *(This rule was changed in 1964 under Canon 919 to 1 hour fasting for the general masses)* But look at this provision in regard to the "unbloody sacrifice" of the mass in the Eleusinian Mysteries, and it is accounted for at once; for there the first question put to those who sought initiation was, "are you fasting?" and unless that question could be answered in the affirmative, no initiation could take place....

Although the god whom Isis or Ceres brought forth, and who was offered to her under the symbol of the wafer or thin round cake, as "the bread of life," was in reality the fierce, scorching Sun, or terrible Moloch, yet in that offering all his terror was veiled, and everything repulsive was cast into the shade. In the appointed symbol he is offered to the benignant mother, who tempers judgment with mercy, and to whom all spiritual blessings are ultimately referred; and blessed by that mother, he is given back to be feasted upon, as the staff of life, as the nourishment of her worshipper's souls. Thus the mother was held up as the favourite divinity and thus, also, and for an entirely similar reason, does the Madonna of Rome entirely eclipse her son as the "Mother of Grace and Mercy."

Having established so far that the Madonna is pagan, the wafer is pagan, and is taken, note, for the spiritual nourishment of souls, not bodies, thence being spiritual food; the worshipers can be partaking of none else than the spiritual body of Satan. Do you understand what this means?

We continue "In regard to the pagan character of the "Unbloody Sacrifice" of the mass, we have seen not little already. But there is something yet to be considered, in which the working of the mystery of iniquity will still further appear. There are letters on the wafer that are worth reading. These letters are I.H.S. What mean those mystical letters? To a Christian these letters are represented as signifying, "Iesus Hominum Salvator," or "Jesus the Saviour of Men," But let a Roman worshipper of Isis (for in the age of the emperors there were innumerable worshippers of Isis in Rome) cast his eyes upon them, and how will he read them? He will read, of course, according to his own well-known system of Idolatry. Isis, Horus, Seb" that is, "The Mother, The Child, and the Father of the gods," in other words, "The Egyptian Trinity." Can the reader imagine that this double sense is accidental? Surely not. The very same spirit that converted the festival of the pagan Cannes into the feast of the Christian Joannes, retaining at the same time all its ancient paganism, has skillfully planned the initials I.H.S. to pay the semblance of a tribute to Christianity, while paganism in reality has all the substance of the homage bestowed upon it."

Here again, one of God's attributes, that of the trinity, has been mimicked by Satan; and this, perhaps, is why the group known as "Jehovah's Witnesses" hold, wrongly so, that any religion today, which teach that there is a heavenly trinity, are as false as the Roman Catholic Church. There is no scriptural authority to suggest that there is no trinity, on the contrary Christ said, "But the comforter, which is the Holy Ghost, whom the Father will send in my name, he shall teach you all things, and bring all things to your remembrance, whatsoever I have said unto you." Luke 14:26.

Further after Jesus was resurrected he said, "Go ye therefore, and teach all nations, baptizing them in the name of the Father, and of the Son, and of the Holy Ghost: Teaching them to observe all things whatsoever I have commanded you: and lo, I am with you alway, even unto the end of the world. Amen." Matt. 28:19-20.

What can be plainer evidence than this for an authentic Heavenly Trinity? Both from scripture, and from the fact that Satan saw fit to counterfeit the true?

We finalise the extract as follows; "When the women of Arabia began to adopt this wafer and offer "the unbloody sacrifice," all genuine Christians saw at once the real character of their sacrifice. They were treated as heretics, and branded with the name of Collyridians, from the Greek name for the cake which they employed. But Rome saw that the heresy could be turned into account: and therefore, though condemned by the sound portion of the church, the practise of offering and eating this "unbloody sacrifice" was patronised by the Papacy; and now, throughout the whole bounds of the Romish Communion, it has superseded the simple but most precious sacrament of the supper instituted by our Lord himself." Two Babylons pp 159-165.

"Where is this wafer kept? "I read the ninth chapter of Hebrews and twenty-fourth verse: For Christ is not entered into the Holy place made with hands (meaning, in the

Roman Catholic Church, the tabernacle that stands in the center of the altar, and in which a consecrated wafer is placed. The same wafer, the priests teach is really and truly the body, soul, and divinity of Christ and is therefore called the real presence. It is to this wafer all Catholics bow as they pass the Altar, believing it to be Christ himself complete in His humanity and divinity)." My life in the Convent by Margaret L Shepherd pg. 217.

Why is it important to have the wafer in the tabernacle on the altar? Remember, the wafer does not represent Christ.

To answer this question we need to remember at least two things. So far it has been proven that Satan has been copying the true, and that he was originally in Heaven. He demands the homage due only to God. We must also remember that not only has he deceived men, but that he also deceived billions of angels. It would be logical then that he would have a system of worship that closely reflects that of the true in Heaven. That there is a tabernacle in Heaven let us read.

"Now of the things which we have spoken this is the sum: We have such an High Priest, who is set on the right hand of the throne of the Majesty in the heavens; A minister of the sanctuary, and of the true tabernacle, which the Lord pitched, and not man." Hebrews 8:1-2.

"For Christ is not entered into the holy places made with hands, which are the figures of the true; but into heaven itself, now to appear in the presence of God for us." Hebrews 9:24. Therefore Christ is our high priest in the heavenly tabernacle, to whom we should request forgiveness of our sins, and to whom we should offer our worship.

Satan in his desire to receive homage, insists that we first confess our sins to a priest, become more corrupted by his priests, then pay homage to him through idolatry, and finally receive him as spiritual food through the consecrated wafer - Eucharist. This is an enormous deception.

Notice the sunburst in the window behind the altar?

We would have read in an earlier chapter that the temples were constructed as the dwelling place of the gods, and how in "Esagila" the chief Babylonian temple was constructed a "Niche" set up on a "Podium" where the god's place was, where he would actually be present, where his "seat" was.

When we examine this further, we will find that we have "Esagila's" counterpart, the "Baldachin" – set on high - Where is this "Baldachin" located?

As was common practise in all the ancient cities, the chief temple was where the chief deity was located. As there are altars in all the Roman churches, the chief public altar of the Roman Catholic Church is in St. Peter's Basilica, Vatican City, known as the Baldachin.

"And I stood upon the sand of the sea, and saw a beast rise up out of the sea, having seven heads and ten horns, and upon his horns ten crowns, and upon his heads the name of blasphemy." Revelation 13:1.

"And the beast which I saw was like unto a leopard, and his feet were as [the feet] of a bear, and his mouth as the mouth of a lion: and the dragon gave him his power, and his seat, and great authority." Revelation 13:2.

How many millions believe that they are worshipping Jesus there but in reality are worshipping the great apostate.

"And I saw one of his heads as it were wounded to death; and his deadly wound was healed: and all the world wondered after the beast." Revelation 13:3.

Revelation 18:2. "And he cried mightily with a strong voice, saying, Babylon the great is fallen, is fallen, and is become the habitation of devils, and the hold of every foul spirit, and a cage of every unclean and hateful bird."
Here as plain as ABC, the scriptures state that the Roman Church, located on the seven hills, is the habitation of devils. - "Dwelling place of the gods?" – The word "Vaticanus" in common latin means, "The place of divination." Which also has its origins from the ancient

Babylonian Magi (priests) of the Babylonian mysteries. The word Magic refers to supernatural powers, and came to us as a direct result of the witchcraft of the ancient Magi, hence, Magic.

Why does Satan demand worship? Allow the scriptures to answer, starting with Satan's original position in Heaven, in the government of God.

"Thou art the anointed cherub that covereth; and I have set thee so; thou wast upon the holy mountain of God; ... Thou wast perfect in thy ways from the day that thou wast created, till iniquity was found in thee." Isaiah 28:14-15.

The scriptures are here describing Satan's position before his fall. What is the meaning of the "cherub that covereth"?

"And make one cherub on the one end, and the other cherub on the other end...and the cherubims shall stretch forth their wings on high ... Covering the mercy seat with their wings... " Exodus 25:19-20.

The covering cherubs are the closest to the mercy seat, therefore Satan being described as the covering cherub was privileged to be the closest to God. The best way to seal his defiance of God he had to steal worship and by deceiving humans into worshipping him he is guaranteeing their fates with him of perishing.

There was a tabernacle on earth when Jesus freed the Israelites from Egyptian slavery and Paul in Hebrews 9:11 confirmed there being a tabernacle in heaven. "But Christ being come an high priest of good things to come, by a greater and more perfect tabernacle, not made with hands, that is to say, not of this building." Satan therefore to make

145

his system of false worship complete, had to set himself up in a place of worship.

The fact of the matter is, that, there at the great altar of St. Peters, the Baldachin, Satan is adored, both in his representation in the Eucharist and in the tabernacle, and his visible representative, the Pope, who as the sovereign of the Vatican state, he possesses his (the Pope's) body, just as he did with the ancient Babylonian kings. Consider this, in order for any man to be the leader of the place of divination, he must be the greatest diviner or devil-worshipper of all mankind. The tabernacles we will discuss in more detail in a later chapter.

Could there be any other pagan practises that the Roman church has adopted as pertaining to Christ? Yes there is.

As the scripture describes her "THE MOTHER OF HARLOTS," and as has been proven, she is nothing else now but the ancient mystery religion cloaked in Christianity, what can we put forward as some of the major aspects of her that most of the world adheres to in their various religions, therefore rendering them daughter harlots? At this juncture it is felt necessary to establish a fact that should be apparent. Some of the customs practised in the Roman church were being practised by other religions before she became Christianised. Some of the festivities and precepts as laid down by the Papacy, through the power and authority of Satan, have been somewhat unknowingly adopted by the majority of Protestants of today.

Mary-Worship

As established earlier, the Eucharist is first offered up to Mary to be blessed, and then it is given back to the penitent to be eaten. Mary, being the Romish name for the mother of the corn, also known as the "Mediatrix," "Mediator," between us and her son.

In paganism this son is known as "the deliverer," it is a biblical fact that there is no other deliverer apart from Christ. Mary is also known as The Madonna etc. "Everyone who studies the Bible, and sees how expressly it declares that, as there is only "One God," so there is only "One Mediator between God and man" (l. Tim. 2:6), must marvel how it could ever have entered the mind of anyone to bestow on Mary, as is done by the church of Rome, the character of the "Mediatrix." But the character ascribed to the Babylonian goddess as Mylitta sufficiently accounts for this. In accordance with the character of Mediatrix, she was called Aphrodite – that is, "The Wrath-subduer" - who by her charms could soothe the breast of Angry Jove, and soften the most ragged spirits of gods or mortal-men.

In Athens she was called Amarusia - that is, "The Mother of gracious acceptance." In Rome she was called "Bona Dea," the "Good goddess," the mysteries of this goddess being celebrated by women with peculiar secrecy. In India the goddess Lakshmi, "The Mother of the universe," the consort of Vishnu, is represented also as possessing the most, gracious and genial disposition; and that disposition is indicated in the same way as in the case of the Babylonian Goddess.

"In the festivals of Lakshmi," says Coleman, "no sanguinary sacrifices are offered." In China, the great gods, on whom the final destinations of mankind depend, are held up to the popular mind as objects of dread; but the goddess Kuanyin, "the goddess of mercy," whom the Chinese of Canton recognise as bearing an analogy to the virgin of Rome, is described as looking with an eye of compassion on the guilty, and interposing to save miserable souls even from torments to which in the world of spirits they have been doomed. Therefore she is regarded with peculiar favour by the Chinese. This character of the goddess-mother has evidently radiated in all directions from Chaldea.

Now, thus we see how it comes that Rome represents Christ, the "Lamb of God," meek and lowly in heart,... who spoke words of sweetest encouragement to every mourning penitent - who wept over Jerusalem – who prayed for his murderers - as a stern and miserable judge, before whom the sinner "might grovel in the dust, and still never be sure that his prayers would be heard," while Mary is set off in the most willing and engaging light, as the hope of the guilty, as the grand refuge of sinners; how is it that the former is said to have "reserved justice and judgment to himself," but to have committed the exercise of all mercy to his Mother! The most standard devotional works of Rome are pervaded by this very principle, exalting the compassion and gentleness of the mother at the expense of the loving character of the Son.

Thus, St. Alphonsus Ligouri tells his readers that the sinner that ventures to come directly to Christ may come with dread and apprehension of his wrath; but let him only employ the mediation of the Virgin with her Son, All this is done to exalt the mother, as more gracious and compassionate than her glorious Son. Now, this was the very case in Babylon: and to this character of the goddess queen her favourite offerings exactly correspond. Therefore, we find the women of Judea represented as simply "burning incense, pouring out drink-offerings, and offering cakes to the queen of heaven." Jeremiah 44:19." Two Babylons pg 157-8.

Mother and child worship:

"In Papal Italy, as travellers universally admit (except where the Gospel has recently entered), all appearance of worshipping the King Eternal and Invisible is almost extinct, while the Mother and the Child are the grand objects of worship. Exactly so, in this latter respect, also was it in ancient Babylon. The Babylonians, in their popular religion, supremely worshipped a Goddess Mother and a Son, who was represented in pictures and in images as an infant or child in his mother's arms. (Figs. 5 & 6). From Babylon, this worship of the Mother and the Child spread to the ends of the earth. In Egypt, the Mother and the Child were worshipped under the names of Isis and Osiris.

Fig. 5.

From Babylon.*

Fig. 6.

From India.†

149

In India, even to this day, as Isi and Iswara; in Asia, as Cybele and Deoius; in Pagan Rome, as Fortuna and Jupiter-puer, or Juiter, the boy; in Greece, as Ceres, the Great Mother, with the babe at her breast, or as Irene, the goddess of Peace, with the boy Plutus in her arms; and even in Thibet, in China, and Japan, the Jesuit missionaries were astonished to find the counterpart of Madonna and her child as devoutly worshipped as in Papal Rome itself; Shing Moo, the Holy Mother in China, being represented with a child in her arms, and a glory around her, exactly as if a Roman Catholic artist had been employed to set her up." Two Babylons, Hislop, p.20.

Need any further comment be added to the facts laid down in connection with the worship of Mary in the Roman church, except the following which shows that the Roman church never changes.

"Pope John Paul II's decision to set aside a special year devoted to Mary reflects his desire to bring back such traditional customs as Pilgrimages to sanctuaries and religious processions, Vatican officials say... The Vatican said the Catholics would gain indulgence, or the pardon of temporal punishment of sin, by devoutly taking part in some of the Marian year activities. ..

From the outset of his pontificate more than eight years ago, John Paul has displayed special devotion to her. He calls Mary the "heavenly mother of the church" and often invokes her intercession in public prayers." The Associated Press, 17th February, 1987.

On this point dear readers, do not be deceived because we find the following in the scriptures, "For there is one God, and one mediator between God and men, the man Christ Jesus." "Jesus saith, I am the way, the truth, and the life: no man cometh unto the Father, but by me." 1 Timothy 2:5, John 14:6, respectively.

Changing of times and laws:

"And he shall speak [great] words against the most High, and shall wear out the saints of the most High, and think to change times and laws:.." Daniel 7:25. How was this fulfilled?

As has been established in previous chapters, there are basically two systems, one true, one false. That the God of Heaven created all that we see, there is no doubt. However, as learned, Satan has also set up his mystery religion, and in setting up that religion he has set up a day specifically as a day of homage to him, in deliberate contrast to the true day of worship and remembrance established by God, as part of His creation.

The God of Heaven blessed and sanctified the Seventh Day to commemorate His six day creation process. Satan through all his various myths and legends, also attempts to claim that he created what we see around us and we can deduce from what we have discovered so far that Satan's homage is very involved with sun worship. Could it be then that "Sun" day (Sunday) is his day of worship? Let us explore. "And he shall speak great words against the Most High, ...and think to change times and laws:.." Daniel 7:25.

This changing attempt is against what God has instituted, and since it is not possible to alter any precept that the Creator Lord has instituted, then the term "think to" is appropriate. Further, that the word "change" is used, proves that some other condition existed before. It is impossible to change something that did not previously exist. Finally, what do the scriptures say that this power would seek to

151

change? The "Times and Laws" of God. This dear readers is the crux of the matter, as it will be the decider between those who serve the true God, and those who serve the false; since you will be worshipping the "holy" day set up by either, as a sign of your allegiance to the one you choose to serve. God is the only being entitled to our allegiance because He created us and He created Lucifer, he became Satan when he decided to rebel against his creator and through his false religion he demands/steals homage. How can a created being worship or follow another created being and expect a truly lasting and good outcome? It may sound simple now, but believe it, the matter will not be that simple, since Satan will make it extremely difficult at the time of the final spiritual battle for any of God's followers to keep the "True Sabbath." But it will not be impossible once you have the Lord of heaven on your side.

All Protestant churches today recognise (or have done so in the past), the Roman church as the whore of revelation. Yet what do we discover? The majority set aside Sunday as their special day of worship, or Sabbath. Some claim Sunday as special by stating that it is in recognition of the resurrection of Christ, "The Lord's day," and/or the Law was nailed to the cross, and that we are no longer under the "Law." Some, like the Jehovah's Witnesses go to the extreme by stating that all the days of the week are for worship, yet they work on them and they also congregate especially on 'Sundays.'? Three questions spring to mind here, where did this idea of "The Lord's Day" originate? And was there a law nailed to the cross? What law are these proponents actually trying to deny?

Sola Scriptura does confirm that there was a law nailed to the cross. "Blotting out the handwriting of ordinances that was against us, which was contrary to us, and took it out of the way, nailing it to his cross." Colossians 2:14.

"Having abolished in his flesh the enmity, even the law of commandments contained in ordinances; for to make in himself of twain one new man, so making peace; and that He might reconcile both unto God in one body on the cross, having slain the enmity thereby." Ephesians 2. 15-16.

These verses of scripture both confirm that the law of ordinances were nailed to the cross, which was our enemy. What was the law of ordinances? They were representative of the ultimate sacrifice of the life of Christ for our sins. They were against us, because, in order to be forgiven our sins we had to supply sheep, doves, etc. and if you had no means of providing or purchasing one you can of course imagine the difficulties a person would find themselves in; in any event, despite the potential inconveniences, the sacrificial system was pointing to Jesus' sacrifice on the cross for humanity and His wider creation, therefore this system was done away with. At the time of the crucifixion of Christ this system was to come to an end.

"Jesus when He had cried again with a loud voice, yielded up the ghost. And, behold, the veil of the temple was rent in twain from the top to the bottom.. Now when the centurion, and they that were with him, watching Jesus, saw the earthquake, and those things that were done, they feared greatly, saying, Truly this was the Son of God."
Matt. 27:50-51, 54.

The veil separated the Holy place from sinners, the renting of the veil at the death of Christ, confirmed the end of that system of sacrifice. The renting (tearing) of the veil (special curtain) from top to bottom was to confirm that it was torn by the hands of angels of God, exposing the area known up until then, as the Most Holy place, that no people were allowed to see except the high priest. The fact that it was

153

now exposed to public view confirmed that that system was now over.

There were two sets of laws given to Moses. What were they? The law of ordinances, (written by Moses and placed on the outside of the ark of the covenant) and the Moral Law as written by the finger of God on tables of stone and handed to Moses (placed in the inside of the ark of the covenant under the mercy seat).

Some Protestants insist that the law written by the finger of God on stone, were nailed to the cross at the crucifixion. If that was the case, what law could the Papacy seek to change? There would not be a law to change, and what in the Moral law could be against us? The Ten Commandments are called the Moral Law, besides teaching us how to serve God they also guide us in the management of our moral lives. According to the dictionary 'moral' is, "concerned with the principles of right and wrong behaviour, holding or manifesting high principles for proper conduct, standards of behaviour; principles of right and wrong."
All the laws of the land are based on those laws, written by the finger of God, otherwise known as the Ten Commandments. The following are a few examples:-

Honour thy father and thy mother - We all are expected to respect our parents.

Thou shalt not kill - You can be imprisoned, hanged, given a lethal injection etc., for taking another human life.

Thou shalt not commit adultery - This is considered by the laws of the land as sufficient cause for divorce.

Thou shalt not steal - Stealing in all its forms is considered a criminal offence, punishable by imprisonment etc.

Thou shalt not bear false witness - This is considered as perjury, and is also punishable by fines or imprisonment.

Would anyone in his or her right mind agree that these laws no longer apply in society? Think of the utter anarchy if our governments should announce tomorrow that no punishment would be dealt out to anyone if they committed any offences relating to those laws? Why then would God abolish them? What type of government would God be running if it was true that the law was abolished? What would be the purpose of striving to live an honest clean life only to be wiped out by anyone that takes pleasure in killing or takes pleasure in depriving you of your heard-earned property? A God of love could not allow this type of crime to exist because if He did there would not have been any purpose in creating life for it to be destroyed or abused by some of the very ones He created.

Here is another example from some protestants that insist that the Sabbath was given only to the Jews because it is part of the old covenant. They make unfounded claims that God's sanctified Seventh Day Sabbath was a ceremonial/ritual law, a description that has no biblical foundation whatsoever. They claim the new covenant is a moral law and is unchangeable. I agree. It is only through God's law can His standards of "Morals" be established. They may quote Hebrews 10 in an attempt to claim that there is a new covenant that does not include God's Sanctified Sabbath. Interestingly the claim is that there is a new law written into the heart. What is that law? Isn't it simply that the new covenant is that God is writing His law into their hearts? Why do criminals attempt to commit crimes using weapons? Simple. Because in their hearts they know it is wrong.

"This is the new covenant that I will make with them after those days, saith the Lord, I will put my laws into their hearts, and in their minds will I write them;"

Yet in a couple of chapters ahead, of the same book i.e, Hebrews 8:10 the Lord states;

"For this is the covenant that I will make with the house of Israel after those days, saith the Lord: I will put my laws in their mind, and write them in their hearts: and I will be to them a God, and they shall be to me a people"

The same declaration with some more information.

Note very carefully, "the House of Israel"

So how is any Gentile entitled to claim they are under the "New Covenant"?

Here dear readers is another example of dishonesty in presenting God's word. The root of the dishonesty is from the fact that the claim is made that the Seventh-day Sabbath found in the old testament belongs to the Jews because it is part of the "Old Covenant" made with the Jews and does not apply to modern Chrstians. However, Hebrews makes it plain that the new covenant is with "the house of Israel." Are you going to ignore this evidence or continue to adhere to deceptive teachings spurred on by the enemy of your soul? You cannot have it both ways, either it applies to the house of Israel or it doesn't.

As the scriptures plainly state "the House of Israel", how then does the covenant include the non-Jews, the Gentiles.

If it does include the Gentiles, as it most definitely does, then what covenants apply to all of mankind? Any of us that describe ourselves as "Christian" Christ-followers become part of the "House of Israel". We are of the "House of Israel" by becoming "Heirs" by being "Grafted in" or "Adopted" See the following verses of scripture.

"But to which of the angels said he at any time, Sit on my right hand, until I make thine enemies thy footstool?
Are they not all ministering spirits, sent forth to minister for them who shall be heirs of salvation? Hebrews 1:13-14
"For as many as are led by the Spirit of God, they are the sons of God.
For ye have not received the spirit of bondage again to fear; but ye have received the Spirit of adoption, whereby we cry, Abba, Father.
The Spirit itself beareth witness with our spirit, that we are the children of God:
And if children, then heirs; heirs of God, and joint-heirs with Christ; if so be that we suffer with [him], that we may be also glorified together." Romans 8:14-17

"For as many of you as have been baptized into Christ have put on Christ.
There is neither Jew nor Greek, there is neither bond nor free, there is neither male nor female: for ye are all one in Christ Jesus.
And if ye [be] Christ's, then are ye Abraham's seed, and heirs according to the promise." Galatians 3:27-29

"Not by works of righteousness which we have done, but according to his mercy he saved us, by the washing of regeneration, and renewing of the Holy Ghost;
Which he shed on us abundantly through Jesus Christ our Saviour;

That being justified by his grace, we should be made heirs according to the hope of eternal life." Titus 3:5-7

"Wherein God, willing more abundantly to show unto the heirs of promise the immutability of his counsel, confirmed [it] by an oath:
That by two immutable things, in which [it was] impossible for God to lie, we might have a strong consolation, who have fled for refuge to lay hold upon the hope set before us:
Which [hope] we have as an anchor of the soul, both sure and stedfast, and which entereth into that within the veil;
Whither the forerunner is for us entered, [even] Jesus, made an high priest for ever after the order of Melchisedec." Hebrews 6:17-20

"For I speak to you Gentiles, inasmuch as I am the apostle of the Gentiles, I magnify mine office:
If by any means I may provoke to emulation [them which are] my flesh, and might save some of them.
For if the casting away of them [be] the reconciling of the world, what [shall] the receiving [of them be], but life from the dead?
For if the firstfruit [be] holy, the lump [is] also [holy]: and if the root [be] holy, so [are] the branches.
And if some of the branches be broken off, and thou, being a wild olive tree, wert grafted in among them, and with them partakest of the root and fatness of the olive tree;" Romans 8:13-17

From Jesus' own lips

"Abide in me, and I in you. As the branch cannot bear fruit of itself, except it abide in the vine; no more can ye, except ye abide in me.

I am the vine, ye [are] the branches: He that abideth in me, and I in him, the same bringeth forth much fruit: for without me ye can do nothing." John 15:4-5

"Jesus saith unto him, I am the way, the truth, and the life: no man cometh unto the Father, but by me." John 14:6
Here, dear readers, can be the only answer to these questions, and that is, the law they are trying to say has been done away with can only be the sabbath law and that they have all fallen into the trap of Popery; that of "think to change times and laws."
As mentioned earlier there are two sabbaths in contention. The true and the false. We state two, as there is one true, and several false; the several false we put together as the false, because the originator of all the false is of the same source, Satan.

The Sabbath, according to Websters third new international dictionary: "a: the day of rest and solemn assembly observed as sacred to God by Jews and some Christian churches on the Seventh day of the week from sunset Friday until sunset Saturday, "six days shalt thou labor and do all thy work: but the Seventh day is the Sabbath of the Lord thy God; in it thou shalt not do any work" b: the day of rest and public worship observed on Sunday by most Christian churches in commemoration of the resurrection of Christ on the first day of the week: specifically, the Lord's Day observed strictly as a day of solemn rest and devotion continuing the old testament sabbath - C: the day of the week regularly set aside by some other religion for public observances, "although it was Friday, the Moslem Sabbath, people were at work..."

From this it is evident that there are several days held as the sabbath. Which is the true? The Seventh day as set aside by the Lord? The lord's Day? or even Friday as the Moslems teach? The Moslems claim to have the angelic faith, and the recipients of the truth as handed down by Abraham. Why then are they keeping a Sabbath that is different to that which Abraham kept, the Seventh day of the week? which is according to the original commmand of Abrahams' God, the God of heaven? Therefore, despite their claims to the truth, this factor alone would put all Muslim claims to the truth into disrepute because they are not honoring the God of heaven. However, the greatest danger that threatens the world in the last days, is that of the sabbath promulgated by the Papacy, because it is that sabbath that will be forced on everyone including Muslims, Pagans, Atheists, New Agers etc. According to Revelation 13 all will fall under the papal mandates. The history of the entrance of this false sabbath we will now examine.

"Sunday. Regular Christian corporate worship on Sunday goes back to the Apostolic age, but new testament writings do not explain how the practise began..." *Paul confirming the mystery already working, also relates to the apostasy entering the early church.* "When the church became predominately Gentile, Sunday remained as the customary day of worship."

"Assemblies for the Eucharist were common on Saturday, however, as well as on Sunday in the eastern churches on into the 5th century... The term Lord's day, signifying the triumph of Christ in his resurrection and the beginning of a new creation, was in use by the end of the first century.. In 321 the Roman Emperor Constantine decreed Sunday to be a legal holiday and forbade all trade and work other than necessary agricultural labour..." Enc. Brit. 16:361:la.

That Constantine was still a Sun-Worshipper after he supposedly became Christian, let us quote the exact words of his decree. "Let all the Judges and Towns people, and the occupation of all trades rest on the Venerable day of the sun; but let those who are situated in the country freely and at full liberty attend to the business of agriculture: because it often happens that no other day is so fit for sowing corn and planting vines; lest, the critical moment being let slip, men should lose the commodities granted by heaven." This is the first Sunday law.

Take note that he stated "Venerable day of the sun" Venerable synonyms include "respected, revered, reverenced, worshipped, honoured, esteemed, hallowed, glorious, …"

"Church councils of the period were more concerned to enforce the obligation of Sunday worship, the earliest being the Spanish council of Elvira (c.300); but a synod of Laodicea (c.381) enjoined Christians not to "JUDAIZE," but to work on the Sabbath and rest, if possible, on the Lord's day.." Enc. Brit. 16:361:la. The extract continues, citing the fact that various kings and protestant churches insisted then, and still do today, upon the moral obligation to attend worship on the Lord's day. It is evident therefore that the Seventh day Sabbath was still being kept, but by man's decrees, it should no longer be reverenced, but that the first day of the week, 'the Lord's day,' should be reverenced in its place.

As has been pointed out earlier that many aspects of the "Moral Law" are still applied in our society. What aspects of that law has the papacy thought to change? When searching their writings, and those of other denominations, we find that the part of that law that they all seek to deny, is the one to do with the Sabbath instituted by God, requiring all men to rest, and also recognising Him as their creator. We will also find that the papacy among "Christian" churches, is almost unique in altering the laws relating to idolatry. Let us now examine the evidence.

The Papacy - "Question: Have you any other way of proving that the church has power to institute festivals of precept?"

"Answer: Had she not such power, she could not have done that in which all modern religionists agree with her: she could not have substituted the observance of Sunday the first day of the week, for the observance of Saturday the Seventh Day, a change for which there is no scriptural authority." - A Doctrinal Catechism, by Rev. Stephan Keenan Pg 174.

Here they plainly admit that there is no scriptural authority for changing the Sabbath; by whose authority then are they changing it? Remember the verse,

"And the Dragon gave him (the Papacy) his power, his seat, and great authority."

"Question : What day was the Sabbath?"
"Answer : Saturday."
"Question : Who changed it?"

"Answer:The Catholic church." Rev. Dr. Butler's Catechism, revised pg. 57.
The Catholics having openly admitted to changing the Sabbath, what do they say about the protestants who also keep Sunday as the Sabbath.

"It was the Catholic church which, by the authority of Jesus Christ, has transferred this rest to the sunday in remembrance of the resurrection of our Lord. Thus the observance of Sunday by the protestants is an homage they pay, in spite of themselves, to the authority of the (Catholic) church." (Emphasis mine [therefore by keeping

162

the pope's Sunday sabbath, a protestant church then becomes a daughter of the harlot church, hence the biblical phrase, Mother of Harlots]) - Plain talk about the protestantism of today. By Mgr. Segur. pg. 213.

Notice how the Catholic church claims that it was by the authority of Christ, that they changed the Sabbath. This authority, if you remember earlier, was vested in the keys of St. Peter, which are none other than the keys of Janus and Cybele. Notice also, that it is the papacy that implies sanctity to Sunday as the sabbath because Sunday was the 'resurrection day', hence the phrase "the Lord's day" that has been adopted by the majority of protestants and who state "in remembrance of the resurrection of our Lord?"

Remember also, that, Sunday is the day of worship of "The Unconquerable Sun," otherwise known as "Baal" - "Lord," therefore that Sunday is a "Lord's Day,"we have no doubt, but what "Lord"?

"The Pope is not only the representative of Jesus Christ, but he is Jesus Christ, Himself, hidden under the veil of human flesh." — Catholic National, July 1895.

Doesn't this confirm that the pope is believed to be inhabited, possessed, by another being?

"All things whatsoever that it was duty to do on the Sabbath, these we have transferred to the Lord's Day." *Commentary on the Psalms, Eusebius; cited in the commentary on the apocalypse, Moses Stuart, Vol.11., 9.40. Andover: Allen, Morrill, and Wardwell, 1845. Bishop Eusebius (A.D. 270-338) who worked with the Emperor Constantine.*

"Question - Which is the Sabbath day?

"Answer - Saturday is the Sabbath day.

"Question - Why do we observe Sunday instead of Saturday?

"Answer - We observe Sunday instead of Saturday because the Catholic Church, in the Council of Laodicea (A.D. 364), transferred the solemnity from Saturday to Sunday." Peter Geiermann, C.S.S.R., The Convert's Catechism of Catholic Doctrine, p. 50, 3rd edition, 1957.

"Perhaps the boldest thing, the most revolutionary change the Church ever did, happened in the first century. The holy day, the Sabbath, was changed from Saturday to Sunday. 'The day of the Lord' was chosen, not from any direction noted in the Scriptures, but from the (Catholic) Church's sense of its own power...People who think that the Scriptures should be the sole authority, should logically ... keep Saturday holy" St. Catherine Church Sentinel, Algonac, Michigan, May 21, 1995.

"Question: How prove you that the Church hath power to command feasts and holy days? "Answer. By the very act of changing the Sabbath into Sunday, which Protestants allow of, and therefore they fondly contradict themselves, by keeping Sunday strictly, and breaking most other feasts commanded by the same Church." Daniel Ferres, manual of Christian Doctrine (1916), p. 67.

"Is Saturday the seventh day according to the Bible and the Ten Commandments? I answer yes. Is Sunday the first day of the week and did the Church change the seventh day - Saturday - for Sunday, the first day? I answer yes . Did Christ change the day'? I answer no!" Faithfully yours,

164

James Cardinal Gibbons, Archbishop of Baltimore (1877-1921), in a signed letter.

"But you may read the Bible from Genesis to Revelation, and you will not find a single line authorizing the sanctification of Sunday. The Scriptures enforce the religious observance of Saturday, a day which we never sanctify." James Cardinal Gibbons, The Faith of our Fathers, 88th ed., p 89.

"And where are we told in the Scriptures that we are to keep the first day at all? We are commanded to keep the seventh; but we are nowhere commanded to keep the first day .... The reason why we keep the first day of the week holy instead of the seventh is for the same reason that we observe many other things, not because the Bible, but because the church has enjoined it." Isaac Williams, Plain Sermons on the Catechism, vol. 1, pp 334,336.

"There is no word, no hint, in the New Testament about abstaining from work on Sunday .... into the rest of Sunday no divine law enters.... The observance of Ash Wednesday or Lent stands exactly on the same footing as the observance of Sunday." Canon Eyton, The Ten Commandments, pp 52, 63, 65.

"For example, nowhere in the Bible do we find that Christ or the Apostles ordered that the Sabbath be changed from Saturday to Sunday. We have the commandment of God given to Moses to keep holy the Sabbath day, that is the 7th day of the week, Saturday. Today most Christians keep Sunday because it has been revealed to us by the [Roman Catholic] church outside the Bible." Catholic Virginian Oct.3, 1947,p. 9, art. "To Tell You the Truth"

"Nowhere in the Bible is it stated that worship should be changed from Saturday to Sunday .... Now the Church ... instituted, by God's authority, Sunday as the day of worship. This same Church, by the same divine authority, taught the doctrine of Purgatory long before the Bible was made. We have, therefore, the same authority for Purgatory as we have for Sunday." Martin J. Scott, Things Catholics are Asked About (1927),p. 136.

"Long before the bible was made?" Interesting comment. Remember Paul stating that "the mystery of iniquity doth already work?"The mystery religion of Babel? Moses put pen to paper beginning with Genesis, centuries after the flood, after the Israelites were freed from Pharoah? Therefore that comment does have credibility.

Incidentally, is purgatory biblical? Answer will be at the end of this chapter.

"Sunday is founded, not of scripture, but on tradition, and is distinctly a Catholic institution. As there is no scripture for the transfer of the day of rest from the last to the first day of the week, Protestants ought to keep their Sabbath on Saturday and thus leave Catholics in full possession of Sunday." Catholic Record, September 17, 1893.

"I have repeatedly offered $1,000 to anyone who can prove to me from the Bible alone that I am bound to keep Sunday holy. There is no such law in the Bible. It is a law of the holy Catholic Church alone. The Bible says, 'Remember the Sabbath day to keep it holy.' The Catholic Church says: 'No. By my divine power I abolish the Sabbath day and command you to keep holy the first day of the week.' And lo! The entire civilized world bows down in a reverent obedience to the command of the holy Catholic Church."

T.Enright, C.S.S.R., in a lecture at Hartford, Kansas, 18th Feb. 1884 - $1,000 offered.

"The Church . . . took the pagan Sunday and made it the Christian Sunday . . . And thus the pagan Sunday, dedicated to Balder, became the Christian Sunday, sacred to Jesus." "Catholic World," (New York), March, 1894, p. 809.

What do the protestants have to say on the matter? Or should we rather be asking, what did they say previously? – Many of these 'Protestant' movements have in recent years signed agreements to come under the jurisdiction of the papacy - Remember Revelation describes the Romish church as the mother of harlots? A mother therefore has daughters? Correct? I must also emphasise that the various stages of the protestant movement was correct, however, scripture also warned us that the Papal wound would heal and that can only happen with the cooperation of Protestants.

A great cloud of witnesses: "Wycliffe, Tyndale, Luther, Calvin, Cranmer; in the seventeenth century, Bunyan, the translators of the King James Bible and the men who published the Westminster and Baptist confessions of Faith; Sir Isaac Newton, Wesley, Whitfield, Jonathan Edwards; and more recently Spurgeon, Bishop J.C. Ryle and Dr. Martin Lloyd-Jones; these men among countless others, all saw the office of the Papacy as the antichrist." — All Roads Lead to Rome, by Michael de Semlyen. Dorchestor House Publications, p. 205. 1991.

Lutheran - "They (the Catholics) allege the Sabbath changed into the Sunday, the Lord's day contrary to the decalogue, as it appears; neither is there any example more boasted of than the changing of the Sabbath Day. Great, say they, is the power and authority of the church, since it dispensed with one of the Ten Commandments." Auxsburg Confession, article XXVIII.

Methodist - "It is true that there is no positive command for infant baptism..... is there any for keeping Holy the first day of the week." Theological compend., Rev. Amos Binney, pg. 180-181, New York: Methodist Book concern, 1902.

Christian - "I do not believe that the Lord's day came in the room of the Jewish Sabbath, or that the Sabbath was changed from the Seventh to the first day, for this plain reason, that where there is no testimony, there can be no faith. Now there is no testimony in the oracles of Heaven that the Sabbath was changed, or that the Lord's day came in the room of it.. There is no divine testimony that the Sabbath was changed, or that the Lord's day came in the room of it; therefore there can be no divine faith that the Sabbath was changed or that the Lord's day came in the room of it." Alexander Campbell (candidus), in Washington (Pa.) Reporter, Oct. 8,1821.

Congregationalist - "Much has been made about the attitude of Christ in speech and deed toward the Sabbath. Some have imagined that by words He uttered and deeds He did, He released the binding nature of the old command. This view, however, is to absolutely misunderstand and misinterpret the doing and the teaching of Jesus." The Ten Commandments, G.Campbell Morgan (Congregationalist) pg 50. New York: Fleming H. Revell.

"It is quite clear that, however rigidly or devoutly we may spend Sunday, we are not keeping the Sabbath.... The Sabbath was founded on a specific divine command. We can plead no such command for the observance of Sunday.... There is not a single sentence in the New

Testament to suggest that we incur any penalty by violating the supposed sanctity of Sunday." The Ten Commandments, R.W. Dale, D.P.(Congregationalist), pp. 106-7, London: Hodder and Stoughton.

Presbytarian - "The Moral Law doth forever bind all, as well justified persons as others, to the obedience thereof and that not only in regard of the matter contained in it, but also in respect of the authority of God the Creator who gave it. Neither doth Christ in the gospel in any way dissolve, but much strengthen this obligation." From the constitution of the Presbyterian church in the U.S.A.

Church of England - "There is no word, no hint, in the New Testament about abstaining from work on Sunday. ..The observance of Ash Wednesday or Lent stands on the same footing as the observance of Sunday... Into the rest of Sunday no Divine Law enters." The Ten Commandments, Canon Eyton (Church of England). London: Trubner.

Baptist - "Dr. Hiscox's solemn question and declaration." "There was and is a Commandment to keep Holy the Sabbath day, but that Sabbath was not Sunday. It will be said, however, and with some show of triumph, that the Sabbath was transferred from the Seventh to the first day of the week, with all its duties, privileges, and sanctions. Earnestly desiring information on this subject, which I have studied for many years, I ask, Where can the record of such a transaction be found? Not in the New Testament, absolutely not. There is no scriptural evidence of the change of the Sabbath Institution from the Seventh to the first day of the week... of course, I quite well know that Sunday did come into use in early Christian history as a religious day, as we learn from the Christian fathers and other sources. But what a pity that it comes branded with the work of Paganism, and Christened with the name of the Sun-god, when adopted and sanctioned by the Papal

169

Apostacy and bequeathed as a sacred legacy to protestantism!" Dr. Edward T Hiscox. Author of the Baptist Manual, in a paper read before a New York Ministers' conference, held Nov. 13, 1893.

It is plainly obvious that the leaders of all these religions acknowledge that the Seventh day Sabbath is the true Sabbath. How fantastic then, that almost the entire world, including the "Christian" world, holds sunday as the Sabbath. Through the papacy Satan was able to institute his false sabbath, "The Venerable day of the Sun," to commemorate his false claims to the creation of our world, acceptance of such a false sabbath would guarantee the eternal death of all those who willingly heed such a deception.

Another point worth consideration at this point is that, although Satan attempts to convince everyone that there is no longer any requirement to honour the laws of God, he still requires the sanctity of the Sabbath to be transferred to Sunday, so that he can receive the homage due only to God. He is a thief and a liar. Who among the protestants are regarded as true Protestants?

"The Church changed the observance of the Sunday... The protestant claiming the Bible to be the guide of faith, has no warrant for observing Sunday. In this matter the Seventh-day Adventist is the only consistent Protestant." The Catholic Universe Bulletin, August 14, 1942. Pg 4.

Who are the Seventh-day Adventists? They, by their descriptive name, believe in and worship on the Seventh day of the week, and also believe in the second, literal return (adventist - advent) of Christ.

"…..all the world wondered after the beast." Rev: 13:3 the change of the sabbath rest to Sunday is so embedded into society that most of the world's population automatically think Sunday is the rest day and Friday evening to Saturday evening, a day of business and secular pleasure.

Some also argue that the Sabbath was made for the Jews. If this was the case, why then do we have the following account in Genesis 2:1-3.

"Thus the heavens and the earth were finished, and all the host of them. And on the Seventh day God ended his work which he had made; and he rested on the seventh day from all his work which he had made. And God blessed the seventh day, and sanctified it: because that in it he had rested from all His work which God had created and made."

God expressly set the Seventh day aside as a Holy day, and in commemoration of His creation. When these verses are compared with Exodus 20:3-11, there can be no doubt what the Lord wanted his followers to understand.

If it were true that the Sabbath was made for the Jews, Adam and Eve would have been Jews, they being the first Human Beings on earth would have rendered us all Jews, wouldn't it? This would then make it obligatory by default to be kept by all of us. *(Interesting that they are defeated by their own words.)* That aside, these verses prove when the first Sabbath was kept and long before the Jews ever existed. Yes, right from the beginning, God instituted the Seventh day Sabbath, day of rest, and sanctified it. The word Sanctified means - made Holy - Set apart to Sacred duty or use. "to set apart to a sacred purpose or to religious use: consecrate, to impart or impute sacred-ness, inviolability, or respect to."

The image on the next page is the comparison between the Ten Commandments as handed down by God, and how it has been changed by the Papacy to suit their Idolatrous and blasphemous ends. Take note also that all businesses and sports are their busiest on God's 7th day sabbath, including Friday evening(clubbing etc,) the evening time of the sabbath, why? Satan's plan!!

In comparing the two, it is plain how the Papacy has removed all reference to their Idolatrous practises in all its forms, and of the Seventh day Sabbath. In order to maintain all the idols that are rampant across catholicism, the second commandment was removed entirely and to make up the number to ten, the last of the original 10 has been divided into two.

This mangling of the Ten Commandments also proves that they were never abolished and nailed to the cross as some claim. Is any further evidence required to prove that the Papacy is the power in scripture, that would think to change times and laws?

The 10 Commandments as given by God		The 10 Commandments as changed by the Catholic church	
1	Thou shalt have no other gods before me.	1	I am the Lord thy God: Thou shalt not have strange gods before me
2	Thou shalt not make unto thee any graven image, or any likeness of any thing that is in heaven above, or that is in the earth beneath, or that is in the water under the earth. Thou shalt not bow down thyself to them, nor serve them: for I the LORD thy God am a jealous God, visiting the iniquity of the fathers upon the children unto the third and fourth generation of them that hate me: And shewing mercy unto thousands of them that love me, and keep my commandments.		(this whole commandment is missing)
3	Thou shalt not take the name of the LORD thy God in vain; for the LORD will not hold him guiltless that taketh his name in vain.	2	Thou shalt not take the name of the LORD thy God in vain;
4	Remember the sabbath day, to keep it holy. Six days shalt thou labour, and do all thy work: But the seventh day is the sabbath of the LORD thy God: in it thou shalt not do any work, thou, nor thy son, nor thy daughter, thy manservant, nor thy maidservant, nor thy cattle, nor thy stranger that is within thy gates: For in six days the LORD made heaven and earth, the sea, and all that in them is, and rested the seventh day: wherefore the LORD blessed the sabbath day, and hallowed it.	3	Remember that thou keep holy the Sabbath day. (Take careful not that all the pointers for the reasons and purpose of the Seventh Day Sabbath, the confirmation of which day is the Sabbath and the fact that is was blessed and made holy by the almighty God have all been deleted)
5	Honour thy father and thy mother: that thy days may be long upon the land which the LORD thy God giveth thee.	4	Honour thy father and thy mother.
6	Thou shalt not kill.	5	Thou shalt not kill.
7	Thou shalt not commit adultery.	6	Thou shalt not commit adultery.
8	Thou shalt not steal.	7	Thou shalt not steal.
9	Thou shalt not bear false witness against thy neighbour.	8	Thou shalt not bear false witness against thy neighbor.
10	Thou shalt not covet thy neighbour's house, thou shalt not covet thy neighbour's wife, nor his manservant, nor his maidservant, nor his ox, nor his ass, nor any thing that is thy neighbour's.	9	Thou shalt not covet thy neighbor's wife. *(notice also that this commandment has been altered and split in two, so the Catholic church can complete 10 commandments).*
		10	Thou shalt not covet thy neighbour's goods.

We have quoted word for word the original 10 Commandments as given by God and quoted word for word the changes made by the Catholic Church as found in their Convert's Catechism of Catholic Doctrine: p.37, edition 1921.

The book of Exodus is the account of God teaching His people that were held in slavery for 400 years, how to come out of the idolatry and lifestyles of the Egyptians and back to where they were before they went into Egypt. That time in Egypt was because of the great famine that resulted in Joseph being put in charge of all Egypt; further confirmation that God's law existed before there was a nation of Israelites or Jews as they are currently known.

As God wanted to take Egypt out of His people, equally so, He wants to take spiritual Egypt out of His people today, yes, our generations.

As it is certain that God instituted the Sabbath from the beginning; He would have instructed Adam and Eve concerning it, along with the rest of His Commandments.

"Adam and Eve transgressed the Lord's requirements, and the terrible result of their sin should be a warning to us not to follow their example. Christ prayed for His disciples in these words: "Sanctify them through thy truth: thy word is truth" (John 17:17). There is no genuine sanctification except through obedience to the truth. Those who love God with all the heart will love all His commandments also. The sanctified heart is in harmony with the precepts of God's law; for they are holy, just, and good.

God's character has not changed. He is the same jealous God today as when He gave His law upon Sinai and wrote it with His own finger on the tables of stone. Those who trample upon God's holy law may say, "I am sanctified"; but to be indeed sanctified, and to claim sanctification, are two different things." To be like Jesus. E G White. Page 67.

Genesis 4:1-8, sums up the birth of Cain and Abel, one serving God correctly (Abel), and suffering death from his brother (Cain), who became annoyed that his (Cain's) sacrifice displeased God. Basically Cain's action said that he would worship God how he (Cain) wanted to. Verses

174

25-26 states "And Adam knew his wife again; and she bare a son, and called his name Seth: for God, said she, hath appointed me another seed instead of Abel, whom Cain slew. *(Cain was so willing to break God's commandment, he committed murder, the thou shalt not kill commandment)* And to Seth, to him also there was born a son, and he called his name Enos: then began men to call upon the name of the Lord."

Those who were calling upon God would have been following His guidelines, and would have been aware that He is the true God. Why? What does Paul in Romans 1: 20 say?

"For the invisible things of Him from the creation of the world are clearly seen, being understood by the things that are made, even His eternal power and Godhead; so that they are without excuse."

The Seventh day Sabbath points to and commemorates God as the creator. It would then have been impossible for men to be calling upon the name of the Lord, without keeping the Seventh day Sabbath. All the sons of God would therefore have passed the same Divine guidelines down through their generations to Noah. We find an excellent example of this in Deuteronomy 6:5-7.

"And thou shalt love the LORD thy God with all thine heart, and with all thy soul, and with all thy might. And these words, which I command thee this day, shall be in thine heart: And thou shalt teach them diligently unto thy children, and shalt talk of them when thou sittest in thine house, and when thou walkest by the way, and when thou liest down, and when thou risest up."

Noah being a righteous person, would have also kept it, he would not have been called a just and perfect man if he was disobeying God. We also find this in James 2:10, "For whosoever shall keep the whole law, and yet offend in one point, he is guilty of all." Therefore, it would have been impossible for Noah to be considered perfect and just, if he did not keep the Seventh day Sabbath. Noah would have received instructions in righteous living from his ancestors.

Enos, Seth's son, was 821 years old, when Noah was born, and he would have received instructions from his father and forefathers. Noah's father, Lamech, lived until 5 years before the great flood, therefore, he could have assisted Noah for 95 of the 100 yrs of warnings the world would have received of the impending disaster, perhaps verbally, but most certainly, in assisting him in the construction of the Ark(a tangible witness of the impending doom), and no, the great ages mentioned here are not ridiculous, we must remember, the human race was living in a perfect environment, fresh from the hands of the Creator.

After the flood, of Noah's three lineages of descent, two turned away from God. Through the lineage of Shem, the true faith was continued. But that of Ham, who fathered Cush, who fathered Nimrod, the Mystery Religion was born; Ham also fathered the nation known as the Canaanites. Japheth fathered the nations known as the gentiles. When the generations of Shem are analysed in Genesis 11, it will be found that Shem was 401 yrs old when Abraham was born, 501 when Isaac was born, 561 when Jacob was born, therefore Abraham, Isaac and Jacob would have had a Patriarch that survived the flood that could have shared amazing information with them.

On analysis, it is also apparent how drastically reduced men's lifespans became. Shem would have buried at least

11 of his generations before he died. How heartrending that must have been for him. His vitality had to have been the result of the food and environment he lived in before the flood.

The planet's perfect environment had been radically altered during the flood. Genesis 7:11 talks about all the fountains of the great deep being broken open and the windows of heaven being opened. We can only conclude that the structure of the habitat before the flood was immensely different from what we have now. Vast subterranean quantities of water erupted from beneath the earth's surface and the canopy of water above the air mass we now describe as the sky broke open and cascaded down to earth. This account of the fountains of the great deep being broken open and the windows of heaven being opened describes the first great catastrophic planet-wide event that drastically changed our climate, because before this, the planet's temperature was regulated evenly by waters above our atmosphere. What we are witnessing now is again the result of humanity turning away from our Creator and worshipping false gods, just as we did before the great flood.

"And God said, Let there be a firmament in the midst of the waters, and let it divide the waters from the waters. And God made the firmament, and divided the waters which [were] under the firmament from the waters which [were] above the firmament: and it was so. And God called the firmament Heaven. And the evening and the morning were the second day." Genesis 1:6-8.

Shem having been alive through 11 generations would have granted Abraham direct access to the truth and history of man's fall in its purest form, passed down to Shem from

Noah and his ancestors before the flood. In Genesis Chapter 12:1-2 God makes Abraham a promise.

"Now the Lord had said unto Abram, get thee out of thy country, and from thy kindred, and from thy father's house, unto a land that I will shew thee: and I will make of thee a great nation, and I will bless thee, and make thy name great; and thou shalt be a blessing."

Where was this land that he was promised? Chapter 13:12. "Abram dwelled in the land of Canaan..." Verses 14-18 "And the Lord said unto Abram,... lift up now thine eyes, and look from the place where thou art, northward, and southward, and eastward, and westward; For all the land which thou seest, to thee will I give it, and to thy seed for ever. And I will make thy seed as the dust of the earth: so that if a man can number the dust of the earth, then shall thy seed also be numbered. Arise, walk through the land... Then Abram removed his tent, and came and dwelt in the plain of Mamre, which is in Hebron, and built there an altar to the Lord."

In Genesis 21:3-5, Isaac is born to Abraham when he was one hundred years old, chapter 25:25-26, Isaac fathered Esau and Jacob. Jacob then being the father of the twelve tribes of Israel, currently known as the Jews, who are now scattered over the earth in almost every nation. The Jews are known to everyone, as keeping the Seventh day as the Holy Sabbath as ordained by God. All these servants of God, after the flood, Noah, Shem, Abraham, Isaac, Jacob to the Jews, kept the Seventh day Sabbath. That the children of Israel kept it even before it was written on tables of stone, read the following. The 15th day of the second month they were instructed to collect 'Manna – bread from heaven' for six days and it would not be available to collect on Sabbath and only in the third month they arrived in the wilderness of Sinai, where Moses would climb the mountain to receive the tables of stone; Exodus 19:1 - in fact the whole of chapter 19 describes the children of Israel getting ready to witness God's appearing on Mount Sinai.

"And they took their journey from Elim, and all the congregation of the children of Israel came unto the wilderness of Sin, which [is] between Elim and Sinai, on the fifteenth day of the second month after their departing out of the land of Egypt....

Then said the Lord unto Moses, behold, I will rain bread from heaven for you; and the people shall go out and gather a certain rate every day, that I may prove them, whether they will walk in my law," (Notice "My Law" [not the Jewish law]) or no.

And it shall come to pass, that on the sixth day they shall prepare that which they bring in; and it shall be twice as much as they gather daily....

And they gathered it every morning, every man according to his eating; and when the sun waxed hot it melted.

And it came to pass, that on the sixth day they gathered twice as much bread, two omers for one man: and all the rulers of the congregation came and told Moses.

And he said unto them, this is that which the Lord hath said, tomorrow is the rest of the Holy Sabbath unto the Lord: bake that which ye will bake today, and seethe that ye will seethe; and that which remaineth over lay up for you to be kept until the morning.

And they laid it up till the morning, as Moses bade: and it did not stink, neither was there any worm therein.

And Moses said, eat that today: for today is a Sabbath unto the Lord: today ye shall not find it in the field.

Six days shall thou gather it; but on the Seventh day, which is the Sabbath, in it there shall be none.

And it came to pass, that there went out some of the people on the seventh day for to gather, and they found none.

And the Lord said unto Moses, how long refuse ye to keep MY COMMANDMENTS and MY LAWS?"

(Emphasis mine, notice God says "My commandments...", I will reiterate, there is nowhere in scripture that states the ten commandments belong to the Jews like some Sunday-keepers assert in order to deny the ten commandments must be kept)

"See, for that the Lord hath given you the Sabbath, therefore He giveth you on the sixth day the bread of two days: abide ye every man in his place, let no man go out of his place on the seventh day. So the people rested on the Seventh day." Exodus:16:1, 4-5, 21-30.

Even there among the Israelites we had the rebellious element, who did not want to obey the word of God and went out on the Sabbath to gather food.

"In the third month, when the children of Israel were gone forth out of the land of Egypt, the same day came they [into] the wilderness of Sinai." Exodus 19:1.

These are the same laws that Jesus spoke of during His ministry on earth. "If ye love me keep my commandments." John 14:15. "Think not that I am come to destroy the law, or the prophets: I am not come to destroy, but to fulfill. For verily I say unto you, till heaven and earth pass, one jot or one tittle shall in no wise pass from the law, till all be fulfilled. Whosoever then shall break one of these least commandments, and shall teach men so, he shall be called the least in the kingdom of heaven: but whosoever shall do and teach them, the same shall be called great in the kingdom of heaven." Matt: 5:17-19.

It was at the arrival of the Israelites at the Mount Sinai, that the Lord gave to Moses the Ten Commandments written on tables of stone. Exodus 20: 3-17 relates the whole of the Ten Commandments.

We now leave the Jews, and examine the actions and sayings of Christ. The Papacy claims that it was by the authority of Christ, that they changed the Sabbath, which claim has been proven as an absolute lie; nevertheless, what did Christ say and do?

"And He (Christ) came to Nazareth... and as His custom was, He went into the synagogue on the Sabbath day..., and came down to Capernaum and taught them on the Sabbath days." Luke 4:16 & 31.

At that time the Christian Sabbath, as we will prove, was the Seventh day of the week; so much so that the Roman church also kept it before changing it. But even when Christ was amongst them, Satan tried to make the Sabbath burdensome through the pompous and proud Pharisees who tried to introduce all sorts of technicalities into the law. Christ had to shew during His ministry how His law was meant to be kept.

"And, behold, there was a man which had his hand withered. And they asked Him saying, is it lawful to heal on the Sabbath days? that they might accuse Him. And He said unto them, what man shall there be among you, that shall have one sheep, and if it fall into a pit on the Sabbath day, will he not lay hold on it, and lift it out? How much then is a man better than a sheep? Wherefore it is lawful to do well on the Sabbath days. Then saith He to the man, stretch forth thine hand. And he stretched it forth; and it was restored whole, like as the other." Matthew 12:10-13.

By this Christ demonstrated that it is good to do acts of kindness on the Sabbath day, which were not to be considered as work.

181

There are rather more interesting interpretations of what is considered work that the Jews still adhere to today, but we will not get into that; this Satan intended very early on, to set the scene for ridiculing the Sabbath when Christianity would gain the ascendancy. Further, Christ intended that the Sabbath was to be kept after His return to heaven. "But pray that your flight be not in the winter, neither on the Sabbath day." Matthew 24:20.

On reading verses 15-20, it will be found that Christ was speaking of the destruction of Jerusalem by the Romans which was yet future. If Christ had this law nailed to the cross why would He have told them to pray that their flight be not in winter or on the Sabbath?, a time yet future, *(note that "nailed to the cross" claimers are happy with the other nine except the sabbath)* when He would no longer be among men. Another point to note is that that prophecy of Jerusalem has a dual application that will have a far greater world fulfillment in the near future. Jesus also said: "If ye love me keep my commandments." "If ye keep my commandments, ye shall abide in my love; even as I have kept my father's commandments, and abide in his love." John 14:15, 15:10. Remember again, we just read earlier in Exodus 16 God describing the commandments as "My Commandments"?

What were those commandments considered to be? "But when the Pharisees had heard that He had put the Sadducees to silence, they were gathered together. Then one of them, which was a lawyer, asked Him a question, tempting Him, and saying, Master, which is the great commandment in the Law? Jesus said unto him. Thou shalt love the Lord thy God with all thy heart, and all thy soul, and with all thy mind. This is the first and great commandment. And the second is like unto it. Thou shalt love thy neighbour as thyself. On these two commandments

182

hang all the law and the prophets." Matthew 22:34-40. God's commandments were written on two tables of stone. These two tables of stone are representative of the two great commandments on which hang all the laws. How?

On the first table of stone, we find the first four of the Ten Commandments that tell us how to express our love for God with all our hearts etc., (having no other gods, not worshipping images, not taking His name in vain, and remembering to keep His Sabbath day holy.) On the second table is found the last six, which deals with loving our neighbours as ourselves, (honoring our parents, not killing, committing adultery, stealing, lying or coveting).

Finally, in connection with Christ, we find that even at His death the Sabbath was kept, which further proves that it was not nailed to the cross. "And when Jesus had cried with a loud voice... gave up the Ghost. And that day was the preparation, and the Sabbath drew on. And the women also, which came with him from Galilee, followed after, and beheld the sepulchre, and how His body was laid. And they returned, and prepared spices and ointments; and rested the Sabbath day according to the commandment." Luke 23:46, 54-56.

It was still recognised as the day before the first day of the week, i.e. the Seventh. "And when the Sabbath was past, Mary Magdalene, and Mary the mother of James, and Salome, had bought sweet spices, that they might come and anoint Him. And very early in the morning the first day of the week, they came unto the sepulchre at the rising of the sun." Mark 16:1-2. Here the first day plainly follows the Sabbath.

Coming nearer to modern times we find both Jews and Gentiles keeping the Sabbath. "And when the Jews were gone out of the synagogue, the Gentiles besought that these words might be preached to them the next Sabbath. And the next Sabbath day came almost the whole city together to hear the word of God." Acts 13:42,44.

Where was this city? "But when they departed from Perga, they came to Antioch in Pisidia, and went into the synagogue on the Sabbath day and sat down." Verse 16. That city was located in present day Turkey.

We move from there to Macedonia on the southern borders of divided and war-torn Yugoslavia. "And from thence to Phillippi, which is the chief city of that part of Macedonia, and a colony: and we were in that city abiding certain days. And on the Sabbath we went out of the city by a river side, where prayer was want to be made; and we sat down, and spake unto the women which resorted thither." And to Thessalonica which still exists today, as the capital city of Macedonia. "Now when they had passed through Amphi-polis and Apollonia, they came to Thessalonica," (Thessalonika)" where there was a synagogue of the Jews: and Paul, as his manner was, went in unto them, and three Sabbaths reasoned with them out of the scriptures." Acts 16:12-13, 17:1-2.

In the following verses we find that Paul takes the gospel to the gentiles as the Jews finally reject Jesus as the Christ, preparing themselves to be caught up in the final great deception we will be discussing in the chapter entitled, Planting of the Tabernacles.

"After these things Paul departed from Athens, and came to Corinth; and he reasoned in the synagogue every Sabbath, and persuaded the Jews and the Greeks. And when Silas and Timotheus were come from Macedonia, Paul was pressed in the spirit, and testified to the Jews that Jesus was the Christ. And when they opposed themselves and blasphemed, he shook his raiment, and said unto them, your blood be upon your heads; I am clean: from henceforth I will go unto the Gentiles. And he continued there a year and six months, teaching the word of God among them." Acts 18:1, 4-6, 11.

This confirms that Paul for one and a half years preached on the Seventh day Sabbath, proof that Christ's disciples kept the Sabbath according to the commandments.

Gen 2:2 And on the seventh[H7637] day[H3117] God[H430] ended[H3615] his work[H4399] which[H834] he had made; [H6213] and he rested[H7673] on the seventh[H7637] day[H3117] from all[H4480 H3605] his work[H4399] which[H834] he had made.[H6213]

H7673

שָׁבַת

shâbath

shaw-bath'

A primitive root; to *repose*, that is, *desist* from exertion; used in many implied relations (causatively, figuratively or specifically): - (cause to, let, make to) cease, celebrate, cause (make) to fail, keep (sabbath), suffer to be lacking, leave, put away (down), (make to) rest, rid, still, take away.

Here, from Genesis Chapter 2:2 it is very plain that God Himself, Sabbathed on the Seventh Day and next in verse 3, He blessed the Seventh Day and sanctified it, making it Holy.

Gen 2:3 And God[H430] blessed[H1288] (H853) the seventh[H7637] day, [H3117] and sanctified[H6942] it: because[H3588] that in it he had rested[H7673] from all[H4480 H3605] his work[H4399] which[H834] God[H430] created[H1254] and made.[H6213]

Even nature obeys the laws of it's creator. Has anyone witnessed a lemon tree produce cucumbers, or a mango tree produce bananas, or a cat produce a dog, or a shark produce an alligator? And I could go on. Most definitely not, why? Because they have a gene code that can only produce what is in that code, how then could we humans, the pinnacle of life-forms on this planet, that has achieved so much with the intelligence we have been blessed with, succumb to the idea that we can tell the creator how to run His creation? It's like paying thousands of dollars purchasing a treasured and longed for motor vehicle or technical equipment and then going about re-writing the manufacturers rules of how to best care for that vehicle or equipment. What is different about us above all the species of the planet is that we have freedom of choice and inherent in that freedom of choice is the opportunity to disobey the guidelines of the best way to live, including the one path to immortality as set down by our Creator.

Widespread in our educational institutions the theory of evolution is taught as if it is fact and regrettably some churches and religious institutions are subscribing to some sort of evolutionary process. This theory compels humans that believe in it to deny there ever was a Creator and this mind-set also means that they will not recognise the day God set aside to acknowledge creation.

Keeping Sunday is worship that is being stolen from God by Satan even though many of the members believe in Jesus but most could be unwittingly serving Satan. Those who have Friday as a holy day also deny their Creator and also make plain statements that He, Jesus, is just another prophet, not their Creator and not special. Atheists go out of their way to deny there is a God. Idol worshippers also deny God through their worship of man-made objects, although many may not know otherwise, here again Satan steals worship from God. All of these things, evolution, atheism, Sunday keeping, Friday keeping or any other day of mankind's choosing as holy days, apart from the seventh, have been designed by Satan to deny God and as a result the earth is mourning and fading away and millions are passing away on an annual basis missing out on the great inheritance that God prepared for all humanity. Satan does not care which belief system of his we adopt as long as it goes against the one and only true option.

"The Celts used a Latin Bible unlike the Vulgate (Roman Catholic) and kept Saturday as a day of rest." Flick, The Rise of the Medieval Church, page 237.

"In 1310, two hundred years before Luther's theses, the Bohemian brethren constituted one-fourth of the population of Bohemia, and that they were in touch with the Waldenses who abounded in Austria, Lombardy, Bohemia, north Germany, Thuringia, Brandenburg, and Moravia. Erasmus pointed out how strictly Bohemian Waldenses kept the seventh-day Sabbath." Armitage, A History of the Baptists, 313.

"The Paulicians, Petrobusians, Passagininians, Waldenses, Insabbatati were great Sabbathkeeping bodies of Europe down to A.D. 1250." Coltheart, The Sabbath of God through the Centuries, 1954.

A few more verses about the Sabbath in the Old Testament.

"Wherefore I caused them to go forth out of the land of Egypt, and brought them into the wilderness.
And I gave them my statutes, and showed them my judgments, which [if] a man do, he shall even live in them.
Moreover also I gave them my sabbaths, to be a sign between me and them, that they might know that I [am] the LORD that sanctify them.
I [am] the LORD your God; walk in my statutes, and keep my judgments, and do them;
  And hallow my sabbaths; and they shall be a sign between me and you, that ye may know that I [am] the LORD your God." Ezekiel 20:10-12, 19-20.

Again these verses remind us of 4 things, 1 - the Law is God's Laws and does not belong to the Jews, 2 - God's sabbaths were a sign between Him and His people, 3 – God's Laws sanctify His people and 4 – That we might know that He is the LORD our God. We can never be sanctified without the Lord and to be the Lord's we need to keep His Sabbath as He set it.

"And he said unto them, The sabbath was made for man, and not man for the sabbath:
Therefore the Son of man is Lord also of the sabbath." Mark 2:27-28.

Since God made Sabbath for us, just as He made the planet, the sun, the moon and the stars we should respect Him by keeping it.

This outline of the Sabbath, we believe is sufficient evidence to prove that the true Sabbath was never lost, and that Satan sought to change it through his false church. Now as to what the future holds for us all, we have yet to discover. The Sabbath will be made the final test of allegiance to the true God. However, it will not be that simple; because Satan will attempt to force the entire world, by the power and influence of the United States, to receive a number, his (Satan's) number, without which no person can transact or conduct any form of business.

The ultimate test will be the honoring of the Sabbath as laid down by the God of Heaven after the creation of this world, thence resting on the Seventh Day, and sanctifying it; or the honoring of the false sabbath as established by Satan.

The other part of the verse at the beginning of this chapter stated "..wear out the saints of the most high.." did this also

188

happen? I will add some brief information, but by all means obtain a copy of the foxes book of martyrs and study it.

Summary of the Inquisition

Of the multitudes who perished by the Inquisition throughout the world, no authentic record is now discoverable. But wherever popery had power, there was the tribunal. It had been planted even in the east, and the Portuguese Inquisition of Goa was, until within these few years, fed with many an agony. South America was partitioned into provinces of the Inquisition; and with a ghastly mimickry of the crimes of the mother state, the arrivals of viceroys, and the other popular celebrations were thought imperfect without an auto da fe. The Netherlands were one scene of slaughter from the time of the decree which planted the Inquisition among them. In Spain the calculation is more attainable. Each of the seventeen tribunals during a long period burned annually, on an average, ten miserable beings! We are to recollect that this number was in a country where persecution had for ages abolished all religious differences, and where the difficulty was not to find the stake, but the offering. Yet, even in Spain, thus gleaned of all heresy, the Inquisition could still swell its lists of murders to thirty-two thousand! The numbers burned in effigy, or condemned to penance, punishments generally equivalent to exile, confiscation, and taint of blood, to all ruin but the mere loss of worthless life, amounted to three hundred and nine thousand. But the crowds who perished in dungeons of torture, of confinement, and of broken hearts, the millions of dependent lives made utterly helpless, or hurried to the grave by the death of the victims, are beyond all register; or recorded only before HIM, who has sworn that "He that leadeth into captivity, shall go into captivity: he that killeth with the sword must be killed with the sword."

Such was the Inquisition, declared by the Spirit of God to be at once the offspring and the image of the popedom. To feel the force of the parentage, we must look to the time. In the thirteenth century, the popedom was at the summit of mortal dominion; it was independent of all kingdoms; it ruled with a rank of influence never before or since possessed by a human scepter; it was the acknowledged sovereign of body and soul; to all earthly intents its power was immeasurable for good or evil. It might have spread literature, peace, freedom, and Christianity to the ends of Europe, or the world. But its nature was hostile; its fuller triumph only disclosed its fuller evil; and, to the shame of human reason, and the terror and suffering of human virtue, Rome, in the hour of its consummate grandeur, teemed with the monstrous and horrid birth of the INQUISITION!" Foxes Book or Martyrs pages 59-60.

There may be attempts at watering down the numbers killed by the Papacy, just as we have folks nowadays who deny that the holocaust ever took place during the second world war, despite current historical evidence. The very description "wear out the saints" must indicate a terrible time attempting to wipe out 'Sola Scriptura' Christians. Estimates are that during the 1,260 year reign of the papacy close to 100 million lost their lives. Is this number absurd? Don't forget that 3 entire nations were also exterminated.

According to R.J Rummel's book – Death by Government (1994), about 110 Million people, foreign and domestic, were killed by Communist democide between 1900 to 1987.
That is a period of 87 years. The Papacy had 1,260 years up until 1798 to "Wear out the saints" of God. 1,260 years is a very, very, very long time in comparison to 87 years. Never forget what has been said about Satan and his angels.

"Therefore rejoice, [ye] heavens, and ye that dwell in them. Woe to the inhabiters of the earth and of the sea! for the devil is come down unto you, having great wrath, because he knoweth that he hath but a short time." Revelation 12:12.

Short time for what? His demise! and he does not want to go alone, he wants to take as many of us humans with him as possible.

"Know that the interest of the Holy See, and those of your crown, make it a duty to exterminate the Hussites. Remember that these impious persons dare proclaim principles of equality; they maintain that all Christians are brethren, and that God has not given to privileged men the right of ruling the nations; they hold that Christ came on earth to abolish slavery; they call people to liberty, that is, to the annihilation of kings and priests! Whilst there is still time, then, turn your forces against Bohemia; burn, massacre, make deserts everywhere, for nothing could be more agreeable to God, or more useful to the cause of kings, than the extermination of the Hussites." L. M. de Cormenin, The Public and Private History of the Popes of Rome, vol. 2, 116-117.

Really? Did God issue such a command to the Papacy? He did not, because it grieved God that His saints were being wiped out through the malicious devices of Satan through the papacy.

"That the Church of Rome has shed more innocent blood than any other institution that has ever existed among mankind, will be questioned by no Protestant who has a complete knowledge of history." William E. H. Lecky, History of the Rise and Influence of the Spirit of Rationalism in Europe, volume 2, page 35.

191

What other organisations have been and are being influential in programming the world to accept the Mystery Religion? **Warning!!** The following content could be disturbing to read and acknowledge as actually real. I propose this question if you doubt their veracity – How will Satan accomplish his goals? Revelation 12 describes him coming down to this earth with great wrath because he knows he has a short time. I will be specifically highlighting the Jesuits and Freemasonry.

The Society of Jesus (Jesuits)

The Society of Jesus, as it is formally known, was begun in the 1530s by Ignatius of Loyola, a Basque soldier who underwent a profound religious transformation while convalescing from war wounds. Ignatius composed the Spiritual Exercises, used to guide the Jesuits' well-known retreats, and in 1540, along with six other theology students at the University of Paris, he won recognition from Pope Paul III as an official church order.

In many ways, the Jesuits are like other religious orders, such as the Franciscans or Dominicans. Jesuits take vows of poverty, chastity and obedience, and they live in community, sharing everything. But unlike diocesan priests, they are not ordained to a particular geographic diocese to serve the local bishop.

Jesuits are an all-male order; there are no Jesuit sisters. The society has an almost military-style structure and ethos, its shock troops willing to go wherever and whenever the church needs them. They are "contemplatives in action," in the words of St. Ignatius, and have an especially lengthy period of study and spiritual preparation before taking vows, usually 10 years or more.

Even then, the process is not complete. After another few years, most Jesuits take a special fourth vow of obedience "in regards to mission" to the pope.

If the church needs priests to reconvert souls lost to the Protestant Reformation, the Jesuits are on it. If they are needed to bring Catholicism to new lands, such as Asia or Latin America, they'll buy a one-way ticket. To advance the church's mission, the Jesuits have shaped generations of minds through universities such as Georgetown, Fordham and Boston College.

Despite their simple beginnings, the Jesuits quickly became (and remain) the largest order in the Catholic Church. Its leader was called "the Black Pope" for his distinctive, austere black cassock as well as his perceived power. ...."
https://www.ncronline.org/news/vatican/understand-pope-francis-look-jesuits

(Jesuits) Extreme Oath of Induction

The following is the Jesuit Extreme Oath of Induction given to high ranking Jesuits only. This oath is taken from the book Subterranean Rome by Carlos Didier, translated from the French, and published in New York in 1843.

"When a Jesuit of the minor rank is to be elevated to command, he is conducted into the Chapel of the Convent of the Order, where there are only three others present, the principal or Superior standing in front of the altar. On either side stands a monk, one of whom holds a banner of yellow and white, which are the Papal colors, and the other a black banner with a dagger and red cross above a skull and crossbones, with the word INRI, and below them the words IUSTUM, NECAR, REGES, IMPIOUS. The

193

meaning of which is: It is just to exterminate or annihilate impious or heretical Kings, Governments, or Rulers. Upon the floor is a red cross at which the postulant or candidate kneels. The Superior hands him a small black crucifix, which he takes in his left hand and presses to his heart, and the Superior at the same time presents to him a dagger, which he grasps by the blade and holds the point against his heart, the Superior still holding it by the hilt, and thus addresses the postulant:"

Superior:

My son, heretofore you have been taught to act the dissembler: among Roman Catholics to be a Roman Catholic, and to be a spy even among your own brethren; to believe no man, to trust no man. Among the Reformers, to be a reformer; among the Huguenots, to be a Huguenot; among the Calvinists, to be a Calvinist; among other Protestants, generally to be a Protestant, and obtaining their confidence, to seek even to preach from their pulpits, and to denounce with all the vehemence in your nature our Holy Religion and the Pope; and even to descend so low as to become a Jew among Jews, that you might be enabled to gather together all information for the benefit of your Order as a faithful soldier of the Pope.

You have been taught to insidiously plant the seeds of jealousy and hatred between communities, provinces, states that were at peace, and incite them to deeds of blood, involving them in war with each other, and to create revolutions and civil wars in countries that were independent and prosperous, cultivating the arts and the sciences and enjoying the blessings of peace. To take sides with the combatants and to act secretly with your brother Jesuit, who might be engaged on the other side, but openly opposed to that with which you might be connected, only that the Church might be the gainer in the end, in the conditions fixed in the treaties for peace and that the end justifies the means.

You have been taught your duty as a spy, to gather all statistics, facts and information in your power from every source; to ingratiate yourself into the confidence of the family circle of Protestants and heretics of every class and character, as well as that of the merchant, the banker, the lawyer, among the schools and universities, in parliaments and legislatures, and the judiciaries and councils of state, and to be all things to all men, for the Pope's sake, whose servants we are unto death.

You have received all your instructions heretofore as a novice, a neophyte, and have served as co-adjurer, confessor and priest, but you have not yet been invested with all that is necessary to command in the Army of Loyola in the service of the Pope. You must serve the proper time as the instrument and executioner as directed by your superiors; for none can command here who has not consecrated his labors with the blood of the heretic; for "without the shedding of blood no man can be saved." Therefore, to fit yourself for your work and make your own salvation sure, you will, in addition to your former oath of obedience to your order and allegiance to the Pope, repeat after me—

The Extreme Oath of the Jesuits:

"1, _ now, in the presence of Almighty God, the Blessed Virgin Mary, the blessed Michael the Archangel, the blessed St. John the Baptist, the holy Apostles St. Peter and St. Paul and all the saints and sacred hosts of heaven, and to you, my ghostly father, the Superior General of the Society of Jesus, founded by St. Ignatius Loyola in the Pontificate of Paul the Third, and continued to the present, do by the womb of the virgin, the matrix of God, and the rod of Jesus Christ, declare and swear, that his holiness the Pope is Christ's Vice-regent and is the true and only head of the Catholic or Universal Church throughout the earth; and that by virtue of the keys of binding and loosing, given to his Holiness by my Savior, Jesus Christ, he hath power to depose heretical kings, princes, states, commonwealths and governments, all being illegal without his sacred confirmation and that they may safely be destroyed. Therefore, to the utmost of my power I shall and will defend this doctrine of his Holiness' right and custom against all usurpers of the heretical or Protestant authority whatever, especially the Lutheran of Germany, Holland, Denmark, Sweden, Norway, and the now pretended authority and churches of England and Scotland, and branches of the same now established in Ireland and on the Continent of America and elsewhere; and all adherents in regard that they be usurped and heretical, opposing the sacred Mother Church of Rome. I do now renounce and disown any allegiance as due to any heretical king, prince or state named Protestants or Liberals, or obedience to any of the laws, magistrates or officers.

I do further declare that the doctrine of the churches of England and Scotland, of the Calvinists, Huguenots and others of the name Protestants or Liberals to be damnable and they themselves damned who will not forsake the same.

I do further declare, that I will help, assist, and advise all or any of his Holiness' agents in any place wherever I shall be, in Switzerland, Germany, Holland, Denmark, Sweden, Norway, England, Ireland or America, or in any other Kingdom or territory I shall come to, and do my uttermost to extirpate the heretical Protestants or Liberals' doctrines

<u>and to destroy all their pretended powers, regal or otherwise.</u>

I do further promise and declare, that notwithstanding I am dispensed with, to assume my religion heretical, for the propaganda of the Mother Church's interest, to keep secret and private all her agents' counsels from time to time, as they may entrust me and not to divulge, directly or indirectly, by word, writing or circumstance whatever; but to execute all that shall be proposed, given in charge or discovered unto me, by you, my ghostly father, or any of this sacred covenant.

I do further promise and declare, that I will have no opinion or will of my own, or any mental reservation whatever, even as a corpse or cadaver (perinde ac cadaver), but will unhesitatingly obey each and every command that I may receive from my superiors in the Militia of the Pope and of Jesus Christ.

That I may go to any part of the world withersoever I may be sent, to the frozen regions of the North, the burning sands of the desert of Africa, or the jungles of India, to the centers of civilization of Europe, or to the wild haunts of the barbarous savages of America, without murmuring or repining, and will be submissive in all things whatsoever communicated to me.

I furthermore promise and declare that I will, when opportunity present, make and wage relentless war, secretly or openly, against all heretics, Protestants and Liberals, as I am directed to do, to extirpate and exterminate them from the face of the whole earth; and that I will spare neither age, sex or condition; and that I will hang, waste, boil, flay, strangle and bury alive these infamous heretics, rip up the stomachs and wombs of their women and crush their infants' heads against the walls, in order to annihilate

197

forever their execrable race. That when the same cannot be done openly, I will secretly use the poisoned cup, the strangulating cord, the steel of the poniard or the leaden bullet, regardless of the honor, rank, dignity, or authority of the person or persons, whatever may be their condition in life, either public or private, as I at any time may be directed so to do by any agent of the Pope or Superior of the Brotherhood of the Holy Faith, of the Society of Jesus.

In confirmation of which, I hereby dedicate my life, my soul and all my corporal powers, and with this dagger which I now receive, I will subscribe my name written in my own blood, in testimony thereof; and should I prove false or weaken in my determination, may my brethren and fellow soldiers of the Militia of the Pope cut off my hands and my feet, and my throat from ear to ear, my belly opened and sulphur burned therein, with all the punishment that can be inflicted upon me on earth and my soul be tortured by demons in an eternal hell forever!

All of which, I, _, do swear by the Blessed Trinity and blessed Sacraments, which I am now to receive, to perform and on my part to keep inviolable; and do call all the heavenly and glorious host of heaven to witness the blessed Sacrament of the Eucharist, and witness the same further with my name written and with the point of this dagger dipped in my own blood and sealed in the face of this holy covenant."

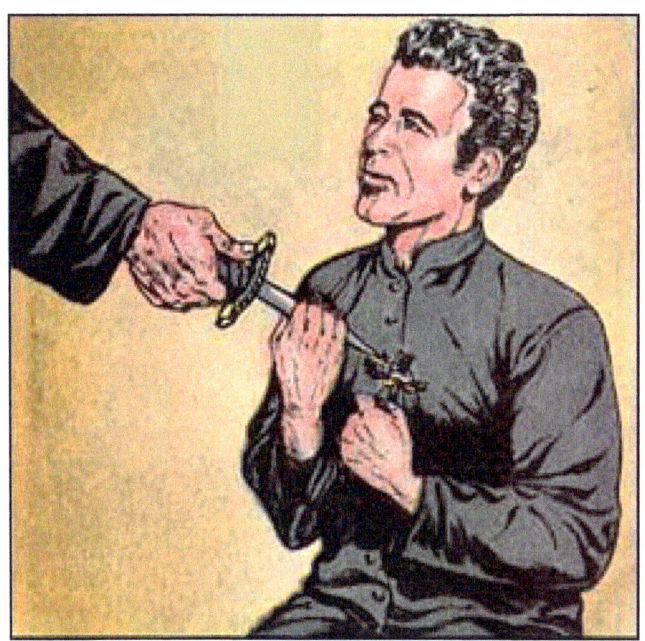

Alberto Rivera taking the Jesuit Oath

(He receives the wafer from the Superior and writes his name with the point of his dagger dipped in his own blood taken from over his heart.)

Superior:

"You will now rise to your feet and I will instruct you in the Catechism necessary to make yourself known to any member of the Society of Jesus belonging to this rank.

In the first place, you, as a Brother Jesuit, will with another mutually make the ordinary sign of the cross as any ordinary Roman Catholic would; then one cross his wrists, the palms of his hands open, and the other in answer crosses his feet, one above the other; the first points with forefinger of the right hand to the center of the palm of the left, the other with the forefinger of the left hand points to the center of the palm of the right; the first then with his right hand makes a circle around his head, touching it; the

199

other then with the forefinger of his left hand touches the left side of his body just below his heart; the first then with his right hand draws it across the throat of the other, and the latter then with a dagger down the stomach and abdomen of the first. The first then says Iustum; and the other answers Necar; the first Reges. The other answers Impious." (The meaning of which has already been explained.)

The first will then present a small piece of paper folded in a peculiar manner, four times, which the other will cut longitudinally and on opening the name Jesu will be found written upon the head and arms of a cross three times. You will then give and receive with him the following questions and answers:

Question —From whither do you come?
Answer — The Holy faith.
Q. —Whom do you serve?
A. —The Holy Father at Rome, the Pope, and the Roman Catholic Church Universal throughout the world.

Q. —Who commands you?
A. —The Successor of St. Ignatius Loyola, the founder of the Society of Jesus or the Soldiers of Jesus Christ.

Q. —Who received you?
A. —A venerable man in white hair.
Q. —How?
A. —With a naked dagger, I kneeling upon the cross beneath the banners of the Pope and of our sacred order.

Q. —Did you take an oath?
A. —I did, to destroy heretics and their governments and rulers, and to spare neither age, sex nor condition. To be as a corpse without any opinion or will of my own, but to

implicitly obey my Superiors in all things without hesitation of murmuring.

Q. —Will you do that?
A. —I will.

Q. —How do you travel?
A. —In the bark of Peter the fisherman.

Q. —Whither do you travel?
A. —To the four quarters of the globe.

Q. —For what purpose?
A. —To obey the orders of my general and Superiors and execute the will of the Pope and faithfully fulfill the conditions of my oaths.

Go ye, then, into all the world and take possession of all lands in the name of the Pope. He who will not accept him as the Vicar of Jesus and his Vice-regent on earth, let him be accursed and exterminated."

Is the account of this oath farfetched? The society of Jesus is very alive and very well. Are you aware that Pope Francis is of Jesuit stock? How pious, holy and friendly does he appear in the eyes of the entire world? If we read between the lines of the following article from the National Catholic Reporter we will understand that it is true.

"To understand Pope Francis, look to the Jesuits"
Mar 12, 2014

VATICAN CITY — Figuring out why Pope Francis has upended so many expectations, how exactly he's changed the Catholic church in his first year and what he might be contemplating for the future has become a Catholic parlor game that is almost as popular as the pontiff himself.

A single key can best answer all of these questions: Francis' longstanding identity as a Jesuit priest.

It's an all-encompassing personal and professional definition that the former Cardinal Jorge Bergoglio brought with him from Buenos Aires, Argentina, and one that continues to shape almost everything he does as Pope Francis.

"He may act like a Franciscan, but he thinks like a Jesuit," quipped Fr. Thomas Reese, a fellow Jesuit who is a columnist for National Catholic Reporter.

In fact, it would be easy to mistake this new pope for a Franciscan, given his emphasis on helping society's outcasts and his decision to become the first pope to take the name of St. Francis of Assisi, the patron saint of the poor. Yet he's the first pope from the Society of Jesus, the religious community whose worldly, wise intellectuals are as famous as its missionaries and martyrs.

Indeed, behind that "Jesuit" label lies a centuries-old history and a unique brand of spiritual formation that go a long way toward understanding who Francis is and where he is taking the church.

From his passion for social justice and his missionary zeal to his focus on engaging the wider world and his preference for collaboration over peremptory action, Francis is a Jesuit through and through. And as the first Jesuit pope, he brings sharply etched memories of being part of a community that's been viewed with deep suspicion by Rome, most recently by his own predecessor, Pope Benedict XVI.

Jesuit priests are explicitly discouraged from becoming bishops, much less pope, and that outsider's sensibility helps to explain Francis' almost breezy willingness to dispense with centuries of closely guarded and cherished tradition.

"We never imagined that a Jesuit could become pope. It was an impossible thing," said Fr. Antonio Spadaro, a Jesuit who conducted a book-length interview with the pope and knows him well. "It sent me into a crisis, in a sense, when he was elected. We Jesuits are supposed to be at the service of the pope, not to be a pope."

What is the focus or purpose of a Jesuit?

We touched on the answer to this question in part of the Jesuit Oath read earlier. I will refer to other writer's because we find in Hebrews 12:1 the inference of the importance of "a cloud of witnesses…"

I am quoting from History of the Jesuits by G.B Nicolini. Published in 1854.

"I trust that in the following pages I have succeeded in the task I proposed to myself, of conveying to my readers a just and correct idea of the character and aims of the brotherhood of Loyola. At least I have spared no pains to accomplish this end. I honestly believe that the book was wanted; for liberal institutions and civil and religious freedom have no greater enemies than that cunning fraternity; while it is equally true, that although the Jesuits are dreaded and detested on all sides as the worst species of knaves, there are few who are thoroughly acquainted with their eventful history, and with all those arts by which the fathers have earned for themselves a disgraceful celebrity. The fault does not altogether lie with the public; for, strange to say, there is no serious and complete history of this wonderful Society. I have done my best to supply the deficiency; and I indulge the hope that, if the book is fortunate enough to challenge public attention, it may be productive of some good. In no other epoch of history, certainly, have the Jesuits been more dangerous and threatening for England than in the present. I am no alarmist. I refuse to believe that England will relapse under the Papal yoke, and return to the darkness and ignorance of the middle ages, because some score of citizens pass over to the Eomish communion; but at the same time I do believe that many bold and less reflective persons make too light of the matter, and are wrong in refusing to countenance vigorous measures, not for religious persecution, but to check the insolence and countermine the plots of these audacious monks. It is true that there exists a great difficulty in deciding what measures are to be adopted for accomplishing this end. It is repugnant, doubtless, to a liberal and generous mind, and it is unworthy of a free and great nation, to persecute any sect, and to make different castes in the same body of citizens. But, it may fairly be asked, are monks, and especially Jesuits, really English citizens, in the strictest sense of the word? Do they recognise Queen Victoria as their legitimate sovereign? Are they prepared to yield a loyal obedience to the laws of the land? To all these questions I answer, No! Even when born in England, they do not consider themselves Englishmen. They claim the privileges which the name confers, but will not accept the obligations it imposes. Their country is Rome; their sovereign the Pope; their laws the commands of their General. England they consider an accursed land; Englishmen heretics, whom they are under an obligation to combat. The perusal of this work will, I imagine, prove beyond the possibility of contradiction that, from their origin, the Jesuits have constantly and energetically laboured towards this object. I cannot too much impress upon the minds of my readers that the Jesuits, by their very calling, by the very essence of their institution, are bound to seek, by every means, right or wrong, the destruction of Protestantism. This is the condition of their existence, the duty they must fulfil, or cease to be Jesuits. Accordingly, we find them in this evil dilemma. Either the Jesuits fulfil the duties of their calling, or not. In the first instance, they must be considered as the bitterest enemies of the Protestant faith; in the second, as bad and unworthy priests; and in both cases, therefore, to be equally regarded with aversion and distrust."

I recommend you acquire a copy of the above Author's book for your personal research. Go to this link https://bit.ly/2U9mPa4

Pope Francis is the First Jesuit Pope in history. We should be very concerned. The Papacy and the Jesuits do not change. They will show courtesy to whoever they need to, but once they are in full power we will experience their wrath again. Never forget their history and purpose. They are working insidiously behind the scenes. Now that we have the Papacy and the Jesuits combined in one individual, we are facing an unprecedented peril. Find and study Fox's Book of Martyrs, you will be astonished.

Freemasonry

"The masonic fraternity is the custodian of the law, it is the home of the mysteries and the seat of initiation. It holds in its symbolism the ritual of Deity, and the way of salvation is pictorially preserved in its work. The methods of deity are demonstrated in the temples, and under the all-seeing-eye the work can go forward. It is a far more occult movment than can be realized, and is intended to be the training school for the coming advanced occultists." The Externalization of the Hierarchy Alice Bailey Lucis Trust. Page 511.

"There is no dissociation between the one universal church, the sacred inner lodge of all true freemasons, and the innermost circles of the esoteric societies. Three types of men have their need met, three major rays are expressed, and the three paths to the master are trodden, leading all three to the same portal and to the same Hierophant." The Externalization of the Hierarchy, Alice Bailey Lucis Trust Page 513.

Take very careful note of the phrase *"leading all three to the same portal and to the same Hierophant"* We can see from these quotes that freemasonry is inextricably linked with the Mysteries, sexual perversions and the master,

206

Satan, just as the Catholic 'Mother' church is actually Satan's church cloaked as 'Christian' a wolf in sheep's clothing.

What are and have been the plans of freemasonry for society and as outlined by Alice A Bailey?

"The Workers in the Field of Religion...[are] to formulate the universal platform of the new world religion. It is a work of loving synthesis and it will emphasize the unity and the fellowship of the spirit....The platform of the new world religion will be built by the many groups, working under the inspiration of THE Christ..." Discipleship In The New Age, Vol 1, p 38, by Alice Bailey.

The New Age Movement

It's main goal is to destroy traditional Judeo Christianity and create a... One world Religion based on a Luciferian system and doctrine.

Alice A Bailey

The leadership to further Lucifer's plans (via Theosophy) was transferred to her. She became the president of the Theosophical Society. She is probably the most important in laying the foundation of the New Age Movement. One day she had a visitation of a spirit, that she thought was Christ at first but the spirit introduced himself as Djwal Khuhl – spirit from Tibetan. Master of Tibetan offered her great success if she could yield herself to be used in cheating the nations of the world and she made a deliberate decision to offer her life in service to Satan. She has so many writings on every sector of life. By the time she had finished her work in 1949 she had written 24 books, a total of 10,469 pages, most of which were allegedly written through her spirit guide, The Tibetan.

She had also established Lucis Trust Goodwill (to which is linked the leadership of the World Constitution and Parliament Association) under the name Lucifer Publishing Company which today boasts of a membership of more than 6000 people. Some of the world's most renowned financial and political leaders have belonged to this organization. The Lucis Trust Headquarters is Located at 866 United nations Plaza, New York City. What is the connection between the UN and the Lucis Trust?

She also describes the Masonic movement as "… the custodian of the law; it is the home of the Mysteries and the seat of initiation. It holds in its symbolism the ritual of Deity, and the way of salvation is pictorially preserved in its work. The methods of Deity are demonstrated in its Temples, and under the All-seeing Eye the work can go forward. It is a far more occult organisation than can be realised, and is intended to be the training school for the coming advanced occultists. In its ceremonials lies hid the

208

wielding of the forces connected with the growth and life of the kingdoms of nature and the unfoldment of the divine aspects in man. In the comprehension of its symbolism will come the power to cooperate with the divine plan. It meets the need of those who work on the first Ray of Will or Power."

Observe carefully their 10 goals for society. Are they another alternative 10 commandments?

1. TAKE GOD AND PRAYER OUT OF THE EDUCATION SYSTEM

Alice Bailey "Change curriculum to ensure that children are freed from the bondage of Christian culture. Why? Because children go to school to be equipped to face life, they are willing to trust and they are willing to value what is being given to them.

If you take God out of education, they will unconsciously form a resolve that God is not necessary to face life. They will focus on those things the school counts them worthy to be passed on and they will look at God as an additional, if one can afford the additional."

I remember when I was a child at school that we had morning assembly, this does not exist any more, yet schools are happy to teach other belief systems, traditions and new ideas apart from Christianity.

Today they introduce Transcendental Meditation (TM) in schools which takes children to altered states of consciousness to meet with demons (spirit guides) New Age.

209

I distinctly remember being shocked to see primary school children practising levitation and playing with ouija boards during lunch break in a primary school classroom.

2. REDUCE PARENTAL AUTHORITY OVER THE CHILDREN

Alice Bailey " Break the communication between parent and child (Why?). So that parents do not pass on their Christian traditions to their children, liberate children from the bondage of their parent traditions (how?)

a) Promote excessive child rights; (1997-1998 South Africa introduced Child rights legislation – UNICEF Charter; Today a child is able to say to parent "I do not want to hear that, I don't want to do what you are telling me." Teachers cannot talk to children, children step up and say "I have my rights, you cannot talk to me like that".

Children as young as 7 are being taught by their schools that they can inform the police if their parents try to discipline them. I, 100% do not support brutality, but it is insane and irresponsible to allow a child to grow up with no discipline. You will only be training tomorrow's criminals.

b) Abolish corporal punishment; (this has been made law). On the other hand the Bible says 'Do not withhold correction from a child, for if you beat him with a rod, he will not die. You shall beat him with a rod and deliver his soul from hell.' (Proverbs 23: 13-14)

c) Teachers are the agents of implementation – from workshops, teachers tell children "your parent has no right to force you to pray or read the Bible, you are yourself, have a right of your own, you need to discover yourself,

self expression, self realization, self fulfillment are all buzz words."

In the West when the child is 7 yrs of age, the teachers begin to say to the child 'you have a right to choose whether you want to follow the faith of your parents or not, parents are not allowed to enforce their faith upon you.' Question is, what type of decision can a 7 year old make?

3. DESTROY THE JUDEO-CHRISTIAN FAMILY STRUCTURE OR THE TRADITIONAL CHRISTIAN FAMILY STRUCTURE (Why?).

It is oppressive and that the family is the core of the nation. If you break the family, you break the nation. Liberate the people from the confines of this structure (How?)

a) Promote sexual promiscuity – Free young people to the concept of premarital sex, let them have free sex, lift it so high that the joy of enjoying it(sex) is the highest joy in life, fantasize it, that everybody will feel proud to be seen to be sexually active, even those outside of marriage.

This is contrary to the word of God which says "… But fornication and all uncleanness or covetousness, let it not even be named among you, as is fitting for saints… for this you know, that no fornicator, unclean person, nor covetous man, who is an idolater has any inheritance in the kingdom of Christ and God." (Ephesians 5: 3-5)

b) Use advertising industry, media – T.V., magazines, film industry to promote sexual enjoyment as the highest pleasure in humanity.

If you want to see whether they have succeeded or not, go to the advertising industry, it does everything to catch your attention and today almost no advert comes out without a sexual connotation.

4. IF SEX IS FREE, THEN MAKE ABORTION LEGAL AND MAKE IT EASY

She said; Build clinics for abortion – Health clinics in schools. If people are going to enjoy the joy of sexual relationships, they need to be free of unnecessary fears, in other words they should not be hampered with unwanted pregnancies.

'Abortion as told by Christians is oppressive and denies our rights, we have a right to choose whether we want to have a child or not. If a woman does not want the pregnancy, she should have the freedom to get rid of that pregnancy painless and as easy as possible'.

5. MAKE DIVORCE EASY AND LEGAL, FREE PEOPLE FROM THE CONCEPT OF MARRIAGE FOR LIFE.

Alice wrote 50 years ago that love has got a mysterious link called the love bond. It is like an ovum that comes out of the ovary, as it travels through your system, it clicks a love favor in you and there's one other person in the world who can respond to that love bond, when you see that person, everything within you clicks, that is your man/woman, if you miss him, you'll never be happy until that love bond cycles past, for many years, so for you to be happy get that person at whatever cost, if it means getting him/her out of that marriage, get him/her that is your man/woman, don't be held in bondage by the Christian values it will never come back, what you need is an easily arranged divorce and allow another love bond to come forth, just like an ovum comes up, and when it comes forth you'll enjoy life again.

6. MAKE HOMOSEXUALITY AN ALTERNATIVE LIFESTYLE

Alice Bailey preached (50 yrs ago) that sexual enjoyment is the highest pleasure in humanity, no one must be denied and no one must be restricted how to enjoy themselves. People should be allowed in which ever way they chose they want, whether it is homosexuality or in incest or bestiality, as long as the two agree."

Is this strategy succeeding? It most certainly is.

I remember as a VIP driver when I was chauffeuring TV Program Planners for a major British Televison organisation back in the 80's, they openly discussed amongst themselves a directive from senior management to write homosexuality into the TV programs so that the homosexual lifestyle would become more acceptable. If such a plan was not going to be effective because it is 'TV' and people would not be influenced, why do companies spend millions on advertising? Isn't it to influence our thought processes to buy products we most of the time don't really need? Therefore on that basis TV definitely has an influence on the masses.

In the world today so many laws have been made that promote homosexuality and give so much freedom to gay rights, that a time will come when it is illegal for a preacher to mention homosexuality as an abomination in the eyes of God, or to read scriptures publicly that talk about homosexuality.

Today many churches marry gays/lesbians, ordain gay priests even appointing transgenders as Church Elders. This is a direct attack on God and it is only corrupt infiltrators and corrupt leaders that are allowing these things into the churches across all denominations. These corruptions were endemic in the Catholic Church and are now being spread into all the churches to destroy the reputation of God's people. This is a cleverly orchestrated plan against the church to bring disrepute and shame to God's cause on earth and honest Christians need to stand against this infiltration and abominations being welcomed into the churches as 'pretend' love.

This is not love. God in His love welcomes all sinners but does not condone remaining in their sins. If we could live as we pleased after joining God's church and remained as we were, then the death of Christ on the cross for our sins was a waste of time. A day of judgment would be a waste of time. The scriptural account of the correct order of things as delivered at creation would be a waste of time, ie, a man and a woman in marriage, not woman and woman or man and man. This also leads into another doctrine and that of evolution because if God did not make us the way He did then evolution would be the only logical alternative therefore there would be no God.

"And there followed another angel, saying, Babylon is fallen, is fallen, that great city, because she made all nations drink of the wine of the wrath of her fornication."

How far have we fallen?

Celine Dion has launched a new clothing label that promotes genderless clothing with the headline "The future is theirs to choose" She states that our children are not really ours but simply links in a never-ending chain of life. Really?

She has them wearing clothes that have New Order printed on them and fashion houses use the phrase "fashion has power to shape people's minds." Do we understand how deep and pervasive their plans are?
What are the goals of these new lifestyle preachers? Our Children are not ours but part of life? They are recruiting more souls into their corrupt lifestyles but the followers of the living God need to stand against this and let their voices be heard. Are our children really choosing or is it adults with ulterior motives thrusting their lifestyles on innocent children? Surely this must be considered child abuse. This is a horrific development!

"Eight-year-old pupils to be told 'boys can have periods too' under new sex education lessons guidelines

- Children will be told that 'all genders' can have periods under new guidelines
- Brighton & Hove City Council issued the guidelines which have faced criticism
- Guidance states: 'Trans boys and men and non-binary people may have periods'

Sex education lessons in which pupils as young as eight will be told 'all genders' have periods were yesterday condemned as unnecessarily confusing for young children.

The classes follow guidelines that were issued to teachers to help them avoid offending girls who identify as boys.

But critics described the guidelines as inappropriate and another example of political correctness gone mad.

The teacher guidance, from Brighton & Hove City Council, states: 'Trans boys and men and non-binary people may have periods.' It says language about menstruation must be inclusive of 'all genders' and orders that 'bins for used period products are provided in all toilets' for children."

7. DEBASE ART, MAKE IT RUN MAD

"How? Promote new forms of art which will corrupt and defile the imagination of people because art is the language of the spirit, that which is inside, you can bring out in painting, music, drama etc.

There is no doubt this goal is being achieved by the music videos, TV Series, Movies etc that are redefining morality.

8. USE MEDIA TO PROMOTE AND CHANGE MINDSET

Alice Bailey said the greatest channel you need to use to change human attitude is media. Use the press, the radio, T.V, cinema.

9. CREATE AN INTERFAITH MOVEMENT

Alice Bailey wrote; Promote other faiths to be at par with Christianity, and break this thing about Christianity as being the only way to heaven, by that Christianity will be pulled down and other faiths promoted. She said promote the importance of man in determining his own future and destiny – HUMANISM. She said tell man he has the right to choose what he wants to be and he can make it happen, he has the right to determine his cause – This takes God off His throne."

The Ecumenical Movement, is this not an Interfaith Movement also? It most definitely is and has gained huge traction in uniting all religions including Islam and pagans.

10. GET GOVERNMENTS TO MAKE ALL THESE LAWS AND GET THE CHURCH TO ENDORSE THESE CHANGES.

Alice Bailey wrote that the church must change its doctrine and accommodate the people by accepting these things and put them into its structures and systems.

Have they succeeded? Yes to some extent, but truth will eventually win because truth is of God. All those that are truly searching for truth will find it and this book is part of the process to help in that search.

Today you wonder why our governments are legislating laws contrary to the Bible and why the church is compromising the Word of God. It is a process of implementing The Plan - A 50 year strategy of the New Age Movement to fulfill its ultimate goal to establish a One World Government, a One World Economic system and a One World Religion. Today the strategy almost in its entirety has been adopted by the United Nations and today a lot of it is already law in many nations. This deception has crept up unobserved on so many people. Source: Bailey, Alice (1922), Initiation, human and solar, Lucifer Pub. Co., OCLC 1882542. The Lucis Trust is the official publisher of Alice Bailey's books.

Our modern society is legislating certain lifestyles onto the statute books of the land. Can man's laws and lifestyles supersede God's laws and lifestyles? Most definitely not.

He knows how best His creation should function successfully.

"Know ye not that the unrighteous shall not inherit the kingdom of God? Be not deceived: neither fornicators, nor idolaters, nor adulterers, nor effeminate, nor abusers of themselves with mankind, nor thieves, nor covetous, nor drunkards, nor revilers, nor extortioners, shall inherit the kingdom of God." 1 Corinthians 6:9-10.

"For if God spared not the angels that sinned, but cast [them] down to hell, and delivered [them] into chains of darkness, to be reserved unto judgment; And spared not the old world, but saved Noah the eighth [person], a preacher of righteousness, bringing in the flood upon the world of the ungodly; And turning the cities of Sodom and Gomorrha into ashes condemned [them] with an overthrow, **making [them] an ensample unto those that after should live ungodly;**" 2 Peter 2:4-6

What is the original meaning of the word ensample?

G5262

ὑπόδειγμα

hupodeigma

hoop-od'-igue-mah

From G5263; an exhibit for imitation or warning ...

An exhibit or warning? We understand an exhibit to mean physical evidence. A warning? Self-explanatory.

If any reader wants to confirm that this evidence exists they only need to visit the area around the salt sea where the five cities were located and the huge layers of gypsum ash and sulphur is clearly evident for all to see. The sulphur residues there are reported to be unique to the area, not found anywhere else on earth.

"For I am not ashamed of the gospel of Christ: for it is the power of God unto salvation to everyone that believeth; to the Jew first, and also to the Greek.
For therein is the righteousness of God revealed from faith to faith: as it is written, the just shall live by faith.
For the wrath of God is revealed from heaven against all ungodliness and unrighteousness of men, who hold the truth in unrighteousness;
Because that which may be known of God is manifest in them; for God hath showed [it] unto them.
For the invisible things of him from the creation of the world are clearly seen, being understood by the things that are made, [even] his eternal power and Godhead; so that they are without excuse: Because that, when they knew God, they glorified [him] not as God, neither were thankful; but became vain in their imaginations, and their foolish heart was darkened.
Professing themselves to be wise, they became fools, And changed the glory of the uncorruptible God into an image made like to corruptible man, and to birds, and four-footed beasts, and creeping things.
Wherefore God also gave them up to uncleanness through the lusts of their own hearts, to dishonour their own bodies between themselves:
Who changed the truth of God into a lie, and worshipped and served the creature more than the Creator, who is blessed for ever. Amen.
For this cause God gave them up unto vile affections: for even their women did change the natural use into that which is against nature:
And likewise also the men, leaving the natural use of the woman, burned in their lust one toward another; men with

men working that which is unseemly, and receiving in themselves that recompense of their error which was meet.

And even as they did not like to retain God in [their] knowledge, God gave them over to a reprobate mind, to do those things which are not convenient;

Being filled with all unrighteousness, fornication, wickedness, covetousness, maliciousness; full of envy, murder, debate, deceit, malignity; whisperers,

Backbiters, haters of God, despiteful, proud, boasters, inventors of evil things, disobedient to parents,

Without understanding, covenant breakers, without natural affection, implacable, unmerciful:

Who knowing the judgment of God, that they which commit such things are worthy of death, not only do the same, but have pleasure in them that do them." Romans 1:16-32.

It is very difficult to understand that even some professed christians are supporting the wider society in claiming that they are unable to find any evidence in scripture for the 'sexual preferences' lifestyles? Paul in Romans as we have just read, makes it very plain that it is condemned, the fires from heaven that destroyed the cities of the plains as an example make it plain that God does not approve.

The old testament in Leviticus 20:13 "If a man also lie with mankind, as he lieth with a woman, both of them have committed an abomination: they shall surely be put to death; their blood [shall be] upon them." In fact the whole chapter describes sexually immoral acts, but classifies homosexuality as an abomination. Sadly the symbol God put in place to represent that He would never again destroy the earth by a global flood is being used by the LGBT movement to attempt to validate their abominations, in other words, in your face God. We will do as we please.

"And I will establish my covenant with you; neither shall all flesh be cut off any more by the waters of a flood; neither shall there any more be a flood to destroy the earth.

And God said, This [is] the token of the covenant which I make between me and you and every living creature that [is] with you, for perpetual generations:

I do set my bow in the cloud, and it shall be for a token of a covenant between me and the earth.

And it shall come to pass, when I bring a cloud over the earth, that the bow shall be seen in the cloud:

And I will remember my covenant, which [is] between me and you and every living creature of all flesh; and the waters shall no more become a flood to destroy all flesh.

And the bow shall be in the cloud; and I will look upon it, that I may remember the everlasting covenant between God and every living creature of all flesh that [is] upon the earth.

And God said unto Noah, This [is] the token of the covenant, which I have established between me and all flesh that [is] upon the earth." Genesis 9:12-17.

Why did God destroy the earth? "And God saw that the wickedness of man [was] great in the earth, and [that] every imagination of the thoughts of his heart [was] only evil continually.

And it repented the LORD that he had made man on the earth, and it grieved him at his heart.

And the LORD said, I will destroy man whom I have created from the face of the earth; both man, and beast, and the creeping thing, and the fowls of the air; for it repenteth me that I have made them." Genesis 6:5-7.

Isn't it ironical that the symbol God has put in the clouds to confirm that He would not destroy the earth again with a flood is being used as a symbol of this abomination of a lifestyle? Is this a proverbial slap in God's face? This is some humans saying to God, we will do what we want. God has warned that He will purify the earth with fire at the end of time. Where we end up will be our choice.

*The rainbow flag **(Depicting the rainbow, God's promise never to destroy the earth again with a flood of water, because of wickedness)** is **(used as)** a symbol of lesbian, gay, bisexual, and transgender (LGBT) pride and LGBT social movements in use since the 1970s.*

In recent times this particular sin was described as Sodomy after the lifestyles of Sodom and Gomorrha, (two cities of 5 that God destroyed with fire) but that lifestyle which our Creator calls an abomination has been renamed 'Sexual Preferences' – what other abominations are following the new legislations? There are those that are now campaigning for paedophilia to be described as a natural sexual orientation.

TEDx Talks: Radical leftists now claiming that pedophilia is a "natural sexual orientation"

Where to next? Reclassify beastiality as a preference? Our Creator has to bring this sin chapter of our planet to a close.

How far has the world now gone in supporting sin instead of encouraging those suffering with these conditions, like many other sin related problems? What does the latest USA President have to say? The President of a 'Christian' Nation? Quoting from *https://il.usembassy.gov/a-proclamation-on-lesbian-gay-bisexual-transgender-and-queer-pride-month-2021/*

".... While I am proud of the progress my Administration has made in advancing protections for the LGBTQ+ community, I will not rest until full equality for LGBTQ+ Americans is finally achieved and codified into law. ....."

NOW, THEREFORE, I, JOSEPH R. BIDEN JR., President of the United States of America, by virtue of the authority vested in me by the Constitution and the laws of the United States, do hereby proclaim June 2021 as Lesbian, Gay, Bisexual, Transgender, and Queer Pride Month. I call upon the people of the United States to recognize the achievements of the LGBTQ+ community, to celebrate the great diversity of the American people, and to wave their flags of pride high.

IN WITNESS WHEREOF, I have hereunto set my hand this first day of June, in the year of our Lord two thousand twenty-one, and of the Independence of the United States of America the two hundred and forty-fifth.

JOSEPH R. BIDEN JR."

Please note dear readers, this is not an attack against anyone, it is calling sin by it's name. God says it is a sin and who are we to question that or attempt to make laws against the God of heaven's laws to legalise sinful actions. Romans 1 clearly adds other sins such as Adultery, lieing, stealing, envy etc as sins that will keep us out of His Kingdom. Not my words, God's words.

"Because that, when they knew God, they glorified [him] not as God, neither were thankful; but became vain in their imaginations, and their foolish heart was darkened.
Professing themselves to be wise, they became fools,
And changed the glory of the uncorruptible God into an image made like to corruptible man, and to birds, and fourfooted beasts, and creeping things.
Wherefore God also gave them up to uncleanness through the lusts of their own hearts, to dishonour their own bodies between themselves:
Who changed the truth of God into a lie, and worshipped and served the creature more than the Creator, who is blessed for ever. Amen.

For this cause God gave them up unto vile affections: for even their women did change the natural use into that which is against nature:

And likewise also the men, leaving the natural use of the woman, burned in their lust one toward another; men with men working that which is unseemly, and receiving in themselves that recompense of their error which was meet.

And even as they did not like to retain God in [their] knowledge, God gave them over to a reprobate mind, to do those things which are not convenient;

Being filled with all unrighteousness, fornication, wickedness, covetousness, maliciousness; full of envy, murder, debate, deceit, malignity; whisperers,

Backbiters, haters of God, despiteful, proud, boasters, inventors of evil things, disobedient to parents,

Without understanding, covenantbreakers, without natural affection, implacable, unmerciful:

Who knowing the judgment of God, that they which commit such things are worthy of death, not only do the same, but have pleasure in them that do them." Romans 1:21-32

Brief discussion on purgatory: Purgatory is a doctrine (teaching) of the Catholic church, which defines purgatory as the place believers go at death to be made perfect, or to be purified, so they can enter Heaven.

Purgatory is not found in Scripture - "And from Jesus Christ, [who is] the faithful witness, [and] the first begotten of the dead, and the prince of the kings of the earth. Unto him that loved us, and washed us from our sins in his own blood," Revelation 1:5.

"And they sung a new song, saying, Thou art worthy to take the book, and to open the seals thereof: for thou wast slain, and hast redeemed us to God by thy blood out of

225

every kindred, and tongue, and people, and nation;" Revelation 5:9.

"For by grace are ye saved through faith; and that not of yourselves: [it is] the gift of God: Not of works, lest any man should boast." Ephesians 2:8-9.

"For the living know that they shall die: but the dead know not anything, neither have they any more a reward; for the memory of them is forgotten. Also their love, and their hatred, and their envy, is now perished; neither have they any more a portion for ever in any [thing] that is done under the sun." Ecclesiastes 9:5-6

It is clear from these verses that Jesus already paid the price of our sins on the cross and we are saved by grace, so these doctrines of purgatory and indulgences are major deceptions and a massive lie against the love our Lord has demonstrated by giving His life on the cross. Furthermore, if the dead don't know anything, how can they be in place called purgatory? Purgatory does not exist.

We are supposed to be able to buy our way out of purgatory via indulgences? and it was because of the 95 theses Martin Luther nailed on the church door in Wittenberg on the 31st of October 1517 that protestantism began in earnest. Most of the 95 theses were focused on indulgences. Today, just over 500 years later the comments that are being made is that protestantism is dead.

I do not need to say any more on this topic as this is not the goal of this book, however, the position on purgatory and indulgences is very clear.

Climate Change – The Truth

We have touched on climate change briefly so far and it would be remiss of me not to devote a whole chapter to it. What we are being sold is one of the biggest lies in history. We have looked at some others already but the information in this chapter is also critical to my readers understanding the much bigger picture. In the early days the "Climate" situation was being described as "Global Warming" but as regular extreme cold events were occurring, it was decided that "Climate Change" was the more appropriate description. Why? Because Warming could not explain extreme cold weather events. They have attempted to explain this away too, but what does the real Science show? CO_2 is not a pollutant.

Let us review some alternative information on the situation which of course will not be popular because it does not fit the agenda of Satan and his henchmen or henchwomen. I will quote from very reputable Scientists, Physicists and NASA scientists amongst others.

NASA declares carbon dioxide is GREENING the Earth… reveals how Green New Death is a DEATH cult that would collapse global ecology.
04/26/2019 / By Mike Adams

"NASA declares carbon dioxide is GREENING the Earth… reveals how Green New Death is a DEATH cult that would collapse global ecology
04/26/2019 / By Mike Adams

In direct contradiction to the scare stories about carbon dioxide being relentlessly pushed by the climate change alarmists, a scientific study published in Nature Climate Change and highlighted by NASA reveals that rising carbon dioxide levels are having a tremendously positive impact on the re-greening of planet Earth over the last three decades, with some regions experiencing over a 50% increase in plant life.

The study, entitled, "Greening of the Earth and its drivers," used satellite data to track and map the expansion of green plant growth across the globe from 1982 – 2015. Published in 2016, this study found that rising atmospheric carbon dioxide causes "fertilization" of plant life, resulting in a remarkable acceleration of increased "greening" across every Earth continent. As the study abstract explains:

We show a persistent and widespread increase of growing season integrated LAI (greening) over 25% to 50% of the global vegetated area... Factorial simulations with multiple global ecosystem models suggest that CO2 fertilization effects explain 70% of the observed greening trend...

In other words, the planet is getting greener, and we have rising CO2 levels to thank for it, since rising CO2 accounts for about 70% of the increase in planet-wide greening, according to scientists. The more CO2 we release into the atmosphere, the more nutrients are available for plants, and the more rapidly the Earth is re-greened.

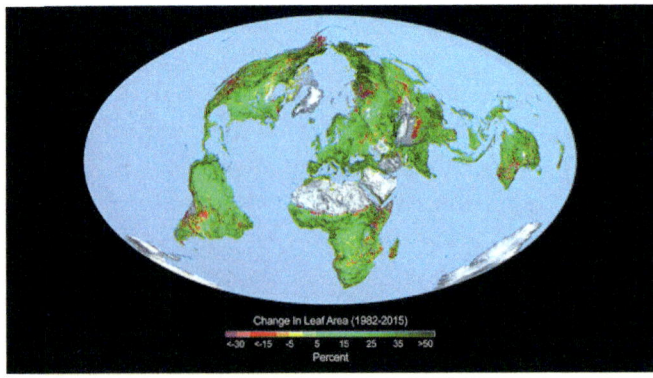

Image credit: Boston University / R. Myeneni

The afore compilation map shows which land masses have experienced expanded greening since 1982. As the legend explains, the light green areas represent a 25% increase in green plants, and the dark green areas represent a 50% or greater increase:

Natural News readers may note this is exactly what we've been reporting for over a decade. It's basic science, of course, since plants use carbon dioxide to thrive. Higher $CO2$ means a greener Earth, since $CO2$ is the single most important molecule for sustaining plant life across the globe. It is beyond astonishing that the entire climate change cult denies the basic science of botany and photosynthesis.

To the shock of many climate change alarmists, even NASA scientists confirmed that carbon dioxide is "greening" the planet. As stated on the NASA.gov website in an article titled, "Carbon Dioxide Fertilization Greening Earth, Study Finds":

From a quarter to half of Earth's vegetated lands has shown significant greening over the last 35 years largely due to rising levels of atmospheric carbon dioxide, according to a new study published in the journal Nature Climate Change on April 25.

An international team of 32 authors from 24 institutions in eight countries led the effort, which involved using satellite data from NASA's Moderate Resolution Imaging Spectrometer and the National Oceanic and Atmospheric Administration's Advanced Very High Resolution Radiometer instruments to help determine the leaf area index, or amount of leaf cover, over the planet's vegetated regions. The greening represents an increase in leaves on plants and trees equivalent in area to two times the continental United States." https://bit.ly/3vhzu7Z

PHYSICIST WILLIAM HAPPER: "THERE IS NO CLIMATE EMERGENCY … RENEWABLE ENERGY IS THE INVERSE ROBIN HOOD STRATEGY … DOUBLING CO2 MAKES NO DIFFERENCE"
MAY 5, 2021 CAP ALLON

William Happer is an American physicist with over 200 published peer-reviews scientific papers. He is the Cyrus Fogg Brackett Professor of Physics, Emeritus, at Princeton University, and has also worked for the U.S. government on two separate occasions: the first was between 1991-1993, where he served as Director of Energy Research, and the second between 2018-2019 under the Trump administration, where he was Deputy Assistant to the President for Emerging Technologies at the National Security Council.

Dr. William Happer spoke at the National Leadership Seminar, sponsored by Hillsdale College, on February 19, 2021, in Phoenix, Arizona. I will refer to some of his talk:

"The best way to think about the frenzy over climate is to consider it a modern version of the medieval Crusades. You may remember that the motto of the crusaders was "Deus vult!", "God wills it!" It is hard to pick a better virtue-signalling slogan than that.

Most climate enthusiasts have not gone so far, but some actually claim that they are doing God's work. After decades of propaganda, many Americans, perhaps including some of you here today, think there really is a climate emergency. Those who think that way, in many cases, mean very well. But they have been misled.

As a scientist who actually knows a lot about climate (and I set up many of our climate research centers when I was at the Department of Energy in the early 1990s) I can assure you that there is no climate emergency. There will not be a climate emergency. Crusades have always ended badly. They have brought discredit to the supposed righteous cause. They have brought hardship and death to multitudes. Policies to address this phony climate emergency will cause great damage to American citizens and to their environment.

Climate frenzy is really heating up recently. On February 4th Senator Bernie Sanders, Congresswoman Alexandra Ocasio-Cortez, and Congressman Earl Blumenauer introduced "legislation mandating the declaration of a national climate emergency.

The National Climate Emergency Act directs the President of the United States to declare a national climate emergency and mobilize every resource at the country's disposal to halt, reverse, mitigate and prepare for the consequences of this climate crisis." (This is from Mr. Blumenauer's website.) But this is utter nonsense. There is no climate crisis, and there will not be a climate crisis

It gets worse when you get to the state levels where there are fewer checks and balances.

These are the remarks made last week by Charles Ismay, the Undersecretary for Climate Change in Massachusetts to the Vermont Climate Council:

"So let me say that again, 60% of our emissions that need to be reduced come from you, the person across the street, the senior on fixed income, right . . . there's no bad guy left, at least in Massachusetts to point the finger at, to turn the screws on, and you know, to break their wills, so they stop emitting. That's you. We have to break your will. Right, I can't even say that publicly."

A few days later Mr. Ismay resigned and had he not, his governor would have fired him. But, that's the way crusades are. This is really not a question of science. This is a question of a secular religion for some. It is a question of money for others. It is a question of power for others. But whatever it is, it is not science. …

So, let's talk about CO2.

Number one, it is not a pollutant at all. We breathe out lots of CO2. Many people are surprised to learn that they exhale a little more than two pounds of CO2 a day. You people in this room are putting out a lot of CO2. I actually brought a CO2 meter here which I am going to turn on. But our breath is not that different from the output of a power plant. Power plants take in normal air, and they consume most of the oxygen by burning coal, or natural gas, or oil. The exhaust that comes out of the stack is mostly the nitrogen that was already there—a little bit of oxygen that was not used up, along with water vapour and CO2.

Our breath is similar, except it has a lot more oxygen. So, you can give mouth-to-mouth resuscitation, but you couldn't if your breath was like the power plant exhaust. Your breath contains about four percent CO2, six percent water. The power plant has a bit more CO2 and correspondingly less oxygen. But our breath is definitely not a pollutant. In fact, our breathing reflex is determined by CO2. It is not determined by oxygen. It is not a lack of oxygen; it is too much CO2 that makes you take another breath of air. …

The Earth is most intensely heated in the tropics. That is the reddish area in the next graphic, where the Sun is most nearly overhead at noon.

Atmospheric circulation transports heat from the equator to the poles

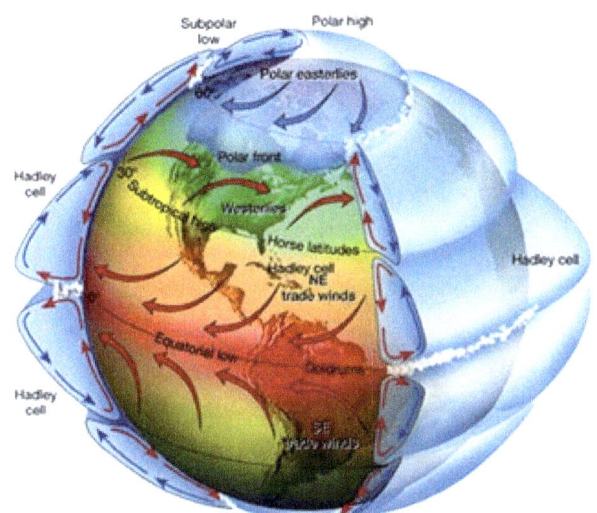

There is more solar energy coming in at the tropics than goes out as cooling radiation to space. The excess heat must be convected to Polar Regions by warm air and ocean water.

Like the Sun, the Earth also radiates. …

Earth maintains its temperature by balancing the solar heating during the day with thermal radiation cooling to cold space, both during the day and night.

Climate involves a complicated interplay of the sunlight that warms us, and thermal infra-radiation that escapes to space. Heat is transported from the tropics to the poles by the motion of warm air and ocean water. We all know about the Gulf Stream that carries huge amounts of heat to northern Europe, even to Russia. Movements of air in the atmosphere also carry a lot of heat, as we know from regular cold spells and hot spells. …

Here is a NASA viewgraph of Earth's energy budget:

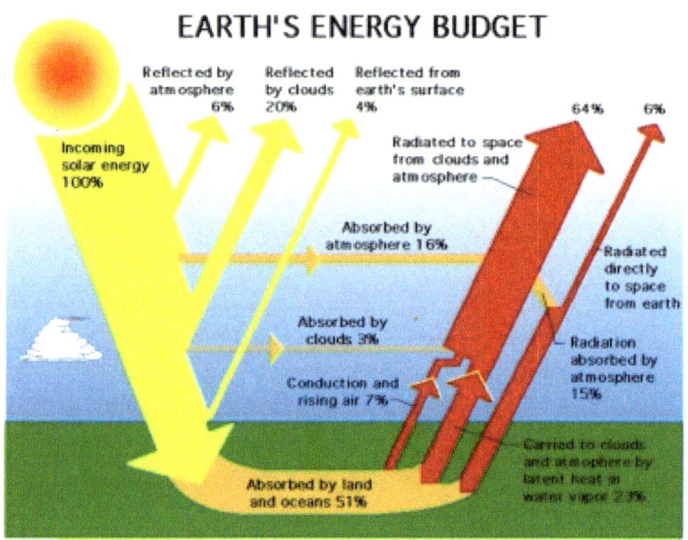

EARTH'S ENERGY BUDGET

A NASA Website

… we are warmed by the Sun. About half of the sunlight eventually gets to the surface. What prevents it all from reaching the surface are clouds and a small amount of scattering and absorption by the atmosphere.

... You can notice that in the afternoon, if you go outside. … you can put your hands in the soil and it is nice and warm. It makes the corn grow. But that heat has to be released. If you keep adding heat to the ground, it gets hotter and hotter. So, the heat is eventually released by radiation into space which is that red arrow going up on the viewgraph. But for the first few kilometres of altitude, a good fraction of that heat is not carried by radiation, but by

234

convection of warm, moist air. CO2 has no direct effect on convection near the surface. But once you get up to 10 kilometres or so, most of the heat is transported by radiation.

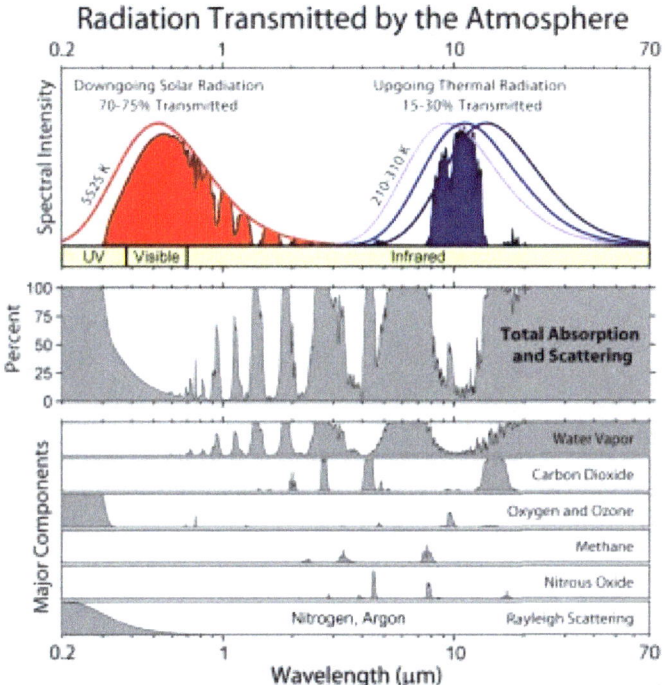

Radiation Transmitted by the Atmosphere

This graph shows the fraction of radiation absorbed or scattered on a vertical path from the top of earth's atmosphere to the surface, or vice versa. The Horizontal scale is the wavelength of the radiation.

The smooth curves on the top panel are "Planck intensities" for various temperatures, 5525 k, the effective temperature of the Sun's surface (red) and the much lower temperatures of the Earth's surface, about 210 k (black) for the South Pole and 310 for a warm day in Phoenix (violet).

Most sunlight (red) is transmitted, only about a quarter of the thermal cooling radiation (blue) is transmitted because of absorption by greenhouse gases, shown in the lower panels.

So, why the frenzy over CO2?

It is because it is a greenhouse gas? That is true. This is a somewhat deceptive picture. What it shows in red (in the above image) is sunlight, and the horizontal scale on the top panel is the wavelength of the sunlight.

Radiation wavelengths for sunlight are typically about a half a micron (half a millionth of a meter). That is green light, the color of green leaves. The thermal radiation that cools the Earth is that blue curve to the right of the upper panel, and that is a much longer wavelength, typically around 10 microns.

So, the wavelength of thermal radiation is 10 to 20 times longer than the wavelengths of sunlight. It turns out that the sun's energy can get through the Earth's atmosphere very easily. So essentially all sunlight or at least 90 percent, if there are no clouds, gets to the surface and warms it. But radiation cooling of the surface is less efficient because various greenhouse gases (most importantly water vapor, which is shown as the third panel down, and CO2, which is the fourth panel down) intercept a lot of that radiation and keep it from freely escaping to space. This keeps Earth's surface temperature warmer than it would be (by about 20 or 30 degrees). The Earth would be an ice cube if it were not for water vapor and CO2. ….

Greenhouse gases were discovered in the 1850s by John Tyndall, who was an Anglo-Irish physicist working in London. He was the first one to discover that water vapor, or carbon dioxide, or ether vapor, or alcohol vapor, intercept thermal radiation. He wrote:

"Aqueous vapour is a blanket, more necessary to the vegetable life of England than clothing is to man. Remove for a single summer-night the aqueous vapour from the air which overspreads this country, and you would assuredly destroy every plant capable of being destroyed by a freezing temperature. The warmth of our fields and gardens would pour itself unrequited into space, and the sun would rise upon an island held fast in the grip of frost" Heat, a mode of motion, fifth edition, 1875 p.359"

Everyone knows that cloudless nights are cooler than cloudy nights and what John Tyndall is saying is without CO2 in the atmosphere we would all freeze to death in one night.

One last graphic with comments from Happer:

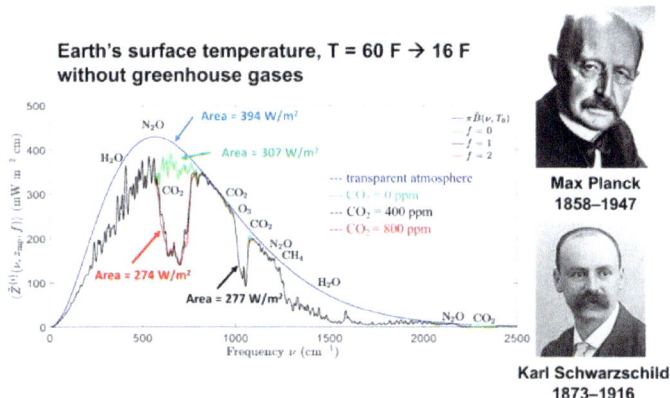

"This is an important slide.

There is a lot of history here and so there are two historical pictures. The top picture is Max Planck, the great German physicist who discovered quantum mechanics. Amazingly,

237

quantum mechanics got its start from greenhouse gas-physics and thermal radiation, just what we are talking about today. Most climate fanatics do not understand the basic physics. But Planck understood it very well, and he was the first to show why the spectrum of radiation from warm bodies has the shape shown on this picture, to the left of Planck.

The horizontal scale, left to right is the "spatial frequency" (wave peaks per cm) of thermal radiation. The vertical scale is the thermal power that is going out to space. If there were no greenhouse gases, the radiation going to space would be the area under the blue Planck curve. This would be the thermal radiation that balances the heating of Earth by sunlight.

In fact, you never observe the Planck curve if you look down from a satellite. We have lots of satellite measurements now. What you see is something that looks a lot like the black curve, with lots of jags and wiggles in it. That curve was first calculated by Karl Schwarzschild, whose picture is below Planck's picture. ...

The important point here is the red line.

This is what Earth would radiate to space if you were to double the CO_2 concentration from today's value. Right in the middle of these curves, you can see a gap in spectrum. The gap is caused by CO_2 absorbing radiation that would otherwise cool the Earth. If you double the amount of CO_2, you don't double the size of that gap. You just go from the black curve to the red curve, and you can barely see the difference. The gap hardly changes.

The message I want you to understand, which practically no one really understands, is that doubling CO_2 makes almost no difference. Doubling would replace the black curve by the red curve. On the basis of this, we are supposed to give up our liberties. We are supposed to give up the gasoline engines of our automobiles. We are supposed to accept dictatorial power by Bernie Sanders and Ocasio-Cortez, because of the difference between the red and the black curve. Do not let anyone convince you that that is a good bargain. It is a terrible bargain. The doubling actually does make a little difference. It decreases the radiation to space by about three watts per square meters. In comparison, the total radiation to space is about 300 watts per square meter. So, it is a one percent effect—it is actually a little less than that, because that is with no clouds. Clouds make everything even less threatening.

Finally, let me point out that there is a green curve. That is what happens if you take all the CO_2 out of the atmosphere. No one knows how to do that, thank goodness, because plants would all die if you took all the CO_2 out of the atmosphere. But what this curve is telling you is that the greenhouse effect of CO_2 is already saturated. Saturation is a jargon term that means CO_2 has done all the greenhouse warming it can easily do. Doubling CO_2 does not make much difference. You could triple or quadruple CO_2 concentrations, and it also would make little difference. The CO_2 effects are strongly saturated."

I have shared some relevant Scientist information, so that you can decide for yourself and become wise to the real reasons behind the "Climate Change" movement. Why are we bombarded with this false spin by the media etc.?

Satan knows the Bible better than any of us humans and he knows his end is soon therefore he will use "any means necessary" to deceive the masses. In the next chapter we will learn about his number and soon to emerge dictatorship managed by his various organisations.

Jesus has already told the world that one of the signs of the end of this sin ravaged earth would be, and I quote:

"And they asked him, saying, Master, but when shall these things be? And what sign [will there be] when these things shall come to pass?

And he said, Take heed that ye be not deceived: for many shall come in my name, saying, I am [Christ]; and the time draweth near: go ye not therefore after them.

But when ye shall hear of wars and commotions, be not terrified: for these things must first come to pass; but the end [is] not by and by.

Then said he unto them, Nation shall rise against nation, and kingdom against kingdom:

And great earthquakes shall be in divers places, and famines, and pestilences; and fearful sights and great signs shall there be from heaven.

And there shall be signs in the sun, and in the moon, and in the stars; and upon the earth distress of nations, with perplexity; the sea and the waves roaring;

Men's hearts failing them for fear, and for looking after those things which are coming on the earth: for the powers of heaven shall be shaken.

And then shall they see the Son of man coming in a cloud with power and great glory.

And when these things begin to come to pass, then look up, and lift up your heads; for your redemption draweth nigh.

And he spake to them a parable; Behold the fig tree, and all the trees;

When they now shoot forth, ye see and know of your own selves that summer is now nigh at hand.

So likewise ye, when ye see these things come to pass, know ye that the kingdom of God is nigh at hand." Luke 21:7-11, 25-31

We have a historical account of Satan attempting to destroy a Man's relationship with God by destroying all that he had including his innocent family. Many people look at disasters around the globe and blame God. They should be placing the blame squarely on its real perpetrator, Satan. That account can be found in the book of Job chapter 1.

"There was a man in the land of Uz, whose name [was] Job; and that man was perfect and upright, and one that feared God, and eschewed evil.

And there were born unto him seven sons and three daughters.

His substance also was seven thousand sheep, and three thousand camels, and five hundred yoke of oxen, and five hundred she asses, and a very great household; so that this man was the greatest of all the men of the east.

And his sons went and feasted [in their] houses, everyone his day; and sent and called for their three sisters to eat and to drink with them.

And it was so, when the days of [their] feasting were gone about, that Job sent and sanctified them, and rose up early in the morning, and offered burnt offerings [according] to the number of them all: for Job said, It may be that my sons have sinned, and cursed God in their hearts. Thus did Job continually.

Now there was a day when the sons of God came to present themselves before the LORD, and Satan came also among them.

And the LORD said unto Satan, Whence comest thou? Then Satan answered the LORD, and said, From going to and fro in the earth, and from walking up and down in it.

And the LORD said unto Satan, Hast thou considered my servant Job, that [there is] none like him in the earth, a perfect and an upright man, one that feareth God, and escheweth evil?

Then Satan answered the LORD, and said, Doth Job fear God for nought?

Hast not thou made an hedge about him, and about his house, and about all that he hath on every side? Thou hast blessed the work of his hands, and his substance is increased in the land.

But put forth thine hand now, and touch all that he hath, and he will curse thee to thy face.

And the LORD said unto Satan, Behold, all that he hath [is] in thy power; only upon himself put not forth thine hand. So Satan went forth from the presence of the LORD.

And there was a day when his sons and his daughters [were] eating and drinking wine in their eldest brother's house:

And there came a messenger unto Job, and said, The oxen were plowing, and the asses feeding beside them:

And the Sabeans fell [upon them], and took them away; yea, they have slain the servants with the edge of the sword; and I only am escaped alone to tell thee.

While he [was] yet speaking, there came also another, and said, The fire of God is fallen from heaven, and hath burned up the sheep, and the servants, and consumed them; and I only am escaped alone to tell thee.

While he [was] yet speaking, there came also another, and said, The Chaldeans made out three bands, and fell upon the camels, and have carried them away, yea, and slain the servants with the edge of the sword; and I only am escaped alone to tell thee.

While he [was] yet speaking, there came also another, and said, Thy sons and thy daughters [were] eating and drinking wine in their eldest brother's house:

And, behold, there came a great wind from the wilderness, and smote the four corners of the house, and it fell upon the young men, and they are dead; and I only am escaped alone to tell thee.

Then Job arose, and rent his mantle, and shaved his head, and fell down upon the ground, and worshipped,
And said, Naked came I out of my mother's womb, and naked shall I return thither: the LORD gave, and the LORD hath taken away; blessed be the name of the LORD.
In all this Job sinned not, nor charged God foolishly."

This historical account of Satan causing all the destruction on Job's family, livestock and assets is being repeated on a grand scale around our planet and he is hiding behind the 'Climate Change' agenda being sponsored by so many organisations including the papacy.

Why is Satan doing this? Because he knows that there is very little time left for him in the universe and he wants to take as many humans with him as possible and deprive them of their future.

"And there was war in heaven: Michael and his angels fought against the dragon; and the dragon fought and his angels,
 And prevailed not; neither was their place found any more in heaven.
And the great dragon was cast out, that old serpent, called the Devil, and Satan, which deceiveth the whole world: he was cast out into the earth, and his angels were cast out with him.
And I heard a loud voice saying in heaven, Now is come salvation, and strength, and the kingdom of our God, and the power of his Christ: for the accuser of our brethren is cast down, which accused them before our God day and night.
And they overcame him by the blood of the Lamb, and by the word of their testimony; and they loved not their lives unto the death.

Therefore rejoice, [ye] heavens, and ye that dwell in them. Woe to the inhabiters of the earth and of the sea! for the devil is come down unto you, having great wrath, because he knoweth that he hath but a short time." Revelation 12:7-12

Satan is causing the disasters on earth then blaming the climate and he is using his people to push his agenda so that he can gain his harvest of humans that will lose out from their greatest opportunity. Do you now understand why we have so many on the bandwagon of "Climate Change?" They have either chosen their side of deception or have been unwittingly deceived. Those that are knowingly deceived must then be part of a much bigger plan. They are in the service of their master, Satan. Pope Francis is also on that bandwagon.

"VATICAN CITY, May 25, 2021 (Reuters) - Pope Francis launched an initiative on Tuesday to make Catholic institutions ranging from families to universities to businesses environmentally sustainable in seven years, saying a "predatory attitude" toward the planet must end.

The Laudato Si Action Platform takes its name from the pope's landmark 2015 encyclical on the need to protect the environment, reduce wasteful lifestyles, stem global warming and protect the poor from the effects of climate change.

At a news conference announcing the initiative, Cardinal Peter Turkson, head of the Vatican's development office, said the pope has been invited to attend the United Nations' Climate Change Conference (COP26) in November in Glasgow, Scotland. Turkson indicated that the pope likely will attend. ……"

Pope Francis leads the Pentecost Mass at St. Peter's Basilica at the Vatican May 23, 2021.

Satan's activities along with mankind's breaking of the covenant as highlighted in Isaiah 24:4-5 confirms the reasons why disasters are on a massive increase on our planet. Humanity is choosing Satan instead of God, so God is gradually removing His protection, this removal of protection will be complete when the planet has reached the end of probationary time. More on this subject and the narrative in the media about the jabs in later chapters.

His number is "666"

"Here is wisdom, let him that hath understanding count the number of the beast for it is the number of a man; and his number is six hundred threescore and six." Rev. 13:18.

This is what we will do in this chapter; count the number. Who does 666 represent? How is this number to be counted? How critical is it to understand this number? This verse indicates that we must have understanding. Where does this understanding come from? God's word and realities in recent history and developments in our present world.

Before we explore the answers to the questions about who '666' represents or how we count the number, I must make a point very, very clear and it is this; We have so far established that Satan is behind the MYSTERY religion and I confirm that Satan is behind the whole grand scheme of things and the Pope of Rome is his visible representative, never lose sight of this because the whole papal system is ramping up its global activities in preparation for its imminent global take over, with the backing of the USA.

I must warn you that this chapter may pose a major challenge to conventional, or should I say, traditional and very prominent protestant thinking with regards to the interpretation of Vicarius Filii Dei being the number 666. I need to repeat this "….Let him that hath understanding, count the number of the beast for it is the number of a man…." The established traditional protestant view is that Vicarius Filii Dei is to be used to calculate the number of the name found in Revelation 13. According to Andreas Helwig, this is the case, but is he correct? Is Vicarius Filii Dei a name? Take careful note about the words "**Vicarius**

Filii Dei" – it is a title, it is not a name. This recognition of it as a title is made very clear in the interpretation by Andreas Helwig. However, **Scripture does not say the number of his title**, it says "… **the number of his name**…" are you with me on this? Do you understand this? The pages of scripture also state "….the number of a man…" Does this mean a series of men or one man? We will explore this in this chapter.

Explaining that the 666 does not actually apply to the title Vicarius Filii Dei but elsewhere, is highly likely to ruffle many feathers. I will be providing the evidence so bear with me. Check out this first quote from the pen of inspiration, there are others in this chapter.

"The mark of the beast is exactly what it has been proclaimed to be. **Not all in regard to this matter is yet understood nor will it be understood until the unrolling of the scroll**.--6T 17 (1900)." Interesting statement.

What is a scroll? It was what the original bible was written on and to help us to understand the phrase "unrolling of the scroll"- to read a scroll it has to be unrolled. What does that mean in relation to the above paragraph? As we see events unfolding (unrolling) we will understand. I believe we are at that point. We do not need a title to confirm the papacy as the whore of Revelation, we actually need to fully "understand" who that number relates to and it is the number of Satan's name in his fallen state. Everything that pertains to him has his 666 number embedded, including the buying and selling system which we will elaborate on later.

What is the history of the interpretation of 666 as relating to the pope? **It was first pointed out** in 1612 in a book entitled "Roman Antichrist" by Andreas Helwig, **that the title** "Vicarius Filii Dei," added up to 666 as follows:

V	=	5	F	=	0	D	=	500
I	=	1	I	=	1	E	=	0
C	=	100	L	=	50	I	=	1
A	=	0	I	=	1			501
R	=	0	I	=	1			
I	=	1			53			
U	=	5						
S	=	0						
		112	+		53	+		501 = 666

All protestants have since then adopted this as the power in the personage of the Pope, that is to be feared as the 666 man. Remember we touched on the fact that the dragon (Satan) gives this Roman church his power, his seat and his great authority? When we trace the history of the "Mystery" we find scripture describing the leader and instigator of the "Mystery," Satan himself.

On closer examination, we will find that there are also three very important points to consider when calculating that number, namely, (1) that John did not write the Revelation in the Latin language. He pointed out where Satan's seat was in Revelation 2, and Paul in 2nd Thessalonians stated that the Mystery was already working (in Paul's time). John and Paul both having clearly understood who this man was, would have been referring to a 'man' who was already in existence, carrying the 666 number, before the Papacy existed and doing so to the end; and secondly (2) that the Pope's Latin title "Vicarius Fillii Dei" **does not** actually **add up to 666 when considering the Roman Numbering system** because the letter 'U' does not actually have a roman numeric value. Yes, it has been explained and argued that the 'U' could be a 'V', but is this trying to make something fit that actually does not? Even if some argue that the 'U' is a "V" it is still the calculation of a title.

Below are the Roman numeral symbols.

1	5	10	50	100	500	1000
I	V	X	L	C	D	M

(3) The verse says "a man" singular, not 'men' there have been numerous popes over the many centuries and it will not be "a man" to come, he was already in existence when written about? And he, Satan, will be very involved in the final showdown. More about this in the chapter, Planting of the Tabernacles…. When we use the Roman numerals exactly as found in the next graphic, what do we find?

$$
\begin{array}{llll}
V &=& 5 & \quad F &=& 0 & \quad D &=& 500 \\
I &=& 1 & \quad I &=& 1 & \quad E &=& 0 \\
C &=& 100 & \quad L &=& 50 & \quad I &=& 1 \\
A &=& 0 & \quad I &=& 1 & \quad & & \underline{501} \\
R &=& 0 & \quad I &=& 1 & \\
I &=& 1 & \quad & & \underline{53} \\
U &=& 5? \\
S &=& \underline{0} \\
& & \underline{112?} &\quad + & & \underline{53} &\quad + & & \underline{501} &= 666 - 5? = 661
\end{array}
$$

How then do we understand the number and who should we be looking out for?

 As we have traced the history of the "Mystery" we 100% acknowledge that the papacy embodies the Mystery religion, however, as it seems clear from the above that there may be something incorrect with the above interpretation we need to understand who is the 666 man John is talking about, if the number is not clearly identified from the "name" of the pope it must therefore relate to some other "Man," this "Man" being none other than the leader and instigator of the "Mystery," Satan himself. How do we count his number?

You may be asking, why would this be important? I suggest to you dear reader that we must look not only to the pope of Rome for what has transpired so far with THE MYSTERY, but all the other organisations and systems that will be doing Satan's bidding. They will all be identified with his number. Time will also confirm why this is important.

I can almost hear you asking, how can Satan be described as a 'Man'? Come with me to the books of Isaiah and Ezekiel.

"That thou shalt take up this proverb against the king of Babylon, and say, how hath the oppressor ceased! The golden city ceased!
He who smote the people in wrath with a continual stroke, he that ruled the nations in anger, is persecuted, [and] none hindereth.
The whole earth is at rest, [and] is quiet: they break forth into singing.
All they shall speak and say unto thee, Art thou also become weak as we? Art thou become like unto us?
How art thou fallen from heaven, O Lucifer, son of the morning! [How] art thou cut down to the ground, which didst weaken the nations!
For thou hast said in thine heart, I will ascend into heaven, I will exalt my throne above the stars of God:
I will sit also upon the mount of the congregation, in the sides of the north: *(This is Lucifer trying to be God)*
I will ascend above the heights of the clouds; I will be like the most High.

Yet thou shalt be brought down to hell, to the sides of the pit.

They that see thee shall narrowly look upon thee, [and] consider thee, [saying, is] this **the man** that made the earth to tremble, that did shake kingdoms;

[That] made the world as a wilderness, and destroyed the cities thereof; [that] opened not the house of his prisoners?" Isaiah 14:4, 6-7, 10, 12-17.

It's interesting how Satan deceives climate change adherents into believing that human activity is entirely the cause of the disasters that are ravaging our cities and towns. Interestingly in one way, this is true because mankind's breaking of the covenant is a contributory cause, but just like the lie to Eve, it is not carbon emissions, therefore this is a lie that is diverting the masses away from the truth of the real cause. *(Pay attention to his climate actions within the laboratories of nature, later in this book, and the biblical confirmation of the real reasons for 'climate change')*

"The word of the LORD came again unto me, saying, Son of man, say unto the prince of Tyrus, Thus saith the Lord GOD; Because thine heart [is] lifted up, and thou hast said, **I [am] a God, I sit [in] the seat of God, in the midst of the seas; yet thou [art] a man,** and not God, though thou set thine heart as the heart of God:

Moreover the word of the LORD came unto me, saying, Son of man, take up a lamentation upon the king of Tyrus, and say unto him, Thus saith the Lord God; Thou sealest up the sum, full of wisdom, and perfect in beauty.

Thou hast been in Eden the garden of God; every precious stone [was] thy covering, the sardius, topaz, and the diamond, the beryl, the onyx, and the jasper, the sapphire, the emerald, and the carbuncle, and gold: the workmanship of thy tabrets and of thy pipes was prepared in thee in the day that thou wast created.

Thou [art] the anointed cherub that covereth; and I have set thee [so]: thou wast upon the holy mountain of God; thou hast walked up and down in the midst of the stones of fire.

Thou [wast] perfect in thy ways from the day that thou wast created, till iniquity was found in thee.

By the multitude of thy merchandise they have filled the midst of thee with violence, and thou hast sinned: therefore I will cast thee as profane out of the mountain of God: and I will destroy thee, O covering cherub, from the midst of the stones of fire.

Thine heart was lifted up because of thy beauty, thou hast corrupted thy wisdom by reason of thy brightness: I will cast thee to the ground, I will lay thee before kings, that they may behold thee.

Thou hast defiled thy sanctuaries by the multitude of thine iniquities, by the iniquity of thy traffic;"

(Take note of the words iniquities and iniquity, remember earlier verses stating [mystery of iniquity?]

"Therefore will I bring forth a fire from the midst of thee, it shall devour thee, and I will bring thee to ashes upon the earth in the sight of all them that behold thee.

All they that know thee among the people shall be astonished at thee: thou shalt be a terror, and never [shalt] thou [be] anymore." Ezekiel 28:1-2, 12-19.

None of the popes were ever in the garden of Eden. None of us were. Satan, also known as Lucifer was there and he was originally at the head of God's government but answerable to Jesus. He rebelled and wanted to be above Jesus. In our present day he has his servants in the form of the papacy and others doing his bidding and claiming to be God on earth.

"Know ye not, that to whom ye yield yourselves servants to obey, his servants ye are to whom ye obey; whether of sin unto death, or of obedience unto righteousness?" Romans 6:16

These statements and verses indicate that the mysterious number identifies the mystery from its beginning and will logically represent Satan himself and his visible servant the pope.

Come with me to one other statement written in 1847 that is to be found in a very rare pamphlet entitled "A word to the Little flock" The authors of that pamphlet included James White, Ellen White and Joseph Bates, although James White was the main contributor. I had to search very diligently from old publications of the writings of Ellen White because the following is not to be found in any other of her current officially published works, **it has been removed**, neither have I been able to find it in current White Estate research software or current published android/mobile apps.

"…Michael is to stand up at the time that the last power in chapter 11, comes to his end, and none to help him.

This power is the last that treads down the true church of God: and as the true church is still trodden down, and cast out by all Christendom, it follows that the last oppressive power has not "come to his end;" and Michael has not stood up. This last power that treads down the saints is brought to view in Revelation 13: 11-18. His number is 666. Much of his power, deceptions, wonders, miracles, and oppression, will doubtless be manifested during his last struggle under the "seven last plagues," about the time of his coming to his end." (*take note of his coming to his end*) "This is clearly shadowed forth by the Magicians of Egypt, deceiving Pharoah and his host, in performing most of the miracles that Moses performed by the power of God. That was just before the deliverance of Israel from Egyptian bondage; and may we not expect to see as great a manifestation of the power of the Devil, just before the glorious deliverance of the Saints?" A word to the little flock Page 8.3 & 8.4. (Unabridged Version).

This quote implies that Satan will be personally involved at the end of time and this quote clearly states "His number is 666". We will explore manifestations of the power of the devil in a later chapter.

The only other 666 statements I have been able to find in Ellen White's writings and they are easily reconcilable to the above 666 statement, because the Pope is servant to Satan and the USA will also serve Satan. They are to be found in the current (abridged) published word to the little flock pg. 19 or 20 (dependent on versions) "I saw all that "would not receive the mark of the Beast, and of his Image, in their foreheads or in their hands," could not buy or sell. [Revelation 13:15-17.] I saw that the number (666) of the Image Beast was made up; [Revelation 13:18.] and that it was the Beast that changed the Sabbath, and the Image Beast had followed on after, and kept the Pope's, and not God's Sabbath. And all we were required to do, was to give up God's Sabbath, and keep the Pope's, and then we should have the mark of the Beast, and of his image." *(This same above quote can be found in {Broadside3, April 7, 1847 par. 5})*
Revelation 13 confirms that at the final battle for souls, only those who accept Satan and his worship system through all his various channels including the Catholic and fallen protestant churches will be able to transact economically through his 666 system, a system invented of all places in the United States. More on this in later in this chapter.

254

God tells us in His word to apply wisdom to, "...count the number of his name..." The man in the prophecies, the number of Satan's name? Let's find out; from these two sets of verses alone you must be getting the picture, but let us not stop here because Jesus told us to count the number of the 'man'.

Pagan and Satanist worshippers also identify with this 666 number as representing Satan himself.

"Religion had close ties with science as well as with literature and art. Astronomy, mathematics and time reckoning are sciences in which the ancient middle east made great strides at an early date,... Heavenly bodies were at the same time both deities and personified numbers... Moreover, all other whole numbers were regarded as multiples of one, representative of the creator... When the Hebrew prophet Zechariah (14:9) proclaimed "on that day the Lord will be one and his name one," he indicated that the Hebrews, like their neighbours, reckoned with sacred numbers and saw in the number one a symbol of the creator. ..." Enc. Brit. 24:63:1c.

"Revelation contains long sections characterized by Greek that is grammatically and stylistically crude, strangely Hebraized to give a unique, almost oriental colour. This may have been deliberate. Although Revelation is replete with Old Testament allusions, there are no direct quotations and they may reflect the seer's conviction that the work is a direct revelation from God...

Mysterious numbers and divisions such as (7, 3, and 12) recur and are part of the theme of assurance, because God has numbers in their order as a sign of His plan of salvation, turning chaos into orderly cosmos. The mysterious name of the Antichrist, 666, in Revelation

13:18, can be calculated by "Gematria" assigning their numerical values to letters of the word and summing them up..." Enc.Brit.14:945:2a, 2c.

"Gematria, similar to numerology is the substitution of numbers for letters of the Hebrew alphabet, a favourite method of exegesis used by Medieval Kabbalists to derive mystical insights into sacred writings or obtain new interpretations of the texts... of the 22 letters in the Hebrew alphabet, the first ten are given number values consecutively from one to ten, the next eight from 20 to 90 in intervals of ten, while the final four letters equal 100, 200, 300 and 400, respectively..." Enc.Brit.5:168:3b.

It is significant that all the alphabets of the languages in which the Mystery is depicted all carry numerical values to their letters. With these points in mind we can trace this mysterious number from Babylon to Rome and the ultimate 666 entity, "Satan", to whom all false organisations both in the past, present and the future, have been and will be subservient to.

Number.	Sound or Power.	Hebrew and Chaldee Letters.		Numerical Value.	
1.	*a* (soft breathing).	א		1.	(Thousands are
2.	*b, bh (v).*	ב		2.	denoted by a
3.	*g* (hard), *gh.*	ג		3.	larger letter;
4.	*d, dh* (flat *th*).	ד		4.	thus an Aleph
5.	*h* (rough breathing).	ה		5.	larger than the
6.	*v, u, o.*	ו		6.	rest of the let-
7.	*z, dz.*	ז		7.	ters among
8.	*ch* (guttural).	ח		8.	which it is,
9.	*t* (strong).	ט		9.	signifies not 1,
10.	*i, y* (as in *yes*).	י		10.	but 1000.)
11.	*k, kh.*	כ	Final = ך	20.	Final = 500
12.	*l.*	ל		30.	
13.	*m.*	מ	Final = ם	40.	Final = 600
14.	*n.*	נ	Final = ן	50.	Final = 700
15.	*s.*	ס		60.	
16.	*O, aa, ng* (gutt.).	ע		70.	
17.	*p, ph.*	פ	Final = ף	80.	Final = 800.
18.	*ts, tz, j.*	צ	Final = ץ	90.	Final = 900.
19.	*q, qh* (guttur.).	ק		100.	(The finals are not
20.	*r.*	ר		200.	always considered as bearing an in-
21.	*sh, s.*	ש		300.	creased numeri-
22.	*th, t.*	ת		400.	cal value.)

Babylonian Alphabet and numerical chart

"Babylon - "As Mystery signifies the Hidden System, so Saturn signifies the Hidden god. To those who were initiated the god was revealed; to all else he was hidden. Now the name Saturn in Chaldee is pronounced Satur; but as every Chaldee scholar knows, consists of only four letters thus - STUR. This name contains the Apocalyptic Number 666:

$$
\begin{array}{lcr}
S & = & 60 \\
T & = & 400 \\
U & = & 6 \\
R & = & \underline{200} \\
& & \underline{666}
\end{array}
$$

257

...still further it turns out, that the original name of Rome itself was Saturnia, "the city of Saturn"... moreover, it is evident that the Romans new that the name "Lateinos" (to whom the Romans or Latin race traced their lineage) signified the "Hidden one", for their antiquarians invariably affirm that Latium received its name from Saturn "lying hid there." Two Babylons pp 269-70.

"It was long ago noticed by Iranaeus, about the end of the second century, that the name Teitan contained the mystic number 666... Iranaeus states "though the name Teitan was originally derived from Chaldee, yet it became thoroughly naturalised in the Greek language. Therefore, to give the more abundant evidence on this important subject, the Spirit of God seems to have ordered it that the number of Teitan should be found according to the Greek computation, while that of Satur is found by the Chaldee."

"...On inquiry, it will actually be found, that while Saturn was the visible head, Teitan was the name of the invisible head of the beast. Teitan is just the Chaldean form of Sheitan, the very name by which Satan has been called from time immemorial by the Devil-Worshippers of Kurdistan."
Two Babylons pp 275-276.

There are only a very small number of protestants that still officially identify the papacy as the whore of Revelation because of her fulfilment of the prophecies in Daniel Chapter 7 of thinking to change times and laws, these laws refer to God's Seventh Day Sabbath that the catholic church boast of having power to change and which most other "protestant" movements actually support and by default become "daughters" because they are following the Pope's (in reality Satan's) Sabbath instead of the heavenly Father's Sabbath.

The number of Teitan is calculated from the Greek as follows:

$$
\begin{array}{rcl}
\mathbf{T} & = & \mathbf{300} \\
\mathbf{E} & = & \mathbf{5} \\
\mathbf{I} & = & \mathbf{10} \\
\mathbf{T} & = & \mathbf{300} \\
\mathbf{A} & = & \mathbf{1} \\
\mathbf{N} & = & \underline{\mathbf{50}} \\
& & \underline{\mathbf{666}}
\end{array}
$$

A	alpha	1	I	iota	10	P	rho	100
B	beta	2	K	kappa	20	Σ	sigma	200
Γ	gamma	3	Λ	lambda	30	T	tau	300
Δ	delta	4	M	mu	40	Y	upsilon	400
E	epsilon	5	N	nu	50	Φ	phi	500
F	digamma	6	Ξ	xi	60	X	khi	600
Z	zeta	7	O	omicron	70	Ψ	psi	700
H	eta	8	Π	pi	80	Ω	omega	800
Θ	theta	9	Ϙ	koppa	90	Ϝ	sampi	900

Greek alphabet and numerical chart

There are numerous other ways of confirming the papacy as the beast of revelation as has been and will be demonstrated in this book.

I need to make a little detour into the music scene to share with you lyrics from one of Satan's musician evangelists just in case you still have challenges with accepting that several of the prophets already quoted have understood that Satan is the 666 'man'. Remember this quote from Ezekiel 28?

"…the workmanship of thy tabrets and of thy pipes was prepared in thee in the day that thou wast created…" this confirms that besides being created the leader of the angelic hosts he was also created as a master musician and musical instrument. Following is a song from the rolling stones album entitled - Sympathy for the devil.

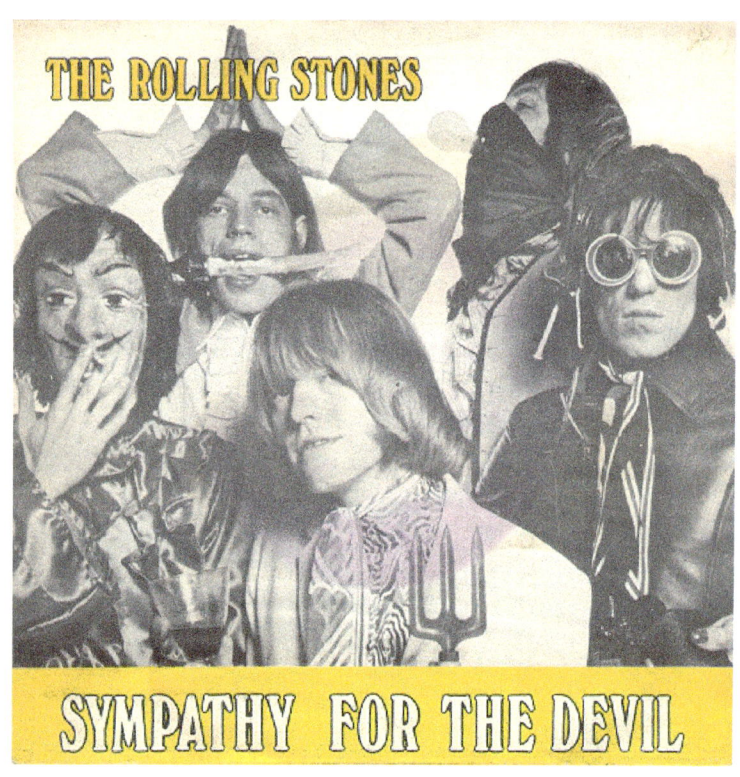

"Please allow me to introduce myself
I'm a man of wealth and taste
I've been around for a long, long year
Stole many a man's soul and faith
And I was 'round when Jesus Christ
Had his moment of doubt and pain
Made damn sure that Pilate
Washed his hands and sealed his fate

Pleased to meet you
Hope you guess my name
But what's puzzling you
Is the nature of my game
I stuck around St. Petersberg
When I saw it was a time for a change
I killed the Czar and his ministers
Anastasia screamed in vain
I rode a tank
Held a general's rank
When the Blitzkrieg raged
And the bodies stank ……
Pleased to meet you
Hope you guess my name, oh yeah
What's puzzling you is the nature of my game, oh yeah
… As heads is tails just call me Lucifer ....
Can papa get a holler now?"

Here **he is clearly calling himself a man**, don't miss this. He also boasts of holding a general's rank whilst riding a tank during the blitzkrieg? He was physically present?

Isaiah and Ezekiel identified him, Paul identified him, John identified him, some of the pioneers of the SDA church identified him and now we are in a position to clearly identify him.

Do the musicians of today know him and his number?

The following images are collages of musicians using their fingers to show the 666 number and various other Satanic symbols. There are numerous other examples of this and many of them boast of having made a deal with the devil for prosperity. They too need to know the truth about who the real leader and creator of the universe is. Lucifer must have some way of deceiving these musicians into believing they have a better future with him. If he was able to deceive holy angels, what about us mere mortals?

I believe that God wants to let even the pagans and devil-worshippers know the truth about the 666 number as identifying Satan as the false god, which is why He shewed it to John in the book of Revelation so that all who are willing to search for and "understand" the truth about that number would be able to find the truth. For those of us that doubt that God is real then the fact that musicians make pacts with the devil is proof enough that the spirit realm exists. Politicians, actors and the Papacy are aware of Satan's Number and symbols.

What about other Satanic Symbols? The Goat?

The first clip in the above image *(enlarged and photoshopped next)* is from a scene in a music video by Rihanna entitled 'Umbrella'. Take note the Pope in this image is also displaying the sign of the goat. He knows who his real master is.

- Here she is seen creating the 'Goat' symbol with her body. The second clip is the Baphomet, (enhanced on the next image) take note of the crosier in the hip and groin area and the Pope carrying the crosier.

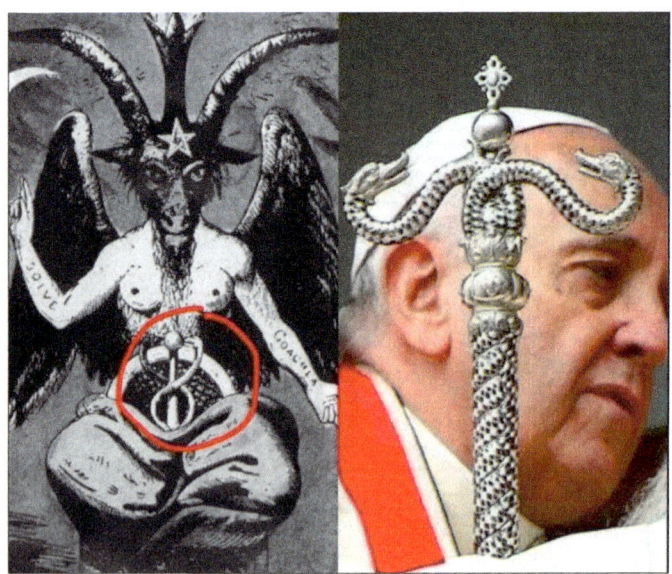

These images confirm the connection between the Catholic Church and Satanism. Remember her description as a den of every unclean and hateful bird? The above picture seems to indicate great intimacy between these two church leaders. This image also confirms the close ties of the Orthodox Church with Catholicism, in fact they are one and the same as they have the same teachings and practises. Is there any surprise with what is coming out about the corruptions and child abuse endemic in the Catholic Church? The scriptures confirmed that the "MYSTERY" will be revealed. This is another horrible side of the Catholic Church that must be told.

"Hundreds of Roman Catholic priests in Pennsylvania have molested more than 1,000 children and senior church officials, including the now archbishop of Washington, D.C., systematically covered up the abuse.

A grand jury report released Tuesday reveals the horrific predatory behavior which included making young boys rinse their mouths with holy water to 'purify' them after they were forced to give oral sex to clergymen and the abuse of one boy who was made to pose naked as Jesus while other priests took pornographic pictures.

Cardinal Donald Wuerl

Cardinal Donald Wuerl, the former longtime bishop of Pittsburgh who now leads the Washington archdiocese, was among the high-ranking clergy who turned a blind eye to the abuse. (Perhaps because he was also involved? – How would the problem be so rampant if he was not involved?)

The priests would mark out which boys had been groomed for abuse by giving them gold crosses to wear as necklaces.

The 800-page report refers to more than 300 priests in six diocese where children were raped, plied with alcohol, or forced to perform for clergymen to produce pornographic material since the mid-1950s. The 'real number' of abused children might be in the thousands since some secret church records were lost, and victims were afraid to come forward, the grand jury said. The 886 page report contains hundreds of examples of horrifying abuse. All were disturbing but some were particularly troubling. They include;

- A priest who raped a seven-year-old girl while visiting her in hospital after she'd had her tonsils removed
- A ring of paedophiles who whipped little boys and allowed other men to rape them for a fee
- Another priest, grooming his middle school students for oral sex, taught them how Mary had to 'bite off the cord' and 'lick' Jesus clean after he was born.
- A priest who went to work at Walt Disney World, with a glowing recommendation letter from the church, after quitting over complaints about him abusing children

Why all of this? The MYSTERY religion.

The next series of pictures show the 2 finger salute of the Baphomet. This idol is clearly worshipped by Satanists and they have clearly identified it in parades etc. as their homage to Satan. Notice that the children are portrayed as admiring the Baphomet? Is this to do with Paedophilia? Does the goat head not only represent Satan but bestiality? Do we wonder why there is such a scandal now coming out of the Catholic Church?

Satanic Temple brings Baphomet statue to Arkansas for rally

AP ASSOCIATED PRESS

August 17, 2018

A sample of popes imitating the Baphomet salute

German Military and Recruits swearing allegiance to Adolf Hitler using the Baphomet salute and Hitler Youth displaying the Baphomet salute

Are you at all surprised that in October 2020 Pope Francis gave his support for same-sex civil unions.

These corrupting Baphomet salutes have also been used in images that are supposedly depicting Jesus

Is there any surprise then why God said "Thou shalt not make unto thee any graven image, or any likeness [of any thing] that [is] in heaven above, or that [is] in the earth beneath, or that [is] in the water under the earth: Thou shalt not bow down thyself to them, nor serve them: for I the LORD thy God [am] a jealous God, visiting the iniquity of the fathers upon the children unto the third and fourth [generation] of them that hate me;" Exodus 20:4-5. The halos and the 'sacred heart' are also pagan in origin.

The '666' number is also present in our buying and selling system and as we have already been warned that there will be monetary pressure applied to coerce the human race into following Satan, then it is very important to explore this.

How will the world be forced to worship Satan besides being deceived by his miracles? Who will police it? More about this question in the chapter entitled, The Papal Military Arm.

"In the last days perilous times shall come. For men shall be lovers of their own selves, covetous, boasters, proud, blasphemers, disobedient to parents, unthankful, unholy, without natural affection, truce-breakers, false accusers,

272

incontinent, fierce, despisers of them that are good, traitors, heady, high-minded, lovers of pleasure more than lovers of God; having a form of Godliness, but denying the power thereof." And in 1 Timothy 4:l, "Now the spirit speaketh expressly, that in the latter times some shall depart from the faith, giving heed to seducing spirits, and doctrines of devils." Finally, Satan will work "....with all powers and signs and lying wonders" that those who did not love the truth should be deceived. 2 Thessalonians 2:9-11.

The scenario foreseen here is that the nations are deceived into making an image to the papacy and as established in revelation 13:17-18, there will be introduced a system whereby no person will be able to transact any form of business whatsoever without being part of the system identified with receiving the "mark of the beast". This dear reader is nothing less than absolute dictatorship.

I must make it very clear that what I am about to share I am not claiming is the "mark of the beast" because the "mark" will be a conscious decision that we all will have to make under pressure of meeting all our economic needs as part of a religious dictatorship masterminded by Satan. There are many ideas floating around about a microchip, RFID and other developments being the mark of the beast. I do not subscribe to any of those ideas and only accept what the scriptures make very clear that the test will be based on worship. God's seventh-day sabbath or Satan's first-day or other day sabbaths. Idol worship, or our Creator God worship. *(Remember we confirmed in earlier pages how the papacy has attempted to change those 2 commandments)*

Here is the point I want to make. Revelation 13: 17 makes it plain that nobody will be able to buy or sell except they have the mark, the name or the number (666) of his name in the forehead or hand. The forehead means a mental decision, the hand means to use the system. Satan being the deceiver that he is, has already organised his "666" number in the "Bar-Coding" that is being used right now in our modern-day electronic merchant system. God has made it very clear to us in His word that the false system would have an identifying mark of false worship, an identifying number of it's name and an identifying number to transact business. That transacting number is the same as the number of his name, 666. I am about to demonstrate this.

It is true that "Bar-Coding" facilitates easy stock controls, pricing etc., and if the system was not going to be attached to a religio-political organisation to be used to force the consciences of men and women, then it would perhaps not be a bad business idea. Located in every Bar-code, no matter what product you have purchased, whether in a corner store supermarket, online etc, the number 666 is embedded in the bar-code. In the above graphic I have highlighted in red 3 un-numbered barcode pairs of lines – These 3 are the 6's in the barcode. You will also notice a slightly taller red highlight that includes an existing number 6 below 2 parallel lines equally distanced as the other 3 parallel lines within the numbers 12268. I have provided this graphic to enable you to compare for yourself.

When you come to the first ever barcode produced (*Troy's Supermarket – upcoming in the next few pages*) you will notice exactly the same pattern. **The number '6' lines** are of the same spacings and thicknesses.

All of the generations born from the 1960's are all familiar with this system and think nothing of it, not realising that it is Satan's number already prepared and embedded in an electronic buying and selling system, decades in advance, just as his mystery religion has been around for millennia. This should give you an idea of how close we are to the end of time, but more so, of how far ahead Satan's plans are laid and that time is running out. If the system was introduced suddenly as a means of living in a new economic order, the nature of us humans being what it is, the majority may perhaps be affronted if such a system was thrust on us over night and would immediately have our suspicions aroused.

The earlier 'eftpos' system and now the 'paywave' and 'paypass' systems, mobile payment apps, in-person microchip technologies that are becoming widespread are many other conditioning mechanisms that are subconsciously preparing everyone for a society that will be devoid of cash and totally reliant on a globalised buying and selling system.

The new economic system and this number is likely to be introduced as the solution to all the economic troubles of the world. Drug dealers will be unable to transact business without the authorities being able to track them down easily. Nobody will be able to dodge income tax payments. Recession hit below-poverty line unemployed people on state benefits will not be able to moonlight. Remember that we have a one world government in the making – The New

World Order - and for it to operate effectively it can only be coupled with a single economy and a single religion.

Another very strong possibility and by far the better strategy is to collapse all the economies of the world in their present form; imagine waking one morning with the news that all the stock markets in the world have gone into meltdown, total, complete and utter collapse; every bank, building society, insurance company, gigantic corporation etc., ceasing to exist as the financial power they once were, all our retirement funds and savings suddenly wiped out (because they are tied into the banks, stock markets, insurance companies and corporations), the governments of all countries suddenly being bankrupted by this unprecented financial collapse, words will fail anyone who will dare to describe the scenes of distress, violence and anarchy that will follow.

This will not happen you may be thinking? Have we forgotten the GFC of 2007/2008? We are still caught up in it now in 2020? Low interest rates etc, How many of us willingly accepted that government "bailouts" were needed? Who footed that bill? We the taxpayers. How many "quantitative easing" initiatives were triggered? These have been in the trillions of dollars globally. The effects of those quantitative easings is the dilution of the real values of all our savings, investments, stocks, shares and pension funds, similar to adding water to fruit juice or soups, they eventually lose their consistency.

The solution to the global economic collapse could be hailed as the only workable solution - a cashless, electronic funds transfer society, controlled by the New World Order, dominated by Satans' 666 code, the list of reasons or excuses could go on and on; however, the real reason behind the whole operation is for Satan to attempt to force everyone to forsake the precepts of God for his, and to destroy as many human beings as possible, because once you have been deceived and remain deceived, there is nothing else that God can do but to let you suffer the same fate as Satan, in that you chose to serve Satan instead of your creator, Jesus Christ, and perish forever with Satan.

Remember that the prophecies confirm nobody being able to buy or sell without the number? You may be asking will it be possible for such a system to exist that will be accepted by humanity and humanity being under the total control of the governments? Well open your eyes, a similar system already exists, but not coupled with Sunday worship as yet. Come with me to an article written by Tyler Grant and published on 05/07/18 entitled "The West could be closer to China's system of 'social credit scoring' than you think"

"China has become the largest surveillance state on the planet. Taking a page out of the Netflix show Black Mirror, the People's Republic of China has begun assigning scores that dictate its citizens' ability to travel, their social mobility, educational opportunities, and where they can live. The totalitarian 1984 of the future is now 2018 China.

China has established a "social credit system" to assign these scores. In June 2014, the National Development and Reform Commission of China issued a State Council Notice initiating the development of a program to "raise the honest mentality and credit levels of the entire society," "build a Socialist harmonious society," and "encourage keeping trust and punish breaking trust." Now fully implemented ahead of the 2020 deadline by the Chinese government, the credit system functions like financial credit scores in America except rather than dictate one's ability to obtain a line of credit, the Chinese social credit score impacts nearly every aspect of one's life.

To date, the implementation and instrumentality of the plan remains largely secret and arbitrarily applied. The best guidance of what to expect from the social score system comes from the 2014 Notice, which better defines several categories of scoring. There are a few troubling areas.

First, online behavior is subject to intense scrutiny. Online speech that "denigrates" others results in score deductions while tattling on fellow citizens can increase scores. The policy goes further than typical online crimes by establishing "online credit black list systems" for behavior considered "grave acts of breaking trust online." Getting blacklisted means Internet usage limitations, public humiliation, or a complete internet ban.

Second, banking and social media information are collected, stored, and evaluated. China has a highly regulated Internet, but anecdotal reports suggest that while some rules are relatively clear like adherence to Chinese law or Communist Party rules, others are more ambiguous such as upholding "social sincerity" and "harmony." Even before scoring, speech in China was highly policed; the difference now is that "bad" speech carries significant consequences.

The freedom to travel will also be highly regulated. Last Tuesday, CBS New York reported that journalist, Liu Hu, is currently unable to fly for failure to sincerely apologize for some of his tweets. The social credit system integrates freedom to use "public roads, railways, waterways, aviation, channels and other such transportation markets" with the other assessment standards to create a holistic "trust-breaking record." High credit score individuals will be rewarded with preferential travel treatment within and out of China. Imagine your low Uber rating means you can no longer take any public transportation.

China collects and calculates scores with the help of large data collection firms downloading on the Chinese people. Wired reports the Chinese government conscripted the assistance from China's Uber equivalent, along with finance companies and others, to create the infrastructure for mass data collection and score algorithms to monitor nearly every aspect of modern life.

Under the guise of creating a utopia, China is now one of the most authoritarian and liberty bereft societies on the planet. The Chinese defend the system as a vehicle to "maintain stability" and "strengthen sincerity." In reality, China views control over its population paramount to liberty. It's tempting to think this government overreach is purely reserved to China, after all they did just forfeit significant freedom by electing Xi Jinping president for life. This is incorrect thinking.

The rest of the world is steps away from trailing the Chinese into a surveillance state.

The attitudes are already in place. The U.K. fines and even imprisons people for hate speech or speech deemed abhorrent to the prevailing norms of society. The U.S. is not far behind. Last week, a Manhattan judge ruled a bar can toss Trump supporters for their political viewpoints. A recent proliferation of politically motivated boycotts seeks to punish "bad" viewpoints; protesters are eager to shout down incorrect speech. In this political climate, it's not difficult to imagine businesses or the government assessing social benefit or worth based upon a variety of factors including political speech.

With incredible data collection, the plumbing is already in place for such a system to take hold. Our tech companies catalogue large quantities of data on everyone. As we saw with Cambridge Analytica in the 2016 election, this data can be used to steer particular viewpoints; it's not a far cry to imagine information being used to control viewpoints.

It's trendy pretending America is enduring a 1984 fascist hellscape, but China is actually implementing the largest surveillance state in the history of civilization with over 1.3 billion people under its watchful eye. The free world is not far behind if we don't protect privacy, deny our policymakers' desire to expand the reach of government, and resist the urge to commercially or socially punish those who don't share our political ideology. Privacy and liberty are never more than one generation away from extinction.

Tyler Grant is an associate at Washington, D.C.-based law firm Clifford Chance. He spent a year as a Fulbright Fellow in Taiwan."

"The History of the Bar Code - Inventor Joe Woodland drew the first bar code in sand in Miami Beach, decades before technology could bring his vision to life. Every few years, the small town of Troy in Miami County, Ohio celebrates an historic occasion that for a few giddy weeks puts it on the world map of the grocery trade. At the time, National Cash Register, which provided the checkout equipment, was based in Ohio and Troy was also the headquarters of the Hobart Corporation, which developed the weighing and pricing machines for loose items such as meat. It was here, at just after 8 a.m. on June 26, 1974, that the first item marked with the Universal Product Code (UPC) was scanned at the checkout of Troy's Marsh Supermarket.

NCR 255 scanning system for super-markets extends computer's power to checkstand. First system installed in U.S. is in Marsh Super Market, Troy, Ohio. Checker passes purchased items over scanning window. Universal Product Code, which appears on package, is read by laser scanner linked to computer. The latter records items and flashes prices on display panel. In supermarket control room, NCR 726 minicomputer controls system and provides detailed operating information for store manager.

The first item marked with the Universal Product Code (UPC) was scanned at the checkout of Troy's Marsh Supermarket. (Courtesy of Yale University Press)

It was treated with ceremonial occasion and involved a little bit of ritual. The night before, a team of Marsh staff had moved in to put bar codes on hundreds of items in the store while National Cash Register installed their scanners and computers. The first "shopper" was Clyde Dawson, who was head of research and development for Marsh Supermarket; the pioneer cashier who "served" him, Sharon Buchanan.

Legend has it that Dawson dipped into his shopping basket and pulled out a multi-pack of Wrigley's Juicy Fruit chewing gum. Dawson explained later that this was not a lucky dip: he chose it because nobody had been sure that a bar code could be printed on something as small as a pack of chewing gum, and Wrigley had found a solution to the problem. Their ample reward was a place in American history.

Joe Woodland said himself it sounded like a fairy tale: he had gotten the inspiration for what became the bar code

281

while sitting on Miami Beach. He drew it with his fingers in the sand. What he was after was a code of some sort that could be printed on groceries and scanned so that supermarket checkout queues would move more quickly and stocktaking would be simplified. That such a technology was needed was not his idea: it came from a distraught supermarket manager who had pleaded with a dean at Drexel Institute of Technology in Philadelphia to come up with some way of getting shoppers through his store more quickly. The delays and the regular stocktaking were costing him his profits. The dean shrugged him off, but a junior postgraduate, Bernard "Bob" Silver, overheard and was intrigued. He mentioned it to Woodland, who had graduated from Drexel in 1947. Woodland was already an inventor, and he decided to take on the challenge."

One other clue to Satan's 666 system being involved in the new economy is found in Revelation 18: 1 - 11 describing the end of this false system where the kings *(leaders)* and merchants of the earth have corrupted themselves because of business and how they will all wail when it all finally collapses. Remember the description given earlier in this book about this false system being the richest organisation on earth? You can refer back to it for a refresher and by this stage in this book I confirm to you that it is the Catholic Church, the wealthiest institution on the planet having accumulated wealth for millennia.

We conclude this chapter with a quote from the Signs of the times, November 19, 1894.

"Satan's chief agent in bringing about the rejection of the fourth commandment, and the institution of the first day of the week as a day of rest, has been the Roman Catholic Church. The Roman Catholic Church does not deny the part she has acted in this change, but makes a boast of her power as shown in the change which she has brought about in the world. Papists acknowledge that the Bible gives no sanction to this change, and that Protestants have no Scriptural authority for Sunday worship. The Catholic Church changed the day of rest from the seventh to the first day, and without the shadow of divine sanction it has been accepted by almost all the Protestant churches, and Rome, pointing to the adherents of her doctrines, claims the supremacy. In changing the fourth precept of God's law, the papal power has thought itself able to exalt itself above all that is called God, or that is worshipped. This was the very work that the prophecy foretold would be done by this power. In trampling upon the fourth commandment, the first commandment is broken. Their idolatry is similar to that of Israel's when she substituted a god which her own hands had made, for the living and true God, and followed after the example of Egypt; for when the Catholics substitute a Sabbath of their own making for that which God commanded, they too worship that which their own hands have made, and follow the example of the heathen who worshiped the sun on the first day of the week.

Through the pope of Rome the same work has been carried on here on earth as was carried on in the courts of heaven before the expulsion of the prince of darkness. Satan sought to correct the law of God in heaven, and to supply an amendment of his own. He exalted his own judgment above that of his Creator, and placed his will above the will of Jehovah, and in this way virtually declared God to be fallible. The pope also takes the same course and, claiming infallibility for himself, seeks to adjust the law of God to meet his own ideas, thinking himself able to correct the mistakes he thinks he sees in the statutes and commands of the Lord of heaven and earth. He virtually says to the world, I will give you better laws than those of Jehovah. What an insult is this to the God of heaven!

Many thousands who have accepted the change made in the day of rest have done so ignorantly, and unwittingly have placed themselves under the banner of the prince of darkness. The Christian church has accepted the false Sabbath but the day of light has now dawned. The times of their ignorance God winked at, but now he commandeth men everywhere to repent. It is demonstrated that no change is necessary in the law of God. Were there a change needed in the law of God, and could such a change be made, the rebellion of Satan would be justified, and the universe would have to concede that Satan was wiser than God, and had a right to supreme authority. But Jesus came to magnify the law and to make it honourable, and his death on Calvary in the sinner's behalf, proves the immutability of the law of heaven."

King of the North

The next phase of this book now needs to examine what exactly is meant by "the king of the north" especially as it relates to the last 5 verses of Daniel 11.

There are numerous other books and studies of the first 39 verses of Daniel 11 therefore I will not be referring to those verses extensively. Our focus is on the last 5. Verses 31 onwards transition from Literal to Spiritual Rome as will be demonstrated in this chapter.

Some hold that Turkey is the King of the North. Seeing that Turkey accepted the protection of the allied powers of Europe on the 11th of August, 1840, I do not see any further role that turkey has to play in the prophetic timeline and therefore Turkey cannot be the king of the north.

Pagan, literal Rome, Invaded Literal Jerusalem in AD 70 and totally destroyed the Temple and drenched the streets of Jerusalem with the blood of it's inhabitants. Interestingly Jesus gave a warning to His people that when the city became surrounded with Roman armies and they planted their banners in the holy place (an area outside of the city), then it would be a sign to flee Jerusalem, therefore none of His believers died in the awful destruction that ensued. They fled the City when the Romans unexpectedly lifted their siege. Similarly there will be an event by the King of the North(Spiritual Rome), that will have global ramifications, more in the Chapter, Planting of the Tabernacles and the Abomination of Desolation. I will elaborate on Jesus warning "When ye therefore shall see the abomination of desolation, spoken of by Daniel the prophet, stand in the holy place, (whoso readeth, let him understand:) Matthew 24:15

"And at the time of the end shall the king of the south push at him: and the king of the north shall come against him like a whirlwind, with chariots, and with horsemen, and with many ships; and he shall enter into the countries, and shall overflow and pass over. He shall enter also into the glorious land, and many [countries] shall be overthrown: but these shall escape out of his hand, [even] Edom, and Moab, and the chief of the children of Ammon. He shall stretch forth his hand also upon the countries: and the land of Egypt shall not escape. But he shall have power over the treasures of gold and of silver, and over all the precious things of Egypt: and the Libyans and the Ethiopians [shall be] at his steps." Daniel 11:40-43.

"The field of Daniel's prophecy embraces five universal kingdoms. These are Babylon, Media and Persia, Grecia, Rome, and the eternal kingdom of God. The ground of the four perishable kingdoms, reaching to, and introducing the immortal kingdom, is covered by four distinct lines of prophecy. These are given in chapters two, seven, eight and eleven. The eleventh chapter of Daniel closes with the close of the fourth monarchy, with these words:

"And he shall plant the tabanacles of his palace between the seas in the .. glorious holy mountain; [mountain of delight of holiness, Heb. Marg.;] yet he shall come to his end, and none shall help him." The twelfth chapter continues:

"And at that time shall Michael [Christ] stand up [reign], the great prince which standeth for the children of thy people; and: there shall be a time of trouble, such as never was since there was a nation even to that same time; and at that time thy people shall be delivered, every one that shall be found written in the book. And many of them that sleep in the dust of the earth shall awake, some to everlasting life, and some to shame and everlasting contempt. And they

286

that be wise shall shine as the brightnest of the firmament, and they that turn many to righteousness as the stars for ever and ever."

The student of prophecy is thus borne down the stream of time from Babylon in the height of the glory of that kingdom, past Media and Persia, the kingdom of Grecia, and the Roman Empire which comes to its end at the second coming of Christ... " James White, Signs of the Times, July 22, 1880. Vol. 6, No. 28.

"And arms shall stand on his part, and they shall pollute the sanctuary of strength, and shall take away the daily [sacrifice], and they shall place the abomination that maketh desolate." Daniel 11:31

By this stage in the prophecy of Daniel 11, Literal Rome has collapsed, verse, 30 and spiritual Rome takes over, verse 31. "And from the time [that] the daily [sacrifice] shall be taken away, and the abomination that maketh desolate set up, [there shall be] a thousand two hundred and ninety days." Daniel 12:11.

"Literal Rome ends with Daniel 11:30 and spiritual Rome takes over in Daniel 11:31:

"And arms shall stand on his part, and they shall pollute the sanctuary of strength, and shall take away the daily [mediation of Christ], and they shall place the abomination that makes desolate [the Papal system of mediation that God abominates because of its idolatry and its cruelty to His people]".

Daniel 8:12 says: "And an host was given him against the daily"

287

Daniel 11:31 says: "And arms shall stand on his part, and they shall pollute the sanctuary of strength, and shall take away the daily." This correct application of Daniel 11:31 in relation to the Papacy and the sanctuary, etc., is further demonstrated by Daniel 12:11, for here we are given the answer relative to the question asked in Daniel 8:13-14 concerning "How long" would the Papal abomination be permitted to tread "under foot" "the sanctuary and the host"? We are informed in Daniel 12:11 that "from the time that the daily [mediatorial service of Jesus in the heavenly sanctuary] shall be taken away [as it was by the Papacy in AD 508] to set up the abomination that makes desolate, there shall be one thousand two hundred and ninety days," margin. Commencing with AD 508, 1290 years brings us to (1798) the termination of Papal power to persecute God's people.

In Revelation 11:1-3 the persecution of God's people during the Dark Ages is explicitly declared to be an attack upon God's "temple" and "the holy city." That is, the Lord in Revelation 11:1-3 applies spiritually in connection with the church that which literal Rome did in connection with the literal city of Jerusalem. Compare Luke 21:24 and Revelation 11:2 and observe that identical language is used in both regarding the treading under foot of the city, Jerusalem.

The persecution of God's people is clearly outlined in Daniel 11:31-35,.... Thus, having introduced in Daniel's last prophecy the Papacy as the power that attacks God's spiritual "temple" and "holy city," the prophecy would naturally continue in this spiritual setting in relation to the church. Thus Paul applies Daniel 11: 36, 37 to the Papacy as if it had succeeded in invading the land of Israel, broken down the walls of "the holy city" and "sits in the temple of

God, showing himself that he is God" (2 Thessalonians 2: 3, 4).

Paul also refers to Daniel 11: 37 when he says of the Papal system: "Forbidding to marry." The 'celibacy' of the Papal priests and nuns is one of the specifications brought to view in the prophecy of Daniel 11. By its celibacy, the Papacy is able more successfully to enslave both priests and people in their false mediatorial system." The King of the North at Jerusalem. Louis F. Were Pg 20.

"In the third year of the reign of king Belshazzar a vision appeared unto me, [even unto] me Daniel, after that which appeared unto me at the first.

And I saw in a vision; and it came to pass, when I saw, that I [was] at Shushan [in] the palace, which [is] in the province of Elam; and I saw in a vision, and I was by the river of Ulai.

Then I lifted up mine eyes, and saw, and, behold, there stood before the river a ram which had [two] horns: and the [two] horns [were] high; but one [was] higher than the other, and the higher came up last.

I saw the ram pushing westward, and northward, and southward; so that no beasts might stand before him, neither [was there any] that could deliver out of his hand; but he did according to his will, and became great.

And as I was considering, behold, an he goat came from the west on the face of the whole earth, and touched not the ground: and the goat [had] a notable horn between his eyes.

And he came to the ram that had [two] horns, which I had seen standing before the river, and ran unto him in the fury of his power.

And I saw him come close unto the ram, and he was moved with choler against him, and smote the ram, and brake his two horns: and there was no power in the ram to stand before him, but he cast him down to the ground, and stamped upon him: and there was none that could deliver the ram out of his hand.

Therefore the he goat waxed very great: and when he was strong, the great horn was broken; and for it came up four notable ones toward the four winds of heaven.

And out of one of them came forth a little horn, which waxed exceeding great, toward the south, and toward the east, and toward the pleasant [land].

And it waxed great, [even] to the host of heaven; and it cast down [some] of the host and of the stars to the ground, and stamped upon them.

Yea, he magnified [himself] even to the prince of the host, and by him the daily [sacrifice] was taken away, and the place of his sanctuary was cast down.

And an host was given [him] against the daily [sacrifice] by reason of transgression, and it cast down the truth to the ground; and it practiced, and prospered." Daniel 8:1-12

These verses, specifically the goat, relates to Alexander the great's empire; after the empire was broken into 4 pieces under 4 generals, through one of their rulers arises a "little horn that waxes great even to the host of heaven. This is the history of the Babel system we have traced coming through the kingdom of Babylon, Pergamum, Greece and eventually becoming the papacy through Rome.

These verses confirm literal and spiritual developments. This king of the North is the Papacy that also rules by virtue of Lucifer who wants to sit on the sides of the north wishing to be God.

"How art thou fallen from heaven, O Lucifer, son of the morning! [How] art thou cut down to the ground, which didst weaken the nations!

For thou hast said in thine heart, I will ascend into heaven, I will exalt my throne above the stars of God: I will sit also

upon the mount of the congregation, in the sides of the north:
I will ascend above the heights of the clouds; I will be like the most High" Isaiah 14:10-12.

These spiritual aspects of Rome will be making strides in the literal world in order to achieve its spiritual goals.

At the time of the end

This chapter is to prove from the pages of past, contemporary, and modern history, that we are living in the time of the end. We will also examine what will happen in this 'time of the end.'

One other prophecy of Daniel that needs attention here with the time of the end also is found in Chapter 12:4. "But thou, O Daniel, shut up the words, and seal the book, *even* to the time of the end: many shall run to and fro, and knowledge shall be increased."

"And at the time of the end shall the king of the south push at him: and the king of the north shall come against him like a whirlwind, with chariots, and with horsemen, and with many ships; and he shall enter into the countries, and shall overflow and pass over." Daniel 11:40.

Pauls' second Epistle to the Thessalonians as quoted in the preface from II Thessalonians 2:4, 7-10, not only referred to their time, but also to something Paul observed was already working. He is found explaining to the Thessalonians that the second coming of Christ was not then imminent as many people taught in their time. He indicated then, that Christ would not return until there came a falling away first, and that the man of sin - the son of perdition and the mystery of iniquity was revealed.

The Apostle Paul understood the sequence of events with regards to the fulfillment of prophecies, it was not possible for Christ to return in Paul's time;

("For I am now ready to be offered, and the time of my departure is at hand. I have fought a good fight, I have finished [my] course, I have kept the faith: Henceforth there is laid up for me a crown of righteousness, which the Lord, the righteous judge, shall give me at that day: and not to me only, but unto all them also that love his appearing" 2:Timothy 4:6-8), therefore placing the falling away, in the future, to the time of the end, and Christ's second coming after the time of the end has concluded.

That event is confirmed in Daniel 12:1 "And at that time shall Michael stand up, the great prince which standeth for the children of thy people: and there shall be a time of trouble, such as never was since there was a nation [even] to that same time: and at that time thy people shall be delivered, every one that shall be found written in the book." (We have been living in the time of the end since 1798).

How do we know we are living in the "time of the end"?

"But thou, O Daniel, shut up the words, and seal the book, [even] to the time of the end: many shall run to and fro, and knowledge shall be increased." Daniel 12:4. He states further "And I heard, but I understood not: then said I, O my Lord, what [shall be] the end of these [things]?" Verse 8 "And he said, Go thy way, Daniel: for the words [are] closed up and sealed till the time of the end. But go thou thy way till the end [be]: for thou shalt rest, and stand in thy lot at the end of the days." Verses 9 & 13.

What is this "....thy lot at the end of days"? Let us go to 1 Thessalonians to find the answer

"But I would not have you to be ignorant, brethren, concerning them which are asleep, that ye sorrow not, even as others which have no hope.
For if we believe that Jesus died and rose again, even so them also which sleep in Jesus will God bring with him.

293

For this we say unto you by the word of the Lord, that we which are alive *and* remain unto the coming of the Lord shall not prevent them which are asleep.

For the Lord himself shall descend from heaven with a shout, with the voice of the archangel, and with the trump of God: and the dead in Christ shall rise first:

Then we which are alive *and* remain shall be caught up together with them in the clouds, to meet the Lord in the air: and so shall we ever be with the Lord."

Here it is very clear that Daniel will rise at the end of time when Jesus returns to take His righteous people home with Him, Daniel will be with his group (lot) of resurrected souls and will join those who at the end of time rejected the false Mystery system and chose Jesus.

It is very clear then that Daniel would not live through the events of his prophecy but see the fulfillment of what he wrote of being with the rest of God's people. As we have already read, Paul came to the same conclusion that he would resurrect at the end of days, the end of the time of the end.

To know what time we are living in we must logically search for the answers from the inspired pages of scripture beginning with the prophetic books writtten by Daniel.

Not only do those verses make it clear that the books of Daniel would not be opened (understood) until the time of the end, those verses also make it very clear that the world would experience an exponential growth in knowledge. Has this happened and is it continuously happening? Are we as a human race migrating from country to country? We can all say without any doubt, YES!!

Our world has gone industrial, our world has developed all types of technology that is catapulting us into things we could not conceive of 50 years ago. Reading this book on a kindle or other forms of media. Facebook, twitter, Instagram etc. are all proof of our advancements.

The World Wide Web that made these social media platforms available was not yet invented. It was as recently as 1983 when TCP/IP was invented and not until 1990 was a recognizable World Wide Web developed. I don't need to go into all the other mammoth leaps mankind has made in the last century; all my readers need to do is visit Google, Bing, Yahoo etc. to learn about them. Our increase in knowledge also includes understanding God's word.

Daniel lays out world history from the time of Kings Nebuchadnezzar and Belshazzar of Babylon, Darius the Mede, Alexander the great and to our very day in Chapters 2, 7, 8 and 11.

King Nebuchadnezzar was greatly disturbed in chapter 2 because of a dream he had of a great image. Daniel informs the king that He is represented as the head of gold of the image, his kingdom would be succeeded by three other world powers, the fourth power being dreadful and terrible crushing all others before it, yet with a weakness in that the feet and toes would be partly iron and clay, therefore, partly strong and weak, eventually all those earthly kingdoms would be replaced by an eternal, heavenly kingdom.

Chapter 7 describes in a little more detail the above four powers and describes the fourth power, verses 7&8 as being dreadful, having ten horns and one of those horns having a mouth speaking great things.

"After this I saw in the night visions, and behold a fourth beast, dreadful and terrible, and strong exceedingly; and it had great iron teeth: it devoured and brake in pieces, and stamped the residue with the feet of it: and it [was] diverse from all the beasts that [were] before it; and it had ten horns. I considered the horns, and, behold, there came up among them another little horn, before whom there were three of the first horns plucked up by the roots: and, behold, in this horn [were] eyes like the eyes of man, and a mouth speaking great things."

Chapter 8 transitions to the time of Belshazzar when Daniel sees in vision another view of the third power of Daniel 2 represented as an he goat with a great horn between its eyes, that horn then breaks into four horns and out of one them a little horn that becomes exceeding great towards the south, the east and the pleasant land even to the host of heaven. In verse 20 of Daniel 8 an explanation of the ram is given as the Kings of Media and Persia, the kingdom that succeeded Babylon, Verse 21 describes the first king of Greece, Alexander the great, verse 22 describes the Grecian empire breaking into four after the death of Alexander the great, verses 23-25 describes the little horn power that arises in the latter times from the influence of Greeks. This is the same mysterious horn power with a mouth of Daniel 7:20. That horn power dominates the world, in verse 25 for "a time, times and dividing of time" This is the same power described in Revelation 13:5 "And there was given unto him a mouth speaking great things and blasphemies; and power was given unto him to continue forty [and] two months."

Revelation 13:1-3 describes the same power as Daniel 7, with a little more detail in that another power described as a dragon gives this incredibly terrifying kingdom his power(dragon's power), seat (dragon's seat) and great

296

authority(dragon's great authority), yet we find that power (not the dragon) receiving a deadly wound (Appendices 2&3) that is subsequently healed. ("And I saw one of his heads as it were wounded to death; and his deadly wound was healed: and all the world wondered after the beast." verse 3)

"In the Revelation, all the books of the Bible meet and end. Here is the complement of the book of Daniel. One is a prophecy; the other a revelation. The book that was sealed is not the Revelation, but that portion of the prophecy of Daniel relating to the last days.." The Acts of the Apostles pg 585.

"In chapter 13 [verses 1-10.] is described another beast, "like unto a leopard," to which the dragon gave "his power, and his seat, and great authority." This symbol, as most Protestants have believed, represents the papacy, which succeeded to the power and seat and authority once possessed by the ancient Roman Empire." Of the leopard-like beast it is declared: "There was given unto him a mouth speaking great things and blasphemies. . . . And he opened his mouth in blasphemy against God, to blaspheme his name, and his tabernacle, and them that dwell in Heaven. And it was given unto him to make war with the saints, and to overcome them; and power was given him over all kindreds, and tongues, and nations." This prophecy, which is nearly identical with the description of the little horn of Daniel 7, unquestionably points to the papacy.

"Power was given unto him to continue forty and two months." And, says the prophet, "I saw one of his heads as it were wounded to death." And again, "He that leadeth into captivity shall go into captivity; he that killeth with the sword must be killed with the sword." The forty and two

297

months are the same as the "time and times and the dividing of time," three years and a half, or 1260 days, of Daniel 7,—the time during which the papal power was to oppress God's people. This period, as stated in preceding chapters, began with the establishment of the papacy, A. D. 538, and terminated in 1798. At that time, when the papacy was abolished and the pope made captive by the French army, the papal power received its deadly wound, and the prediction was fulfilled, "He that leadeth into captivity shall go into captivity." The Great Controversy pg 440.

"Said the angel of the Lord: "The holy city [the true church] shall they tread under foot forty and two months. And I will give power unto my two witnesses, and they shall prophesy a thousand two hundred and threescore days, clothed in sackcloth. . . . And when they shall have finished their testimony, the beast that ascendeth out of the bottomless pit shall make war against them, and shall overcome them, and kill them. And their dead bodies shall lie in the street of the great city, which spiritually is called Sodom and Egypt, where also our Lord was crucified. . . . And they that dwell upon the earth shall rejoice over them, and make merry, and shall send gifts one to another; because these two prophets tormented them that dwelt on the earth. And after three days and a half the Spirit of life from God entered into them, and they stood upon their feet; and great fear fell upon them which saw them." [Revelation 11:2-11.]

The periods here mentioned—"forty and two months," and "a thousand two hundred and threescore days"—are the same, alike representing the time in which the church of Christ was to suffer oppression from Rome. The 1260 years of papal supremacy began with the establishment of the papacy in AD 538, and would therefore terminate in 1798. At that time a French army entered Rome, and made the pope a prisoner, and he died in exile...." GC 267. This event marked the "time of the end."

This exile of the Pope was the deadly wound prophecied to take place in 1798AD exactly 1260 years after the Emperor Justinians decree in 538AD..

Revelation 13:10 Prophecies the captivity and death of the Pope under General Berthier ("He that leadeth into captivity shall go into captivity: he that killeth with the sword must be killed with the sword. Here is the patience and the faith of the saints") and as this event unfolds with the Papacy, another event that was taking place "at the time of the end" was the rising of another power as highlighted in revelation 13:11-12.

"And I beheld another beast coming up out of the earth; and he had two horns like a lamb, and he spake as a dragon. And he exerciseth all the power of the first beast before him, and causeth the earth and them which dwell therein to worship the first beast, whose deadly wound was healed."

In a later chapter we will confirm who this power is.

Interestingly the Papacy is confirmed here as becoming healed from its deadly wound. This event took place in 1929 (Appendix 3) when Mussolini signed a concordat with the Vatican restoring the Papal estates back to the Pope, from then on we have witnessed the relentless rising of Papal power all over the world. "And I saw one of his heads as it were wounded to death; and his deadly wound was healed: and all the world wondered after the beast." Revelation 13:3

The disciples of Christ were as curious as Daniel for an explanation of the time of the end. Shouldn't we also be very curious as to what is about to happen with our world seeing as we are actually living "at the time of the end"?

"And as he sat upon the mount of Olives, the disciples came unto him privately, saying, Tell us, when shall these things be? and what [shall be] the sign of thy coming, and of the end of the world?
And Jesus answered and said unto them, Take heed that no man deceive you.
For many shall come in my name, saying, I am Christ; and shall deceive many.
And ye shall hear of wars and rumours of wars: see that ye be not troubled: for all [these things] must come to pass, but the end is not yet.
For nation shall rise against nation, and kingdom against kingdom: and there shall be famines, and pestilences, and earthquakes, in divers places.
 All these [are] the beginning of sorrows.
Then shall they deliver you up to be afflicted, and shall kill you: and ye shall be hated of all nations for my name's sake. "

(Persecution of the true followers of Christs for approximately 1260 years of the dark ages)

"And then shall many be offended, and shall betray one another, and shall hate one another. And many false prophets shall rise, and shall deceive many. And because iniquity shall abound, the love of many shall wax cold. But he that shall endure unto the end, the same shall be saved.

(and a persecution that will be revived at the time of the end)
And this gospel of the kingdom shall be preached in all the world for a witness unto all nations; and then shall the end come."

(Make special note of this verse, a more detailed explanation will be given later in this book)

"When ye therefore shall see the abomination of desolation, spoken of by Daniel the prophet, stand in the holy place, (whoso readeth, let him understand:) Then let them which be in Judaea flee into the mountains: Let him which is on the housetop not come down to take any thing out of his house: Neither let him which is in the field return back to take his clothes. And woe unto them that are with child, and to them that give suck in those days! But pray ye that your flight be not in the winter, neither on the sabbath day: For then shall be great tribulation, such as was not since the beginning of the world to this time, no, nor ever shall be. And except those days should be shortened, there should no flesh be saved: but for the elect's sake those days shall be shortened."

(8 more very significant verses, with dual prophecies)

"Wherefore if they shall say unto you, Behold, he is in the desert; go not forth: behold, [he is] in the secret chambers; believe [it] not."

(more on the secret chambers later also)

"For as the lightning cometh out of the east, and shineth even unto the west; so shall also the coming of the Son of man be."

(One of the most significant of these verses that will tie in with Daniel 11:44-45)

For wheresoever the carcase is, there will the eagles be gathered together.

Immediately after the tribulation of those days shall the sun be darkened, and the moon shall not give her light, and the stars shall fall from heaven, and the powers of the heavens shall be shaken:

And then shall appear the sign of the Son of man in heaven: and then shall all the tribes of the earth mourn, and they shall see the Son of man coming in the clouds of heaven with power and great glory." *(another significant verse that ties in with Daniel 12:1)* Matthew 24:3-30.

In the time of the end, Satan will be organising and promoting his greatest deceptions. The papacy will make its last desperate attempt at surviving and in the process will bring the greatest calamities in the spiritual world on all its inhabitants.

There will be scenes of utter disaster, of unimaginable crimes and the lowest of mans inhumanity to man.

During the scenes of utter chaos in this time of the end, the heavens will part and Jesus will return with billions of His angels to take His believers home with Him. In the next few chapters I will share with you what to look out for and how to be one of those who choose to follow Jesus and reject Satan's 'MYSTERY' 666 system.

Planting of the Tabernacles & the Abomination of Desolation

"And he shall plant the tabernacles of his palace between the seas in the glorious holy mountain; yet he shall come to his end, and none shall help him." Daniel 11:45.

"When ye therefore shall see the abomination of desolation, spoken of by Daniel the prophet, stand in the holy place, (whoso readeth, let him understand:)" Matthew 24:15

We will begin first with the glorious holy mountain. Is it a literal place? Is it a Spiritual place? Is it both? Let us find out.

We have already established in earlier chapters the spiritual aspect of the papacy in this end of time prophecy. **In this chapter we are dealing with the literal location of the Holy Mountain, so if you have not yet read the earlier explanation of the spiritual aspects, please do not go any further until you have gone back and studied it.** Warning - The events that will be outlined in this chapter are not to be taken lightly.

Firstly we need to determine the location of the literal glorious holy mountain that the verse is referring to and one of the clues is "between the seas" There are very few people today that do not recognise Jerusalem as the Holy Mountain, the image on the next page places Jerusalem between the Dead sea and the Mediterranean sea and no I am not ignoring the spiritual application.

"O Lord, according to all thy righteousness, I beseech thee, let thine anger and thy fury be turned away from thy city Jerusalem, thy holy mountain..." Daniel 9:16.

"Blow ye the trumpet in Zion, and sound an alarm in my holy mountain: let all the inhabitants of the land tremble: for the day of the Lord cometh, for it is nigh at hand." Joel 2:1.

"So shall ye know that I am the Lord your God dwelling in Zion, my holy mountain: then shall Jerusalem be holy, and there shall no strangers pass through her any more." Joel 3:17

Between the seas:

"But I say unto you, swear not at all, neither by heaven; for it is God's throne: Nor by the earth; for it is his footstool: neither by Jerusalem; for it is the city of the great king." Matthew 5:34-35.

"Beautiful for situation, the joy of the whole earth, is mount Zion, on the sides of the north, the city of the great king." Psalms 48:2.

Therefore the "Holy Mountain," referred to in Daniel 11 is none other than present day Jerusalem. As has already been determined, the last power of Daniel 11 and Revelation 13 is Satan. What steps have been taken by the Pope to secure Jerusalem? and why would he want to "plant the tabernacles of his palace" in Jerusalem? We will answer part 1 of this question first.

The prophecy emphasises that "he shall plant" does that imply that "he" has been trying for a while and will at last succeed? I have researched various concordances and the following are the results:

Dan 11:45 And he shall plant[H5193] the tabernacles[H168] of his palace[H643] between[H996] the seas[H3220] in the glorious[H6643] holy[H6944] mountain; [H2022] yet he shall come[H935] to[H5704] his end, [H7093] and none[H369] shall help[H5826] him.

H5193

נָטַע
nâta‘
naw-tah'
A primitive root; properly to *strike* in, that is, *fix*; specifically to *plant* (literally or figuratively): - fastened, plant (-er).

These confirm that the events taking place are spiritual and literal. The spiritual goals driving the literal accomplishments. The verse describes the event as striking in, fixing, fastening. This seems different to digging into the ground for the purpose of growing a plant. This planting is driving something into. For example driving a metal or other solid object into the soil with another implement, ramming it into the soil or other object?

How far back in history can we go to understand how long the papacy has been trying to establish itself in Jerusalem? Or should I say Satan trying to do so through the Pope? Remember he wants to imitate the Most High. We have examined aspects of the Spiritual history of the "MYSTERY" but what else is there to know. Our earthly Jerusalem was God's special City and the new city, God's special, more glorious, holy and eternal city, descending from heaven will be called 'New Jerusalem'.

The following account is by former Jesuit Priest – Alberto Rivera (Indications are that Rivera was assassinated in 1997):

"Long before the Crusades, the Vatican secretly negotiated and financed Mohammed (through a Roman Catholic relative), to help them annihilate the Jews, but when the Islamic forces captured Jerusalem in the name of the prophet Mohammed, the Pope was blocked from moving the Vatican there because Mohammed turned around and called the Pope and the Jews, infidels.

The ultimate goal of the Roman Catholic church is to get control of the Holy city of Jerusalem. The Vatican helped to finance the three Islam armies of old, in exchange for three favors: One was to eliminate the Jews and Bible Believers. One was to protect the Augustinian monks and the Roman Catholics, and the last reason was the most important; to conquer Jerusalem for the Pope. The Muslim army conquered Jerusalem, but refused to co-operate with the Vatican. This started the hatred between the two heathen religions, but because of their shady past, this was never made public knowledge. Muslims went on to conquer the world in the name of their god "Allah", while the Catholics went on to conquer the world in the name of Mary. Both factions (religions) played an essential part in the creation of the "prophet" Muhammad.

Roman Catholics wanted Jerusalem at the end of the third century. Because of its religious history and its strategic location, the Holy City was considered a priceless treasure. A scheme had to be developed to make Jerusalem a Roman Catholic city. The great untapped source of manpower that could do this job was the children of Ishmael. The poor

Arabs fell victim to one of the most clever plans ever devised by the Powers of Darkness.

Early Christians went everywhere with the gospel, setting up small churches, but they met heavy opposition. Both the Jews and the Roman government persecuted the believers in Christ to stop their spread. But the Jews rebelled against Rome, and in 70 A.D. Roman armies under General Titus smashed Jerusalem and destroyed the great Jewish temple which was the heart of Jewish worship – in fulfillment of Christ's prophecy in Matthew 24:2. In this "holy" place, *(where the temple is alleged to have stood – more on this later),* the Dome of the Rock Mosque stands today as Islam's second most holy place.

Sweeping changes were in the wind. Corruption, apathy, greed, cruelty, perversion, and rebellion were eating at the Roman Empire, and it was ready to collapse. The persecution against Christians was useless, as they continued to lay down their lives for the gospel of Christ. The only way Satan could stop this thrust was to create a counterfeit "Christian" religion to destroy the work of God. The solution was in Rome. Their religion had come from ancient Babylon, and all it needed was a face-lift. This didn't happen overnight, but began in the writings of the "early church fathers". It was through their writings that a new religion would take shape. The statue of Jupiter in Rome was eventually called St. Peter, and the statue of Venus was changed to the Virgin Mary. The site chosen for its headquarters was on one of the seven hills called "Vaticanus" – the place of the divining serpent where the Satanic Temple of Janus stood. (Revelation 17:9)

The great counterfeit religion was Roman Catholicism, called "Mystery, Babylon the Great, the Mother of Harlots and Abominations of the Earth" (Revelation 17:5). She was raised up to block the gospel, slaughter the believers in

Christ, establish religions, create wars, and make the nations drunk with the wine of her fornication as we will see. Three major religions have one thing in common – each has a holy place where they look for guidance. Roman Catholicism looks to the Vatican as the Holy City. The Jews look to the wailing wall in Jerusalem, and the Muslims look to Mecca as their Holy City. Each group believes that they receive certain types of blessings for the rest of their lives for visiting their holy place. In the beginning, Arab visitors would bring gifts to the "House of God" and the keepers of the Kaaba were gracious to all who came. Some brought their idols and, not wanting to offend these people, their idols were placed inside the sanctuary. It is said that the Jews looked upon the Kaaba as an outlying tabernacle of the Lord with veneration, until it became polluted with idols.

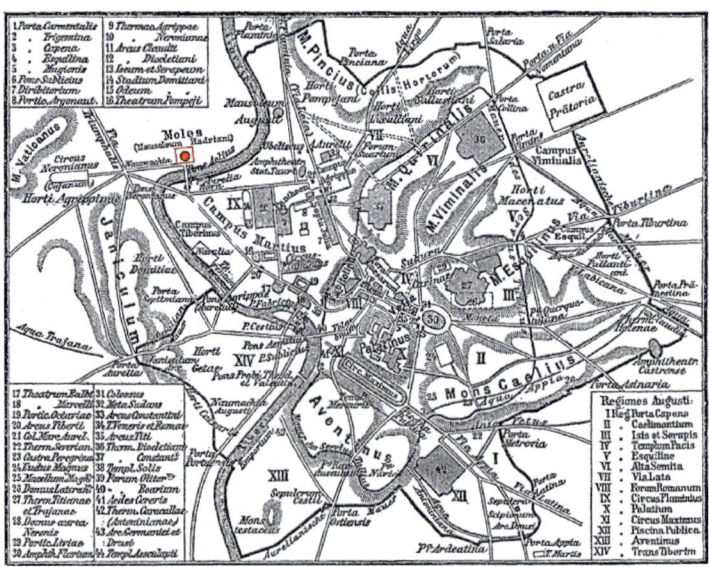

Ancient map of the seven hills – Mons Vaticanus top left of image.

In a tribal contention over a well (Zamzam) the treasure of the Kaaba and the offerings that pilgrims had given were dumped down the well and it was filled with sand; it disappeared. Many years later Adb al-Muttalib was given visions telling him where to find the well and its treasure. He became the hero of Mecca, and he was destined to become the grandfather of Muhammad. Before this time, Augustine became the bishop of North Africa and was effective in winning Arabs to Roman Catholicism, including whole tribes. It was among these Arab converts to Catholicism that the concept of looking for an Arab prophet developed. Muhammad's father died from illness, and sons born to great Arab families in places like Mecca were sent into the desert to be suckled and weaned and spend some of their childhood with Bedouin tribes for training and to avoid the plagues in the cities. After his mother and grandfather also died, Muhammad was with his uncle when a Roman Catholic monk learned of his identity and said:

"Take your brother's son back to his country and guard him against the Jews, for by God, if they see him and know of him that which I know, they will construe evil against him. Great things are in store for this brother's son of yours."

The Roman Catholic monk had fanned the flames for future Jewish persecutions at the hands of the followers of Muhammad. The Vatican desperately wanted Jerusalem because of its religious significance, but was blocked by the Jews.

Another problem was the true Christians in North Africa who preached the gospel. Roman Catholicism was growing in power, but would not tolerate opposition. Somehow the Vatican had to create a weapon to eliminate both the Jews and the true Christian believers who refused to accept

Roman Catholicism. Looking to North Africa, they saw the multitudes of Arabs as a source of manpower to do their dirty work. Some Arabs had become Roman Catholic, and could be used in reporting information to leaders in Rome. Others were used in an underground spy network to carry out Rome's master plan to control the great multitudes of Arabs who rejected Catholicism. When "St. Augustine" appeared on the scene, he knew what was going on. His monasteries served as bases to seek out and destroy Bible manuscripts owned by the true Christians. The Vatican wanted to create a messiah for the Arabs, someone they could raise up as a great leader, a man with charisma whom they could train, and eventually unite all the non-Catholic Arabs behind him, creating a mighty army that would ultimately capture Jerusalem for the pope.

In the Vatican briefing, Cardinal Bea told us this story:

A wealthy Arabian lady who was a faithful follower of the pope played a tremendous part in this drama. She was a widow named Khadijah. She gave her wealth to the church and retired to a convent, but was given an assignment. She was to find a brilliant young man who could be used by the Vatican to create a new religion and become the messiah for the children of Ishmael. She found and married Muhammad, she was 40, he was 25. Khadijah had a cousin named Waraquah, who was also a very faithful Roman Catholic, and the Vatican placed him in a critical role as Muhammad's advisor. He had tremendous influence on Muhammad. Teachers were sent to young Muhammad and he had intensive training. Muhammad devoured the works of St. Augustine, which prepared him for his "great calling". The Vatican had Catholic Arabs across North Africa spread the story of a great one who was about to rise up among the people and be the chosen one of their God. While Muhammad was being prepared, he was told that his enemies were the Jews and that the only true Christians were Roman Catholic. He was taught that others calling themselves Christians were actually wicked impostors and should be destroyed. Many Muslims believe this.

Muhammad began receiving "divine revelations" and his wife's Catholic cousin Waraquah helped interpret them. From this came the Koran. In the fifth year of Muhammad's mission, persecution came against his followers because they refused to worship the idols in the Kaaba. Muhammad instructed some of them to flee to Abysinnia, where Negus, the Roman Catholic king, accepted them because Muhammad's views on the virgin Mary were so close to Roman Catholic doctrine. These Muslims received protection from Catholic kings because of Muhammad's revelations. Muhammad later conquered Mecca and the Kaaba was cleared of idols.

History proves that before Islam came into existence, the Sabeans in Arabia worshiped the moon-god who was married to the sun-god. They gave birth to three goddesses, who were worshipped throughout the Arab world as "Daughters of Allah". An idol excavated at Hazor in Palestine in the 1950s shows Allah sitting on a throne with the crescent moon on his chest. Muhammad claimed he had a vision from Allah and was told: "You are the messenger of Allah." This began his career as a prophet and he received many messages. By the time Muhammad died, the religion of Islam was exploding. The nomadic Arab tribes were joining forces in the name of Allah and his prophet, Muhammad. Some of Muhammad's writings were placed in the Koran, others were never published. They are now in the hands of high ranking holy men (Ayatollahs) in the Islamic faith.

When Cardinal Bea shared this information in the Vatican, he said:

"These writings are guarded because they contain information that links the Vatican to the creation of Islam."
.

Both sides have so much information on each other that, if exposed, it could create such a scandal that it would be a disaster for both religions. In their "holy" book, the Koran, Christ (Jesus(Eesa)) is regarded as only a prophet. If the pope was his representative on Earth, then he also must be a prophet of God. This caused the followers of Muhammad to fear and respect the pope as another "holy man". The pope moved quickly and issued bulls granting the Arab generals permission to invade and conquer the nations of North Africa.

The Vatican helped to finance the building of these massive Islamic armies in exchange for three favors:

I. Eliminate the Jews and Christians (the latter were regarded as true believers, which they called infidels)
II. Protect the Augustinian monks and Roman Catholics
III. Conquer Jerusalem for "His Holiness" in the Vatican
As time went by, the power of Islam became tremendous. Jews and true Christians were slaughtered, and Jerusalem fell into their hands. Roman Catholics were never attacked, nor were their shrines, during this time. But when the pope asked for Jerusalem, he was surprised at their denial! The Arab generals had such military success that they could not be intimidated by the pope – nothing could stand in the way of their own plan.

Under Waraquah's direction, Muhammad wrote that Abraham offered Ishmael as a sacrifice. The Bible says that Isaac was the sacrifice, but Muhammad removed Isaac's name and inserted Ishmael's name. As a result of this and Muhammad's vision, the faithful Muslims built a mosque, the Dome of the Rock, in Ishmael's honor, on the alleged site of the Jewish temple that was destroyed in 70 A.D. This made Jerusalem the second most holy place in the Islamic faith. How could they give such a sacred shrine to the pope without causing a revolt? The pope realized what they had created was out of control when he heard they were calling "His Holiness" an infidel. The Muslim generals were determined to conquer the world for Allah, and now they turned toward Europe. Islamic ambassadors approached the pope and asked for papal bulls to give them permission to invade European countries. The Vatican was outraged; war was inevitable. Temporal power and control of the world was considered the basic right of the pope. He wouldn't think of sharing it with those whom he considered heathens.

The pope raised up his armies and called them "crusades" to hold back the children of Ishmael from grabbing Catholic Europe. The crusades lasted for centuries and Jerusalem slipped out of the pope's hands. Turkey fell, and Spain and Portugal were invaded by Islamic forces. In Portugal, they called a mountain village "Fatima" in honor of Muhammad's daughter, never dreaming it would become world famous. Years later, when the Muslim armies were poised on the islands of Sardinia and Corsica, to invade Italy, there was a serious problem. The Islamic generals realized they were too far extended. It was time for peace talks. One of the negotiators was Francis of Assisi. As a result, the Muslims were allowed to occupy Turkey in a "Christian" world, and the Catholics were allowed to occupy Lebanon in the Arab world. It was also agreed that the Muslims could build mosques in Catholic countries without interference, as long as Roman Catholicism could flourish in Arab countries.

Cardinal Bea told us in Vatican briefings that both the Muslims and Roman Catholics agreed to block and destroy the efforts of their common enemy: Bible-believing Christian missionaries. Through these concordats, Satan blocked the children of Ishmael from a knowledge of scripture and the truth. The Islamic community looks on the Bible-believing missionary as a devil who brings poison to the children of Allah. This explains years of ministry in those countries with little results. The Vatican also engineered a campaign of hatred between the Muslim Arabs and the Jews. Before this, they had co-existed peacefully. A tight control was kept on Muslims – from the Ayatollah, down through the Islamic priests, nuns, and monks. The next plan was to control Islam. In 1910, Portugal was going Socialistic. Red flags were appearing and the Catholic Church was facing a major problem. Increasing numbers were against the Church. The Jesuits wanted Russia involved, and the location of this vision at Fatima could play a key part in pulling Islam to the Mother Church. In 1917, the Virgin appeared in Fatima. "The Mother of God" was a smashing success, playing to overflow crowds. As a result, the Socialists of Portugal suffered a major defeat. Roman Catholics worldwide began praying for the conversion of Russia, and the Jesuits invented the novenas to Fatima, which they could perform throughout North Africa, spreading good public relations to the Muslim world.

The Arabs thought they were honoring the daughter of Muhammad, which is what the Jesuits wanted them to believe. As a result of the vision of Fatima, Pope Pius XII ordered his Nazi army to crush Russia and the Orthodox religion, and make Russia Roman Catholic. A few years after he lost World War II, Pope Pius XII startled the world with his phony "dancing Sun" vision to keep Fatima in the news (1950). It was great religious show biz and the world swallowed it. Not surprisingly, Pope Pius was the only one to see this vision. As a result, a group of followers has grown into a Blue Army worldwide, totaling millions of faithful Roman Catholics ready to die for the Blessed Virgin. But we haven't seen anything yet. The Jesuits have their Virgin Mary scheduled to appear four or five times in China, Russia, and major appearance in the U.S. What has this got to do with Islam? Note Bishop Sheen's statement:

"Our Lady's appearances at Fatima marked the turning point in the history of the world's 350 million Muslims(1917). *(1.8 billion Muslims 2017?)* After the death of his daughter, Muhammad wrote that she 'is the most holy of all women in Paradise, next to Mary.' He believed that the Virgin Mary chose to be known as Our Lady of Fatima as a sign and a pledge that the Muslims who believe in Christ's virgin birth, will come to believe in his divinity."

Bishop Sheen pointed out that the pilgrim virgin statues of Our Lady of Fatima were enthusiastically received by Muslims in Africa, India, and elsewhere, and that many Muslims are now coming into the Roman Catholic Church. There is no question that we are seeing the push for a global peace plan that will not just come with Israel, but with every other religion in the world, including Islam. What can we look forward to is anyone's guess, but I do know this, at some point in the distant future, either this current Pope, or the one which will follow after him, will bring the world into some sort of spiritual darkness where all men will become deceived." Alberto Rivera.

You may be thinking does the account by Alberto Rivera have any credibility? Let's dig a little deeper into root commonalities of Catholicism and Islam and this should confirm how intertwined both religions are.

The following images confirm similarities between Catholic and Islamic worship implements (excluding relics worship):

"The crescent moon cradle used in the monstrance (which is always in the form of a sunburst) to hold the Eucharist signifies the joining of the sun (Eucharist) with the moon (the crescent cradle). That same symbolism is found in Islam, where flags often depict a star and crescent moon, which symbolises the sun joining with the moon. In both the Catholic monstrance and the Islamic flags, the representation has an occult meaning that celebrates the generative power of the procreative act where the sun is the lingam and the moon is the yoni."

Monstrance With Crescent Moon Cradle

Ancient Idol of the Moon Deity, Allah, With Crescent Moon on His Chest

Catholic Monstrance   *Pakistan Flag*   *Moon god, Allah*

Pope John Paul publicly kissing the Koran. Why would he do that? This confirms that popery is heavily involved with Islam.

Catholic Prayer Beads

Islamic Prayer Beads

"The misogyny and pederasty in both the Catholic priesthood and among Islamic males may be caused by the fact that both Islam and Catholicism are deviant phallic religions that flow from Babylon. All ancient mystery religions are based upon phallicism. Phallicism is the pantheistic worship of procreation in nature, with a focus on genitalia. Phallicism is a fetish theology, wherein the generative principle is represented through images of phalli and yonis. That is why there is a phallic obelisk in St. Peter's Square and Islamic mosques are surrounded by phallic minarets."

Phallicism was the central theme of the ancient mystery religions flowing from Babylon. Martin Wagner explains:

"The phalluse was an essential part in the rites and symbolism of the mysteries. Its office was to convey to the initiated a profound and sacred meaning. It was a common object of worship and of ornament. Originally it had no other meaning than that of union of male and female upon which depended the procreation of life."

(Take note that the worship ceremony in St. Peter's Square is organised around the obelisk. This 326 tonne obelisk was brought to Rome From Egypt by Gaius Caligula in 37 AD.)

"The gods were male and female, and the worship of the sexual was prominent in these cults. The religious ideas were based upon the sexual facts, and grew out of a profound veneration for the generative principle. Ritual prostitution which was possibly a decadence, was a recognized and widespread institution, and grew out of a purely religious point of view. At the shrine of Baal and Astarte in Phoenicia and similar sanctuaries elsewhere, sexual intercourse was a part of the rite."

"...Rivera's account seems so fantastic and incredible; it is hard to believe, There is one way to verify its truth. He claims that as part of the concordat, Catholic Churches would be allowed in Arab countries. Let us look at the most conservative Islamic country, Saudi Arabia {which follows the ultra-conservative Hanbali school of Sunni Islam) and

319

see if the concordat is being put into force. Nina Shea, who is director of Hudson Institute's Center for Religious Freedom and co-author of *Persecuted: The Global Assault on Christians* states that "Saudi Arabia is the only state in the world to ban all churches and any other non-Muslim houses of worship." She further stated that "distributing Bibles in Saudi Arabia is illegal," The persecution of Christian churches has continued unabated.

For example, in September 2014, Benjamin Weinthal reported for Fox News that 28 people were arrested at a prayer meeting in a home church in Kalji, Saudi Arabia, by hard-line Islamists from the Commission for the Promotion of Virtue and Prevention of Vice. The arrests were based solely upon the fact that the arrestees were practicing their Christian faith, Weinthal reported that "an article posted on the Arabic-language news website Akhbar 24 said the arrests came after the Kingdom's religious police got a tip about a home-based church. It seems that the concordat is being enforced against bible-believing Christians.

What about the protection of the Catholic Church? In 2008, the Saudi Arabian government allegedly refused to allow the building of a Catholic Church in Saudi Arabia. Shea, writing in 2014, claimed that the Catholic Church was among the persecuted churches. "Priests must go undercover, pretending to be cooks or mechanics, to celebrate underground Masses for the estimated 1.5 million Filipino, Indian and other Catholics working or living there. Furthermore, the Roman Catholic Apostolic Vicariate of Northern Arabia explains on its website:

As Saudi Arabia is home to Islam's holiest sites, it does not permit churches to be built, as a result there are no Christian churches or places of worship. Non-Islamic religion is not recognized and its public display or activity is prohibited.

That suggests that there might not be a concordat that protects the Catholic Church in Islamic countries. Further checking, however, reveals that the alleged Catholic persecution is carefully contrived false propaganda. The persecution of churches is aimed solely at bible-believing Christians. The proof that the persecution of the Catholic Church is a myth is found on a Roman Catholic website that contains a worldwide directory of Roman Catholic Churches. Lo-and-behold, what do we find? There are listed the names, addresses, phone numbers, fax numbers, and web addresses of four (4) Roman Catholic churches in Riyadh, which is the capital city of Saudi Arabia. That is not including the Lady of Fatima Catholic Church located at 1st Fahad Street, Ash Sharqiyah 31932. In the city of Khobar, Saudi Arabia, that is particularly notable, since even clandestine attempts at Christian worship by bible-believing Christians in secret home churches results in arrest if the Islamic authorities are tipped off, yet, the Roman Catholic Church has openly publicised addresses for their churches. The Catholic Church, obviously, is not concerned about arrest or persecution in Saudi Arabia.

It seems that the Vatican is engaged in a sophisticated media deception designed to conceal their hidden hand behind the persecution of bible-believing Christians in Islamic countries. They are falsely portraying the persecution of Christian churches as including the Roman Catholic Church, when in fact the Roman Church can operate freely and openly, in fact, a review of the Catholic Church Directory reveals that there is not a single Islamic country that does not have a Catholic Church that is allowed to practice freely and openly. All the while, bible believing Christians are hunted down and persecuted. The fact that the Roman Catholic Churches are allowed to operate openly in Islamic countries supports Alberto

Rivera's information that there is a concordat between Islam and the Vatican to allow Catholic Churches to operate in Islamic countries while those Islamic countries persecute the true Christian church.

Raymond Ibrahim and Scott Allswang revealed how the official Muslim theology calls for the elimination of biblical Christianity in Islamic countries, which makes it the perfect religion to do the dirty work for the Vatican in North Africa and the Middle East.

The Grand Mufti of Saudi Arabia, one of the Islamic world's highest religious authorities, declared that it is necessary to destroy all the churches of the region. He made his assertion in response to a question posed by a delegation from Kuwait, where a parliament member recently called for the "removal" of all churches: the delegation wanted to confirm Sharia's position on churches with the Grand Mufti, who "stressed that Kuwait was a part of the Arabian Peninsula, and therefore it is neccessary to destroy all churches in it," basing his verdict on a saying (or hadith) of Muhammad.

Upon visiting the global directory of Catholic churches we find that there are thriving Catholic churches in Kuwait in the cities of Ahmadi, Kuwait City, Moroni, and Salmiya. The Catholic Churches proudly post their addresses, phone numbers, fax numbers, and websites. One of the Catholic churches, Our Lady of Arabia Catholic Church," (check avona.org) "even has its weekly Mass schedule posted on the directory. The Roman Catholic churches seem not to have been affected at all by the fatwa from the Grand Mufti of Saudi Arabia calling for the elimination of all the churches in the region.

There have heen instances where Catholic priests, nuns, and churches have been attacked by Muslims in Arab countries. However, such incidents seem to be collateral consequences of the confusion among the rank and file Muslims, who equate Catholicism with Christianity, Mobs, once set in motion, are hard to control. The real target of the Muslim attacks is biblical Christianity.

According to the U. S. State Department's International Religious freedom Report for 2012, in Afghanistan "there are no public Christian churches. The report states that, because there are no public churches, "Afghan Christians worship alone or in small congregations in private homes. Oddly, the religious persecution of the Christian church in Afghanistan has increased since the arrival of U.S. troops. According to a news reports "Afghanistan has seen a decrease in religious liberty in the past decade, especially since American troops have been active there, The U.S. Government was instrumental in drafting and installing the 2004 Constitution of Afghanistan, which provided for an inviolable Islamic state, with no freedom of religion. At the time the Constitution of Afghanistan was approved, the country was under U.S. Military occupation. It is almost as if part and parcel of the military mission was to remove any Christian influence. That has certainly been the effect. Raymond Ibrahim and Scott Allswang reported:

Ten years after the LLS, invaded and overthrew the Taliban—at a cost of more than 1,700 U.S. military lives and S440 billion in taxpayer dollars the State Department revealed that Afghanistan's last Christian church was destroyed. The report further makes clear that the Afghan government - installed by the U.S. - is partially responsible for such anti-Christian sentiments, for instance, by upholding apostasy laws, which make it a criminal offence for Muslims to convert to other religions.

Apparently, the Catholic Church has been given a pass on the persecution. At the time the U.S. State Department reported that there were no longer any public churches in Afghanistan, there was (and still is today) a publicly listed Catholic Church in the capital city of Kabul, Afghanistan. The Catholic directory listing for the church includes its schedule of Masses for every day of the week, including 10 services on Sundays from (6:15 am to 12:00 pm), that open listing on the internet can be seen by any Afghanistan government official or Islamic leader, yet the church remains unmolested.

Certainly the U. S. State Department was aware of the existence of the Catholic church in Kabul when it announced that there were no public churches in Afghanistan. Why would the U.S. State Department make such a statement in the face of clear contrary evidence? One could hope that it is because the U.S. State Department did not consider the Catholic religion a Christian religion and therefore did not count it as such when stating that there were no Christian churches in Afghanistan. However, that certainly is not the reason the Catholic church in Kabul was not mentioned in the State Department report. The reason it was not mentioned is because to report that there was only one church in Afghanistan, a Catholic church, would reveal too much. That information, would give away the fact that only Protestant churches were targeted for destruction. That must be kept secret. The evidence of the targeting and wiping out of public Christian churches, while leaving Roman Catholic churches untouched, is yet more contemporary evidence that confirms the claim by former Jesuit Alberto Rivera of a secret concordat between the Vatican and Islamic leaders to act in concert against their common enemy, biblical Christianity.

Alberto Rivera's assertion regarding the secret concordat between Islam and the Vatican, wherein Catholics were allowed to occupy Lebanon in the Arab world, is also supported by the evidence. For example, since 1943, Lebanon has operated as a consociational government under an informal agreement known as the "National Pact," with power sharing between Maronite "Christians" (a Roman Catholic sect) and Muslims. This informal agreement was memorialized, with some changes, in the 1989 Taif Agreement, which gave more authority to the Muslim majority in Lebanon, but maintained the hegemony of the Catholic minority over the Lebanese government. In Lebanon, the President must be a Maronite "Christian.'" Furthermore, "Christians" are guaranteed at least 50% of the seats in the Lebanese Parliament, even though they make up less than 40% of the population." Antichrist: The beast Revealed by Edward Hendrie.

The image on the next page is another recorded example confirming that the papacy did not give up after Islam with attempts at planting their tabernacles in Jerusalem. That article was placed in The Review and Herald 13th of May, 1862 by Uriah Smith. Again, you will not find that article in today's officially printed versions of the SDA Review and Herald volumes.

THE REVIEW AND HERALD.

BATTLE CREEK, MICH., THIRD-DAY, MAY 13, 1862.

WILL THE POPE REMOVE THE PAPAL SEAT TO JERUSALEM.

"A CORRESPONDENT of the Liverpool Mercury, writing from Rome, states that French officers have latterly been very busy in obtaining information respecting Jerusalem, and the state of things in that quarter. He adds that they had been taking measurements in several localities, particularly the ground that lies about the Mosque of Omar, on Mount Moriah. From Jerusalem they had gone on to Hebron, Gaza, and other points, for the like purpose. It was also currently reported that a body of French troops were shortly to come to Jerusalem, while another would be stationed at Jaffa, and a third on mount Carmel. At Beyrout, he says, the French officers openly affirmed that their government had no intention of withdrawing the force sent out, but were about to employ them shortly on a new and very different errand to that for which they ostensibly came. The French were also actively employed in making a road from the Holy City to Damascus, along which they were erecting houses at certain intervals. It is said that such a scheme as this intelligence shows to be in course of development, points to the realizing of Pio Nono's favorite plan of *removing the seat of the Papacy to Jerusalem.*"

Is not the above item significant, taken in connection with Dan. xi, 45 ?   u. s.

Recent underhand manouevres by the papacy to shape events along with it's world view:

Can you remember or are you aware of all the trouble that developed in Poland around the Solidarity movement? Are you aware of the real reasons for Solidarity's existence? If not the following may come as a shock to you, and should give an idea of the manipulations taking place behind the scenes.

"The first instrument the Pope fomented - Solidarity was devised purely and simply as a model of sociocultural liberty. The sociocultural model in and of itself was not an original idea. It traced back at least as far as the argument set out by Thomas Aquinas seven hundred years ago to the effect that the two seminal and ineradicable loves of any individual human being are the love of God and the love of one's native country; and, further, that these can live and flourish only within the framework of a religious nationalism.

The greatest significance of Solidarity, therefore, was to be its function as a modern laboratory of sociocultural liberty rooted entirely and sufficiently in religious nationalism. If it was totally successful, it would be an important new ingredient introduced into the dough of international affairs that would produce a slow leavening of the materialist mind dominating East and West alike. To some degree, then, Solidarity was the first international arena in which John Paul's early idea – his early vision, if you will, of religious nationalism as the vehicle for sociocultural freedom – made its debut in the hostile territory of the Soviet Union, and at the same time went head-to-head with the basic premise of the capitalist superpower.

Solidarity alone would not do the trick, of course, the melting of the Soviet iceberg of materialist, anti-church and anti-God intransigence would, as John Paul saw the matter in 1979, be an intricate affair of papal policy that he would begin. But it would continue into another pontificate after he himself had joined his predecessors in the papal crypt beneath the altar of St. Peter's Basilica.

The policy toward the Soviet Union initiated in 1959-60 by Pope John XXIII, and subsequently elaborated from 1963 to 1978 into the well-known Ostpolitik of the Vatican under Pope Paul VI, presented a practical problem for John Paul.. Its essence was to contain Soviet aggression; to react to Soviet moves; and to wait for some favorable evolution within the Soviet system.

The solution for John Paul lay in the fact that there was nothing in the Vatican's Ostpolitik and nothing in the Vatican protocols, to keep him from attempting an end run around the Soviet Party-State. In precisely such a move, the new Holy Father set about building closer and ever closer ties with the Russian Orthodox Church and with Orthodoxy in general. This papal end run included certain overt moves – John Paul visited the Greek Orthodox center in Istanbul, for example; and he received and openly favored visits to the Vatican by Orthodox prelates. But there were also constant covert moves originating in Poland and radiating into western parts of the USSR, moves that fostered a common religious bond between Eastern European Catholics and Russian Orthodox communities.

By the opening of the eighties, about half of the Orthodox prelates were already secretly prepared, if the opportunity were afforded, to place themselves under the ecclesial unity of the Roman Pope. John Paul achieved some remarkable successes in the dynamic pursuit of his independent policies to sow the seeds of sociocultural change in the geopolitical soil of the East. Indeed, his assault on the Soviet monolith was key to the 1989 liberation of the Eastern European states. And by 1990 – almost overnight, as it seemed to the inattentive; - whole blocs of Russian believers voted themselves and their church property back into the Roman Catholic fold.

328

Nevertheless this was not a pope for halfhearted ventures, nor for half an international policy. His end run around Soviet officialdom was not a religious gambit, but a geopolitical strategy, and it was therefore joined to a twin policy to the West. The deepest and broadest effects of John Paul's policies were produced in the West as a direct consequence of his crisscrossing lines of world travel.

Within a brief time, it became so clear that Pope John Paul had taken his due place among the nation's leaders – even the United States reestablished formal diplomatic relations between Washington and the Vatican." Keys of this blood pp 42-45

Remember where it was noted earlier how the papal church regards miracles as a sign of the true church; the following account, even if it may seem a minor miracle is just an example. It is firmly connected to a failed attempt on John Paul's life in 1981.

"The attempted assassination of John Paul shocked the world as a planned act of high sacrilege. In its immediate intent, however, that most vile act had no religious significance. For it was an act committed against the Pope not as a religious leader but as a geopolitician well along on the highroad of success. The wrath that had boiled up in homicidal anger, and that by the remotest and most covert control had guided the actions of Ali Agca on that day, was the wrath of hegemonic interests separated from St. Peter's Square by huge distances of land and water, interests unwilling to see this Pope reintroduce the Holy See as an independent an uncontrollable force in international affairs.

Already John Paul's successes in Poland had jiggered alliances presumed to have been inviolable. As he had widened the ambit of his attention and his energies, he had consistently shown himself to be a leader capable of carrying out his intention to shape events, and to determine the success or failure of secular policies for the New World Order. He had not opened the new game of nations by chance, as some had originally thought. He was not some papal Alice who had carelessly fallen down a geopolitical rabbit hole and then wondered where he had landed. He was a purposeful contender for power, who cast a shadow that had already blocked the light of success from the eyes of some of diametrically opposed plans for the geopolitical future of the society of nations. Better, then, to cut that shadow down to the abject shades of death in the noonday glare of the Italian sun.

Given the fact that the attempt to murder him was itself a badge of his geopolitical success, there was no earthly reason to expect John Paul to change his vision of the new world order or his agenda to influence it. It was not lost on him, however, that the attempt on his life had taken place on May 13. Or that a series of very curious supernatural events - events of intimate interest to the papacy - had begun on May 13, 1917, in the obscure Portugeuse hamlet of Fatima, and had ended there on October 13 of the same year with a miracle centered on the Virgin Mary and her apparent power to control the sun in spectacular ways. Nor, finally, was it lost on him that, but for the picture of the Virgin of Fatima pinned to the blouse of the little girl, his skull would have been shattered by the first bullets of Ali Agca's gun.

Given such circumstances, it would have been a stony papal heart indeed that could have refused to re-examine the compelling events that had taken place over five months, from spring to fall, in 1917.

Like most Catholics the world over, Karol Wojtyla had been acquainted for as long as he could remember with most of the facts about Fatima. The Virgin Mary had appeared several times to three peasant children; she had confided to them certain admonishments and instructions, including a detailed set of instructions and predictions that were intended for papal action at a certain time in the future; and she had ended her visits in October with a miracle that recalled for many the Bible verse that tells of a "Woman clothed with the Sun, and giving birth to a Son who will rule the Nations with a scepter of iron."

It is very important to mention that this prophecy alluded to this event describes the persecuted church, and the irony is, that the Papal Church was the persecuting church, and will be a persecuting church again in the future, more on this later.

"Once elected Pope in 1978, John Paul had become privy to the papal instructions and predictions Mary had entrusted in confidence to the children at Fatima. That part of her message dealt with matters of tribulation for the Roman Catholic institutional organization, and with the troubled future of mankind in general.

Like his two predecessors, John XXIII and Paul VI, Pope John Paul had long since accepted the authenticity of the Fatima events of 1917. In fact, he had been rooted and reared in a certain special intimacy Poles have always cultivated with Mary as the mother of God; and his papal motto reflected his personal and public dedication to her. Still, as those same predecessors had done, John Paul had always taken the papal instructions and predictions of Fatima as a matter for the future. "This matter." John XXIII had written of Fatima in 1960, "does not concern Our time." This matter. Pope John Paul had concluded in 1978, does not concern my pontificate. Based on the facts available, it seemed a legitimate judgment call at the time.

Now, however – after what were arguably the very pointed events that had taken place in St. Peter's Square; after exhaustive examination of the documents and living witnesses and participants connected with the Fatima events themselves; and after nothing less than a personal communication from heaven during his long convalescence - John Paul was all but forced to face the full meaning of Stefan Cardinal Wyszynski's familiar maxim that "certain events are willed by the Lord of History, and they shall take place."

More, he came face-to-face with the realization that, far from pointing to some distant future time, the contents of the now famous Fatima message - and, specifically, the secret contents directed to papal attention - amounted to a geopolitical agenda attached to an immediate timetable.

Gone was the Pope's agenda in which Central Europe figured as the primary springboard for lasting geopolitical change, ... Instead, there was now no doubt in John Paul's mind that Heaven's agenda had located the catalyst of geopolitical change in Russia.

Gone, too, was the pope's presumed time frame involving a leisurely and relatively peaceful evolution from the traditional system of sovereign and interacting nation-states to a veritable New World Order. Instead, there was now no doubt in John Paul's mind that in Heaven's agenda, all would be thrown into the cauldron of human judgment gone awry; of human evil sanctioned by men as normal; of unparalled natural catastrophes, ...

When Pope John Paul had left the Apostolic Palace to greet and bless the people in St. Peter's Square that May 13 of 1981, he had done so as the leading practitioner of the geopolitics of power. By the time he took up his papal schedule again six months later, his entire papal strategy had been raised to the level upon which the "Lord of History" arranges the geopolitics of faith.

In its essence, ..Fatima became for John Paul something like the famed Heavenly mandate and guarantee of success proffered to Constantine on the eve of his battle at the Milvian Bridge. Suddenly, Constantine had seen the Sign of the Cross appear in the sky, accompanied by the latin words In hoc signo vinces. "In this sign you will conquer." Improbable as it was, Constantine took that sign as anything but unrealistic or unworldly. He took it as a guarantee. With miraculous confidence, he not only conquered at the Milvian Bridge but proceeded to conquer his entire world, transforming it into what became the new civilisation of Christianity.

True, Pope John Paul was not a sword-toting conqueror; and at Fatima, Mary hadn't exactly said, "In this sign you will conquer." But she had given a mandate that was every bit as clear. And as a consequence, in the light of what he now understood his situation to be, the millenium endgame became as important and as urgent for John Paul as the international situation had become for Constantine in his time."

For those who do not know the scriptural truth on the matter of Mary still being alive, they would be deceived by this touching story. Mary is not alive, but as dead as all other human beings who have gone before, and will be when we pass away. Since Mary is dead, the vision could have come from none else than Satan.

"With stunning clarity, the Pope now knew that there was even less time left than he had thought for the old adversarial juxtaposition of East and West that still held sway in 1981 across the face of Europe and the wide world. Within a scant four years of the change in John Paul's geopolitical outlook, thrust so brusquely upon him between the spring and fall of 1981, Mikhail Gorbachev emerged from the heartland of Russia, right on schedule, as the agent of unimagined and unimaginable change in the old world order. Suddenly, nothing – not even the Kremlin fortress in Moscow itself – seemed permanent. Suddenly, the whole world was expectant.

Clearly, the new agenda - Heaven's agenda; the Grand Design of God for the New World Order - had begun. And Pope John Paul would stride now in the arena of the millenium endgame as something more than a geopolitical giant of his age. He was, and remains, the serene and confident Servant of the Grand Design." KOB pp 46-50.

Notice the words "Servant of the Grand Design." Whose grand design?

"From the outset of his pontificate, John Paul has found increasing awareness among his peers about what is happening in world affairs. Though some were as articulate in their practical judgment about those affairs as John Paul, all have demonstrated at least a growing intuition about the two primary forces that are reshaping the world in the final decade of the millenium. Everyone he has spoken to agrees with the pope at some level that there is in the making nothing less than a world system, determining relationships between all the nations that constitute human society.

And predictably enough, all agree with him that this world system – this newly minted and all-encompassing interdependence that is coming into existence – includes economic, political, cultural and sectarian elements.

What was less predictable for many onlookers was the success John Paul has achieved in hammering home what he is certain is the most basic fact of all: the fact that interdependence among nations must be based upon some common agreement as to moral good and moral evil in modern life. And, further, that if such common agreement cannot be reached as a working basis of globalism, then all attempts at establishing a new world order will end only in disaster." KOB 159.

That it will end in disaster John the Revelator states: "And the ten horns which thou sawest are ten kings, which have received no kingdom as yet," (ten in prophetic symbolism denotes universal) "but receive power one hour with the beast." (this beast is the same whore of revelation) "And the ten horns which thou sawest upon the beast, these shall hate the whore, and shall make her desolate and naked, and shall eat her flesh, and burn her with fire. For God hath put it in their hearts to fulfill his will, and to agree, and give their kingdom unto the beast, until the words of God shall be fulfilled." Revelation 17:12, 16-18.

John foresaw that all the nations of the earth will give their kingdoms to the beast.

"What captures the unwavering attention of the secular leaders of the world in this remarkable network of the Roman Catholic Church is precisely the fact that it places at the personal disposal of the Pope a supranational, supracontinental, supra-trade-bloc structure that is so built and oriented that if tomorrow or next week, by a sudden miracle, a one-world government were established, the Church would not have to undergo any essential structural change in order to retain its dominant position and to further its global aims." KOB p 143.

Again John confirms this development "How much she hath glorified herself, and lived deliciousiy, .. and the kings of the earth who have committed fornication with her and lived deliciously with her, ..and the merchants of the earth ..which were made rich by her..." Revelation 18:7-15.

Therefore many of the leaders and businessmen will make a conscious decision to join with the papacy in his supposed answer for the problems of mankind. Many of the large corporations and conglomerates already have a global view with regards to their expansion plans, as they regard this as the only way forward. Others on the religious sphere also regard unity of religions as the only way forward, to eliminate all religious wars etc. Pope John Paul places them all under the banner of globalist groups, and maintains an intimate knowledge of them all. He analyzes them in terms of categories and subcategories and has spoken about many of them publicly from time to time. He has met both publicly and privately, on his world travels and in the Vatican, with leaders and representatives of all of them.

"From his vantage point at the hub of the Vatican – the world's greatest listening post – Pope John Paul is so acutely aware of the daily moves and long-range plans of each major globalist group, that it is as though each of these groups maintained a "situation room." A sort of high-command headquarters in which tactics and strategies and ultimate aims are laid out across the maps and action models on display. It is as though the Pope himself could enter those imaginary "situation rooms," unseen in his white robes .... It is as though he could listen to all the discussions and debates about the shape of the coming world and about each group's hoped-for system of global order." KOB p 282.

Do you begin to see how all the world will fall in with the pope? It is because they already want to form some system of a unified world; when a solution is presented to them all which looks feasible, they will accept it. What or who, are some of the major groups that the pope eyes so closely?

"The Angelists (Muslims). – They number over 700 million, (1.8bn 2017) and are all united under the light of faith and the law of Islam, even though they may vary in terms of moderates or extremists. They all regard the West especially America as the Great Satan. They also regard Israel as an enemy, making it presently impossible to guarantee peace in that area.

Despite all this, Pope John Paul considers their faith as genuinely religious, and preserves certain fundamental truths that the Holy Spirit reveals or speaks to all people of good will. He expects that in God's providence that the adherents of Islam, because of the Holy Spirit aspect, will be prepared to accept the only historical revelation made by God to this world. The pope believes that there will come a day when the heart of Islam already attuned to Christ and his mother Mary, will receive the illumination it needs. Presently though, the pope realises that Islam stands against his vision of global power." *(yes, the papacy will need to bring unwitting muslims back into line with their leaders first secret plans, it will be very interesting to see how that unfolds)*

"As for the next groups of Christians and non-Christians, who he regards as minimalists, because they expect to be the remnant who will remain out of a world of corrupt or sinful peoples. They are considered to be in the upper economic income brackets, and number in the region of 7 million per grouping, namely Baptists, Evangelists, Seventh-Day Adventists, excepting Jehovah's Witnesses

337

who number in six figures and who he considers, as well as Mormons and Christian scientists, as non-Christian.

He has problems with these groups in different ways; with the Seventh-Day Adventists, Advent Christians, Abrahamic faith and others, in that they all regard the papacy as the whore of revelation; the Mormons and Scientists on the other hand deny the central tenet of Catholicism, the divinity of Christ. He also states that they have all at some stage disembarked from the battered but ever advancing caravan of the Roman Church. Each group has remained where they got off, and continue to retain deep objections to the authority of the Pope.

However, he maintains that like the Angelists, they also have some element of the full revelation made by God to his Church, and that on the day of reward, will be integrated into the full faith of Christ, before the last day comes. It is axiomatic for John Paul that no one has the right – democratic or otherwise – to a moral wrong, as these groups hold; (since God has left us the freedom of choice) and no religion based on divine revelation has a moral right to teach such a moral wrong or to abide by it.

He also places the Animists, Shintoists, Hindus and Buddhists in another grouping; Non-Christians. It is interesting though, that New Agers are deriving a lot of their ideas from these groups.

The final grouping is of The Jews, Chinese, and Japanese. It is believed that you can only be of those nations if you are born of them, even though any of them can become proper Americans or Englishmen etc.. The Jews allow you to convert, to Judaism, but you can never become a Jew. These, according to him pose a big problem.

John Paul is constantly engaged in dialogue with representatives of all these groups, and his vision is that the best in all these groups, i.e. their sense of dignity and mission, will become a potent element in the building of a genuinely God-blessed structure for all nations."

Do I need to add anything more to this? Yes, just a little more. October 31, 2017 supposedly marked the death of protestantism.

"Pope Francis has praised the move on the part of the World Communion of Reformed Churches (WCRC), the largest association of Reformed Churches representing 80 million members in 108 nations. The WCRC has joined the Methodist Church and the Lutheran Church by signing their names to the Joint Declaration on the Doctrine of Justification.

This declaration was an agreement between the Lutheran Church and the Roman Catholic Church that basically ended the protest raised by Martin Luther just over 500 years ago. It states that the churches now share a "common understanding" on justification, God's grace and salvation – the very doctrinal issues for why the Protestant Reformation began in the first place.

The 74-million strong World Lutheran Federation, and the Roman Catholic Church signed the agreement between the two faiths on October 31, 1999.

The World Methodist Council, with its 80.5 million members, unanimously decided to adopt the same agreement with the Catholic Church in 2006.

The World Communion of Reformed Churches, includes members of the Congregational, Presbyterian, Reformed,

United, Uniting, and Waldensian churches that have adopted the joint declaration with Rome.

Roman Catholics, Lutherans, Methodists, and now various Reformed Protestant Churches have united in their basic understanding and teachings of the "gospel."

This signing ceremony between Protestants and Roman Catholics took place in the town of Wittenberg, Germany. It was in Wittenberg that Martin Luther nailed his 95 Theses to the door of the Roman Catholic Church on October 31, 1517 protesting the corruption of the church. 500 years later Protestants have come full circle. And in the very place where Protestantism was born, Protestantism has 'died.'

A new era of cooperation and unity has begun. Rome is now experiencing a time of healing and reconciliation with this latest signing. Rome has overcome the divisions of the past and is coming into full unity with the Protestant Churches. These churches have now accepted each other's faith as equally valid. Even though Christians are called to unity, this unity should not be achieved by sacrificing the clear Biblical teachings of Scriptures. Doctrine is paramount, especially when it concerns the principles of the faith."
"God is a Spirit and they that worship him must worship him in spirit and in truth." John 4:24.

Notice the reasons why millions of sincere Christians during the Dark Ages left the fellowship of the Roman Catholic Church in the first place.

"After a long and severe conflict, the faithful few decided to dissolve all union with the apostate church if she still refused to free herself from falsehood and idolatry. They saw that separation was an absolute necessity if they would obey the word of God. They dared not tolerate errors fatal to their own souls, and set an example which would imperil the faith of their children and children's children. To secure peace and unity they were ready to make any concession consistent with fidelity to God; but they felt that even peace would be too dearly purchased at the sacrifice of principle. If unity could be secured only by the compromise of truth and righteousness, then let there be difference, and even war. The Great Controversy p45." Advent Messenger, July 8, 2017.

The ecumenical movement and the emerging church are also great tools of THE MYSTERY's deception being used in our modern times to bring about 'unity' amongst protestant churches, Satan, through the pope, has been engineering during the past millenia. How many times do we hear 'love' as the most important doctrine nowadays? How extensive is the Islamisation of Britain and Europe becoming since the rise of Isis and the scattering of millions of muslims into Britain and Europe, is this also another deliberate ploy?

The real truth about the emerging church's underlying doctrine of panentheism is that God is in everything and is looking to emerge from being in everything to becoming physically present amongst us as a separate entity. I wonder who will be appearing? Or do I need to wonder? The Angel of Light? Lucifer? And where best if not in Jerusalem?

In order to succeed in planting his tabernacles, the Pope needs the support of a military power, we will discuss this in the next chapter. However, he may well need the Jews. Didn't the pope want to destroy the Jews? Was the holocaust a smokescreen or part of a grand scheme?

What do some of the Jews believe about Jesus and what have they been up to in recent years?

There are Jews that believe and teach that the Messiah has not come yet. Have they forgotten the wise men from the east who followed a star, visited Jerusalem and enquired of Herod where the King of the Jews was to be born? All the chief priests and scribes gathered together and told Herod that according to the prophets, Jesus was to be born in Bethlehem? There are also over 300 prophecies about the coming of the Messiah that were fulfilled in the First Advent of Jesus. Incredible but true. These Jews can be described as Mashiach Jews. I'm quoting from their sources.

"Mashiach: The Messiah - I believe with perfect faith in the coming of the mashiach, and though he may tarry, still I await him every day. - Principle 12 of Rambam's 13 Principles of Faith

The Messiac Idea in Judaism - Belief in the eventual coming of the mashiach is a basic and fundamental part of traditional Judaism. It is part of Rambam's 13 Principles of Faith, the minimum requirements of Jewish belief. In the Shemoneh Esrei prayer, recited three times daily, we pray for all of the elements of the coming of the mashiach: ingathering of the exiles; restoration of the religious courts of justice; an end of wickedness, sin and heresy; reward to the righteous; rebuilding of Jerusalem; restoration of the line of King David; and restoration of Temple service.

Modern scholars suggest that the messianic concept was introduced later in the history of Judaism, during the age of the prophets. They note that the messianic concept is not explicitly mentioned anywhere in the Torah (the first five books of the Bible).

However, traditional Judaism maintains that the messianic idea has always been a part of Judaism. The mashiach is not mentioned explicitly in the Torah, because the Torah was written in terms that all people could understand, and the abstract concept of a distant, spiritual, future reward was beyond the comprehension of some people. However, the Torah contains several references to "the End of Days" (acharit ha-yamim), which is the time of the mashiach; thus, the concept of mashiach was known in the most ancient times.

The term "mashiach" literally means "the anointed one," and refers to the ancient practice of anointing kings with oil when they took the throne. The mashiach is the one who will be anointed as king in the End of Days.

The word "mashiach" does not mean "savior." The notion of an innocent, divine or semi-divine being who will sacrifice himself to save us from the consequences of our own sins is a purely Christian concept that has no basis in Jewish thought. Unfortunately, this Christian concept has become so deeply ingrained in the English word "messiah" that this English word can no longer be used to refer to the Jewish concept....

Some gentiles have told me that the term "mashiach" is related to the Hebrew term "moshiah" (savior) because they sound similar, but the similarity is not as strong as it appears to one unfamiliar with Hebrew. The Hebrew word "mashiach" comes from the root Mem-Shin-Chet, which means to paint, smear, or annoint. The word "moshiah" comes from the root Yod-Shin-Ayin, which means to help or save. The only letter these roots have in common is Shin, the most common letter in the Hebrew language. The "m" sound at the beginning of the word moshiah (savior) is a common prefix used to turn a verb into a noun. For example, the verb tzavah (to command) becomes mitzvah (commandment). Saying that "mashiach" is related to "moshiah" is a bit like saying that ring is related to surfing because they both end in "ing."

The mashiach will be a great political leader descended from King David (Jeremiah 23:5). The mashiach is often referred to as "mashiach ben David" (mashiach, son of David). He will be well-versed in Jewish law, and observant of its commandments (Isaiah 11:2-5). He will be a charismatic leader, inspiring others to follow his example. He will be a great military leader, who will win battles for Israel. He will be a great judge, who makes righteous decisions (Jeremiah 33:15). But above all, he will be a human being, not a god, demi-god or other supernatural being.

It has been said that in every generation, a person is born with the potential to be the mashiach. If the time is right for the messianic age within that person's lifetime, then that person will be the mashiach. But if that person dies before he completes the mission of the mashiach, then that person is not the mashiach.

When Will the Mashiach Come? - There are a wide variety of opinions on the subject of when the mashiach will come. Some of Judaism's greatest minds have cursed those who try to predict the time of the mashiach's coming, because errors in such predictions could cause people to lose faith in the messianic idea or in Judaism itself. This actually happened in the 17th century, when Shabbatai Tzvi claimed to be the mashiach. When Tzvi converted to Islam under threat of death, many Jews converted with him. Nevertheless, this prohibition has not stopped anyone from speculating about the time when the mashiach will come.

Although some scholars believed that G-d has set aside a specific date for the coming of the mashiach, most authority suggests that the conduct of mankind will determine the time of the mashiach's coming. In general, it is believed that the mashiach will come in a time when he is most needed (because the world is so sinful), or in a time when he is most deserved (because the world is so good). For example, each of the following has been suggested as the time when the mashiach will come:

if Israel repented a single day;
if Israel observed a single Shabbat properly;
if Israel observed two Shabbats in a row properly;
in a generation that is totally innocent or totally guilty;
in a generation that loses hope;
in a generation where children are totally disrespectful towards their parents and elders;

What Will the Mashiach Do? - Before the time of the mashiach, there shall be war and suffering (Ezekiel 38:16)

The mashiach will bring about the political and spiritual redemption of the Jewish people by bringing us back to Israel and restoring Jerusalem (Isaiah 11:11-12; Jeremiah 23:8; 30:3; Hosea 3:4-5). He will establish a government in Israel that will be the center of all world government, both for Jews and gentiles (Isaiah 2:2-4; 11:10; 42:1). He will rebuild the Temple and re-establish its worship (Jeremiah 33:18). He will restore the religious court system of Israel and establish Jewish law as the law of the land (Jeremiah 33:15)." Does this sound like plans for a world government?

Israeli Rabbi Says He's already holding Meetings with Messiah

"A snapshot of Israel's spiritual hunger as biggest rabbis are afraid to leave the country lest they miss Messiah's coming" October 15, 2020, Ryan Jones.

A recent interview on Israeli radio again featured prominent rabbis explaining that the Messiah is just about to reveal himself.

Rabbi Yaakov Zisholtz told religious broadcaster Radio 2000 that Rabbi Rabbi Chaim Kanievsky recently told him that he (Kanievsky) is already in direct contact with the Messiah.

To understand why religious Jews are taking this seriously, it's important to know that Rabbi Chaim Kanievsky is considered one of the two or three top rabbis of the ultra-Orthodox Jewish community in Israel.

And Rabbi Zisholtz says that Kanievsky and others of the mystical *"concealed" rabbis* have now tasked him with informing the public of the Messiah's imminent arrival.

Rabbi Zisholtz began his explosive three-hour interview with a warning:

"...the process of redemption is about to start happening very quickly and at a fast pace. It is important that people remain calm and steady to act properly in the right time.

"There is a potential Messiah in every generation and there are righteous men who know precisely who it is. This is, of course, true in this generation.
"Getting the word out now that the Messiah is closer than ever is a matter of life and death. Haven't you heard of Gog and Magog? That is what is going to happen very soon. Right now, the situation is explosive more than you can possibly imagine. Everyone needs to know whether they are on the inside or if they are going to be left out."

He went on to reiterate a number of signs of which prominent rabbis have *taken note* and that they firmly believe to be evidence of the coming of Messiah.

"Rabbi Dov Kook, as everyone knows, is a very righteous man. He is one of the greatest men of our generation… [and] ten years ago, when Israel was suffering from a horrible drought, someone asked Rabbi Kook when the Sea of Galilee will again be full," recounted Rabbi Zisholtz. "Rabbi Kook responded that when the Messiah arrives, the Sea of Galilee will be full. In a few weeks, the Sea of Galilee will be full for the first time since Rabbi Kook made this statement."

"Another righteous rabbi said that according to the current situation in heaven, there will not be Israeli elections – rather, there will be a war," cautioned Zisholtz. "If the elections do take place, it's pointless since it will end like the other elections; no government will come out of it. No one will take the government away from Netanyahu."

Decades ago, Rabbi Yitzhak Kaduri, one of modern Israel's most revered sages, as well as the Lubavitcher Rebbe, Rabbi Menachem Schneerson, both predicted that Benjamin Netanyahu would be the State of Israel's last prime minister prior to the Messianic Age. A great many, if not most of the ultra-Orthodox Jews in Israel continue to believe that to be true." https://bit.ly/3q53tOf

"Olam Ha-Ba: The Messianic Age - The world after the messiah comes is often referred to in Jewish literature as Olam Ha-Ba (oh-LAHM hah-BAH), the World to Come. This term can cause some confusion, because it is also used to refer to a spiritual afterlife. In English, we commonly use the term "messianic age" to refer specifically to the time of the messiah.

Olam Ha-Ba will be characterized by the peaceful co-existence of all people (Isaiah 2:4). Hatred, intolerance and war will cease to exist. Some authorities suggest that the laws of nature will change, so that predatory beasts will no longer seek prey and agriculture will bring forth supernatural abundance (Isaiah 11:6-11:9). Others, however, say that these statements are merely an allegory for peace and prosperity.

All of the Jewish people will return from their exile among the nations to their home in Israel (Isaiah 11:11-12; Jeremiah 23:8; 30:3; Hosea 3:4-5). The law of the Jubilee will be reinstated.

In the Olam Ha-Ba, the whole world will recognize the Jewish G-d as the only true G-d, and the Jewish religion as the only true religion (Isaiah 2:3; 11:10; Micah 4:2-3;

Zechariah 14:9). There will be no murder, robbery, competition or jealousy. There will be no sin (Zephaniah 3:13). Sacrifices will continue to be brought in the Temple, but these will be limited to thanksgiving offerings, because there will be no further need for expiatory offerings.

Some gentiles have tried to put an ugly spin on this theology, claiming that Jews plan to force people to convert to our religion, perhaps based on their own religion's history of doing exactly the same thing. That is not at all how Jews understand the messianic age. We believe that in that future time, everyone will simply know what the truth is, in the same way that we know that 2+2=4, and there will no longer be any reason to argue about it. It is much like a situation I witnessed at work once: two computer programmers were arguing loudly and at length about whether it was possible for a user to input data at a certain point in a program. Finally someone pressed a key and they all saw that nothing happened. Now they knew the truth, end of argument. When mashiach comes, theological truths will be equally obvious to mankind, and there will be no reason to argue about it.

What About Jesus? – Some Jews do not believe that Jesus was the mashiach. Assuming that he existed, they state, and assuming that the Christian scriptures are accurate in describing him, he simply did not fulfill the mission of the mashiach as it is described in the biblical passages cited above. Jesus did not do any of the things that the scriptures said the messiah would do."

(The above statement is incredible, what history are those Jews reading?)

"On the contrary, another Jew born about a century later came far closer to fulfilling the messianic ideal than Jesus

349

did. His name was Shimeon ben Kosiba, known as Bar Kokhba (son of a star), and he was a charismatic, brilliant, but brutal warlord. Rabbi Akiba, one of the greatest scholars in Jewish history, believed that Bar Kokhba was the mashiach. Bar Kokhba fought a war against the Roman Empire, catching the Tenth Legion by surprise and retaking Jerusalem. He resumed sacrifices at the site of the Temple and made plans to rebuild the Temple. He established a provisional government and began to issue coins in its name. This is what the Jewish people were looking for in a mashiach; Jesus clearly does not fit into this mold. Ultimately, however, the Roman Empire crushed his revolt and killed Bar Kokhba. After his death, all acknowledged that he was not the mashiach.

Throughout Jewish history, there have been many people who have claimed to be the mashiach, or whose followers have claimed that they were the mashiach: Shimeon Bar Kokhba, Shabbatai Tzvi, Jesus, and many others too numerous to name. Leo Rosten reports some very entertaining accounts under the entry for meshiekh in The New Joys of Yiddish. But all of these people died without fulfilling the mission of the mashiach; therefore, none of them were the mashiach. The mashiach and the Olam Ha-Ba lie in the future, not in the past."

How about Papal assertion that the Apostle Peter was the first Pope? What was Peter, a gentile or Jew? Remember also the Mashiach Jews are insisting that the Mashiach must be a descendant of King David? Are we then to expect that the Pope that will succeed will be a Jew? Have their been Jewish Popes? There are some indications, somewhat speculative, that there have been several Jews that have been Popes. Cardinals are the priests that can be elected as Pope through their selection process and we do have information that we did have a Cardinal who was of the line of David, although now deceased, he could have been selected as Pope in our modern times if the situation allowed it.

"Cardinal O'Connor Was a Jew - Does it really matter?
by Rabbi Nechemia Coopersmith

So it turns out the Cardinal John Joseph O'Connor, the Catholic Church's top official in New York for 16 years until his death in 2000, was a Jew.

Mary O'Connor Ward, the cardinal's 87-year-old sister, recently discovered that their mother was Jewish, a daughter of an Orthodox rabbi, while digging into her genealogical roots. Their Prussian-born maternal grandparents were Gustave Gumpel and Tina Ruben, who are buried in a Jewish cemetery in Fairfeld, Conn.

New York's Cardinal John J. O'Connor shakes hands with Israeli prime minister Yitzhak Shamir during a meeting in Jerusalem, Jan. 5, 1992.

According to the New York Times, Gustave Gumpel was the rabbi of B'nai Israel and a butcher in the late 1800s. His

351

first wife died in 1890, and his second wife, Tina, died 10 years after coming to the United States, leaving Rabbi Gumpel to raise a large blended family on his own. Cardinal O'Connor's mother, (Deborah on her 1887 birth certificate, Dora in the 1900 census, and Dorothy when she converted to Catholicism in 1908) was a toddler when her mother died. She was raised by two half sisters in difficult circumstances and fled from home as soon as she came of age, never to come back. Apparently two other sisters also left the family and their Jewish heritage behind.

My gut reaction to reading about Cardinal O'Connor's Jewish roots was one of sadness (different than the JTA who wrote, "Is this really a big deal? Let's say the cardinal really was Jewish. It runs in the family, because so was his boss"). This is not a "cool" story. It's a human tragedy: a young girl, bereft of her mother, flees from her home. And it's a Jewish tragedy: a Jewish girl abandons her religion and people.

Cardinal O'Connor was a powerful leader who was a staunch defender of the Jewish people. He spoke often about what he had seen at Dachau as a Navy chaplain, fought for Soviet Jewry, and played a role in the Vatican's recognition of Israel. Upon his death the New York Times wrote that he was a "towering presence, a leader whose views and personality were forcefully injected into the great civic debates of his time, a man who considered himself a conciliator, but who never hesitated to be a combatant."

Imagine what he would have accomplished for the Jewish people if his mother would have remained committed to Judaism and given her son a strong Jewish education.
Just imagine what the Cardinal would have accomplished for the Jewish people if his mother would have remained

committed to Judaism and given her son, Yochanan Yosef, a strong Jewish education. Of course we can't judge his mother, but we can mourn the loss to the Jewish nation. The reality of assimilation isn't fully expressed through statistics alone. Every Jew is an entire world. The toll of assimilation is more acutely felt when you think about the mindboggling loss of Jewish individuals, families and future descendants who could have made enormous contributions to the Jewish people.

Link in the Chain - The same day I read about Mary O'Connor's discovery through genealogy of her family's Jewish lineage I received a file from my wife's cousin that conveys the thorough research into my wife's grandmother's family tree. It turns out that even though she herself wasn't especially religious, she was a direct descendant of some of the greatest rabbinic figures in the last 1000 years. Rashi, the foremost commentator on the Chumash and Talmud, is her 25th great grandfather. The Shach, Rabbi Shabtai HaCohen, and the Rema, Rabbi Moshe Isserles, are her 11th great grandfathers. The list includes a wide range of European Jewish leaders, judges, and authors since the Middle Ages. We were amazed. Who knew?

Chances are very likely that if any Jew today would trace their direct lineage back 25 generations they would also discover that they are descendants of some of the greatest leading scholars and Jewish leaders in Jewish history.

What difference does it make? Two things strike me.

One, it makes the chain of Jewish history far more vivid when I see plotted out on paper the ancestral sequence linking my wife's grandmother, who died this year, directly to Rashi. I am not just a Jew living in the present in a vacuum; I am part of dynamic chain of transmission that stretches a few thousand years, and I am the present link in the chain.

And knowing the illustriousness of my family's personal lineage gives me a greater sense of the privilege and responsibility to carry that legacy forward.
I wonder if things would have been different if Cardinal O'Connor had discovered as a young child that he was a direct descendant of the Vilna Gaon, Rashi or King David."

"…According to halachah, or traditional Jewish law, anyone with a Jewish mother is considered Jewish.

O'Connor had close ties with New York's Jewish community and co-authored a book with the late New York City mayor, Ed Koch, who was Jewish. O'Connor often described Jews as Catholics' "elder brothers," marched in protests to free Soviet Jews, visited the site of the Dachau concentration camp and joined Jews in commemorating the Holocaust. A native of Philadelphia, O'Connor became an auxiliary bishop in 1979 and bishop of Scranton, Pa., in 1983. In 1984, Pope John Paul II named him archbishop of New York, a position he held until his death, and O'Connor was made a cardinal in 1985…."

What else are the Jews involved in that will assist the Papacy with its goals. They are either ignorant that their initiatives will assist the Papacy or they are complicit?

The Green Sabbath Project:

Opening Statement – "In the face of the urgent environmental crises that the world faces, multiple solutions are necessary: technological, political, economic, ethical and behavioral."

Mission

"Welcome to the Green Sabbath Project! Our main focus is education and advocacy. Our mission is to spark a mass movement of observance of a weekly day of rest -- shabbat, sabbath, a green sabbath or a weekly earth day -- on which impact on the environment is minimized as much as possible. We envision individuals and groups choosing whichever day is most meaningful to them. While inspired by ancient religious sources, the green sabbath is a self-consciously refashioned ritual practice aimed at addressing current realities. As taken up by individuals and communities, it may or may not be connected to organized religion or God.

Our website features readings, crowd-sourced liturgy, graphics for advocacy campaigns available for use, suggestions for sabbath activities, a global calendar regarding local (green) sabbath get-togethers and actions links to related campaigns and organizations, and more. Our materials and events span the range of approaches: religious, spiritual, pantheistic, agnostic and materialist."

(Take careful note that all belief systems are catered for. This confirms that this project is not Godly. If it was Godly it would only promote the one and only Sabbath as instituted by our Creator)

The propositions from the Green Sabbath Project were foretold to occur as far back as 1888.

"The mark of the beast is to be presented in some shape to every institution and every individual." Ellen G White 1888 Materials 477.2. This is exactly what is happening, I quote "Our materials and events span the range of approaches: religious, spiritual, pantheistic, agnostic and materialist."

What does the "Green Sabbath" initiative prove? There is a Sabbath that was instituted in the past, created by God just as He created everything else.

We continue -
Vision

"The multidimensional nature of our environmental crises demands holistic responses. We believe that our sabbath days must become a time of active avoidance of environmental vandalism, a time for programmatic congregational and individual reflection on how we are undoing creation. We intend green sabbaths to be a radical ritual within which we can digest anew the biblical prophets' warnings against the corruption of the rich and powerful, the oppression of the poor and the self-centered pursuit of short-sighted pleasures, understanding how relevant such warnings are to the ecological devastation wrought by hypercapitalism. Sabbath properly practiced offers a weekly investment in family and local community, a weekly interruption of the suicidal econometric fantasy of infinite growth, a weekly divestment from fossil fuels, a weekly moment of rewilding. As Greta Thunberg reminds us, we already know what the solutions are for our environmental crises. Green sabbaths provide a recurring weekly greenhouse for incubating the required collective consciousness and willpower — the ultimate renewable energies — to make the solutions reality. Green sabbaths will constitute both a model of the ecologically-sane world to come and an actual foretaste of it."

The majority members of the Advisory Board are Jews. *(I'm not against the Jews, I'm only confirming who is*

356

*driving this and shockingly some of the leaders,(Rabbis) of the Jewish nation, a Nation that historically was selected by God as the guardians of God's only True Sabbath. Through this initiative are confirming their consistency in betraying that sacred trust that was given to their forefathers, Abraham, Isaac and Jacob. They were supposed to spread God's truth to all the nations around them, but they didn't. The Rabbis over 2,000 years ago orchestrated the betrayal of Christ and demanded Barabbas be freed and Christ to be crucified. All of their support will play directly into the hands of the Papacy because of the Papacy's usurped "**Moral Authority over the world**") I must add at this point that there are many Jews that have accepted Jesus as their Messiah and Saviour.*

Rabbi Ellen Bernstein (Holyoke, MA)
Dr. Jeremy Benstein
The Heschel Center for Sustainability, Tel Aviv

Rabbi Michael Cohen
Arava Institute for Environmental Studies

Center for the Advancement of Public Action, Bennington College

Einat Kramer
Founder and Executive Director, Teva Ivri

Bill McKibben
Schumann Distinguished Scholar, Middlebury College
Rabbi Yonatan Neril
Founder and Executive Director, Interfaith Center for Sustainable Development

Rabbi Micha Odenheimer

Founder and Director Emeritus, Tevel B'Tzedek
David W. Orr
Paul Sears Professor of Environmental Studies and Politics
Emeritus, Oberlin College

Nigel Savage
Founder and Executive Director, Hazon

Rabbi David Mevorach Seidenberg, Alon Tal.
Professor, Dept. of Public Policy, Tel Aviv University
Rabbi Jonathan Wittenberg
Senior Rabbi, Masorti UK

Rabbi, New North London Synagogue

Next is the leadership of a Rothschild in seeking the Moral guidance of the Pope through a newly established group of Elite Businesses named "The Council for Inclusive Capitalism. The Rothschilds are Jews and have been funding entire nations for Centuries. They are fabulously and incredibly wealthy. They are again playing into the hands of the papacy or are very aware of what they are doing.

"Pope Francis gives his blessing to Council for Inclusive Capitalism Alliance marks an embrace of big business and finance by the Vatican

Pope Francis once called unfettered free markets the 'dung of the devil' Andrew Edgecliffe-Johnson in New York December 8, 2020. Interesting comment from the Pope. We know by now that his rhetoric is only a smokescreen.

Pope Francis is giving his blessing to a coalition of large investors, companies, unions and foundations that are pledging to make capitalism less socially and environmentally damaging.

The Vatican will on Tuesday lend its name to the Council for Inclusive Capitalism, whose members must commit to measurable action to create a more equitable and trusted economic system, including adherence to the UN's sustainable development goals.

The alliance marks an embrace of big business and finance by a head of the Roman Catholic Church who has warned of the idolatry of making profit one's only purpose and called unfettered free markets the "dung of the devil".

In a statement, Pope Francis said that a fair, trustworthy economic system that could address humanity's biggest challenges was "urgently needed". The group's leaders had taken up the challenge of making capitalism "a more inclusive instrument for integral human wellbeing", he said.

The council's founding members, who will hold annual meetings with the Pope, include the managers of $10.5tn of assets, companies with a combined market capitalisation of more than $2tn and groups representing more than 200m workers around the world.

They include the leaders of companies including Bank of America, BP, EY, Johnson & Johnson, Salesforce and Visa. The investment groups Calpers, State Street and TIAA are also members, alongside the Ford and Rockefeller Foundations, OECD secretary-general Angel Gurría and Mark Carney, the UN special envoy for climate finance.

"Neither the Vatican nor the CEOs that I know need another meeting. We need action and we need to reform capital markets," **Lady Lynn Forester de Rothschild, the council's founder, told the Financial Times**. The Pope's support was significant, she said, because "it's a positive embrace of doing the right thing for capitalism, but it's also a challenge".

She said she had been confident that she could enlist leaders in business and finance to advance a more inclusive form of capitalism, but approached the Vatican because **"we needed moral guidance"**.

The third temple? - Are there plans for it's construction?

Yes there is sufficient evidence now to confirm that the Jews are preparing to build the third temple. I am not going into elaborate detail about this because there is a great deal of information about this from the temple institute of which I will quote only a few paragraphs from the TEMPLE INSTITUTE in Jerusalem, Israel.

"The Temple Institute is dedicated to every aspect of the Holy Temple of Jerusalem, and the central role it fulfilled, and will once again fulfill, in the spiritual wellbeing of both Israel and all the nations of the world. The Institute's work touches upon the history of the Holy Temple's past, an understanding of the present day, and the Divine promise of Israel's future. The Institute's activities include education, research, and development. The Temple Institute's ultimate goal is to see Israel rebuild the Holy Temple on Mount Moriah in Jerusalem, in accord with the Biblical command-ments.....

THE SCHOLARS OF THE TEMPLE INSTITUTE have dedicated their lives to raising public awareness of the importance of the Holy Temple in the life of all mankind, both Israel and the nations of the world. The Institute seeks to disseminate this knowledge, rekindle the desire and yearning for the rebuilding of the Holy Temple, and help to prepare as much as possible for the actual rebuilding. At this site you can view educational articles and essays about the Holy Temple, as well as an archive of newsletters and news items. You can also subscribe to the Temple Institute's free email newsletters. Also available are many online video teachings.

THE TEMPLE INSTITUTE CONSIDERS IT OF PRIMARY IMPORTANCE to educate about the great significance of Mount Moriah, the Temple Mount in Jerusalem, the only site in the world that is considered holy by the Jewish people, and the only site in the world which G-d chose to rest His presence through the establishment of the Holy Temple. … learn more about the sacred Temple Mount. … find out how to request a tour of the Temple Mount according to halacha, Jewish law, without treading upon the actual site of the Temple, which is Biblically forbidden for all people, whether Jew or Gentile."

There are some problems with the assumption that where the Mosques are built is actually Holy Ground.

What did Jesus have to say about the temple whilst He was present on earth?

"And Jesus went out, and departed from the temple: and his disciples came to [him] for to show him the buildings of the temple. And Jesus said unto them, See ye not all these things? verily I say unto you, There shall not be left here one stone upon another, that shall not be thrown down." Matthew 24:1-2.

As we all know that Jesus cannot lie, and that He prophesied that there would not be one stone left upon another, that prophecy was fulfilled to the letter in AD 70, so what are those walls standing where they are as the alleged site of the temple? This cannot be the original temple site because the temple was utterly destroyed and levelled by the Romans and current researchers affirm that those walls currently standing there are the outer walls of what used to be Fort Antonio, built by the Roman soldiers.

For an exegesis on this you can refer to the great research of Ernest L. Martin in his book entitled, The Temples that Jerusalem forgot.

The correct site of the temple? Even if it is placed where it was originally, in the city of david, will the Jews accept two muslim mosques overshadowing their temple? Quite unlikely. Will it be a Catholic collaboration? Let's keep an eye on developments there.

The temple that they will be attempting to build is not of God because when Jesus gave His life on the cross the sacrificial system that represented His sacrifice was ended. And if they succeed in building a temple, then the only god they will be sacrificing to will be Satan, the man of the Mystery. The God of heaven will not recognise that temple.

"Seventy weeks are determined upon thy people and upon thy holy city, to finish the transgression, and to make an end of sins, and to make reconciliation for iniquity, and to bring in everlasting righteousness, and to seal up the vision and prophecy, and to anoint the most Holy.
Know therefore and understand, [that] from the going forth of the commandment to restore and to build Jerusalem unto the Messiah the Prince [shall be] seven weeks, and

threescore and two weeks: the street shall be built again, and the wall, even in troublous times.

And after threescore and two weeks shall Messiah be cut off, but not for himself: and the people of the prince that shall come shall destroy the city and the sanctuary; and the end thereof [shall be] with a flood, and unto the end of the war desolations are determined.

And he shall confirm the covenant with many for one week: and in the midst of the week he shall cause the sacrifice and the oblation to cease, and for the overspreading of abominations he shall make [it] desolate, even until the consummation, and that determined shall be poured upon the desolate." Daniel 9:24-27.

Here, as plain as ABC is confirmation that the sacrificial system would come to an end. To deny that Jesus was ever here is to deny their own prophet Daniel in the old testament.

Here is some further proof that the sacrificial system that represented Jesus' death on the cross was finished.

"Jesus, when he had cried again with a loud voice, yielded up the ghost. And, behold, the veil of the temple was rent in twain from the top to the bottom; and the earth did quake, and the rocks rent;" Matthew 27:50-51

"And Jesus cried with a loud voice, and gave up the ghost. And the veil of the temple was rent in twain from the top to the bottom. And when the centurion, which stood over against him, saw that he so cried out, and gave up the ghost, he said, Truly this man was the Son of God." Mark 15:37-39.

Is there a true sanctuary in our current age and if so, where is it?

363

"Wherefore he is able also to save them to the uttermost that come unto God by him, seeing he ever liveth to make intercession for them. For such an high priest became us, [who is] holy, harmless, undefiled, separate from sinners, and made higher than the heavens; Who needeth not daily, as those high priests, to offer up sacrifice, first for his own sins, and then for the people's: for this he did once, when he offered up himself." Hebrews 7:25-27.

Jesus offered up Himself and therefore the daily sacrifices were no longer needed. As the above verses describe Him as a priest, where is he carrying out His priestly role?

"Now of the things which we have spoken [this is] the sum: We have such an high priest, who is set on the right hand of the throne of the Majesty in the heavens; A minister of the sanctuary, and of the true tabernacle, which the Lord pitched, and not man." Hebrews 8:1-2.

Aha! There you have it, the true tabernacle that the Lord pitched (built, placed etc), not humans, is in heaven.

When did Jesus start His priestly ministry? "But Christ being come an high priest of good things to come, by a greater and more perfect tabernacle, not made with hands, that is to say, not of this building;

Neither by the blood of goats and calves, but by his own blood he entered in once into the holy place, having obtained eternal redemption [for us].
For if the blood of bulls and of goats, and the ashes of an heifer sprinkling the unclean, sanctifieth to the purifying of the flesh: How much more shall the blood of Christ, who through the eternal Spirit offered himself without spot to

364

God, purge your conscience from dead works to serve the living God?

For Christ is not entered into the holy places made with hands, [which are] the figures of the true; but into heaven itself, now to appear in the presence of God for us: And as it is appointed unto men once to die, but after this the judgment: So Christ was once offered to bear the sins of many; and unto them that look for him shall he appear the second time without sin unto salvation." Hebrews 9:11-14, 24, 27-28.

Jesus begun His priestly ministry in heaven after his death and resurrection, He will be coming a second time, to take those that believe that he died and rose again, home with Him.

"For if we believe that Jesus died and rose again, even so them also which sleep in Jesus will God bring with him.

For this we say unto you by the word of the Lord, that we which are alive [and] remain unto the coming of the Lord shall not prevent them which are asleep.

For the Lord himself shall descend from heaven with a shout, with the voice of the archangel, and with the trump of God: and the dead in Christ shall rise first:

Then we which are alive [and] remain shall be caught up together with them in the clouds, to meet the Lord in the air: and so shall we ever be with the Lord. Wherefore comfort one another with these words." 1 Thessalonians 4:14-18.

Clearly then from these verses, if you don't believe that Jesus died and rose again then you will not be brought to God and will have missed Jesus' second coming.

Sadly this will include (unless they come to understand and change their mind-sets) the Mashiac Jews, the Muslims who do not regard Jesus as their Creator and Saviour and that place Mohammed higher than Jesus. Those that adhere to other ideologies, such as paganism, atheism, evolution etc that do not believe in Jesus, or those in other 'Christian' organisations that do not heed the call to come out of Babylon. (See appendix 1 for Secular History records that Jesus was physically present here on earth 2,000+ years ago and that He did resurrect).

Another important point on this second visit to earth, Jesus will not be touching down on this planet as we just read earlier; ("Then we which are alive and remain shall be caught up together with them in the clouds, to meet the Lord in the air: and so shall we ever be with the Lord." 1 Thessalonians 4:17) but He will touch down on His third visit with the New Jerusalem as described in Revelation 21:2.
"And I John saw the holy city, new Jerusalem, coming down from God out of heaven, prepared as a bride adorned for her husband."

These verses leave no room for the so-called 'rapture' as some churches teach. The righteous dead will be resurrected and along with the living saints will meet Jesus in the air. The 'left behind' people are those that have chosen Satan and his beast mark and will be forever lost. At that second coming of Christ all of humanity will have had their eternal destinies sealed. 'Another opportunity' doctrine is another lie of Satan.

Does the construction of the temple mean that animal sacrifices will be resumed? and if so, are there precedents in our modern times that would not make it a surprise that animal sacrifices are conducted? The sacrifices of the Jews were conducted with fire.

Yes, animal sacrifices are being performed in our day and age and we will take a look at Islam, because according to the Pew Research Center, Islam is the worlds fastest growing religion (currently 1.8 billion). The festivals where the sacrifices are conducted are Eid-ul-Fitr (celebrated for three days after a month of fasting in Ramadan) & Eid-ul-Adha (celebrated for three days every year after the annual Holy Pilgrimage to Mecca for Muslims who can afford it).

"Muslims engaged in the Hajj (pilgrimage) are obliged to sacrifice a lamb or a goat or join others in sacrificing a cow or a camel during the celebration of the Eid al-Adha, an Arabic term that means "Feast of Sacrifice", also known as al-Id al-Kabir (Great Feast), or Qurban Bayrami (Sacrifice Feast) in Turkic influenced cultures, Bakar Id (Goat Feast) in Indian subcontinent and Reraya Qurben in Indonesia. Other Muslims not on the Hajj to Mecca also participate in this sacrifice wherever they are, on the 10th day of the 12th lunar month in the Islamic calendar. It is understood as a symbolic re-enactment of Abraham's sacrifice of a ram in place of his son. Meat from this occasion is divided into three parts, one part is kept by the sacrificing family for food, the other gifted to friends and family, and the third given to the poor Muslims. The sacrificed animal is a sheep, goat, cow or camel. The feast follows a communal prayer at a mosque or open air.

The animal sacrifice during the Hajj is a part of a nine step pilgrimage ritual. It is, states Campo, preceded by a statement to intention and body purification, inaugural circumambulation of the Kaaba seven times, running between Marwa and Safa hills, encampment at Mina, standing in Arafat, stoning the three Mina Satanic pillars with at least forty nine pebbles. Thereafter, animal sacrifice, and this is followed by farewell circumambulation of the Kaaba. The Muslims who are not on Hajj also perform a simplified ritual animal sacrifice. According to Campo, the animal sacrifice at the annual Islamic festival has origins in western Arabia in vogue before Islam. The animal sacrifice, states Philip Stewart, is not required by the Quran, but is based on interpretations of other Islamic texts.

Other occasions when Muslims perform animal sacrifice include the 'aqiqa, when a child is seven days old, is shaved and given a name. It is believed that the animal sacrifice binds the child to Islam and offers protection to the child from evil."

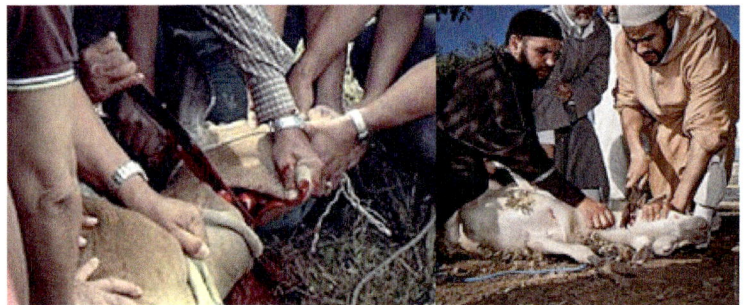

Cattle sacrifice at Eid. Goat sacrifice.

The Eid al-Adha is a major annual festival of animal sacrifice in Islam. In Indonesia alone, for example, some 800,000 animals were sacrificed in 2014 by its Muslims on the festival, but the number can be a bit lower or higher depending on the economic conditions. According to Lesley Hazleton, in Turkey about 2,500,000 sheep, cows and goats are sacrificed each year to observe the Islamic festival of animal sacrifice, with a part of the sacrificed animal given to the needy who didn't sacrifice an animal."

Animal sacrifices at the Eid al-Adha Islamic festival in Pakistan (left) and India (right)

"According to The Independent, nearly 10,000,000 animals are sacrificed in Pakistan every year on Eid. Countries such as Saudi Arabia transport nearly a million animals every year for sacrifice to Mina (near Mecca). The sacrificed animals at Id al-Adha, states Clarke Brooke, include the four species considered lawful for the Hajj sacrifice: sheep, goats, camels and cattle, and additionally, cow-like animals including the water buffalo, domesticated banteng and yaks. Many are brought in from north Africa and parts of Asia.

The tabernacles of the palace of the popes?:

"What is a tabernacle? Catholic Answers Staff August 05, 2011.

Full Question
One of my students asks why they keep the Eucharist in the tabernacle. What is the tabernacle?

Answer

The tabernacle is a liturgical furnishing used to house the Eucharist outside of Mass. This provides a location where the Eucharist can be kept for the adoration of the faithful and for later use (e.g., distribution to the sick).

It also helps prevent the profanation of the Eucharist. Thus the law requires, *see (CIC 938 §3) below.*

The word tabernacle means "dwelling place." Any place someone dwells is a tabernacle. The term is also sometimes used for a temporary dwelling place. Thus the tent-like sanctuary that the Jews used before the Temple was built was called the Tabernacle, because God dwelt there. Similarly, for the feast of Sukkot the Hebrews erected temporary shelters to live in for the festival, which is often called "the feast of tabernacles" or "the feast of booths" as a result. The tabernacle in Church is so named because it is a place where Christ dwells in the Eucharist."

and directly from the Vatican:

"THE RESERVATION AND VENERATION OF THE MOST HOLY EUCHARIST

Can. (Canon) 934 §1. The Most Holy Eucharist:

1/ must be reserved in the cathedral church or its equivalent, in every parish church, and in a church or oratory connected to the house of a religious institute or society of apostolic life;

2/ can be reserved in the chapel of the bishop and, with the permission of the local ordinary, in other churches, oratories, and chapels.

§2. In sacred places where the Most Holy Eucharist is reserved, there must always be someone responsible for it and, insofar as possible, a priest is to celebrate Mass there at least twice a month.

Can. 936 In the house of a religious institute or some other pious house, the Most Holy Eucharist is to be reserved only in the church or principal oratory attached to the house. For a just cause, however, the ordinary can also permit it to be reserved in another oratory of the same house.

Can. 937 Unless there is a grave reason to the contrary, the church in which the Most Holy Eucharist is reserved is to be open to the faithful for at least some hours every day so that they can pray before the Most Blessed Sacrament.

Can. 938 §1. The Most Holy Eucharist is to be reserved habitually in only one tabernacle of a church or oratory.

§2. The tabernacle in which the Most Holy Eucharist is reserved is to be situated in some part of the church or oratory which is distinguished, conspicuous, beautifully decorated, and suitable for prayer.

§3. The tabernacle in which the Most Holy Eucharist is reserved habitually is to be immovable, made of solid and opaque material, and locked in such a way that the danger of profanation is avoided as much as possible.

§4. For a grave cause, it is permitted to reserve the Most Holy Eucharist in some other fit-ting and more secure place, especially at night.

§5. The person responsible for the church or oratory is to take care that the key of the tabernacle in which the Most Holy Eucharist is reserved is safeguarded most diligently.

Can. 939 Consecrated hosts in a quantity sufficient for the needs of the faithful are to be kept in a pyx or small vessel; they are to be renewed frequently and the older hosts consumed properly.

Can. 940 A special lamp which indicates and honors the presence of Christ is to shine continuously before a tabernacle in which the Most Holy Eucharist is reserved.

Can. 942 It is recommended that in these churches and oratories an annual solemn exposition of the Most Blessed Sacrament be held for an appropriate period of time, even if not continuous, so that the local community more profoundly meditates on and adores the eucharistic mystery. Such an exposition is to be held, however, only if a suitable gathering of the faithful is foreseen and the established norms are observed.

Can. 943 The minister of exposition of the Most Blessed Sacrament and of eucharistic benediction is a priest or deacon; in special circumstances, the minister of exposition and reposition alone without benediction is the acolyte, extraordinary minister of holy communion, or someone else designated by the local ordinary; the prescripts of the diocesan bishop are to be observed.

Can. 944 §1. When it can be done in the judgment of the diocesan bishop, a procession through the public streets is to be held as a public witness of veneration toward the Most Holy Eucharist, especially on the solemnity of the Body and Blood of Christ.

§2. It is for the diocesan bishop to establish regulations which provide for the participation in and the dignity of processions."

"If we are to know the lord, we must go to him. Listen to him in silence before the tabernacle and approach hin in the sacraments" – Pope Francis.

St. Peter's Basilica - Tabernacle containing the sacrament.

Tabernacle of St. John Lateran.

High Altar (Baldachin) Mass in St. Peter's.

John the Revelator states: "Woe to the inhabiters of the earth... for the devil is come down unto you, having great wrath, because he knoweth that he hath but a short time." Revelation 12:12.
How is he to manifest his great wrath?

He is angry because he knows what he has lost, and what we stand to gain. Therefore he will use all means possible, and by any means necessary to ensure that we do not gain access to what he has lost. Another point to consider is, that because he so utterly hates Christ, that he will do all in his power to destroy all that Christ has created. With these points in mind we will continue.

"And he shall plant the tabernacles of his palace between the seas in the glorious holy mountain; yet he shall come to his end and none shall help him." Daniel 11:45.

Who else does this "he" that the prophet Daniel saw, refer to? Verse 45 completes the 11th chapter of Daniel.

Various authors have commented on the possible meanings of Daniel 11:45. Some have interpreted, with uncertainty, that power as being the final struggle of the Ottoman Empire; as I consider the Ottoman Empire to have no further significant role to play in prophecy since 1840, I could not reconcile this view.

We will refer again to the very small pamphlet produced by the early pioneers of the Seventh-Day Adventist church (A word to the Little Flock – unabridged). I have already shared part of the following quotation in an earlier chapter of this book, but here, I will share the whole quotation with you because of it's relevancy and because repetition is a good learning tool.

"We are taught by some, that the standing up of Michael, the time of trouble, and the delivering of the saints are in the future; and that all these events are to be accomplished at the second appearing of Christ. Others teach, that Michael stood up on the 10th day of the 7th month, 1844, and that since that time we have been passing through the "time of trouble such as never was;" and that the deliverance of the Saints, is at the first resurrection. But as I cannot harmonize either of these views with the Bible, I wish to humbly give my brethren and sisters my view of these events. It is clear to me, that here are four distinct events, all in the future. 1st, The standing up of Michael. 2nd, The time of trouble. 3rd, The deliverance of the Saints. and 4th, The resurrection of the just to everlasting life.

That Jesus rose up, and shut the door, and came to the Ancient of Days, to reconcile his kingdom, at the 7th month 1844, I fully believe. See Luke 13:25; Matt:25:10; Dan:7:13-14. But the standing up of Michael, Dan:12:l, appears to be another event, for another purpose. His rising up in 1844, was to shut the door, and come to His father, to receive His kingdom, and power to reign; but Michael's standing up, is to manifest His kingly power, which He already has, in the destruction of the wicked, and in the deliverance of His people. Michael is to stand up at the time that the last power in chapter 11, comes to his end, and none to help him.

This power is the last that treads down the true church of God: and as the true church is still trodden down, and cast out by all Christendom, it follows that the last oppressive power has not "come to his end;" and Michael has not stood up. This last power that treads down the saints is brought to view in Revelation 13: 11-18. His number is 666. Much of his power, deceptions, wonders, miracles, and oppression, will doubtless be manifested during his last struggle under the "seven last plagues," about the time of his coming to his end. This is clearly shadowed forth by the Magicians of Egypt, deceiving Pharoah and his host, in performing most of the miracles that Moses performed by the power of God. That was just before the deliverance of Israel from Egyptian bondage; and may we not expect to see as great a manifestation of the power of the Devil, just before the glorious deliverance of the Saints?" A word to the little flock Page 8.3 & 8.4 (Unabridged Version)

Two key points present themselves here; his number is 666, and manifestation of the power of the Devil. We have already identified the various connections of the 666 number. Here we can understand clearly that Satan, the papacy, the USA etc will all be working together at the end of the time of the end.

When all the evidence is placed before us, we should begin to realise the enormity of the final deception that confronts us all. Daniel was told to shut up the book and seal it until the "time of the end." As we have already discovered, the time of the end began in 1798 when the Papacy, in Revelation 13:3, received its deadly wound and when the second beast, the United States, began rising to power, verse 11. Therefore the books of Daniel are now unsealed, open for understanding.

How is he (Satan) to manifest his power ultimately? Why would Satan, the Pope and Apostate Protestant Churches want Jerusalem?

Remember Jesus' warning in Matthew 24:15 "When ye therefore shall see the abomination of desolation, spoken of by Daniel the prophet, stand in the holy place, (whoso readeth, let him understand:)"

The abomination of desolation was when the Roman armies would set up, plant? their idolatrous standards in the holy ground that extended some furlongs around Jerusalem's city walls. Their pagan banners were to indicate their assumed authority over a territory. Those banners, flags etc was their display.

This warning had a fulfillment in AD 70 and will have a second fulfillment in Spiritual Jerusalem. However, the prophets Daniel and John the Revelator seem to indicate that there will be literal events in Jerusalem around the "abomination of desolation"

Will we be witnessing events in literal Jerusalem that will give credence to a grand deception of the papacy and it's pagan practises specifically to deceive the world, spiritual Jerusalem, that will also be a warning to God's true followers?

Remember also, the prophet Isaiah in chapter 14:4 speaking of the king of Babylon? Let us read on in verses 12-13.

"How art thou fallen from heaven, O Lucifer, son of the morning! How art thou cut down to the ground, which didst weaken the nations! For thou hast said in thine heart, I will ascend into heaven, I will exalt my throne above the stars of God: I will sit also upon the mount of the congregation, in the sides of the north." Heaven he cannot reach, but the verses plainly state he has a throne and we have already traced the history of that throne.

The prophet Ezekiel also noted his actions there, in chapter 28 verses 1-2. "The word of the Lord came again unto me, saying. Son of man, say unto the prince of Tyrus, thus saith the Lord God; because thine heart is lifted up, and thou hast said, I am a God, I sit in the seat of God, in the midst of the seas; yet thou art a man, and not God, though thou set thine heart as the heart of God."

Several things become apparent here, he says "I am a God," through his various systems of false worship, and especially through his creation myths, he has claimed to be God. "I sit in the seat of God," he will actually be present there. "In the midst of [between, in the middle of] the seas," again the same location as viewed by the other prophets.

Now the final part of Daniel 11:45, points out his coming to his end and none to help him. So does Isaiah and John the Revelator. "He who smote the people in wrath with a continual stroke, he that ruled the nations in anger, is persecuted, and none hindereth." "Yet thou shalt be brought down to hell, to the sides of the pit." "And I saw an angel come down from heaven, having the key of the bottomless pit... And he laid hold on the dragon, that old serpent, which is the Devil, and Satan, ... and cast him into the bottomless pit." Isaiah 14:6,15. Revelation 20:1-3.

All these prophets are viewing the same event, the end of Satan's kingdom. Remember hs is using the papacy. (His final end will be after another 1,000 years when the New Jerusalem descends, an entirely separate study). The big question probably now on your mind is, what is so important about Jerusalem that he would want to set himself up there in such a prominent manner?

Remember Satan's habits? He does not have any originality. He must copy his Creator. Let's read from Exodus 25:8 & 9.

"And let them make me a sanctuary; that I may dwell among them. According to all that I show thee, [after] the pattern of the tabernacle,....."

Coming back to our time (or more specifically, the time of the end), Satan succeeds in establishing his tabernacle there in Jerusalem? What did our God in heaven do to prove that he accepted the first sacrificial offering in the wilderness?

By all means read the whole of Leviticus 9, but I will only quote verses 5 to 7 and 24.

"And they brought [that] which Moses commanded before the tabernacle of the congregation: and all the congregation drew near and stood before the LORD. And Moses said, This [is] the thing which the LORD commanded that ye should do: and the glory of the LORD shall appear unto you.
And Moses said unto Aaron, Go unto the altar, and offer thy sin offering, and thy burnt offering, and make an atonement for thyself, and for the people: and offer the offering of the people, and make an atonement for them; as the LORD commanded.

379

And there came a fire out from before the LORD, and consumed upon the altar the burnt offering and the fat: [which] when all the people saw, they shouted, and fell on their faces."

"And David built there an altar unto the Lord, and offered burnt offerings and peace offerings, and called upon the Lord; and he answered him from heaven by fire upon the altar of burnt offering." 1 Chronicles 21:26.

Perhaps even more relevant to the coming events is the account of Solomon's dedication of the First Temple found in 2 Chronicles 7:1.

"Now when Solomon had made an end of praying, the fire came down from heaven, and consumed the burnt offering and the sacrifices; and the glory of the LORD filled the house."

One more example of the authority and confirmation of the true God is in the account of Elijah and the false prophets of Baal at their confrontation on Mount Carmel found in 1 Kings 18:17-40, however, although I am only going to quote verses 36-39, I recommend you read all the verses to understand the whole event that took place.

The Mount Carmel event.

"And it came to pass at [the time of] the offering of the [evening] sacrifice, that Elijah the prophet came near, and said, LORD God of Abraham, Isaac, and of Israel, let it be known this day that thou [art] God in Israel, and [that] I [am] thy servant, and [that] I have done all these things at thy word.
Hear me, O LORD, hear me, that this people may know that thou [art] the LORD God, and [that] thou hast turned

their heart back again. Then the fire of the LORD fell, and consumed the burnt sacrifice, and the wood, and the stones, and the dust, and licked up the water that [was] in the trench. And when all the people saw [it], they fell on their faces: and they said, The LORD, he [is] the God; the LORD, he [is] the God." Remember the prophecy in revelation 13:13-14?

(Take note that those baal priests were Satan's false prophets and that Satan is the chief of baals, baalzebub.)

"And he doeth great wonders, so that he maketh fire come down from heaven on the earth in the sight of men. And deceiveth them that dwell on the earth by [the means of] those miracles which he had power to do in the sight of the beast; saying to them that dwell on the earth, that they should make an image to the beast, which had the wound by a sword, and did live."

"… he doeth great wonders, so that he maketh fire come down from heaven on the earth in the sight of men." Wouldn't this be an awesome event to witness? What is the result of this? Verse 14. He deceives earth's inhabitants, through the second beast, to make an image to the first beast.

According to the Thayer Definition from Strong's concordance, the word "wonders" includes in its meanings:

"1. a sign, mark, token that by which a person or a thing is distinguished from others and is known a sign, prodigy, portent, i.e. an unusual occurrence, transcending the common course of nature of signs portending remarkable events soon to happen of miracles and wonders by which God authenticates the men sent by him, or by which men prove that the cause they are pleading is God's.

G4592

σημεῖον
sēmeîon,
say-mi'-on;
Neuter of a presumed derivative of the base of G4591; an indication, especially ceremonially or supernaturally:— miracle, sign, token, wonder.

It is very clear from the above verses that the fire from heaven event is to deceive the world and this time God will allow Satan to do it.
To answer part 2 of the earlier question as to why Satan, the Pope and Apostate Protestant Churches would want Jerusalem? Is it that they can have a false Mount Carmel type "fire from heaven" event? An event to demonstrate that our eternal God 'supposedly' approves the change of the Sabbath from the Seventh to the first day of the week? and to validate their false system of worship?

"The last great delusion is soon to open before us. Antichrist is to perform his marvelous works in our sight. So closely will the counterfeit resemble the true, that it will

382

be impossible to distinguish between them except by the Holy Scriptures. By their testimony every statement and every miracle must be tested." Great Controversy pg 593.

The major confrontation on mount Carmel between Elijah - God in heaven's servant, and the 450 prophets of Baal and the 400 prophets of the groves - Satan's servants related in 1 Kings 18:17- 40 confirm that God did not allow Satan to bring fire down from heaven.

How is it possible then that Satan is shown as being able to call fire down from heaven? He was unable to do it for his priests of Baal way back then, and remember Satan is known as Baalzebub, the chief of the devils; why is he at the time of the end able to do so?

I submit to you, that God will allow him to do it, so that those who do not love the truth will be deceived. "And with all deceivableness of unrighteousness in them that perish; because they received not the love of the truth, that they might be saved. And for this cause God shall send them strong delusion, that they should believe a lie." II Thessalonians 2:10-11.

"For the invisible things of him from the creation of the world are clearly seen, being understood by the things that are made, [even] his eternal power and Godhead; so that they are without excuse: Because that, when they knew God, they glorified [him] not as God, neither were thankful; but became vain in their imaginations, and their foolish heart was darkened. Professing themselves to be wise, they became fools, And changed the glory of the uncorruptible God into an image made like to corruptible man, and to birds, and fourfooted beasts, and creeping things. Wherefore God also gave them up to uncleanness through the lusts of their own hearts, to dishonour their own bodies between themselves: Who changed the truth of God into a lie, and worshipped and served the creature more than the Creator, who is blessed for ever. Amen." Romans 1:20-25.

In Revelation 13:14, Satan is described as having power to do the miracles that will deceive; in other words what will be seen will not be pretence, but real miracles; Satan has tremendous supernatural powers, but he has not been granted the ability to create life.

This is an example of where type meets antitype, where history repeats itself. Mount Carmel was a literal and spiritual event with literal Israel. Satan's fire event will be a literal and spiritual event in the sight of spiritual Israel, global spiritual Israel, all those who profess to serve God, those that have decided to follow a false god and those yet undecided. The result will be deception or salvation. "Choose you this day who you will serve"? This is not going to be pretty, it will be very traumatic.

Dear readers, the God of heaven is at present restraining Satan, just like He did on Mt.Carmel when his priests and prophets wanted to demonstrate to all present that Baal was the all-powerful god by the calling down of fire from Heaven to consume the sacrifice, but this time God will allow Satan to do it.

Another point worthy of consideration, is the fact that deities such as Marduk, Zeus, Jupiter, Bel etc., all have as their attributes, the Thunderbolt or lightning. What is the truth then on this matter? Jesus said "If any man shall say unto you, lo, here is Christ, or there; believe it not, for there shall arise false Christs and false prophets, and shall shew great signs and wonders, insomuch that if it were possible, they shall deceive the very elect."

These delusions then are very close to scriptural truth, however, the elect will be able to discern the difference, since a sure sign of a counterfeit Christ, is that he will be reported to be in different places. The true Christ, by contrast, will be seen by all at the same time, and He will not be walking on the earth, His coming will be only to receive His own, who have already been sealed.

What has all this to do with the tabernacles? We already know that Satan has two forms of tabernacles; one in which the eucharist is placed, and the great altar of St. Peter's Basilica, the Baldachin. What other types of altars were in use for the worship of Satan? All of the nations that worshipped him, in some form or other built ziggurats like the first built in Babylon, they were altars to him as the sun god. The Aztecs regularly sacrificed 20,000 victims annually to the sun-god, in order to receive blessings and propitiation for their sins.

Does the next headline provide an example of how the United States will be very instrumental in assisting the papacy to succeed in its plans? I must state that I do not believe there will be a need to replace the Al Aqsa mosque because it is not built on the site of the second temple. Time will tell. I have added it to demonstrate the intentions of the powers that be to build a temple in Jerusalem.

The sacrificial altar of Solomon's temple was in the open air and if they are to be true to rebuilding it as the previous ones then the altar will be in the open air. This is important because the fire coming down from heaven needs to be in plain sight.

U.S. Ambassador David Friedman receives a controversial photo showing a putative Third Temple in place of the Al Aqsa mosque compound. Bnei Brak, Israel, May 22, 2018. Credit: Israel Cohen / Kikar Hashabat

U.S. Ambassador to Israel Pictured With Controversial Image of Jerusalem Third Temple Replacing Muslim Mosque

Again, this will only be as our eternal God allows it and His true followers will not be deceived by it or any actions that take place in Jerusalem that are contrary to sola scriptura.

At this point we need to refer back to the chapter (at the time of the end) and now examine the statement made by Paul about "the son of perdition"(the papacy), sitting in "the temple of god" the question is what exactly does Paul mean? There are many scriptural references to "temples". Our bodies are regarded as a temple of the Holy Ghost (1 Corinthians 6:19-20), there was solomon's temple in Jerusalem, there is the original temple in heaven that Moses had to pattern after (Exodus 25:9, Hebrews 8:2), and the

New Jerusalem will not need a temple because God the Father and God the Son reign from there (Revelation 21:22). The fact of the matter is, temples are and always have been regarded as dwelling-places for the gods.

I say gods, because even the false system has copied the original by setting up temples for the false gods. Since the pope cannot be understood to be sitting inside a human body and that he cannot be sitting in the temple in heaven, neither the one in Jerusalem, because it no longer exists, (yes, the Jews are trying to build a third temple and even if they do it will not be of God) we can draw the only conclusion that since the Lord always called the earthly Jerusalem His holy mountain etc, has Paul described the "Son of perdition" sitting in "the temple of God" as sitting in literal Jerusalem?

Paul therefore marvelled at the fact that the "Son of perdition" would "sit" there at the end of time, just like he saw the "Mystery" already existed and that "Satan" would deceive those who did not love the truth. The papacy, the Mystery, and the powers of Satan are to reach their climax at the end of time, just before the second advent of Christ. One meaning of the word "sit" according to Merriam-Webster's dictionary is "to occupy a place as a member of an official body" and this fits well with the view of the papacy/Satan sitting in the temple of God, "occupying Jerusalem as a member of an official body."
Isaiah 14:13, we have Satan sitting on the mount of the congregation, in the sides of the north. Ezekiel 28:2, Satan says in his heart, "….I sit in the seat of God, in the midst of the seas…"Daniel 11:45, he plants the tabernacles of his palace between the seas, in the glorious holy mountain. Paul in 2 Thessalonians 2:4 sees the son of perdition sitting in the temple of God showing himself that he is God.

John in Revelation 13:13-14 sees him bringing fire down from heaven to deceive the inhabitants of earth. All these prophets would not have seen these events for the sake of seeing them, they confirm significant developments yet to come and they are all in agreement with each other. In fact God has revealed these events to several of His prophets. They are warnings to earth's inhabitants.

The roman church insists that it is the true church by virtue of "the keys (allegedly) given to Peter," etc., by Jesus Christ. Jesus Christ was crucified in the vicinity of Jerusalem. Jerusalem was the main battleground between Christ and Satan when Christ was on earth. Jerusalem is regarded as one of the centers of Christianity. What the scriptures are definitely saying, is that dramatic events are to take place around and or in Jerusalem.

I submit to you that God will allow Satan to make it appear that he can bring fire down from heaven, because the world's unbelievers in His Son will be looking for someone of miraculous powers to take them through to the "next" stage.

He will perform those miracles, just as he did at Fatima, pretending that he is Christ and has come to confirm that he changed the sabbath to Sunday, and that all those who do not keep his Sunday sabbath are to be destroyed. "And no marvel; for Satan himself is transformed into an angel of light." 2 Corinthians 11:14.

Will we be witnessing type meets anti-type in Jerusalem? When Jesus came the first time, Pagan Rome was in control of Jerusalem. The Jews despised the Romans and wanted Jesus to use supernatural powers to rid Jerusalem of the Romans and be their King. This time around will it be Spiritual Rome in charge of Jerusalem and will they be accepting the false Messiah in the form of Lucifer as an

Angel of light stating he is Christ and that he changed the Sabbath from Saturday to Sunday along with his many other deceptions? Will the Jews accept Satan as the Messiah?

Jesus has told us in Revelation 1:7 how He (Jesus) will be coming and He has warned us in Matthew 24: 23-27 as follows:

"Then if any man shall say unto you, Lo, here is Christ, or there; believe it not. For there shall arise false Christs, and false prophets, and shall shew great signs and wonders; insomuch that, if it were possible, they shall deceive the very elect. Behold, I have told you before. Wherefore if they shall say unto you, Behold, he is in the desert; go not forth: behold, he is in the secret chambers; believe it not Behold, he cometh with clouds; and every eye shall see him, and they [also] which pierced him: and all kindreds of the earth shall wail because of him. Even so, Amen."

Jesus' second coming will be a globally supernaturally viewable event, not a localised one.

And for clarity I will repeat a quote already in this book to confirm that on His second coming He will not descend to the planet's surface.

"For the Lord himself shall descend from heaven with a shout, with the voice of the archangel, and with the trump of God: and the dead in Christ shall rise first:
Then we which are alive [and] remain shall be caught up together with them in the clouds, to meet the Lord in the air: and so shall we ever be with the Lord" 1 Thessalonians 4:16-17.

Come with me to a very well written and inspired book originally written in 1858.

"Fearful sights of a supernatural character will soon be revealed in the heavens, in token power of miracle – working demons. The spirits of devils will go forth to the kings of the earth and to the whole world, to fasten them in deception, and urge them on to unite with Satan in his last struggle against the government of heaven. By these agencies, rulers and subjects alike will be deceived. Persons will arise pretending to be Christ himself, and claiming the title and worship which belong to the world's redeemer. They will perform wonderful miracles of healing and will profess to have revelations from Heaven contradicting the testimony of scriptures.

As the crowning act in the great drama of deception, Satan himself will personate Christ. The church has long professed to look to the Saviour's Advent as the consummation of her hopes. Now the great deceiver will make it appear that Christ has come. In different parts of the earth, Satan will manifest himself as a majestic being of dazzling brightness, resembling the description of the Son of God given by John in the Revelation 1:13-15.

The glory that surrounds him is unsurpassed by anything that human eyes have yet beheld. The shout of triumph rings out upon the air: "Christ has come! Christ has come!" The people prostrate themselves in adoration before him, while he lifts up his hands and pronounces a blessing upon them, as Christ blessed His disciples when he was upon the earth. His voice is subdued, yet full of melody. In gentle, compassionate tones, he presents some of the gracious, heavenly truths which the Saviour uttered; he heals the diseases of the people, and then, in his assumed character of Christ, he claims to have changed the Sabbath to

Sunday, and commands all to hallow the day which he has blessed. He declares that those who persist in keeping holy the Seventh Day are blaspheming his name by refusing to listen to his angels sent to them with light and truth. This is the strong, almost overmastering delusion. Like the Samaritans, who were deceived by Simon Magus, the multitudes, from the least to the greatest, give heed to these sorceries, saying: this is "the great power of God." Acts 8:10.

But the people of God will not be misled. The teachings of this false Christ are not in accordance with the scriptures. His blessing is pronounced upon the worshipers of the beast and his image, the very class upon whom the Bible declares that God's unmingled wrath shall be poured out. And, furthermore, Satan is not permitted to counterfeit the manner of Christ's Advent. The Saviour has warned his people against deception upon this point, and has clearly foretold the manner of His second coming.. Matthew 24:24-27, 31; 25:31; Revelation l:7; 1 Thess:4:16-17.

This coming there is no possibility of counterfeiting. It will be universally known - witnessed by the whole world. Only those who have been diligent students of the scriptures and who have received the love of the truth will be shielded from the powerful delusion that takes the world captive. By the Bible testimony these will detect the deceiver in his disguise. To all the testing time will come. ..." The Great Controversy pp. 624-5.

Apparently there are certain things the Lord will not allow Satan to do such as creating life. His calling of fire down from heaven is something the Lord will allow Satan to do so that he can deceive his followers. Cast your mind back to the verses from Leviticus and II Chronicles, where the glory of God also accompanied the manifestation of His power by fire. The earlier article citing the fact that Satan will appear as a being of dazzling brightness is interesting when comparing it with the following:-

"As spiritualism more closely imitates the nominal Christianity of the day, it has greater power to deceive and ensnare. Satan himself is converted, after the modern order of things. He will appear in the character of an angel of light. Through the agency of spiritualism, miracles will be wrought, the sick will be healed, and many undeniable wonders will be performed. And as the spirits will profess faith in the Bible, and manifest respect for the institutions of the church, their work will be accepted as a manifestation of divine power.

The line of distinction between professed Christians and the ungodly is now hardly distinguishable. Church members love what the world loves and are ready to join with them, and Satan determines to unite them in one body and thus strengthen his cause by sweeping all into the ranks of spiritualism. Papists, who boast of miracles as a certain sign of the true church, will be readily deceived by this wonder-working power; and protestants, having cast away the shield of truth, will also be deluded. Papists, Protestants, and worldlings will alike accept the form of godliness without the power, and they will see in this union a grand movement for the conversion of the world and the ushering in of the long-expected millenium." Great Controversy pp 588-9.

Take very careful note of what you have just read "....**Papists**, who boast of miracles as a certain sign of the true church, will be readily deceived by this wonder-working power; **and protestants, having cast away the shield of truth, will also be deluded**..." by whose miracles? Satan's

Now compare the above with the prophecy related to us in Revelation 13:14, which continues from the calling down of fire from heaven. "And deceiveth them that dwell on the earth by the means of those miracles which he had power to do in the sight of the beast; saying to them that dwell on the earth, that they should make an image to the beast, which had the wound by a sword and did live."

I submit to you that the power in this verse will deceive those in the United States; the beast mentioned first in the verse, to make an image to the beast which had the wound (the papacy). This image will make the world enforce the false Sabbath as set up by the papists, in reality Satan's sabbath. Again, compare this with this extract also from GC 588, paragraph 1.

"Through the two great errors, the immortality of the soul and Sunday sacredness, Satan will bring the people under his deceptions. While the former lays the foundation of spiritualism, the latter creates a bond of sympathy with Rome. The protestants of the United States will be foremost in stretching their hands across the gulf to grasp the hand of spiritualism; they will reach over the abyss to clasp the hands of the Roman power; and under the influence of this threefold union, this country (United States) will follow in the steps of Rome in trampling on the rights of conscience."

We will all have to watch the sequence of events as they unfold. Human nature being what it is though, Satan cannot just appear suddenly on the scene with his grand deceptions. He must worm his way, behind the scenes, through his servants. The Papacy is plainly one of his servants, and there are and will be others, we will examine a few of them, beginning with various views of the AntiChrist.

"Dajjal, Ad (Arabic "The Deceiver"), is mentioned in Islamic Eschatology, the AntiChrist who will come forth before the end of time. ...he will be destroyed by Christ.... Ad Dajjal will appear during a period of great tribulation; he will be followed by the Jews and will claim to be God in Jerusalem. He will work false miracles, and most people will be deceived. At this moment will occur the second coming of Christ. ..." Enc. Brit. 3:852:3a.

This will not be the first time that the Jews will have been deceived. When Christ was amongst them, they did not receive Him, as He was of too lowly birth, too poor, they expected Him to come as a King, ridding them of the Roman yoke, and making their nation the Capital of the then known world, with all the wealth that was controlled by the Roman Empire. The prophecies relating to His coming in great splendour, which apply to His second and third coming, were misapplied, and brought forward to their time. Therefore, when Satan makes his appearance there with dazzling brightness, it will be very easy for those deceived ones, to hail him as Christ.

"AntiChrist, the chief enemy of Christ. The earliest mention of the name AntiChrist, which was probably first coined in Christian Eschatological literature (concerned with the end of time) is in the letters of St. John (1 John 2:18,22, 2 John 7).. Yet the conception of a mighty ruler who will appear at the end of time and whose essence will be enmity with God is older and was taken over by Christianity from Judaism.

A Christian view of the AntiChrist is given in II Thessalonians 2. Here AntiChrist appears as a tempter who works signs and wonders and seeks to obtain divine honours; it is further significant that this "Man of Lawlessness" will obtain credence, especially among the Jews because they have not accepted the truth? (See John 5:43)." Enc. Brit. 1:450:1a.

Within, or an off-shoot of the Seventh-Day Sabbath keeping church, "Seventh Day Adventists," there is a group known as "Davidian Seventh Day Adventists," or "Shepherd's Rods," who actively teach and insist that there will be a physical purification of the Seventh Day Adventist church by God (removal of the tares, by a literal slaughter); then those who remain alive from all over the world, (the 144,000?) will be headquartered in Jerusalem, then they would go out to evangelise the world and then Jesus will come? This is an errant fable that is being propogated by this group, which is not a teaching of the Seventh Day Adventist church. This lie is only another ploy of Satan to deceive, as Jesus will not walk amongst men at his Second Advent, therefore the person they (the rod believers) will meet, will be none other than Satan himself.

New agers also speak of a Messiah - Maitreya. - "New Agers hearken to the teachings of a founding father. In 1931, Japan's Meishu Sama claimed to have received a special revelation... Complete with detailed instructions, plans for the New Age of mankind. A New Age of light was coming soon, said Sama. It would be introduced by catastrophes on land and sea - "Negative Vibrations." he called them – that would purify our present age, the old age of darkness. Both the purification of the old age, claimed Sama, and the establishment of the new age would be supervised by a "Maitreya," or Messiah. Endowed with superhuman wisdom and fantastic psychic abilities, the Maitreya would bring to heel all powers of the universe and would establish the global village.

Lest Humanists or Mega-Religionists be alarmed that a non-materialistic, transcendent heresy is afoot in New Age, let them be of good heart. According to Sama, the great Maitreya to come will be as much a part of the material human universe as, say, Moses or Buddha or Shiva or Baha'U'llah or any of those great religious leaders of past ages. In fact, all those people – Moses and Shiva and all of that crowd – were Maitreyas too. And so was Christ, according to New Age doctrine. All were Maitreyas who came to teach us.

The whole point, in fact, is that the final and all-powerful Maitreya to come will correct the distortions mankind has wreaked upon the originally pure message of all those former Maitreyas. When it comes to materialism, therefore, New Age will give Humanism a run for its money. And it will beat Mega-Religionists hands down. For, where Mega-Religionist groups are willing to accommodate certain malleable aspects of this or that transcendental religion for the sake of peace, comfort and consolation, New Age doctrine is rock-hard on two core principles that permit no such compromise.

The first point is that there is no reality beyond this world. No cheating, and no pretending. Everything presumably including Sama's revelation – is exclusively human. Even the coming Maitreya and his attendant spirits, of which he has many, belong to this human universe. The second principle is .. even more important than the first for the New Age outlook. Man, according to that principle, is an animal evolving on an upward curve of increasing, all-inclusive perfectings that will result, very soon now, in millenial conditions for all mankind." Keys of this Blood (KOB) by Malachi Martin 1990 pp306-7.

How many deceptions can you find in the above statements?
"A New Age of light was coming soon, ... it would be introduced by catastrophes on land and sea." How do the scriptures describe conditions before Christ returns?

"And there shall be signs in the sun, and in the moon, and in the stars; and upon the earth distress of nations, with perplexity; the sea and the waves roaring; men's hearts failing them for fear, and for looking after those things which are coming upon the earth: for the powers of heaven shall be shaken. And then shall they see the Son of Man coming in a cloud with power and great glory. And when these things begin to come to pass, then look up, and lift up your heads; for your redemption draweth nigh." Luke 21:25-28.

Matthew 24: 6-7, describes scenes before Jesus' second coming and this following verse 8, makes a very particular statement. "All these [are] the beginning of sorrows"

Matt 24:8 (G1161) All^{G3956} these^{G5023} *are* the beginning^{G746} of sorrows. ^{G5604}

G5604

ὠδίν
ōdin
o-deen'
Akin to G3601; a *pang* or *throe*, especially of childbirth: - pain, sorrow, travail.

Jesus is telling us here, that the closer we get to the end the more intense these events will be, just as when a woman is about to deliver a child that the birth pangs become more frequent and intense.

"The establishment of the New Age would be supervised by a Maitreya or Messiah., endowed with superhuman wisdom and fantastic psychic abilities, bringing to heel all powers of the universe, and establishing the global village.

There is the audacity of grouping our Creator, Lord and Saviour amongst the Buddhas and Shivas of this world, who were all mere mortals, and of the pagan kind, not even to be classed with such mortals as Moses, who was a true child of God. On examination Baha'u'allah claims to have been a manifestation of Christ (remember Christ has said that there shall be many false Christs), Buddha is regarded as one of a series of enlightened beings, his teachings include rewards for good or evil in a succession of rebirths. (In other words Reincarnation). The Bible teaches that once you die, that's it, no re-birth. Shiva is part of the Indian trinity of gods, and he is exactly comparable to the trinity of Isis, Horus, and Seb, the Sun-god. It is obvious where this New Age doctrine hails from and where it is leading."

The coming Maitreya has many attendant spirits? This is true because Satan has millions of evil angels, devils, who are united with him in his work.

"Although New Age may seem on the surface of it to be a little cog in the machinery of deception when examining the prophecies regarding the whore of revelation, how does the Papacy describe the New Age movement?

Though they appear to be in the thrall of the utter marvel of their own vision of what is to come. Pope John Paul sees in the New Agers something more practical for our near-future world. He sees in them the ideological ground troops of the Piggyback Globalists. ..their success is practical proof that they have an appeal for the common man in all of us that is undeniable." KOB pg 306.

A prominent Catholic New Ager quotes Witch Starhawk approvingly. "The New Age ... will be one in which "no one is ruled or ruler, where no promise of Heaven offers us false compensation for our present pain, but where we tend together the earth's living, fruitful flesh."

He is pleased to denounce the promises made by Christ of the glories of Heaven. What a tragedy! So far it seems that New Age only affects those outside of mainstream Christian religions, although it is clear that Catholicism already acknowledge their usefulness.

"John Randolph Price, one of the acknowledged world leaders of the New Age movement, claims that "there are more than half a billion (yes 500 million) advocates on the planet at this time, working among various religious groups." Given the subindustry of New Age publications thriving around the world, it is not surprising that even the most conservative estimate place the number of New Agers in the hundreds of millions, and find them sprouting like mush-rooms not only in western populations, but among the Chinese, the Japanese, the Indians and the Africans.

Further, where the Humanists and Mega-Religionists tend to appeal to the middle and upper-middle classes, New Agers seem to have something for everyone. Millions of individuals engage in self-training techniques at dawn and dusk each day. Individuals who run the gamut from laborers to laboratory geniuses, and from youths to senior citizens, all perform the same meditations. ..all nourish wild hopes for "the new world of man that is just around the corner, for the global village of the New Age.

No religion is immune from the zeal of the enthusiasts, converts and disciples of the New Age movement. New Age simply borrows all the words, melts them down like so many gold chalices and crosses, and pours them into the mold of their New Age globalism. Networked throughout the Roman Catholic church and all the mainline Protestant Churches in the United States, for example, are teams of former Christian believers - bishops, priests and laity - who are subtly and gradually transforming the meaning of Baptism, Confirmation, the Eucharist, Marriage, Confession of Sins. ..

Generally speaking. New Age also rides especially well on the shambles left in the wake of the Anti-God accomplishments of the Humanists and the religion-leveling accomplishments of the Mega-Religionists. Perhaps the firm if tatterdemalion teachings of New Age concerning "spirits" and "devas" give some measure of comfort to the former believers of the major Christian denominations."

It is necessary, at this juncture, to remind the reader of the origin of the word "deva." It was first mentioned in this work where it was noted that in the time of Xerxes, that the temples and statues of Marduk, where "devas" were worshipped, were destroyed. In further elucidation it was established that deva means devil. Let us proceed.

"The function of these "spirits" and "devas" is to aid men and women to enter the New Age. Chief among them all is Lucifer, the one whom all Christian denominations unjustly pillory and excoriate. "Lucifer," writes David Spangler, a former co-director of the Findhorn New Age Center," is the Angel of man's inner light..."

Now you see. New Agers openly admit that Lucifer is their leader. Compare the term "The Angel of man's inner light." to 2 Corinthians 11:14 "And no marvel; for Satan himself is transformed into an Angel of light." Well, what more can we say. What a wonderful book is the Bible, for no matter how Satan disguises himself, we have already been forewarned. Notice how it is stated that no religion is immune? Be careful what you listen to in your church, even if you are of the true Sabbath keeping church, because he has designs especially against that church, as many of its members attempt to cling to the truth and the truth only.

"Lucifer, like Christ," we continue, "stands at the door of man's consciousness and knocks... If man says, "come in." Lucifer becomes... the being who carries.. the light of wisdom.. - Lucifer is literally the Angel of experience... He is an agent of God's love and we move into a New Age... each of us is in some way brought to that point which I term the Luciferic initiation... We must say, "Thank you, beloved, for all these experiences... they have brought me to you.".. At some point each of us faces the presence of Lucifer... Lucifer comes to give us the final gift of wholeness. If we accept it, then he is free and we are free. That is the Luciferic initiation. It is one that many people now, and in the future days ahead, will be facing, for it is the initiation into the New Age."

Blasphemies, all of it! What about the term "he is free and we are free"? There is as usual with Satan's speeches, a truth and a lie. If we accept him he is truly free, but from what? The heaping of our sins upon his head as represented by the scapegoat in Leviticus 16:20-22 where all the sins of Israel were laid on the head of the goat on the Day of Atonement. At the final Day of Atonement when Jesus comes to claim His own, all the sins of the redeemed will then be placed upon Satan's head; that we submit to you, is what he will be free from if you accept him, for in accepting him you must reject your saviour Jesus Christ and you must pay for your own sins, (*the biggest tragedy here is the loss of eternal life)* and no we will not be free, we will die for our sins and he will be free from having our sins heaped on his head, do you get it? A truth and a lie at the same time, just like he did to Eve in the garden of Eden. Isn't it interesting that he is represented as a goat in his baphomet?

"Whether because or in spite of its belief in Lucifer and the lesser "devas" and "spirits," such New Age spirituality has demonstrated its attraction not only for former Christians, but for men and women of all religious groups, and of no religion .... As cult expert David Fletcher concludes, in plainer, un-co-opted language, the aim for everyone is "to act like God, because you are God." KOB pp 308-310.

So we have come full circle. The first lie in Eden, "Ye shall become as gods," has come down to us "act like God, because you are God."

Despite the support Pope John Paul admits to the New Age movement, he still insists to them that there is no salvation outside the Roman Church. Interesting? Truly, she is "The Mother of Harlots." Catholicism never changes, she merely assimilates any and everything to ensure she retains her supremacy.

Finally, "Like many other "One World" groups, New Agers look forward to the elimination of existing political systems and national boundaries. They are prepared to welcome the subsequent blending of all nations and peoples into one planetary culture, with a single court of Justice a single police force, a single economic and educational system - all under a single government dominated by a superbureau of "enlighted ones." KOB pp 311-12.

Part of the following has been quoted in the introduction, but will be enlarged on here.

"Willing or not, ready or not, we are all involved in an all-out, no-holds-barred, global competition. Most of us are not competitors, however. We are the stakes. For the competition is about who will establish the first one-world system of government that has ever existed in the society of nations. It is about who will hold and wield the dual power and authority and control over each of us as individuals and over all of us together as a community; over the entire six billion people expected by demographers to inhabit the earth by early in the third millenium. The competition is all-out because, now that it has started, there is no way it can be reversed or called off. No holds are barred because, once the competition has been decided, the world and all that's in it-our way of life as individuals and as citizens of the nations; our families and our jobs; our trade and commerce and money; our educationals systems and our religions and our cultures; even the badges of our national identity, which most of us have always taken for granted – all will have been powerfully and radically altered forever. No one can be exempted from its effects. No sector of our lives will remain untouched.

It is not too much to say, in fact, that the chosen purpose of John Paul's pontificate – the engine that drives his papal grand policy and that determines his day-to-day, year-by-year strategies - is to be the victor in that competition, now well under way. For the fact is that the stakes John Paul has placed in the arena of geopolitical contention include everything - himself; his papal persona; the age-old Petrine Office he now embodies; and his entire Church Universal, both as an institutional organization unparalled in the world and as a body of believers united by a bond of mystical communion.

John Paul II is adamant on one capital point: No system will ensure and guarantee the rights and freedoms of the individual if it is not based on the laws of human behaviour revealed by God through the teaching of Christ, as proposed by Christ's Church. This is the backbone principle of the New World Order envisaged by the Pontiff.

The contemporary world order over which Pope John Paul casts his wide-sweeping gaze is not a tidy place. It is cluttered with all manner of groups, large and small, able to command greater or lesser publicity, all making their own globalist claims.

The members and spokesmen of these groups wax poetic about their vision. In their imagined grand design, the new world order will be one great Temple of Human Understanding. The truly global home of all nations will still resound with the languages of every nation and tribe; but they will be roofed over with the all-inclusive allegiance to the common good. Its walls will be decorated with the icons of the new values, peacefulness; healthfulness; respect for Earth and environmental devotion. But over all, there will be the great icon of Understanding. What divinity exists will be accepted as incarnate in man; divinity of, for and by-and only within-mankind. All other shapes and concepts of divinity will melt - are already melting; fusing gently and irresistibly into the Understanding of mankind's own inherent and godly power to fashion it's own destiny.

Intent upon predisposing as many minds as possible to the task of achieving heaven on earth, they have developed infiltration to a high art. Chameleon-like, they are to be found basking at the height of power everywhere in the West – in Transnationalist boardrooms and Internationalist bureaucracies: in the hierarchies of the Roman, Orthodox and other Christian churches; in major Jewish and Islamic

enclaves already dedicated to the total westernization of culture and civilisation."
Keys of this Blood. 15, 17, 19, 38-39.

Jesus warned us through His word that the deadly wound received by the Papacy would be healed and there is truly a major healing taking place.
So, with all the billions controlled by the Vatican, backed up by the Superpower status of Apostate America, the inevitable route we will be heading down is the final confrontation between good and evil. Satan has prepared a gigantic monolith to ensure that you do not find the escape route, but God has also made it possible to find the route.

Do not lose heart though, because Jesus Christ having died on the cross and shed his blood for our sins, was resurrected and is now in heaven; overcame Satan and has promised us that whosoever calls on His name and whosoever loves Him and keeps His commandments will be saved.

The battle will be between the commandments of God and the commandments of men. There will be those who will be victorious over the beast and its image etc., and those that will not.

Will you follow Jesus Christ, and abandon all your temporary worldly wealth, face the possibility of suffering from hunger, thrust out in the freezing cold or other weather? Will you be prepared to suffer the humiliation of imprisonment and mockery, even the threat of, or actual death? Or would you accept the number of Satan just to have access to all his supposed but very temporary kingdom?

"Satan works through the elements also to garner his harvest of unprepared souls. He has studied the secrets of the laboratories of nature, and he uses all his power to control the elements as far as God allows. When he was suffered to afflict Job, how quickly flocks and herds, servants, houses, children, were swept away, one trouble succeeding another as in a moment. It is God that shields His creatures and hedges them in from the power of the destroyer.

But the Christian world have shown contempt for the law of Jehovah; and the Lord will do just what He has declared that He would—He will withdraw His blessings from the earth and remove His protecting care from those who are rebelling against His law and teaching and forcing others to do the same. Satan has control of all whom God does not especially guard. He will favor and prosper some in order to further his own designs, and he will bring trouble upon others and lead men to believe that it is God who is afflicting them.

While appearing to the children of men as a great physician who can heal all their maladies, he will bring disease and disaster, until populous cities are reduced to ruin and desolation. Even now he is at work. In accidents and calamities by sea and land, in great conflagrations, fierce tornados and terrific hailstorms, in tempests, floods, cyclones, tidal waves, and earthquakes, in every place and in a thousand forms, he is exercising his power. He sweeps away the ripening harvest, and famine and distress follow. Destruction will be upon man and beast."

"The earth mourneth and fadeth away, the haughty people... do languish. The earth also is defiled under the inhabitants thereof;" (Why?) "because they have transgressed the laws, changed the ordinance, broken the everlasting covenant." Isaiah 24:4-5. Darkness before Dawn Pages 33-34.

"And the Lord said unto Satan, Whence comest thou? Then Satan answered the Lord, and said, From going to and fro in the earth, and from walking up and down in it. Job 1:7. Satan was "a murderer from the beginning." John 8:44. His temptations are leading multitudes to ruin. Intemperance dethrones reason; sensual indulgence, strife, and bloodshed follow. Satan delights in war; for it excites the worst passions of the soul, and then sweeps into eternity its victims steeped in vice and blood. It is his object to incite the nations to war against one another; for he can thus divert the minds of the people from the work of preparation to stand in the day of God.

In accidents and calamities by sea and by land, in great conflagrations, in fierce tornadoes and terrific hailstorms, in tempests, floods, cyclones, tidal waves, and earthquakes, in every place and in a thousand forms, Satan is exercising his power. He sweeps away the ripening harvest, and famine and distress follow. He imparts to the air a deadly taint, and thousands perish by the pestilence.(*an example,* Covid-19?) These visitations are to become more and more frequent and disastrous." The Faith I live By pg 328

Satan's activities along with mankind's breaking of the covenant as highlighted in Isaiah 24:4-5 confirms the reasons why disasters are on a massive increase on our planet. Humanity is choosing Satan instead of God, so God is gradually removing His protection, this removal of protection will be complete when the planet has reached the end of probationary time.

What though will be the end of the vast 'Mystery, 666' system and the effects it will truly have on the world?

Remember in Revelation 17:12, 16-18 that John saw the ten horns (earth's kingdoms) hating the whore, making her desolate, naked, eating her flesh and burning her with fire? How and why is that to happen?

I submit to you that it is through her usurpation of power and her greed for wealth, that the nations will discover her deception, but perhaps for most, too late, because their eternal destinies will have by then been forever sealed.

All of the calamities will be blamed on the people of God. and the sentence of death will be pronounced against them to finally rid the earth of those who continually call upon the name of the Lord.

Jesus Christ says "I call heaven and earth to record this day against you, that I have set before you life and death, blessing and cursing: therefore choose life, that both thou and thy seed may live." Deuteronomy 30:19.

The Cause of Evil Falsely Identified

To elaborate on a verse quoted earlier in this book I need to repeat it. "And the dragon was wroth with the woman, and went to make war with the remnant of her seed, which keep the commandments of God, and have the testimony of Jesus Christ" Revelation 12:17

No matter how popular the explanations or denials will be from both the papacy and fallen protestants that keep Sunday as the Sabbath it will not confirm that a remnant that are following the true sabbath are wrong. The above verse along with verse 12 ("Therefore rejoice, [ye] heavens, and ye that dwell in them. Woe to the inhabiters of the earth and of the sea! for the devil is come down unto you, having great wrath, because he knoweth that he hath but a short time.") confirms that it is a remnant of the planet that will stick to the truth. You dear reader are welcome to stick to the truth. Jesus died for all of humanity, unfortunately many will reject Him. Remember Noah's flood? How many came through alive? 8. The destruction of Sodom and Gomorrha and the other 3 cities of the plains for all the abominations committed there? How many came out alive? Lot's family of 4, but Lot's wife turned around to see and she also didn't survive, so only 3 survived.

Satan hates all of humanity with a passion and he hates with the deepest vehemence and rage those that choose to **keep God's commandments and have the testimony of Jesus Christ.**

The words 'keep' and 'testimony' described in the verse are very important to understand so I will refer to the concordance once more.

Keep

G5083

τηρέω

tēreō

tay-reh'-o

From τηρός teros (a *watch*; perhaps akin to G2334); to *guard* (from *loss* or *injury*, properly by keeping *the eye* upon; and thus differing from G5442, which is properly to *prevent* escaping; and from G2892, which implies a *fortress* or full military lines of apparatus), that is, to *note* (a prophecy; figuratively to *fulfil* a command); by implication to *detain* (in custody; figuratively to *maintain*); by extension to *withhold* (for personal ends; figuratively to *keep unmarried*): - hold fast, keep (-er), (ob-, pre-, re) serve, watch.

Those people are keeping an eye on God's commandments, they are guarding it, preventing it to escape? Why escape? So a fortress is built around it with full military lines of defence? In order to have lines of defence there has to be enemies and defenders. The remnant are the defenders of God's true sabbath. The enemies naturally are against God's true Sabbath. Enemies and defenders mean there will be a battle over it. The remnant, defenders, will be holding fast, keepers, preservers, watchers.

Testimony

G3141

μαρτυρία

marturia

mar-too-ree'-ah

From G3144; *evidence* given (judicially or generally): - record, report, testimony, witness.

This means the evidence, records, report, testimony and witness given by Jesus Himself. Dear friends we should tremble when we read this. Our Creator Himself is sharing with us the truth about the situation of planet earth and Satan's aims. What else do we need to understand to choose the right path and how to be one of God's eternal saints? To do that we need to open our eyes and act on the warnings and evidence. Take very special note of the word '**witness**' I will shed some more light on it in the next chapter.

Let's pay attention to the following from Darkness before dawn p34.

"And then the great deceiver will persuade men that those who serve God are causing these evils. The class that have provoked the displeasure of Heaven will charge all their troubles upon those whose obedience to God's commandments is a perpetual reproof to transgressors. It will be declared that men are offending God by the violation of the Sunday sabbath; that this sin has brought calamities which will not cease until Sunday observance shall be strictly enforced; and that those who present the claims of the fourth commandment, thus destroying reverence for Sunday, are troublers of the people, preventing their restoration to divine favor and temporal prosperity. Thus the accusation urged of old against the servant of God will be repeated and upon grounds equally well established:

"And it came to pass, when Ahab saw Elijah, that Ahab said unto him, Art thou he that troubleth Israel? And he answered, I have not troubled Israel; but thou, and thy father's house, in that ye have forsaken the commandments of the Lord, and thou hast followed Baalim." 1 Kings 18:17, 18. As the wrath of the people shall be excited by false charges, they will pursue a course toward God's ambassadors very similar to that which apostate Israel pursued toward Elijah."

Notice that apostate Israel forsook Gods' commandments just like apostate humans and the apostate churches will forsake Gods' commandments.

"The miracle-working power manifested through spiritualism will exert its influence against those who choose to obey God rather than men. Communications from the spirits will declare that God has sent them to convince the rejecters of Sunday of their error, affirming that the laws of the land should be obeyed as the law of God. They will lament the great wickedness in the world and second the testimony of religious teachers that the

411

degraded state of morals is caused by the desecration of Sunday. Great will be the indignation excited against all who refuse to accept their testimony.

Satan's policy in this final conflict with God's people is the same that he employed in the opening of the great controversy in heaven. He professed to be seeking to promote the stability of the divine government, while secretly bending every effort to secure its overthrow. And the very work which he was thus endeavoring to accomplish he charged upon the loyal angels. The same policy of deception has marked the history of the Roman Church. It has professed to act as the vicegerent of Heaven, while seeking to exalt itself above God and to change His law.

Under the rule of Rome, those who suffered death for their fidelity to the gospel were denounced as evildoers; they were declared to be in league with Satan; and every possible means was employed to cover them with reproach, to cause them to appear in the eyes of the people and even to themselves as the vilest of criminals. So it will be now. While Satan seeks to destroy those who honor God's law, he will cause them to be accused as lawbreakers, as men who are dishonoring God and bringing judgments upon the world."

"The Special Point of Controversy

When the Sabbath shall become the special point of controversy throughout Christendom, the persistent refusal of a small minority to yield to the popular demand will make them objects of universal execration. Satan will excite indignation against the humble remnant who conscientiously refuse to accept the customs and traditions of error. Blinded by the prince of darkness, popular

412

religionists will see only as he sees, and feel as he feels. They will determine as he determines, and oppress as he has oppressed. Liberty of conscience, which has cost this nation so great a sacrifice, will no longer be respected. The church and the world will unite, and the world will lend to the church her power to crush out the right of the people to worship God according to His Word. {ST, February 22, 1910 par. 4}

It will be urged that the few who stand in opposition to an institution of the church and a law of the state, ought not to be tolerated; that it is better for them to suffer than for whole nations to be thrown into confusion and lawlessness. This argument will appear conclusive; and against those who hallow the Sabbath of the fourth commandment will finally be issued a decree denouncing them as deserving of the severest punishment, and giving the people liberty, after a certain time, to put them to death. {ST, February 22, 1910 par. 5}

At this point I need to bring my readers back to the Covid situation. Can you identify a similar language in the following press article to what you have just read about Sabbath keepers at the end of time and note how the intended methods are meant to justify the outcome?

"A more controversial issue is over restrictions on social interaction. Over the last two years policy argument has raged about the balance to be struck between curbing personal freedoms in order to stop the transmission of the virus, hospitalisation and deaths, and the economic and wider costs of those curbs.

The parameters of that debate are however quite different to a year ago. The success of the vaccination roll-out in Britain and most other developed economies has changed

413

the balance of the argument in two key respects. First, the level of vaccination, with boosters, combined with the antibodies of the many millions who have had Covid, protects a large majority from the risk of further serious infection. Consequently, Covid has become a disease we can live with.

Secondly, the threat to society at large from omicron comes not from the virus itself but from pressures on the NHS from rapidly growing numbers of serious infections among the unvaccinated. The pressures are felt by NHS staff but also those whose treatment for other diseases is disrupted or postponed. There is therefore a big divide opening between the vaccinated, who want to get on with their lives, and the unvaccinated who are at growing risk and are responsible for restrictions affecting everyone.

The harm caused to society by the unvaccinated is partly that there is increased transmissibility. The evidence is contested but there are clear findings from the research conducted at Imperial College by Professor Lalvani's team and the UK Health Security Agency, published in The Lancet, that while vaccinated people can pass on the disease, they do so at lower rates (about half). Then, additionally, because they are unprotected, unvaccinated people are themselves at greater risk of becoming very unwell and placing serious pressures on the NHS.

A head of steam is therefore building up behind the idea that further curbs on freedoms should mainly apply to the unvaccinated. A recent article by Andrew Neil in the Mail spelt out very forcefully the logic which leads inexorably to some form of discrimination through vaccine passports.

The idea that unvaccinated people should be treated differently and discriminated against as a conscious policy

414

runs into several objections. The first is widely heard but weak: that people have a basic right to exercise a choice not to be jabbed. But if that exercise of choice harms others, it is not a valid choice. We do not allow motorists to choose to drive the wrong way down a motorway or allow people to choose to hold noisy, all-night, parties whenever they wish.

A more serious point is that there are some people who have genuine health reasons for not being vaccinated, because of allergies or compromised immune systems. But ways can be found to accommodate them, such as GP certification to explain any exemption.

The most difficult objection is that there are distinct groups who have refused injection not as a result of laziness or bloody-mindedness but because of widespread suspicion, based on experience, that the authorities are not to be trusted. In the US, some black Americans cite the history of being used for scientific experiments. Others have been fed plausible misinformation by community leaders. But these arguments are wearing a little thin. Elected ethnic minority figures, such as the Mayor of London, have given strong, clear leadership on the need for vaccination. And indulgence of anti-vax sentiment may do more to inflame ethnic divisions than to insist on conformity.

This is a classic case of the distinction between "freedoms from" and "freedoms to". It is objectionable that the freedom of a majority from restrictions on their daily lives might be removed by the freedom of a minority to refuse vaccination.

Furthermore, the experience of France and other European countries is that, faced with serious barriers, large numbers of unvaccinated people drop their objections to vaccination very quickly. France was regarded as implacably anti-vax; but quite suddenly that has changed.

As we consider what to do about the unvaccinated here, there are three options – compulsion through employment conditions; changes to rights of treatment under the NHS; and a more comprehensive vaccine passport system.

It is, of course, impractical and unacceptable to have refuseniks dragged away, held down and forcefully injected. However, compulsion as a condition of employment is already happening for NHS and care staff in the UK and elsewhere. There is a risk of losing some quality staff who, for whatever reason, refuse to comply. But that risk must be set against the wider public interest including maintaining the confidence of patients and those who use care services.

Another approach is to penalise the unvaccinated by restricting their access to the NHS. As things stand, large numbers of unvaccinated people who present themselves at A&E with severe Covid symptoms will get preferential treatment over those with lethal but slowly evolving diseases like cancer. Most of us, and I suspect most medical professionals, would regard that as fundamentally unjust.

However, doctors have a professional duty to treat the patients in front of them. People who put themselves at risk by base jumping, climbing vertical rock faces without support or getting seriously drunk can expect the same treatment as everyone else. A pandemic is however quite different from individual eccentricities or indulgence. The sheer numbers of infected cases prevents other patients receiving the care they need."
https://www.scribd.com/article/547863844/Voices-What-To-Do-About-The-Anti-Vaxxers-There-Are-Three-Options

I cannot complete this chapter without addressing the situation in many of our religious institutions that are capitulating to the global narrative, however, I must also add that not all our Pastors are acquiescing to the narrative and I will quote from one of them.

"An Appeal to Church Members

The majority of voices in our church keep assuring us that vaccine mandates are not the dreaded "mark of the beast." So does that mean that we should not be concerned about these mandates? Is the "mark of the beast" the totality of the third angel's message? So as long as we are not at that "mark of the beast" stage of prophetic development all is well?

It is true that vaccine mandates are not the "mark of the beast," however they are a very significant assault on liberty of conscience, especially in America. Think about this for a minute if you will. The US government is forcing millions of thinking people to receive into their bodies a substance that:

1. Is new technology
2. Is emergency use only
3. Has unlisted ingredients
4. Has unknown long term affects
5. Does not always prevent infection
6. Does not always prevent death
7. Does not prevent transmission
8. Loses efficiency in months
9. Requires booster shots
10. Caused adverse effects and even death in hundreds of thousands of people.

At the same time the US government:
1. Ignores the well-established science of natural immunity
2. Dismisses other effective science based treatments
3. Discredits those who question the vaccine narrative with proven science as sharing "fake news" and misinformation."

Additionally we are being asked to comply with this political narrative which is anti-science for the "common good."

Our church seems so focused on credibility that those who ask science based questions like "what about natural immunity" or "vaccinated break-through infection rates and transmission" must be listening to wack conspiracy theories and ignoring "the science" (there is true and false science - evolution is backed by "the science").

Then there are the supposedly wise words of conventional wisdom, "Save your credibility for the real 'mark of the beast' crisis." As if to say, "kindly consider saving your exemption letters for the time just before the end of the world when you'll really need to keep your job to pay your bills.
You certainly don't want to risk losing your job, career, educational and public access - your ability to buy and sell now." If you lose everything now you'll have nothing to lose when the media and all the institutionally faithful social justice watchmen alert us to the real "mark of the beast" crisis. As if we will be filing religious exemption letters when the "mark of the beast" crisis comes (Daniel and his friends were first tested on what they put into their bodies. They asked for and received religious exemptions for their health crisis, but there were no religious exemptions for the worship tests - the fiery furnace or the den of lions).

Dear friends, please prayerfully consider:

The third angel's message is much more than the "mark of the beast."

The first angel heralds the everlasting gospel of God's love for the entire world which calls us to liberty of conscience. Free choice - to choose God or the devil - is central to the Great Controversy. The third angel's message calls us to fear God and not man. It calls us to glorify God in what we take into our bodies, in eating or drinking or whatsoever we do (1 Corinthians 10:31). It calls us to worship God because we were created in His image and our bodies belong to Him by creation and redemption.

The second angel announces the fall of Babylon, code word for a world-wide religio-political system that has deceived the nations, in part, by her sorceries (Revelation 18:23- "sorceries - pharmakeia- from Strong's G5332; medication - "pharmacy").

The third angel warns against worshiping the beast and the image to the beast. This is, in principle, the action of church/state unity compelling the conscience by economic sanctions in matters that belong solely between the individual and God.

No, the world-wide vaccine mandates are not the final "mark of the beast" crisis, but they certainly portend that event for they bring with them a clear and present danger of liberty of conscience threatened.

The last movements will be rapid ones. The enemy of souls is moving us as close as he can to these final movements, hoping we will not be alerted to our danger.

Read The Great Controversy chapters 35 to 39. Note specifically the order (and content) of these chapters:

35. Liberty of Conscience Threatened
36. The Impending Conflict
37. The Scriptures a Safeguard
38. The Final Warning
39. The Time of Trouble

Notice that "liberty of conscience threatened" leads us into the final crisis - it precedes the "mark of the beast" threat. And that only makes sense. The "mark of the beast" cannot gain momentum with liberty of conscience alive and well. That old battle cry from Patrick Henry - "give me liberty or give me death" - must be decimated in the hearts and minds of present-day Americans before the "mark of the beast" can have its way.

Please think prayerfully about your life, your present priorities, how you spend the majority of your time, how you feel about the second coming of Jesus and if you are truly preparing yourself and others for this long looked for event. Ask God to search your heart claiming His promise:

"Search me, O God, and know my heart: try me, and know my thoughts: And see if there be any wicked way in me, and lead me in the way everlasting" (Psalm 139:23-24 KJV).

Thank you for taking the time to consider this appeal. In Jesus' name. Amen.

Spirit of Prophecy -

"The exercise of force is contrary to the principles of God's government; He desires only the service of love; and love cannot be commanded; it cannot be won by force or authority. Only by love is love awakened" (DA 22).

"Compelling power is found only under Satan's government. The Lord's principles are not of this order. His authority rests upon goodness, mercy, and love; and the presentation of these principles is the means to be used. God's government is moral, and truth and love are to be the prevailing power" (DA 759).

Pastor James Rafferty

Rev 9:21 Neither[G2532] [G3756] repented[G3340] they of[G1537] their[G848] murders,[G5408] nor[G3777] of[G1537] their[G848] sorceries,[G5331] nor[G3777] of[G1537] their[G848] fornication,[G4202] nor[G3777] of[G1537] their[G848] thefts.[G2809]

Rev 18:23 And[G2532] the light[G5457] of a candle[G3088] shall shine[G5316] no more at all[G2089] [G3364] in[G1722] thee;[G4671] and[G2532] the voice[G5456] of the bridegroom[G3566] and[G2532] of the bride[G3565] shall be heard[G191] no more at all[G2089] [G3364] in[G1722] thee:[G4671] for[G3754] thy[G4675] merchants[G1713] were[G2258] the[G3588] great men[G3175] of the[G3588] earth;[G1093] for[G3754] by[G1722] thy[G4675] sorceries[G5331] were all[G3956] nations[G1484] deceived.[G4105]

G5331

φαρμακεία

pharmakeia

far-mak-i'-ah

From G5332; *medication* ("pharmacy"), that is, (by extension) *magic* (literal or figurative): - sorcery, witchcraft.

φαρμακεύς

pharmakeus

far-mak-yoos'

From φάρμακον pharmakon (a *drug*, that is, spell giving *potion*); a *druggist* ("pharmacist") or *poisoner*, that is, (by extension) a *magician*: - sorcerer.

We can choose to ignore the fulfilments of the above prophecies or pay attention to them. Are not the nations of the earth being deceived by what is happening under Covid? Is liberty of conscience being threatened and destroyed? Are families and livelihoods being destroyed? There are places in the world already where you cannot buy or sell without being jabbed, so how much easier will be it to translate these practises against those who choose to show their allegiance to the God of heaven by rejecting Satan's worship system?

Words of warning to the last days church:

"The remnant church will be brought into great trial and distress. Those who keep the commandments of God and the faith of Jesus, will feel the ire of the dragon and his hosts. Satan numbers the world as his subjects; he has gained control of the apostate churches; but here is a little company that are resisting his supremacy. If he could blot them from the earth, his triumph would be complete. As he influenced the heathen nations to destroy Israel, so in the near future he will stir up the wicked powers of earth to destroy the people of God. All will be required to render obedience to human edicts in violation of the divine law. Those who will be true to God and to duty will be betrayed "both by parents, and brethren, and kinsfolks, and friends."

Testimonies, vol. 9, p. 231. {ChS 157.1}

"The time is not far distant when the test will come to every soul. The observance of the false sabbath will be urged upon us. The contest will be between the commandments of God and the commandments of men. Those who have yielded step by step to worldly demands, and conformed to worldly customs, will then yield to the powers that be, rather than subject themselves to derision, insult, threatened imprisonment, and death. At that time the gold will be separated from the dross. . . . Many a star that we have admired for its brilliance will then go out in darkness. Those who have assumed the ornaments of the sanctuary, but are not clothed with Christ's righteousness, will then appear in the shame of their own nakedness"
Prophets and Kings, p. 188. {ChS 157.2}

We can understand that Romanism in the Old World, and apostate Protestantism in the New, will pursue a similar course toward those who honour all the divine precepts. This is the mystery of iniquity, the devising of satanic agencies, carried into effect by the man of sin. Remember whilst Jesus was in the wilderness for forty days and nights that amongst Satan's temptations were, that Jesus should bow down and worship him? If he has the audacity to demand worship from his Creator, don't you think he will do the same with humanity? To say no to this question would deny all the evidence laid out in this book and to defy logic. Did he not use food, material things and worship as part of his arsenal of temptations?

"Satan claims the world as his kingdom, and counts as his subjects those who unite with him in opposition to the God of heaven, because they have chosen him as their ruler. He is unable to dethrone Jehovah; but he exalts himself as the ruler of this world, and plants his throne between the soul

423

who would worship toward heaven, and the divine being Jehovah, who alone is worthy of all honor, glory, and praise, to whom alone belong all power, dominion, and might. Satan arranges his plans in such a way as to intercept the worship due to God, and to transfer to himself the adoration due to God alone. But the Lord did not leave the fallen race to the mercy of the devices of the enemy. He selected a people for himself, and gave directions for the erection of a temple for the benefit of those who would be his true worshipers, in order that the presence and the name of the Lord might not be forgotten in the earth. This temple of the true God was to stand as a protest against the usurpation of the enemy, a testimony to the fact that there is a living and true God, a proclamation of the character of Jehovah, and his right to the supreme regard of men. Satan was stirred with enmity toward the worshipers of God, and determined to seduce this people into idolatry, and cause the name of God to be blotted from the earth.
{ST, Special Testimonies, June 13, 1895 par. 2}

Satan determined to sit upon the throne of God in the earth, to sit in the temple of God, showing himself to be God. For ages he seemed to rule as though the world was entirely his own, and his assumption to supreme authority seemed undisputed. The powers of hell seemed to hold men under their control, and Satan revealed his hellish principles in taking possession of the human body, and plunging his subjects into misery and crime. To all appearances the world had become his subjects, with the exception of a small minority who dared to withstand his power and to dispute his authority. Through his agents he invented instruments of torture, and put his victims to cruel suffering, and then he charged his own attributes upon God, and indicted the law of God as the cause of men's misery. Temptation became a science in his hands, and men were educated to be sinners. The confederacies of evil were numerous, and every demon power had a part to act in carrying out the plottings of evil, and every worker was to be ready to spring into action to do his assigned work at an instant's notice. Could the curtain have been withdrawn so that men could have seen what measures were being taken to gain access to the human soul, could they have realized how successful the demoniacal plottings were to prove, they could have stood back with horror, and would have broken with Satan without delay. {ST, June 13, 1895 par. 3}

But though men failed to see the deep plottings of the enemy of God and men, these plottings were not hidden from the hosts of heaven. They were known to God, and a way of escape was provided for all who would believe in the plan of salvation, devised from the foundation of the world. Jesus came to our world to oppose the usurper, and Christ was the object of Satan's hate. Christ was the rightful sovereign of the world, and Satan proposed to seduce him from his loyalty to the law of God. He led him into the wilderness of temptation, and tempted Christ, saying that if Jesus would bow down and worship him he would make him the king of the world. He declared: "All this power will I give thee, and the glory of them; for that is delivered unto me; and to whomsoever I will, I give it. If thou therefore wilt worship me, all shall be thine." But Christ had come to the world to dispute the assumed authority of Satan, and to overthrow his claims to the kingdom of this world. "And Jesus answered and said unto him, Get thee behind me, Satan; for it is written, Thou shalt worship the Lord thy God, and him only shalt thou serve." {ST, June 13, 1895 par. 4}

Christ came to reveal to the world, in the sight of heavenly intelligences, the true character of the Father, and to present his claims to the sovereignty of the universe.

425

Jesus represented the character of the Father in a way to disprove the lying representations of the enemy, for the Son of God revealed the Father as a being full of mercy, compassion, goodness, truth, and love. Far from casting off the fallen sons of Adam, Jesus had come to take upon himself their guilt, woe, and misery, and to suffer the penalty of the law which man had transgressed. In him dwelt all the fullness of the Godhead bodily. He was the express image of his Father's person, the brightness of his glory. {ST, June 13, 1895 par. 5}

Christ was the way, the truth, and the life. He came down from the royal courts of heaven, and appeared in untarnished glory, in perfection of beauty, in holiness of character, the chiefest among ten thousand, and the One altogether lovely. So unblemished was he that he could say, "Satan cometh, and hath nothing in me." {ST, June 13, 1895 par. 6}

But though no taint of evil could be found in the Son of God, though no flaw could be detected, though men could find no fault in him, yet, controlled by the Satanic hate of their leader, men rose up against the Prince of life, and with demoniacal fury they cried, "Away with him, away with him, crucify him." When Pilate brought forth Jesus and Barabbas, and asked, "Whether of the twain will ye that I release unto you? They said, Barabbas." They preferred a robber and a murderer to the Son of God, and when asked what should be done with Jesus, they cried, "Let him be crucified." But the great object for which Christ had come to the earth was not defeated by his death and suffering. Though he was led as a lamb to the slaughter, and as a sheep before her shearers is dumb, so he opened not his mouth, yet he revealed the love of God for a fallen world; for "God so loved the world, that he gave his only-begotten Son, that whosoever believeth in him should not perish, but have everlasting life."

Satan is attempting to disassemble all that has been established for our eternal happiness. The day to worship God, the sanctity of the marriage is now corrupted by Satan's children of disobedience, (Ephesians 2:1-5) and he has society trumpeting that humans are genderless and simply binary units. If God did not come to end this madness, eventually there would not be any humans, maybe even any life left on this planet.

"And I saw another sign in heaven, great and marvellous, seven angels having the seven last plagues; for in them is filled up the wrath of God.

 And I saw as it were a sea of glass mingled with fire: and them that had gotten the victory over the beast, and over his image, and over his mark, [and] over the number of his name, stand on the sea of glass, having the harps of God.
And they sing the song of Moses the servant of God, and the song of the Lamb, saying, Great and marvellous [are] thy works, Lord God Almighty; just and true [are] thy ways, thou King of saints." Revelation: 15:1-3.

Dear readers the solution is quite simple, when did Jesus say He would return? Matthew 24:14 "And this gospel of the kingdom shall be preached in all the world for a **witness** unto all nations; and then shall the end come" What exactly is this verse saying? I will enlighten you in the next chapter.

His contract between us and Him has been declared to all the world and everyone will come to know the truth of the matter, then Jesus will come. Jesus has made it plain "And ye shall hear of wars and rumours of wars: see that ye be not troubled: for all [these things] must come to pass, but the end is not yet..... and there shall be famines, and pestilences, and earthquakes, in divers places..." Matthew 24:6-7.

 In other words the wars and disasters etc. are not the final sign of His coming that we should be looking for, although these will get worse and worse, but we should be looking out for the truth of the gospel of His kingdom being spread to every corner of the globe. That's great news dear friends. Unfolding events will ensure that this truth will be made known and that everyone will have had the opportunity to make an informed decision.

The Abomination of Desolation:

Why did Jesus tell us in Matthew 24:15 and Mark 13:14 that we that read these verses must understand? What is there that needs to be understood?
"When ye therefore shall see the abomination of desolation, spoken of by Daniel the prophet, stand in the holy place, (whoso readeth, let him understand:)"
"But when ye shall see the abomination of desolation, spoken of by Daniel the prophet, standing where it ought not, (let him that readeth understand,) then let them that be in Judaea flee to the mountains:"

The abomination of desolation Jesus spoke about has 2 fulfilments, the first happened to the literal Jews and the 2nd will affect the Spiritual Jews.
Time of the Jews 70AD – "When the idolatrous standards of the Romans should be set up in the holy ground, which extended some furlongs outside the city walls, then the followers of Christ were to find safety in flight. When the warning sign should be seen, those who would escape must make no delay. Throughout the land of Judea, as well as in Jerusalem itself, the signal for flight must be immediately obeyed. He who chanced to be upon the housetop must not

go down into his house, even to save his most valued treasures. Those who were working in the fields or vineyards must not take time to return for the outer garment laid aside while they should be toiling in the heat of the day. They must not hesitate a moment, lest they be involved in the general destruction." Great Controversy p 88.

Not a single Christian died when the Romans returned and utterly destroyed Jerusalem and the Temple. What does that mean for modern day Christians? The Jews faced judgment for turning against Jesus, will there be a judgment too for modern-day Christians? Yes, but how? Remember Jesus' directive to "understand."

The planting of the Papal standards or tabernacles? In literal Jerusalem to vindicate its position in Spiritual Jerusalem (the world) are the laws of Satan that betray and deny Jesus Christ. Laws that the papacy changed as we have described in previous chapters will be forced on the inhabitants of earth. Those laws combined with the financial blackmail of earth's inhabitants under the new buying and selling regime are the abominations that will make the earth desolate. You need to remember the other verse that is directly connected to this event, Revelation 13:18, also tells us to understand "….let him that hath understanding count the number of the beast…." Man's breaking of God's laws even before its church and state enforcement have already caused the earth to "mourn and fade away" and when it is made a global law, everything will come to a climax as described by Daniel in Chapter 12:1.

"And at that time shall Michael stand up, the great prince which standeth for the children of thy people: and there shall be a time of trouble, such as never was since there was a nation [even] to that same time: and at that time thy people shall be delivered, every one that shall be found written in the book."

Truly this time period will be an immense time of trouble that nobody currently on planet earth can possibly imagine. But how are we to be found written in the book? God's book? We can only be written in a book because we have been found worthy. What does that imply? There will be a judgment. There has to be one, otherwise the God of heaven will not be a God of order or of process. This judgment will be around the mark of the beast. Receive Satan's number, name etc. and you will not be in God's book. Reject Satan's number, name etc. and you will be in God's book.

We have quoted this verse before but need to repeat it because it is the same church that is described as the Mother of … Abominations (that we have been warned about from Christ's own lips and who gave in the book of Revelation to John Rev:1:1 "The Revelation of Jesus Christ, which God gave unto him, to show unto his servants things which must shortly come to pass; and he sent and signified [it] by his angel unto his servant John") that will be planting, driving, it's abominations into the world. "And upon her forehead [was] a name written, MYSTERY, BABYLON THE GREAT, THE MOTHER OF HARLOTS AND ABOMINATIONS OF THE EARTH." Rev: 17:5. Do you see the connection from tracing the history and plans and do you UNDERSTAND? (Emphasis mine)

Time of the end – "The time is not far distant, when, like the early disciples, we shall be forced to seek a refuge in desolate and solitary places. As the siege of Jerusalem by the Roman armies was the signal for flight to the Judean Christians, so the assumption of power on the part of our nation [the United States] in the decree enforcing the papal Sabbath will be a warning to us. It will then be time to leave the large cities, preparatory to leaving the smaller ones for retired homes in secluded places among the mountains. Maranatha p 180.

Was there an occasion when the United States and Sunday keeping church organisations attempted to plant their banners of the mark of the beast around a law upholding Sunday?

Yes there was, around the late 1800's and early 1900's, read appendix 4. You will find in appendix 4 that those proposing a Sunday law were defeated. Because of that defeat they proposed that it should be put forward as a "Federal blue law that would serve a public-welfare purpose and promote the interest of the labouring man." The second version is now being put forward not only to include the interests of labouring mankind, but under the premise of climate change. Appendix 5.

Does that mean that the first warning to the world has already been given and that the second time around they will succeed and that this attempt to plant their banners will be the final one?

"And in the days of these kings shall the God of heaven set up a kingdom, which shall never be destroyed: and the kingdom shall not be left to other people, [but] it shall break in pieces and consume all these kingdoms, and it shall stand for ever. Forasmuch as thou sawest that the stone was cut out of the mountain without hands, and that it brake in pieces the iron, the brass, the clay, the silver, and the gold; the great God hath made known to the king what shall come to pass hereafter: and the dream [is] certain, and the interpretation thereof sure." Daniel 2:44-45.

431

Popery will come to an end and many will have discovered the truth and chosen Jesus.

"And the ten horns which thou sawest are ten kings, which have received no kingdom as yet; but receive power as kings one hour with the beast. These have one mind, and shall give their power and strength unto the beast. These shall make war with the Lamb, and the Lamb shall overcome them: for he is Lord of lords, and King of kings: and they that are with him [are] called, and chosen, and faithful. And he saith unto me, the waters which thou sawest, where the whore sitteth, are peoples, and multitudes, and nations, and tongues. And the ten horns which thou sawest upon the beast, these shall hate the whore, and shall make her desolate and naked, and shall eat her flesh, and burn her with fire. For God hath put in their hearts to fulfil his will, and to agree, and give their kingdom unto the beast, until the words of God shall be fulfilled. And the woman which thou sawest is that great city, which reigneth over the kings of the earth." Revelation 17:11-18.

Note the sequence of events from the Mount Carmel type event:

Verse 14, he has power to do the miracles in the sight of the beast. An image is then made to the beast.

Verse 15, The image of the beast is setup. The False Sabbath and system of worship is elevated. Threats of the death sentence is promoted against all who will not subscribe to the false system of worship.

Verses 16–17, All members of society will be forced to receive a number for all transactions, be they economic, medicinal, educational, you name it.

Verse 18, the wise will know that this system is from none else but Satan with his MYSTERY 666 number.

Strong's Lexicon concordance on the word 'count' in Rev:13:18 means:

1) to count with pebbles, to compute, calculate, reckon
2) to give one's vote by casting a pebble into the urn

3) to decide by voting – Satan will deceive the world into voting for his false system just as in current times he is deceiving the masses to vote into law, corruptions and immorality under the guise of 'equality' and 'preferences' He will engineer 'climate change' calamities and events to deceive the world into voting for the papal solution as the answer.

How significant is this meaning of 'vote'? our politicians, through the media, have a huge influence on matters that will indirectly and directly affect our futures. Consider the British 'Brexit' referendum. Many members of the British public thought it a wonderful idea to vote Britain out of the EU thinking it would be great, but is it? It is going horribly wrong and so it will be when the whole world is deceived into passing laws and putting processes in place believing it will be the best move to make for humanity without realising that they are being deceived and not realising the repercussions of what they are voting for. My hope is that not only one person will be better informed after studying the contents of this book, but that many millions will at last be given an opportunity to understand the bigger picture and choose the correct path.

A few more clear cut quotes as we conclude this chapter.

Satan will be deified

"In this age antichrist will appear as the true Christ, and then the law of God will be fully made void in the nations of our world. Rebellion against God's holy law will be fully ripe. But the true leader of all this rebellion is Satan clothed as an angel of light. Men will be deceived and will exalt him to the place of God, and deify him. But Omnipotence will interpose, and to the apostate churches that unite in the exaltation of Satan, the sentence will go forth, "Therefore shall her plagues come in one day, death, and mourning, and famine; and she shall be utterly burned with fire: for strong is the Lord God who judgeth her" Testimonies to Ministers page 62.

"As the second appearing of our Lord Jesus Christ draws near, Satanic agencies are moved from beneath. Satan will not only appear as a human being, but he will personate Jesus Christ, and the world that has rejected the truth will receive him as the Lord of lords and King of king." Last Day events page 169.

"Satan will come in to deceive if possible the very elect. He claims to be Christ, and he is coming in, pretending to be the great medical missionary. He will cause fire to come down from heaven in the sight of men to prove that he is God." Medical Ministry 87, 88.

Those who refuse to join Satan and his false system will incur his wrath and through the papacy, the apostate churches and the Papal military arm, he, Satan, will set out to 'make away many' of God's people.

Why?

Because:

"Multitudes Will Join the Armies of the Lord. -- Many . . . will be seen hurrying hither and thither, constrained by the Spirit of God to bring the light to others. The truth, the Word of God, is as a fire in their bones, filling them with a burning desire to enlighten those who sit in darkness. Many, even among the uneducated, now proclaim the words of the Lord. Children are impelled by the Spirit to go forth and declare the message from heaven. The Spirit is poured out upon all who will yield to its promptings, and, casting off all man's machinery, his binding rules and cautious methods, they will declare the truth with the might of the Spirit's power. Multitudes will receive the faith and join the armies of the Lord. -- Review and Herald, July 23, 1895.

Utterly make away many

"But tidings out of the east and out of the north shall trouble him: therefore he shall go forth with great fury to destroy, and utterly to make away many." Daniel 11:44.

We need to examine and compare these verses, scripture with scripture because this is where things can appear complicated. Remember that we are dealing with a spiritual power and that these are the final series of events that will take place at the end of this known world. We have previously discovered that verse 45 confirms that this spiritual power will succeed in planting his tabernacles in the glorious holy mountain.

How do we understand the meaning of "utterly make away many"?

Part of understanding those words is the reason, "tidings out of the east and out of the north shall trouble him: therefore he shall go forth with great fury to destroy..."

Those who fell by the hand of popery during the dark ages fell because they understood the papacy as a fallen church, and they refused to obey the papacy by a "thus saith the Lord or Sola Scriptura" and they paid for that with their lives.

"And they that understand among the people shall instruct many: yet they shall fall by the sword, and by flame, by captivity, and by spoil, [many] days, And [some] of them of understanding shall fall, to try them, and to purge, and to make [them] white, [even] to the time of the end: because [itis] yet for a time appointed." Daniel 11: 33 & 35.

They gave their lives because they understood salvation came not from works as the papal system taught, such as absolution, penance, indulgences, confessions to mortal priests etc; but those people would not have known about the "tidings out of the east and out of the north" because the book of Daniel was sealed until "the time of the end" These "tidings" were yet future.

What are these tidings? To answer this we need to go to the book of Revelation (revealing). We'll begin in chapter 14 verses 6-12.

"And I saw another angel fly in the midst of heaven, having the everlasting gospel to preach unto them that dwell on the earth, and to every nation, and kindred, and tongue, and people,"

"Saying with a loud voice, Fear God, and give glory to him; for the hour of his judgment is come: and worship him that made heaven, and earth, and the sea, and the fountains of waters.

And there followed another angel, saying, Babylon is fallen, is fallen, that great city, because she made all nations drink of the wine of the wrath of her fornication.

And the third angel followed them, saying with a loud voice, If any man worship the beast and his image, and receive [his] mark in his forehead, or in his hand,

The same shall drink of the wine of the wrath of God, which is poured out without mixture into the cup of his indignation; and he shall be tormented with fire and brimstone in the presence of the holy angels, and in the presence of the Lamb:

And the smoke of their torment ascendeth up for ever and ever: and they have no rest day nor night, who worship the beast and his image, and whosoever receiveth the mark of his name.

Here is the patience of the saints: here [are] they that keep the commandments of God, and the faith of Jesus."

These are clear messages of warning to the world that the papal system is a fallen system and God is about to bring it to an end, but not before His people have delivered the messages of warning to the entire world.

This is it dear readers, any organisation that denies God's laws, denies the Messiah as the Son of God, that encourages the worshipping of Idols all fall under the same "MYSTERY" religious system that God warns about, however, the papal system is the fortress of all of this evil and God wants His truth-seeking people to come out of her so they will not receive her plagues. Are there any other verses of scripture in the new testament that make it very plain that your life will depend on accepting this truth as the ultimate qualifier for eternity?

"And this gospel of the kingdom shall be preached in all the world for a witness unto all nations; and then shall the end come."

"When ye therefore shall see the abomination of desolation, spoken of by Daniel the prophet, stand in the holy place, (whoso readeth, let him understand:)" Mark 13:14.

"But when ye shall see the abomination of desolation, spoken of by Daniel the prophet, standing where it ought not, (let him that readeth understand,)" What do these verses mean?

Gospel?
G2098

εὐαγγέλιον
euaggelion
yoo-ang-ghel'-ee-on
From the same as G2097; a *good message*, that is, the *gospel:* - gospel.

G2097

εὐαγγελίζω
euaggelizō
yoo-ang-ghel-id'-zo

From G2095 and G32; to *announce good* news ("evangelize") especially the gospel: - declare, bring (declare, show) glad (good) tidings, preach (the gospel).

Kingdom?

G932
βασιλεία
basileia
bas-il-i'-ah

From G935; properly *royalty*, that is, (abstractly) *rule*, or (concretely) a *realm* (literally or figuratively): - kingdom, + reign.

G935
βασιλεύς
basileus
bas-il-yooce'
Probably from G939 (through the notion of a *foundation* of power); a *sovereign* (abstractly, relatively or figuratively): - king.
Preached?

G2784
κηρύσσω
kērussō
kay-roos'-so
Of uncertain affinity; to *herald* (as a public *crier*), especially divine truth (the gospel): - preach (-er), proclaim, publish.

Witness?

Usually we consider the word "witness" to mean the following: (and yes, you would be correct)

Witness

verb (used with object)
1. to see, hear, or know by personal presence and perception: *to witness an accident.*
2. to be present at (an occurrence) as a formal witness, spectator, bystander, etc.: *She witnessed our wedding.*
3. to bear witness to; testify to; give or afford evidence of.
4. to attest by one's signature: *He witnessed her will.*

However, **there is something very unusual and exciting about the word "witness" in Matthew 24:14** that I alluded to in the previous chapter that is quite unique amongst all the other incidences to be found in the bible. **Please do not miss it.** I will quote the verse again as found in e-sword with the corresponding concordance numbers.

"And this gospel[G2098] of the kingdom[G932] shall be preached[G2784] in all the world for a witness[G3142] unto all nations; and then shall the end[G5056] come."

What does witness in Matthew 24:14 mean?

G3142
μαρτύριον
marturion
mar-too'-ree-on
... something evidential, that is, (generally) evidence given or **(specifically) the Decalogue** (in the sacred Tabernacle): - to be testified, testimony, witness.

With this in mind let us re-read the verse.

The good news of the kingdom will be proclaimed, published in all the world for evidence unto all nations, specifically the Decalogue, Deca? Ten? (God's original ten commandments that has the Sabbath as the sign of His Lordship.)

"For [in] six days the LORD made heaven and earth, the sea, and all that in them [is],..." - Buried in Matthew 24:14 is the fact that the Decalogue is to be honoured. Note also 5056(and then shall the end come) explanation from the concordance. **This is the final and uttermost event.**

G5056
τέλος
telos
tel'-os

441

From a primary word τέλλω tellō (to *set out* for a definite point or *goal*); properly the point aimed at as a *limit*, that is, (by implication) the *conclusion* of an act or state (*termination* [literally, figuratively or indefinitely], *result* [immediate, ultimate or prophetic] .... **finally, uttermost.**

Here, dear reader is a prophecy spoken from the lips of Jesus Himself *(that you may have never seen in this light)* while He was on earth, that at the end of time, the good news of His kingdom that will replace all earthly kingdoms and the Sabbath truth as a witness, will be made plain throughout the whole world, then He will return.

Remember Revelation 12:17 talking about the testimony of Jesus Christ? He being a witness? Giving evidence judicially? Don't miss this either because He is our judge and advocate.

"My little children, these things write I unto you, that ye sin not. And if any man sin, we have an advocate with the Father, Jesus Christ the righteous:
And he is the propitiation for our sins: and not for ours only, but also for [the sins of] the whole world.
And hereby we do know that we know him, if we keep his commandments.
He that saith, I know him, and keepeth not his commandments, is a liar, and the truth is not in him."
1 John 2:1-4

What better judge to have than a judge that is also our advocate, lawyer, attorney? If our judge is also our attorney, how could we lose our case? He already paid the price for our sins on the cross, he has paid the charges for defending our cases, he gave His life, what better payment could there ever be? Isn't this a done deal? All we need to do is accept His offer, "come to me as you are and I will give you rest" He doesn't mean, stay as you are after you have accepted Him. Who would wait for their broken leg to mend before they went to the hospital to straighten it out, surely we would need help to get it done correctly. Jesus will mend our defects no matter what they are but we need to go to Him first. This mending equals change.

How is this final and uttermost event to be enforced? Through the buying and selling religio-politico organisation described in previous chapters.

Revelation 15:2 adds another element not found in Revelation 13:16-17, "And I saw as it were a sea of glass mingled with fire: and them that had gotten the victory over the beast, and over his image, and over his mark, [and] over the number of his name, stand on the sea of glass, having the harps of God."

In this verse we find the prophet seeing that there are those that got victory over the beast (popery) his image (USA and fallen protestant churches) his mark (Sunday Sabbath) and over the number of his name (Satan's name). Victory over all of them, notice there is no "or" in this verse to describe the various elements, only and's. The victories are over all four of them, together. Why would anyone need to get the victory over the number unless they consciously decided not to use it? A very smart move of the one-world government plotters would be to introduce the system as a solution to a global economic collapse as mentioned before then gradually withdraw all rights to all those who would not comply with the new papal religious laws. Make sense? More on this in the second to last chapter.

The world would need voices to warn others and explain to them the real reasons for the collapse, the true meaning and repercussions of accepting the buying and selling system and the impending grand finale.

Here is the scenario; there will be those who will preach the Sabbath and imminent second coming of Christ and there will be those who will as a result be converted to the truth (*who had already been given access to the new buying and selling regime, without Sunday Law Conditions*) and those who may abandon the truth because of the hardships without financial support and cross over to Satan's side before the final day of probation. All those who refuse to abide by the false Sabbath will be blamed for the increased calamities on earth and will be branded heretics, troublers of the planet and worthy of economic sanctions, imprisonment and eventually the death penalty. All who reject popery will receive the mark of God and they will also gain the victory over Satan's number.

Satan, the papacy and the other fallen churches etc. will be enraged and this will catalyse them into their attempt at utterly making away many.

For reference purposes I will quote the only other 3 verses in scripture that you will find where "witness" has the same meaning as Matthew 24:14:

"And with great power gave the apostles witness of the resurrection of the Lord Jesus: and great grace was upon them all." Acts 4:33 - "Our fathers had the tabernacle of "witness" in the wilderness, as he had appointed...." Acts: 7:44.

"Your gold and silver is cankered; and the rust of them shall be a witness against you, and shall eat your flesh as it were fire. Ye have heaped treasure together for the last days." James 5:3

Acts 4 speaks of the tabernacle of witness in the wilderness. This refers to the Ark of the Covenant and inside that Ark of the Covenant were the tables of stone written by the finger of God Himself, the great I AM.

"At that time the LORD said unto me, Hew thee two tables of stone like unto the first, and come up unto me into the mount, and make thee an ark of wood. And I will write on the tables the words that were in the first tables which thou brakest, and thou shalt put them in the ark." Deuteronomy 10:1-2.

Was this event an example that God's law cannot be changed, and so important that He wrote them again on stone as before?

The gold and silver in acts 7 that will become cankered is the same that is accumulated by all the kings of the earth that have committed fornication with the harlot as party to the trampling of God's Mark and Sign of Authority, the Seventh-Day Sabbath, and for further clarification, treasures heaped together for the last days.

"Think not that I am come to destroy the law, or the prophets: I am not come to destroy, but to fulfil.

For verily I say unto you, Till heaven and earth pass, one jot or one tittle shall in no wise pass from the law, till all be fulfilled.

Whosoever therefore shall break one of these least commandments, and shall teach men so, he shall be called the least in the kingdom of heaven: but whosoever shall do and teach [them], the same shall be called great in the kingdom of heaven." Matthew 5:17-19.

Is the papacy now making moves in connection with the "tidings from the east"? He most definitely is and this fact will give us an indication of where we are in the warnings given in Daniel 11:40-45, specifically verse 44 with the following news articles:

"Don't listen to the 'prophets of doom,' Pope Francis insists." Inés San Martín. Nov 14, 2016 ROME BUREAU CHIEF

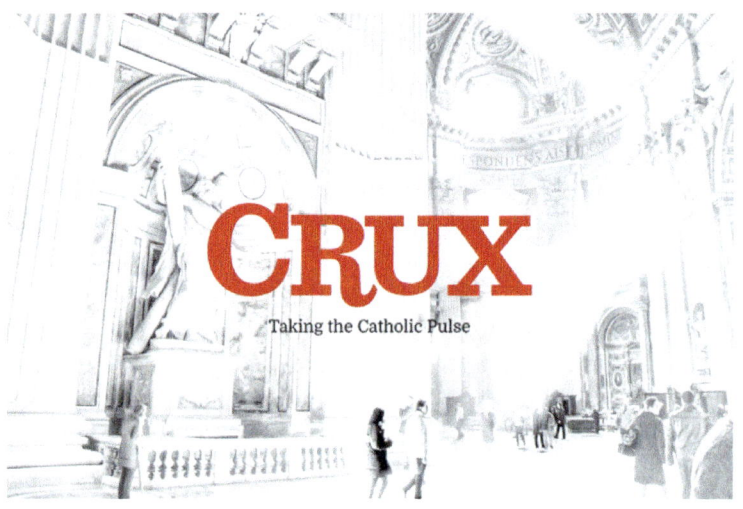

"ROME— Pope Francis on Sunday called for the faithful not to be driven by end-times curiosities or apocalyptic preachers, urging them to focus on what is truly important: "The Lord and our neighbor."

"Those who follow Jesus pay no heed to prophets of doom, the nonsense of horoscopes, or frightening sermons that distract from the truly important things," Francis said.

It is important, he continued, to distinguish "the word of wisdom that God speaks to us each day" from the shouting of those who use "God's name to frighten, to nourish division and fear."

"Warning about fake preachers" The Church 2021/06/23

"The Pope recalled that years after the Apostle's evangelization, other Christians who had come from Judaism began telling the Galatians that they had to be circumcised and that Paul was not an apostle.

POPE FRANCIS
"They begin with doctrine, then they denigrate the apostle. It's always the same way: to take the apostle's authority".

The Pope warned that this happens still today, especially on social media. Supposed evangelizers sell themselves as protectors of the doctrine.

POPE FRANCIS
"How can we recognize these people? For example, one of their characteristics is rigidity in the way they preach the Gospel, which should make us free and joyful. These people are rigid. Always rigid: You have to do this, you have to do that. Rigidity. That's typical of these people".

What rigid people is he referring to? It can only be those who are adhering to the Gospel and warnings as delivered by Jesus in His word. What else is the Pope saying?

VATICAN
"Pope Francis warns against preachers who sow division online"

Catholic News Agency. Angelus Jun 23, 2021

"At his general audience on Wednesday, Pope Francis warned against preachers who sow division and mistrust online.

"There is no shortage of preachers who, especially through the new means of communication, can disturb communities. They present themselves not primarily to announce the Gospel of God who loves man in Jesus, Crucified and Risen, but to insist, as true 'keepers of the truth,' ... what is the best way to be Christians," the pope said June 23.

"And they strongly affirm that the true Christianity is the one they adhere to, often identified with certain forms of the past, and that the solution to the crises of today is to go back so as not to lose the genuineness of the faith. Today too, as then, there is a temptation to close oneself up in some of the certainties acquired in past traditions."

Pope Francis said that these "new preachers" can be recognized by their "rigidity," which contrasts with "preaching the Gospel that makes us free, makes us joyful."
....

Pope Francis greets people during his general audience in the San Damaso Courtyard of the Apostolic Palace at the Vatican June 23, 2021. The pope began a new series of audience talks focused on St. Paul's Letter to the Galatians and its lessons about evangelization, faith and freedom. (CNS photo/Paul Haring)

Why would Jesus say His gospel will be for a witness? Is that all we are seeking a sensation of being "Joyful" or do we want to know how to escape Satan's wicked plans?

"Indeed, some Christians who had come from Judaism had infiltrated these churches, and began to sow theories contrary to the Apostle's teaching, even going so far as to denigrate him. They began with doctrine -- 'No to this, yes to that,' and then they denigrated the Apostle," he said.

"It is the usual method: undermining the authority of the Apostle. As we can see, it is an ancient practice to present oneself at times as the sole possessor of the truth, the pure, and to aim at belittling the work of others, even with slander."

Pope Francis said that this is exactly the way that "the evil one" seeks to divide Christian communities today.

"Let us think about how some Christian communities or dioceses first begin with stories, and then they end by discrediting the priest or the bishop. It is precisely the way of the evil one, of these people who divide, who do not know how to build. And in this Letter to the Galatians, we see this process," he said."

Interesting statements coming from the mouth of the servant of the man of sin himself.

Dear readers - **God's law cannot be changed. It is part of His character.** Why are we so ready to keep all the others, "don't steal?" because it protects our property? "don't lie?" because it protects our reputation? "don't commit adultery?" it protects our relationship with our husband or wife? Do you get the point? Why then are we so willing to break the one that clearly maintains our relationship with our Creator, that points to His Lordship that demonstrates our accountability to Him? Friends Satan or his agents statements that the law has been changed has been forewarned when Jesus made it plain "I am not come to destroy the law.... But to fulfil, Till heaven and earth pass, one jot or one tittle shall in no wise pass from the law...Thou shalt worship the Lord thy God, and him only shalt thou serve." Matthew 4:10.

It is those who obey that will be blessed of God. He says that He will bless your children and your lands and all that you lay your hand unto. Do you think that Satan is going to allow this without making a struggle for the mastery?

The enemy is working just as sharply and decidedly now as he worked upon the minds of Adam and Eve in Eden. The people are gathering under his banner, and he is encircling them with his power. But everyone who sees that the law of God is changeless in its character will decide on the side of Christ. If God could have changed one precept of His law to meet the fallen human race, then Jesus Christ need never have come to our earth to die.

Did Christ die to let loose the whole of humanity to worship idols, when the commandment said, "Thou shalt worship the Lord thy God, and him only shalt thou serve"? And "the Lord made heaven and earth," and what then? "And rested the seventh day" and "sanctified it," and gave it to you to observe as God's memorial—a memorial that He is the living God who created the heavens overhead and the earth upon which we stand. He made the lofty trees and put the covering upon every flower. He gave to each one its tints, and the Lord of heaven made human beings and gave them the Sabbath. What for? For all the posterity of Adam; it was a gift to all his posterity. If they had always obeyed the fourth commandment there never would have been an infidel in the world, because it testified that "the Lord made heaven and earth, the sea, and all that in them is."...

His hands are over His created works. Can you wonder that the devil wants to make void the law of God, the standard of His character? It will be the standard in the judgment when the books shall be opened and every person judged according to the deeds that are done. And the names are written—what does He say?—engraven "upon the palms of my hands." The marks of the crucifixion have engraven them. Humans are His property, and they are God's by creation and by redemption....

What do we give to Satan when we concede the point that the law of God needs to be taken away? We give the whole creative universe a defective God, a God that made a law and it was so defective that He had to take it away. That is all Satan wants. Can we afford to be working on any side but that of God?"—Manuscript 10, 1894 (Sermons and Talks, 1:234-235).

I believe this is the most important piece of prophecy that relates specifically to our time. We must preach the truth of the Sabbath linked to Jesus' kingdom. This is the final decider before He returns. The Sabbath is the great divider, the key to God's Kingdom. The battle for our souls, will be fought, on this point. We have no other way for salvation but through Jesus Christ, by loving Him and keeping ALL of His commandments as He directed them to be kept. The Sabbath command is what identifies us with our Creator, which indicates that we accept His lordship over our lives.

If we want to fully surrender to Jesus we will cease all earthly labour and business activities on God's holy day, not a day of man's or the devil's making. If we are unwilling to worship as Jesus asks us to then we cannot be in His kingdom because sin will never be allowed to raise its ugly head again. Do you, dear reader understand this? There is no final truth but this. Can you with an honest heart after studying all of this material continue to say I will follow a Friday or Sunday Sabbath or any other form of worship or belief system?

These truths that will be proclaimed all across the globe will infuriate the papacy and will result in it doing everything in it's power to suppress it. This is why I believe Jerusalm is key to Satan attempting to make his final stand.

The preaching of the Sabbath truth to the world and the warnings to the world not to receive the mark of Popery or Satan, the warnings describing Popery as the whore and the beast of Revelation, will enrage the papacy and it's false religious supporters to seek out the true sabbath keepers to attempt to wipe them out.

With the calamities wreaking havoc on the planet and the preaching of God's messages warning of the consequences of following the papal sabbath and God's soon appearing from the east, the pope will seek to utterly make away many from God's spiritual Jerusalem, His faithful church comprising of His faithful followers, just like Satan tried under pagan Rome in the time of the Caesars to wipe out true Bible believers and through the Pope's 1260 year reign of terror (AD 538 to 1798) tried to wipe out true Christianity and when Satan will through the Pope in the not too distant future fulfill these verses from Revelation 6:9-11.

"And when he had opened the fifth seal, I saw under the altar the souls of them that were slain for the word of God, and for the testimony which they held:

And they cried with a loud voice, saying, How long, O Lord, holy and true, dost thou not judge and avenge our blood on them that dwell on the earth?

And white robes were given unto every one of them; and it was said unto them, that they should rest yet for a little season, until their fellowservants also and their brethren, that should be killed as they [were], should be fulfilled."

Take courage though, when the final decisions have been made and the eternal destinies of all humans have been sealed, Satan and his gang will not be able to raise a finger on the righteous as there will be no more need of witnessing with their lives.

"I saw that God had children who do not see and keep the Sabbath. They have not rejected the light upon it. And at the commencement of the time of trouble, we were filled with the Holy Ghost as we went forth and proclaimed the Sabbath more fully. This enraged the churches and nominal Adventists, as they could not refute the Sabbath truth. And at this time God's chosen all saw clearly that we had the truth, and they came out and endured the persecution with us. I saw the sword, famine, pestilence, and great confusion in the land. The wicked thought that we had brought the judgments upon them, and they rose up and took counsel to rid the earth of us, thinking that then the evil would be stayed.

In the time of trouble we all fled from the cities and villages, but were pursued by the wicked, who entered the houses of the saints with a sword. They raised the sword to kill us, but it broke, and fell as powerless as a straw. Then we all cried day and night for deliverance, and the cry came up before God.

The sun came up, and the moon stood still. The streams ceased to flow. Dark, heavy clouds came up, and clashed against each other. But there was one clear place of settled glory, whence came the voice of God like many waters, which shook the heavens and the earth. The sky opened and shut, and was in commotion. The mountains shook like a reed in the wind, and cast out ragged rocks all around. The sea boiled like a pot, and cast out stones upon the land.

And as God spoke the day and the hour of Jesus' coming, and delivered the everlasting covenant to His people, He spoke one sentence, and then paused, while the words were rolling through the earth. The Israel of God stood with their eyes fixed upward, listening to the words as they came from the mouth of Jehovah, and rolled through the earth like peals of loudest thunder. It was awfully solemn. And at the end of every sentence the saints shouted, "Glory! Alleluia" Their countenances were lighted up with the glory of God; and they shone with the glory, as did the face of Moses when he came down from Sinai. The wicked could not look on them for the glory. And when the never-ending blessing was pronounced on those who had honored God in keeping His Sabbath holy, there was a mighty shout of victory over the beast and over his image." Christian Experience and teachings pgs 95-96. E G White.

Who will help the Papacy in this dastardly attempt?

The Papal Military Arm

The papacy does not have it's own military. We have alluded to the nation that will be the military/state arm of this church and state New World Order, we will now confirm its identity.

Jesus, through His prophet John, makes it very clear that at the time that the Papacy would temporarily lose it's horrendous grip on power in 1798, that another power would be rising.

"He that leadeth into captivity shall go into captivity: he that killeth with the sword must be killed with the sword. Here is the patience and the faith of the saints.
And I beheld another beast coming up out of the earth; and he had two horns like a lamb, and he spake as a dragon.
And he exerciseth all the power of the first beast before him, and causeth the earth and them which dwell therein to worship the first beast, whose deadly wound was healed." Revelation 13:10-12.

Who or what is this beast?

The word 'before' has a couple of meanings. During the time preceding and in front of - therefore at some stage it can be at the same time as, so who is the other beast?

Exercising all the power of the first beast implies becoming just as much a persecutor and dictator like the first beast. It will become church and state to force everyone to worship the first church and state beast.

"And I stood upon the sand of the sea, and saw a beast rise up out of the sea, having seven heads and ten horns, and upon his horns ten crowns, and upon his heads the name of

455

blasphemy.   And the beast which I saw was like unto a leopard, and his feet were as [the feet] of a bear, and his mouth as the mouth of a lion: and the dragon gave him his power, and his seat, and great authority.

And I saw one of his heads as it were wounded to death; and his deadly wound was healed: and all the world wondered after the beast." Revelation 13:1-3.

I quote these verses because numerous other studies have already concluded this first beast as the papacy that received a deadly wound in 1798 and according to the prophecy would also be healed. This healing is taking place at a rapid pace, the first stages being the 1929 Lateran Treaty between Mussolini and Cardinal Gaspari.

Since then healings have been happening, but in the last few years especially in 2017 there were significant healings happening, but let us answer who the second beast is because it will exercise all the power of the papacy and cause the earth and every one in it to worship the papacy.

How do we understand the book of Revelation? From cross-referencing other books of the Bible. If we are on a journey we need a map to provide directions to enable us to arrive at our destination, therefore we need a starting point, in between points, and a destination point. To keep a map simple we also need symbols, graphics, a universal language of sorts that we all understand, indicating hospitals, significant places of interest etc. Different line colours to indicate major highways, minor routes, waterways, railway lines, bridges etc. With this in mind we will let the Bible explain itself.

Clue number 1

Let's continue in Revelation 13:10-11.

"He that leadeth into captivity shall go into captivity: he that killeth with the sword must be killed with the sword. Here is the patience and the faith of the saints.

And I beheld another beast coming up out of the earth; and he had two horns like a lamb, and he spake as a dragon."

So we need to look for a nation that was rising at the same time the papacy was falling.

The United States of America was the only nation "coming up" to power in 1798, as the first beast received its deadly wound. The Constitution had been voted in 1787, and the Bill of Rights adopted in 1791. Also, it was in 1798 that America was first recognized by a world power. Historians record that there was something wonderful and providential about the rise of this country.

Let us read a statement by John Wesley, a marvelous student of the Bible, and the architect of the Methodist Church. Writing in 1754 in his New Testament with Explanatory Notes after applying the first beast of Revelation 13 to the papacy, he said, "Another … beast … But he is not yet come, though he cannot be far off; for he is to appear at the end of the forty-two months of the first beast." Page 427. Please note that Wesley was looking for a nation to be rising within a very short time that would meet the description of the prophecy. Only the United States could have fulfilled his expectation.

Clue number 2

This power has Lamb-Like horns with an absence of crowns. What does this mean? Horns represent kings and kingdoms, or governments as the verses in Daniel explain. In this case, they represent America's two governing principles: civil and religious liberty. These two governing principles have also been labeled "republicanism" (a government without a king) and "Protestantism" (a church without a pope). Other nations since ancient times had taxed people to support a state religion. Most had also oppressed religious dissidents. But America established something entirely new: Freedom to worship as you wish without government interference or control--and with government protection.

Absence of crowns signifies a republican form of government, rather than a monarchy.

Lamb-like horns denote an innocent, young, non-oppressive, peace-loving, and spiritual nation. Jesus is referred to as a lamb 28 times in Revelation. So this new government was trying to uphold His principles. No other power on earth could possibly fit the characteristics and time slot of the lamb-horned beast, except America. The United States was born out of a population fleeing religious persecution from the papacy in Europe, and the forefathers had seen enough of the evils of a church/state government. Therefore one nation and only one meets the specifications of this prophecy. The symbol points unmistakably to the United States.

Arising steadily into power at the close of the eighteenth century, giving promise of strength and greatness, she soon attracted the attention of the whole world. The orator and the historian, in describing the rise and growth of this nation, have again and again unconsciously employed the thought of the sacred writer, almost the exact words, "Coming up out of the earth."

G. A. Townsend, describing the rise of the United States, speaks of "the mystery of her coming forth from vacancy,"

and says: "Like a silent reed we grew into empire."—The New World Compared With the Old, p. 462.
A European newspaper, The Dublin Nation, in 1850 spoke of the United States as a wonderful empire, which was "emerging," and "amid the silence of the earth daily adding to its power and pride."

"Did they look," said the orator, Edward Everett, of the Pilgrim founders of this nation, "for a retired spot, inoffensive for its obscurity, and safe in its remoteness, where the little church of Leyden might enjoy freedom of conscience? Behold the mighty regions over which, in peaceful conquest . . . they have borne the banners of the cross!"—Speech delivered at Plymouth, Massachusetts, December 22, 1824, p. 11.

Right now you are probably thinking, hold on a minute, we are talking about the great United States of America, "land of the free and home of the brave," it is crazy to think that America is set to support a dictatorship, surely that cannot be true? America is truly a great country--with its freedom of conscience, press, speech, and enterprise; the protection it provides; its golden opportunities; its sense of fair play; its sympathy for the underdog; and its strong Christian orientation. It is not perfect, but even still a host of people from other countries hasten to become American citizens every year. If America's doors were opened wide, a vast portion of the people of the world would move to the United States at once--to "heaven on earth" as they perceive it. Sadly, this richly blessed country will change drastically in the days just ahead, precipitating unparalleled heartache and distress for all people, especially God's people.

That the United States is firmly involved in this New World Order note the following extract from U.S. President George Bush Senior's speech in his State of the Union address, as reported in the Los Angeles Times, February 18, 1991.

Is America changing? In order to compel the world to worship the papacy, America must repudiate its constitution. It must speak like a dragon. Is it doing that? Most definitely yes.

Defiant Donald Trump confirms US will recognise Jerusalem as capital of Israel

"My announcement marks the beginning of a new approach to the conflict"

Donald Trump has defied overwhelming global opposition by recognising Jerusalem as the capital of Israel, but insisted that the highly controversial move would not derail his own administration's bid to resolve the Israeli-Palestinian conflict.

In a short speech delivered at the White House, Trump directed the state department to start making arrangements to move the US embassy from Tel Aviv to Jerusalem – a process that officials say will take at least three years.

"I have determined that it is time to officially recognize Jerusalem as the capital of Israel," Trump said. "While previous presidents have made this a major campaign promise, they failed to deliver. Today, I am delivering."

Trump said: "My announcement today marks the beginning of a new approach to the conflict between Israel and the Palestinians."

The president's announcement provoked condemnation from US allies, and a furious reaction from Palestinian leaders and the Muslim world. Within minutes of Trump's announcement, US embassies in Turkey, Jordan, Germany and Britain issued security alerts urging Americans to exercise caution.

The United Nations Security Council is likely to meet on Friday to discuss the move, after a request by eight countries on the 15-member body, including the UK, Italy and France.

"Nikki Haley: The US is 'taking names' on Jerusalem resolution

US Ambassador to the United Nations Nikki Haley warns the US will be "taking names" of the countries that vote in favor of a resolution that condemns the Trump administration's decision to recognize Jerusalem as the capital of Israel.

"At the UN, we're constantly asked to do more and give more -- in the past we have. So, when we make a decision, at the will of the American people, about where to locate OUR embassy, we don't expect those we've helped to target us,"

Haley wrote on Facebook and Twitter on Tuesday evening. "On Thursday, there will be a vote at the UN criticizing our choice. And yes, the US will be taking names."

President Donald Trump backed his ambassador's tough talk at a Cabinet meeting in Washington on Wednesday. "We're watching those votes," the President said. "Let them vote against us, we'll save a lot. We don't care. But this isn't like it used to be where they could vote against you and then you pay them hundreds of millions of dollars and nobody knows what they're doing."

Trump indicated that he and Haley had agreed on her message beforehand. "Nikki, that was the right message that you and I agreed to be sent yesterday," he said. "People that live here, our great citizens that love this country -- they're tired of this country being taken advantage of and we're not going to be taken advantage of any longer."

On Monday, the US exercised its veto power at the UN to sink a Security Council resolution critical of the White House's unilateral move to recognize the city as Israel's capital. Haley cast the veto, blocking the resolution introduced by Egypt, despite the 14 other members of the Security Council voting in favor.

"What we witnessed here today in the Security Council is an insult. It won't be forgotten. It's one more example of the United Nations doing more harm than good in addressing the Israeli-Palestinian conflict," Haley said in remarks following her veto.

The Palestinians are now moving the resolution before the UN's General Assembly, where the US cannot unilaterally avoid censure. It is scheduled for a vote on Thursday.

In addition to her admonition on social media, Haley also sent a letter to fellow nations warning them of the potential impact of their vote.

"As you consider your vote, I want you to know that the President and U.S. take this vote personally." she wrote.

"The President will be watching this vote carefully and has requested I report back on those countries who voted against us."

President Donald Trump announced in early December that the US would recognize Jerusalem as the capital of Israel and would move its embassy there. The controversial move upended decades of foreign policy precedent and inflamed protests across the region.

14th May 2018. "US opens new embassy in Jerusalem as dozens are killed in Gaza.

The US officially relocated its embassy in Israel from Tel Aviv to Jerusalem … formally upending decades of American foreign policy in a move that was met with clashes and protests along the Israeli-Gaza border.

At least 58 Palestinians were killed and more than 2,700 injured in Gaza as deadly protests took place ahead of, during and after the ceremony in Jerusalem, making it the deadliest day there since the 2014 Gaza war.

The violence could deepen Tuesday, when Palestinians mark what they call the "Nakba," or Catastrophe, in memory of the more than 700,000 Palestinians who were either driven from or fled their homes during the Arab-Israeli war that accompanied the creation of the state of Israel in 1948.

On Monday, which marked the 70th anniversary of the founding of the state of Israel, US and Israeli leaders hailed the embassy move as a sign of the enduring relationship between the two countries and of US trustworthiness. American officials said it could create an honest foundation for an eventual peace agreement between Israelis and Palestinians.

President Donald Trump did not attend the ceremony in Jerusalem's Arnona neighborhood, but in a video message broadcast at the event he congratulated Israel, saying the opening had been "a long time coming."

"Today, Jerusalem is the seat of Israel's government. It is the home of the Israeli legislature and the Israeli Supreme court and Israel's Prime Minister and President. Israel is a sovereign nation with the right, like every other sovereign nation, to determine its own capital, yet for many years we failed to acknowledge the obvious, the plain reality that Israel's capital is Jerusalem," Trump said in the pre-recorded remarks. "As I said in December, our greatest hope is for peace," he added..."

Donald Trump has even been likened to King Cyrus of Ancient Persia. An organisation known as the Mikdesh Educational Center has created 1,000 coins with Donald Trump's image placed alongside King Cyrus. The idea is to sell the coins to assist in raising funds for the construction of the Third Temple describing the third temple as important for Jerusalem and the entire world. The coin has actually been called "Temple Coin" Unfortunately they have been deceived. It will not be a good thing for Jerusalem or the world because if it is constructed it likely to be part of the final grand deception of the world.

What was the actions of King Cyrus that they are alluding to?

"Now in the first year of Cyrus king of Persia, that the word of the LORD [spoken] by the mouth of Jeremiah might be accomplished, the LORD stirred up the spirit of Cyrus king of Persia, that he made a proclamation throughout all his kingdom, and [put it] also in writing, saying,

Thus saith Cyrus king of Persia, All the kingdoms of the earth hath the LORD God of heaven given me; and he hath charged me to build him an house in Jerusalem, which [is] in Judah. Who [is there] among you of all his people? The LORD his God [be] with him, and let him go up." 2 Chronicles 36:22-23

I must make it clear that this prophecy will not be fulfilled again.

Revelation 13:11-12 describes one of the characteristics of the USA:

465

"And I beheld another beast coming up out of the earth; and he had two horns like a lamb, and he spake as a dragon. And he exerciseth all the power of the first beast before him, and causeth the earth and them which dwell therein to worship the first beast, whose deadly wound was healed."

The USA was established because of Papal persecutions yet it will be the protestant churches of America who will first hand over their freedoms to the papacy, and this is very clear in actions taken by many of the protestant churches of America with the "Joint declaration on the doctrine of Justification" (JDDJ) which many of them have now signed.

"By the decree of enforcing the institution of the Papacy in violation of the law of God, our nation will disconnect herself fully from righteousness. When Protestantism shall stretch her hand across the gulf to grasp the hand of the Roman power, when she shall reach over the abyss to clasp hands with Spiritualism, when, under the influence of this threefold union, our country shall repudiate every principle of its Constitution as a Protestant and Republican government, and shall make provision for the propagation of papal falsehoods and delusions, then we may know that the time has come for the marvelous working of Satan, and that the end is near." -- Testimonies vol. 5, p. 451.

The papacy has always used the military might of a country or countries and The United States is the military arm that will support and uplift the papacy in all of its plans and designs against the true church of God. The fallen churches according to Revelation 13:13 will be deceived into supporting the papacy through the powers that will be demonstrated by Satan.

466

The enforcement of religious laws would be directly opposed to the constitution as it presently reads. "Congress shall make no law respecting an establishment of religion, or prohibiting the free exercise thereof, no religious test shall ever be required as a qualification to any office of public trust under the United States.

For the constitution to be done away with, there has to be a spirit of apostasy throughout protestantism, and that such is the case, we only have to take into account the effects of ecumenism, and such ideas like the "love" doctrine, that teaches that we are all generally believing in the same thing anyway, from various view-points, and all we should be doing really is to love one another. Yes, Jesus did say that we should love one another, but not if we have to sacrifice our principles or disobey His commandments.

Impending Global Financial Collapse – The Why, The Maths

There is not a single person who is at the rational age where they are either studying or in some form of employment or business, or now retired and relying on their pensions funds or savings, who is not aware of the unsettled state of their local and the global economy. When the Reserve banks lower their rates of interest, the retirees that are depending on returns on their savings lose out.

The decline of the value of money is a matter of concern for all. Again our loving God has spoken to us about this concern of ours so that we can put it to rest and that we can know how to act, behave, know what to do and understand what is taking place in today's world.

Let's go again to Rev:13:16-17. "And he causeth all, both small and great, rich and poor, free and bond, to receive a mark in their right hand, or in their foreheads: And that no man might buy or sell, save he that had the mark, or the name of the beast, or the number of his name."

Note these words, causeth (forces) all, all means everyone and for further emphasis, no man, nobody, might buy or sell.

There are some points that we need to pay special attention to:

- Satan's last effort to gain control of the people of the world is going to be through the economy, based on the principle that "if you control the man's money, you control the man." In other words, every man has his price. Satan cannot understand people who cannot be bought or cannot be sold, a person

468

that cannot and will not compromise their ethics or their principles for the sake of a profit. Remember the millions through the dark ages that preferred to die for their faith rather than compromise?

- It's not just God's people that will not be able to buy or sell. The scriptures state plainly "**all**." It will not matter if you are the CEO of a major Corporation, A lawyer or a judge, a factory worker or a slave. A prisoner or a pauper. It wouldn't make the slightest difference. All will come under some form of economic bondage or part of an economic plan. This means that there is going to exist an absolute dictatorship including rulership of the global economy. The scenario where "**all**" will receive a number is that "**all**" human beings will be allocated a number in the system irrespective of their atheistic, evolutionist, theist, religious convictions or any type of persuasion; the test of allegiance will be if you decide to use or not to use the number. Refusing to use the number means that you have chosen to join the Creator and reject the usurper's system.

- Once these controls are established they will ultimately be used to harass and persecute the people of God. People cannot be legally and globally persecuted with non-existent laws, the laws have to be put in place before the harassment can take place.

- The bible is a global book. What is contained in its pages applies to every inhabitant of the planet whether they believe it or not. Disbelief of something does not mean it does not exist. For example, if you do not believe in the law of gravity, you will still realise its effects if you jump off a 20 storey building without a parachute or any other safety device. You will come in contact with the ground, concrete, fence pailings, vehicle or whatever object is in the path of your descent and your body will be highly likely pulverised.

- In order for the prophecy to be fulfilled of no man being able to buy or sell (financial transactions), there must be a crisis of Global Proportions. All who are reading this will realise that we are now facing a Global Financial Crisis, (the 1980 GFC was a tea party in comparison to what's coming) a crisis that did not exist when John wrote about it nearly 2,000 years ago.

- The prophecies were placed there for us as maps of the future so that we would know where we are. God in His mercy wanted us to know when the struggle would finally be over and that we would be aware of the truth of what is happening and outline a way of escape for all who wanted it.

- The mark of the beast – It will come into the world at a time of great economic distress. The nearer we get to severe wage and price controls, what we can now call "austerity measures" the closer we are to the dreaded mark of the beast. There is a close connection between, economic, political and religious freedom. If we lose the first of these, we will also lose both of the last two. It is inevitable

With these points in mind let us take a brief review of some recent economic wars history: Napoleon rose to power as a result of the bankruptcy of the French Economy, most of the collapse attributed to numerous wars fought by France.

470

France was at war almost continually under Kings Louis XIV, XV & XVI. The final war to break France was the American Revolutionary war.

Following the 1st world war the German economy fell to pieces and a wheelbarrow full of cash was needed to buy a loaf of bread. In fact there is an account of a person going into a store, leaving their wheelbarrow outside full of cash, they returned to find the cash on the ground and the wheelbarrow gone, the wheelbarrow had more value than the cash.

The reason that cash lost its value was because Germany tried to solve its problems by printing money (QE - Quantitative Easing). As a result Adolf Hitler raised his hands and said "I have solutions" For his first election he received 12,000 votes, the next he received 12 million. Why was he so successful? He promised the German nation economic security. The results we can say is history. Everyone wants financial security. The Germans sold their freedoms for financial security. Despite this history, will the world's population do the same? Absolutely, there will hardly be a choice.

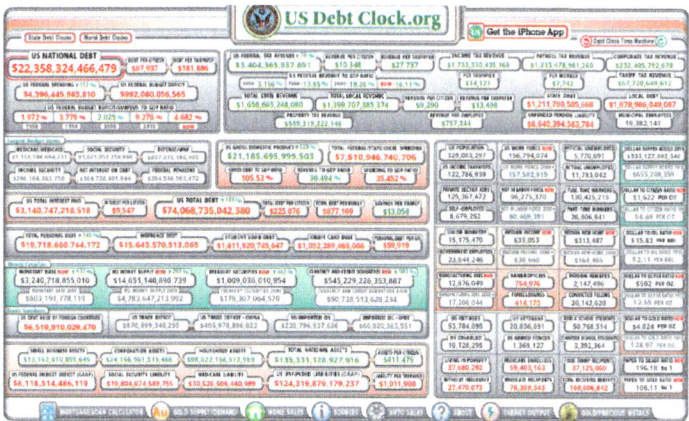

What about global debt?

Here is what the daily Reckoning had to say on April 11th 2018

"The Global Debt Bomb: Debt + Derivatives = Over 1 Quadrillion Dollars"

"How cartoonish, how completely unreal, have counterparty obligations gotten around the world? When you include financial derivatives, those murky casino bets bankers love to make and hate to account for, total global debt is now over one quadrillion dollars.

A quadrillion dollars is 1,000 trillion dollars. **About 15x the GDP of the world**. If you placed one quadrillion British pound coins on top of each other, they'd reach beyond our solar system.

Which, at this rate, is where we will all need to look for sustainable fiscal policy before long.

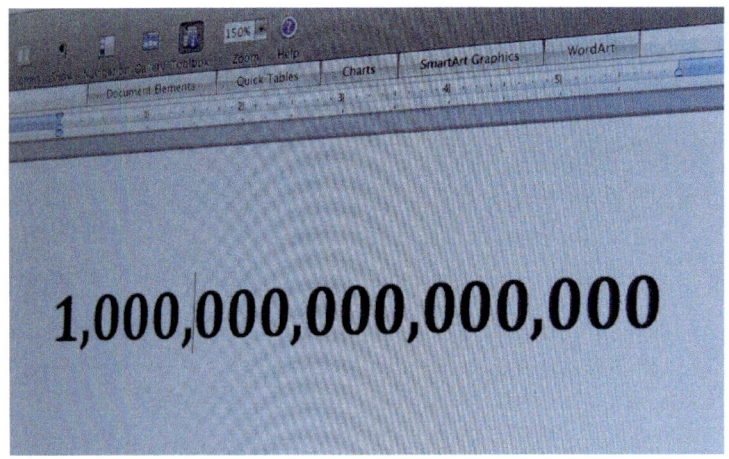

Total global debt now exceeds $233 trillion. Another way to express that figure is about a quarter-quadrillion dollars (a quadrillion is 1,000 trillion). The **global debt-to-GDP**

ratio is about 318%, a dangerously high level, especially if interest rates start to rise.

This debt is in addition to approximately $750 trillion of bank derivatives as reported by the Bank for International Settlements (BIS).

Adding the debt and derivatives together produces over $1 quadrillion of financial obligations of various kinds. This is far more than the amount of debt and derivatives outstanding before the last financial crisis in 2008.

That fact alone means that the next financial crisis will be exponentially greater than the last one. Regulators won't admit this and investors are unprepared for it, but it's true.

It's difficult to get economists to agree on anything, but in this rare instance five prominent economists are in total agreement.

How much has the largest economy on earth spent on defence and is spending in 2019?

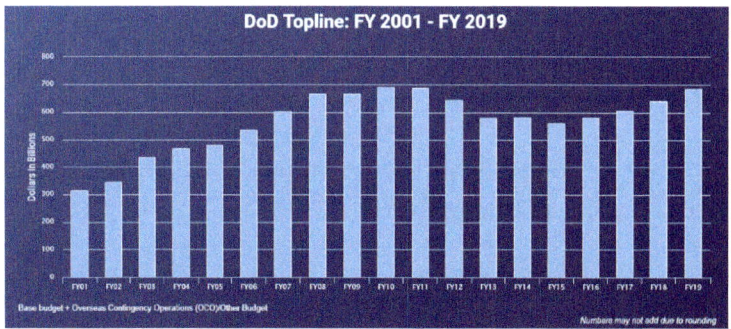

For 2019 the US defence budget (DoD) stands at $US686Billion. For the last 2 decades $US 10,765Billion.

US National debt stands at $US22,358,0823,106,000 in 2019, $22 Trillion, 358 Billion and was rising at $2.8billion daily, growing exponentially.

You can visit the US debt clock here for yourself. www.usdebtclock.org and other world debt clocks here, www.usdebtclock.org/world-debt-clock.html below is a print screen of the US debt situation as of June 2019.

Unfortunately, the issue they agree on is that the U.S. is going broke.

That the U.S. is heading quickly toward $1 trillion annual deficits, probably by next year, and that these deficits will continue at that level as far as the eye can see.

They also warn that government debt will increase by $5 trillion in the next few years on top of the $20 trillion already outstanding. Higher interest on the debt will just add to the burden.

These are the warnings not of a fringe doomsday blogger but of the establishment itself. My own estimate is that the actual debt and deficit numbers will be worse than these projections, pushing the U.S. closer toward a true crisis of confidence in the dollar.

This path is unsustainable. Something has to give — and probably sooner rather than later."

What are derivatives? Here is one description:

"Hedging with derivatives - Financial institutions and corporations use derivative financial instruments to hedge their exposure to different risks, including commodity risks, foreign exchange risks, and interest rate risks.

Basically hedging consists of taking a risk position that is opposite to an actual position that is exposed to risk. A company that takes variable-interest, short-term loans or that reissues commercial paper as it matures faces interest rate risk. In such cases, the firm might hedge its position by entering into a transaction that would produce a gain of almost the same amount as the potential loss if interest rates do increase. Forwards, futures, and options can be used to hedge exposure to the effects of changing interest rates. Foreign exchange futures contracts can be used by firms to hedge foreign exchange risks. Interest rate swaps, which form a major chunk of derivatives, is used to hedge interest risk. In interest rate swaps, the fixed interest payments are exchanged for floating rate payments or vice versa without exchanging the underlying principal amounts. Derivatives hedging techniques using interest rate swaps and interest rate caps can help institutions retain core longer-duration assets to manage interest rate risk."

Basically it is a smart way of saying "we are gambling"

I'm sure most of us have heard the phrase "Hedge your bets"

"Lessen one's chance of loss by counterbalancing it with other bets, investments, or the like. For example, I'm hedging my bets by putting some of my money in bonds in case there's another drop in the stock market. This term transfers hedge, in the sense of "a barrier," to a means of protection against loss."

The shear lunacy of this is that banks lend money to organisations to hedge bets via derivatives and this has now become the largest debt bubble in the world. 1,000 trillion minus 233 trillion leaves us with 767 trillion in derivatives debts.

What is GDP? Gross Domestic Product and can be measured in three ways:

☐ Output measure: This is the value of the goods and services produced by all sectors of the economy; agriculture, manufacturing, energy, construction, the service sector and government.

☐ Expenditure measure: This is the value of the goods and services purchased by households and by government, investment in machinery and buildings. It also includes the value of exports minus imports.

☐ Income measure: The value of the income generated mostly in terms of profits and wages. In theory all three approaches should produce the same number.

At what stage would GDP/Debt ratios begin to have an effect on the economy?

The European Central Bank prepared a working Paper NO 1237 / August 2010:

"...This paper investigates the average impact of government debt on per-capita GDP growth in twelve euro area countries over a period of about 40 years starting in 1970. It finds a non-linear impact of debt on growth with a turning point—beyond which the government debt-to-GDP ratio has a deleterious impact on long-term growth—at about 90-100% of GDP. Confidence intervals for the debt turning point suggest that the negative growth effect of high debt may start already from levels of around 70-80% of GDP, which calls for even more prudent indebtedness policies...."

What is this telling us? At 90-100% of GDP there is a deleterious impact on long-term growth. We now know that our global debt is 15 x global GDP. Not 1 x Global GDP but 15 x GDP. This is a catastrophic situation and can only result in a complete and utter global financial collapse.

I can hear you saying, but wait, what is the value of all properties in the world, of stocks and shares, would they not counterbalance this debt situation?

The following comes from Yolande Barnes, head of Savills world research.

"Add up all the property in the entire world, and you get $217 trillion (£152.2 trillion) of assets, a new report has suggested – that's 2.7 times the world's GDP.

"To give this figure context, the total value of all the gold ever mined is approximately $6 trillion, which pales in comparison to the total value of developed property by a factor of 36 to one," said Yolande Barnes, head of Savills world research.

The research, by Savills, showed residential property makes up by far the biggest portion of real estate, worth $162 trillion.

Homes also have the largest "spread of ownership" – i.e. the largest number of owners – with approximately 2.5bn households.

Meanwhile, commercial property made up $29 trillion, while agricultural and forestry land was worth about $26 trillion.

By comparison, the total value of world equities is $55 trillion – while outstanding securitised debt is worth about $94 trillion.

Not surprisingly, China accounts for nearly a quarter of the total value (and a fifth of the world's population), while 21 per cent of the world's total residential asset value is in North America – despite the fact it only has five per cent of the world's population.

"Real estate is the pre-eminent asset class which will be most impacted by global monetary conditions and investment activity and which, in turn, has the power to most impact national and international economies," added Barnes."

Do the maths, 1,000 trillion minus 217 trillion leaves us with a deficit of 783 trillion, so either way we look at it the planet is broke and the New World Order backed by the biblically foretold Religio-Politico organisation is poised and just about ready to pounce on us all with a solution that very few realise the full impact of until we are all thoroughly enmeshed in it.

Hot on the heels of this already disastrous financial scenario is the lockdowns of the Covid-19 pandemic, destroying thousands upon thousands of businesses and millions of jobs, resulting in the inability of debtors to service their debts and now talks of "The Great reset" as the great debt management solution. Is Covid-19 the vehicle that will be used to finally take us all across the line? Whatever system that is brought to the world that is coupled with a religious dictatorship needs to be rejected for what it is. Lucifer's final attempt to dominate the world, but it will fail. Fortunately, not everyone will fall victim of his final desperate plan.

It will become very clear that the promoters of the "Great reset" are singing the same tune as the Papacy and must therefore be in cahoots. As it has become very clear that the Babylonian system has existed for millennia, we can then conclude that the promoters of the great reset, climate change, LGBTQI+ etc. all lead to or come from that one Babylonian source, aptly described as THE MOTHER OF HARLOTS AND ABOMINATIONS OF THE EARTH. The plans of the Great Reset to take away private property has been promoted by the papacy for centuries, cite the following:

Theft, Needs, and Private Property

Because the goods of some are due to others according to Catholic natural law, it is not considered sinful for the poor to take the goods of their neighbours. Thomas Aquinas, pivotal 13th-century Catholic philosopher, says this:

"In cases of need, all things are common property, so that there would seem to be no sin in taking another's property, for need has made it common."

Not only is such taking of another's property not a sin, it is not even a crime, according to Thomas:

"...it is lawful for a man to succour his own need by means of another's property by taking it either openly or secretly; nor is this, properly speaking, theft and robbery...It is not theft, properly speaking, to take secretly and use another's property in a case of extreme need; because that which he takes for the support of his life becomes his own property by reason of that need...In a case of a like need, a man may also take secretly another's property in order to succour his neighbour in need."

According to this statement, your neighbour determines whether they need your stuff. And, according to Thomas

Aquinas' article, it is even lawful for you to steal for your neighbour's need!

Stealing based on need is more than just the musings of a 13th-century mystic. Paul VI made the point quite clear in his 1967 encyclical:
"...each man has therefore the right to find in the world what is necessary for himself. The recent Council [Vatican II] reminded us of this: "God intended the earth and all that it contains for the use of every human being and people. Thus, as all men follow justice and unite in charity, created goods should abound for them on a reasonable basis." All other rights whatsoever, including those of property and of free commerce, are to be subordinated to this principle."

This principle is being espoused in government thought and policy around the world. In the late 1960s, American President Lyndon Johnson said this:

We are going to try to take all the money that we think is unnecessarily being spent and take it from the "haves" and give it to the "have nots" that need it so much.

The Roman Catholic Church-State and Wealth Redistribution

John Robbins sums up the Papacy's views on wealth redistribution this way:

"Whoever needs property ought to possess it. Need makes another's goods one's own. Need is the ultimate and only moral title to property. Neither possession, nor creation, nor production, nor gift, nor inheritance, nor divine commandment (with the exception of Roman Church-State property) grants title to property that is immune to the prior claim of need."

Pius XI says in his encyclical Quadragesimo Anno (1931) that the work of "picked men" to indoctrinate people and governments with Catholic economic views since the late 1800s, had a profound effect on 20th-century politics:

"Under the guidance and in light of Leo's encyclical was thus evolved a truly Christian social science, which continues to be fostered and enriched daily by the tireless labours of those picked men whom we have named the auxiliaries of the Church...The doctrine of Rerum Novarum began little by little to penetrate among those who, being outside Catholic unity, do not recognize the authority of the Church; and these Catholic principles of sociology gradually became part of the intellectual heritage of the whole human race...Thus too, we rejoice that the Catholic truths proclaimed so vigorously by our illustrious Predecessor [Leo XIII in 1891's Rerum Novarum], are advanced and advocated not merely in non-Catholic books and journals, but frequently also in legislative assemblies and in courts of justice"

This key quote is proof that Roman Catholic policies, principles, and doctrine have penetrated secular venues to such an extent that individuals who otherwise have no allegiance to the Roman Catholic Church are promoting its agenda. How many of those individuals don't even know that they have been influenced to think as someone else would have them think?

These "picked men," "auxiliaries of the Church," can be none other than the Jesuits. They have sworn allegiance to the Pope, swearing to take any guise, even that of the Protestant, in order to achieve the Catholic Church's aims.

Fyodor Dostoyevsky puts the role of the Jesuits into perspective for us:

The Jesuits...are simply the Romish army for the earthly sovereignty of the world in the future, with the Pontiff of Rome for emperor...that's their ideal... It is simple lust of power, of filthy earthly gain, of domination; something like a universal serfdom with them as masters; that's all they stand for. They don't even believe in God perhaps. We could add Climate Alarmists? New World Order Promoters etc.? To the list of "picked men"

According to Pope Benedict's most recent encyclical, Caritas in Veritate, Pope Paul VI's encyclical Populorum Progressio "deserves to be considered 'the Rerum Novarum of the present age'".

Rerum Novarum is one of the Roman Church-State's most influential statements on economic matters, in which it lays down "unerring rules for the right solution of the difficult problem of human solidarity."

So what does Populorum Progressio have to say that is so pivotal for our day?

"...each man has therefore the right to find in the world what is necessary for himself. The recent [Vatican II] Council reminded us of this: "God intended the earth and all that it contains for the use of every human being and people. Thus, as all men follow justice and unite in charity, created goods should abound for them on a reasonable basis." All other rights whatsoever, including those of property and of free commerce, are to be subordinated to this principle."

Today's "unerring rules" for humanity are that every person should abound with manufactured goods, even at the expense of all other rights?

Here is a statement from Vatican II Council document Gaudium et Spes:

"If one is in extreme necessity he has the right to procure for himself what he needs out of the riches of others...Therefore, because private property is immoral, all men - individuals and governments - have the moral obligation to redistribute goods held unjustly by property owners."

In this Vatican statement, stealing is clearly endorsed. And we are told by Pope Benedict that this document and its principles codified at Vatican II are to be considered today's definitive statement on social doctrine.

Pope John Paul II echoed this statement in 1981 and again in 1987:

"[all men must have] access to those goods which are intended for common use: both the goods of nature and manufactured goods.

...the goods of this world are originally meant for all. The right to private property is valid and necessary, but it does not nullify the value of this principle. Private property, in fact, is under a 'social mortgage', which means that it has an intrinsically social function, based upon and justified precisely by the principle of the universal destination of goods."

In the same document, John Paul also wrote that in today's world "we are faced with a serious problem of unequal distribution of the means of subsistence originally meant for everybody"

One key element of fascist feudalism is the governmental control of property. Redistribution of this wealth to the poor is at the discretion of those in power, and crimes such as theft can be excused if a personal need is found.

Accrding to Pope Pius XI:

"Under fascism, property owners may keep their property titles and deeds, but the use of their property is, as Leo XIII wrote, "common"...Under fascism, property titles and deeds are intact, but the institution of private property has disappeared." Adapted from amazingdiscoveries.org

We are on the cusp of global fascism.

Toward an Effective World Authority

"Such international collaboration among the nations of the world certainly calls for institutions that will promote, coordinate and direct it, until a new juridical order is firmly established and fully ratified. We give willing and wholehearted support to those public organizations that have already joined in promoting the development of nations, and We ardently hope that they will enjoy ever growing authority. As We told the United Nations General Assembly in New York: "Your vocation is to bring not just some peoples but all peoples together as brothers. . . Who can fail to see the need and importance of thus gradually coming to the establishment of a world authority capable of taking effective action on the juridical and political planes?" Popularum Progressio March 1967

"However much society worldwide shows signs of fragmentation, expressed in the conventional names First, Second, Third and even Fourth World, their interdependence remains close. When this interdependence is separated from its ethical requirements, it has disastrous consequences for the weakest. Indeed, as a result of a sort of internal dynamic and under the impulse of mechanisms which can only be called perverse, this interdependence triggers negative effects even in the rich countries. It is precisely within these countries that one encounters, though on a lesser scale, the more specific manifestations of under development. Thus it should be obvious that development either becomes shared in common by every part of the world or it undergoes a process of regression even in zones marked by constant progress. This tells us a great deal about the nature of authentic development: either all the nations of the world participate, or it will not be true development." https://www.vatican.va/ content/john-paul-ii/en/encyclicals/ documents/hf_jp-ii_enc_30121987_sollicitudo-rei-socialis.html

The Use of Private Property

"He who has the goods of this world and sees his brother in need and closes his heart to him, how does the love of God abide in him?" Everyone knows that the Fathers of the Church laid down the duty of the rich toward the poor in no uncertain terms. As St. Ambrose put it: "You are not making a gift of what is yours to the poor man, but you are giving him back what is his. You have been appropriating things that are meant to be for the common use of everyone. The earth belongs to everyone, not to the rich." These words indicate that the right to private property is not absolute and unconditional.

No one may appropriate surplus goods solely for his own private use when others lack the bare necessities of life. In short, "as the Fathers of the Church and other eminent theologians tell us, the right of private property may never be exercised to the detriment of the common good." When "private gain and basic community needs conflict with one another," it is for the public authorities "to seek a solution to these questions, with the active involvement of individual citizens and social groups." https://www.vatican.va/content/ paul-vi/en/encyclicals/documents/hf_p-vi_enc_26031967_populorum.html

"I encourage financial experts and political leaders to ponder the words of [Saint John Chrysostom], one of the sages of antiquity: "Not to share one's wealth with the poor is to steal from them and to take away their livelihood. It is not our own goods which we hold, but theirs.""

"The private ownership of goods is justified by the need to protect and increase them, so that they can better serve the common good; for this reason, solidarity must be lived as the decision to restore to the poor what belongs to them." https://www.crs.org/stories/pope-francis-care-poor

Would it surprise you to know that by the year 2000 the Catholic Church was expected to control 1/3rd of the worlds wealth. I am going to quote the Preface of a book entitled Vatican Billions written by Avro Manhattan giving us some indication of the Catholic Church's vast wealth and they want to preach to the world about the poor stealing from the rich? One of Gods' commandments is thou shalt not steal. Yes, there are many rich that rob the poor in order to accumulate wealth, but that's not the point I am discussing here. I'm giving you some idea of the shear hypocrisy and fraud of that organisation. The fraud is again stated plainly in Revelation 18:7 "How much she hath glorified herself, and lived deliciously, so much torment and sorrow give her: for she saith in her heart, I sit a queen, and am no widow, and shall see no sorrow." Please find the book and read it for yourself. I hope by now I would have encouraged you to embark on your own path of research. Here is the book's intro:

"Christ was born, lived and died in poverty. His church, *(Papal system clearly isn't – Christ does have a true church that is governed by Sola Scriptura - my emphasis)* is a multi-, multi-, multi-billion concern. How come that although she claims to be preoccupied with the riches of heaven, she is in reality one of the most formidable accumulators of the riches of the earth?

When did it all begin? Where? How? What was the Church's economic empire in the past? One thousand, five hundred or one hundred years ago? How vast is it now? Is it true that it is the most powerful financial entity of all times?

If so, how many thousand millions does it handle? How much real estate? How much stock, trusts and bonds? How many shares in oil, motors, automation, electronics, hotels, air lines, chemicals, engineering and space corporations? Is it true that she has vast deposits of gold in Swiss, American and other banks? That she has more dollar assets than the most powerful corporations of the U. S. A., larger monetary reserves than France, Belgium, Italy and Great Britain put together? That by the end of the present century she will control at least one third of the total wealth of Europe and America?

What are her tangible and intangible financial funds in most of the major countries of the world? Such questions have never been answered before. This book answers them. In a vast, up-to-date piece of history, stretching from the time of St. Peter to the Dark Ages; from the Renaissance to the Reformation and the Counter-Reformation; from the French Revolution in the eighteenth century to the Industrial in the nineteenth. From the birth of Bolshevik Russia to the rise of Fascist Europe and to the Second World War. And from there to the landing of the first man on the moon, and thus to the Space Age.

Two thousand years of astonishing wealth accumulation, highlighted by dazzling deeds of private greed and of public philanthropy, of saintly sacrifices and of evil meanness, of individual generosity and of collective usury, carried out by popes, kings, prelates, rebellious churches, fiery reformers, holy men and villains, in the recent past; by revolutions, dictatorships, political parties, national and international banks, inter-continental corporations and global syndicates, in our times.

The whole is supported by names, dates, figures and facts. It is written in a simple, clear, racy style. This book is a unique disclosure of the most formidable financial empire the world has ever seen, and which is still in full operation. Now!" AVRO MANHATTAN, London.

St. Peter's Basilica was built from the sale of indulgences, the idea that you could buy your way out of purgatory (a place that does not actually exist – a fabrication of the papacy) buy your dead relatives out of purgatory or even pay for future crimes. How absurd and deceptive.

When Jesus Christ died on the cross He paid for all our sins so why would we pay money to a deceptive system? Why would we confess our sins to another human being that is completely impotent in being able to cleanse us from our sins and grant us eternal life?

If you were not interested in the good old book, maybe now you may be interested to open its pages to fully understand what is about to happen. It is inevitable. All of our properties, assets, savings, retirement funds will be swallowed up in this maelstrom of a global financial collapse, following on from that a great solution will then be presented by the powers that be. Maybe, then, the populations of the world may want to wake and listen to what the good old book has to say, will it be too late by then? Do you want to wait that long to find out? Your time will be up, either when that day comes or when you fall asleep as a result of our human mortality. The good old book tells us the following:

"Behold, the days come, saith the Lord GOD, that I will send a famine in the land, not a famine of bread, nor a thirst for water, but of hearing the words of the LORD:

And they shall wander from sea to sea, and from the north even to the east, they shall run to and fro to seek the word of the LORD, and shall not find [it]." Amos 8:11-12.

"Seek ye the LORD while he may be found, call ye upon him while he is near: Let the wicked forsake his way, and the unrighteous man his thoughts: and let him return unto the LORD, and he will have mercy upon him; and to our God, for he will abundantly pardon." Isaiah 55:6-7.

"For as in the days that were before the flood they were eating and drinking, marrying and giving in marriage, until the day that Noe entered into the ark,

And knew not until the flood came, and took them all away; so shall also the coming of the Son of man be." Matthew 24:38-39.

Don't get caught out like the populations of the world before Noah's flood.

What's Next - Final Victory, Final Reward

In this final chapter it is important to recap verse 45 of Daniel 11 and go on to Verses 1 – 3 of Daniel 12.

"And he shall plant the tabernacles of his palace between the seas in the glorious holy mountain; yet he shall come to his end, and none shall help him

And at that time shall Michael stand up, the great prince which standeth for the children of thy people: and there shall be a time of trouble, such as never was since there was a nation [even] to that same time: and at that time thy people shall be delivered, every one that shall be found written in the book.

And many of them that sleep in the dust of the earth shall awake, some to everlasting life, and some to shame [and] everlasting contempt.

And they that be wise shall shine as the brightness of the firmament; and they that turn many to righteousness as the stars for ever and ever."

These are very serious verses folks because when the last power succeeds in planting the tabernacles of his palace, and his system finally collapses, then **the end, of the time of the end** will have come. The first 3 verses of Daniel 12 make it very plain that Michael, Jesus, will stand up at that collapse for His people, and there will then occur on this earth a terrible time of trouble such as never was seen since the planet existed and by then it will have been too late for anyone to decide, just as it was too late for many of the inhabitants of the earth before Noah's flood that constantly ridiculed him, to enter the ark. The doors were sealed shut by God's holy angels.

"When the third angel's message closes, mercy no longer pleads for the guilty inhabitants of the earth. The people of

God have accomplished their work. They have received "the latter rain," "the refreshing from the presence of the Lord," and they are prepared for the trying hour before them. Angels are hastening to and fro in Heaven. An angel returning from the earth announces that his work is done; the final test has been brought upon the world, and all who have proved themselves loyal to the divine precepts have received "the seal of the living God."

Then Jesus ceases his intercession in the sanctuary above. He lifts his hands, and with a loud voice says, "It is done;" and all the angelic host lay off their crowns as he makes the solemn announcement: "He that is unjust, let him be unjust still; and he which is filthy, let him be filthy still; and he that is righteous, let him be righteous still; and he that is holy, let him be holy still." [Revelation 22:11.] Every case has been decided for life or death. Christ has made the atonement for his people, and blotted out their sins. The number of his subjects is made up; "the kingdom and dominion, and the greatness of the kingdom under the whole heaven," is about to be given to the heirs of salvation, and Jesus is to reign as King of kings, and Lord of lords.

When He leaves the sanctuary, darkness covers the inhabitants of the earth. In that fearful time the righteous must live in the sight of a holy God without an intercessor. The restraint which has been upon the wicked is removed, and Satan has entire control of the finally impenitent. God's long-suffering has ended. The world has rejected his mercy, despised his love, and trampled upon his law. The wicked have passed the boundary of their probation; the Spirit of God, persistently resisted, has been at last withdrawn. Unsheltered by divine grace, they have no protection from the wicked one. Satan will then plunge the inhabitants of the earth into one great, final trouble. As the angels of God cease to hold in check the fierce winds of human passion, all the elements of strife will be let loose. The whole world will be involved in ruin more terrible than that which came upon Jerusalem of old." Great Controversy 613-614.

Is the above statement far-fetched? I say no. Consider again the scenario. The merchants of the earth collaborate with the papacy to collapse the global economy to usher in their buying and selling religious regime, the world gets sucked in by it all, many being unaware of the real reasons of the powers that be until they come to know the truth, many will become very angry with the system, it will fall apart abruptly, as for sure it will, because of the prophecy in Revelation that we read in the first chapter of this book:

"Standing afar off for the fear of her torment, saying, Alas, alas that great city Babylon, that mighty city! for in one hour is thy judgment come.
And the merchants of the earth shall weep and mourn over her; for no man buyeth their merchandise any more:
The merchants of these things, which were made rich by her, shall stand afar off for the fear of her torment, weeping and wailing,
And saying, alas, alas, that great city, that was clothed in fine linen, and purple, and scarlet, and decked with gold, and precious stones, and pearls!
For in one hour so great riches is come to nought. And every shipmaster, and all the company in ships, and sailors, and as many as trade by sea, stood afar off,
And cried when they saw the smoke of her burning, saying, What [city is] like unto this great city!
And they cast dust on their heads, and cried, weeping and wailing, saying, Alas, alas, that great city, wherein were made rich all that had ships in the sea by reason of her costliness! for in one hour is she made desolate."
Revelation 18: 10-11, 15-19.

Nobody buys any merchandise any more, why? Because a real financial collapse has occurred and nobody can buy because all the businesses have collapsed, no buying equals no selling, no selling equals no manufacturing or shipping and transport etc. no manufacturing or shipping or transport equals no employment, no employment equals no income for anybody and no revenue for the taxman/government which in turn equals no pay for the police force, the armies, the prisons etc. this will then precipitate a complete and utter breakdown of society. I don't think that any human being alive today can possibly imagine what will happen when that time comes.

I will also propose another factor that collapses the entire system. **No electricity**. The entire electronic system, with whatever enforcement processes that will be implemented, will rely on power that God can shut down at will. Electricity is a part of nature to some extent because vast amounts of it is released in thunderstorms. Consider the generation of electricity as an element that is released through power distribution equipment, turbines, nuclear etc. then fed in to our homes and places of work or industry, similar to us turning on the taps. Water is from nature, we pipe it to wherever we need it. The internet, computers, pay wave, microchips, RFID's, mobile phones etc. cannot operate without electricity.

The outcome of this great struggle will be two separate and distinct groups of people. Those that <u>choose</u> Jesus Christ, the Holy Spirit and The Father as truly entitled to be worshipped and receive the seal of God and those that <u>choose</u> and worship Satan and receive his seal/mark.

If one does not choose God through conscience or by indecision or deny that God or Satan exists, they will by default choose Satan. There is no middle ground, no sitting on the fence.

Both groups will receive rewards accordingly. But the Lord of heaven has warned of the consequences of worshiping the beast and his image. "And the third angel followed them, saying with a loud voice. If any man worship the beast and his image, and receive his mark in his forehead or in his hand. The same shall drink of the wine of the wrath of God, which is poured out without mixture into the cup of his indignation;" Revelation 14:9-10.

"For I testify unto every man that heareth the words of the prophecy of this book. If any man shall add unto these things, God shall add unto him the plagues that are written in this book: And if any man shall take away from the words of the book of this prophecy, God shall take away his part out of the book of life, and out of the holy city, and from the things which are written in this book." Rev: 22:18-19.

What are these plagues that God is warning us of? We find them detailed in the 16th chapter of Revelation. But the Lord being the merciful God that He is, gives us enough warning of these plagues and how to escape them. "And after these things I saw another angel come down from heaven, having great power; and the earth was lightened with his glory. And he cried mightily with a strong voice, saying, Babylon the great is fallen, is fallen,... And I heard another voice from heaven saying, come out of her, my people, that ye be not partakers of her sins, and that ye receive not of her plagues." Revelation 18: 2 to 4.

The first of these plagues, as described in verse 2 of chapter 16, a terrible scourge of grievous sores, falls on those who have received the mark of the beast and worshipped his image. Grievous sores mean huge, horrible, putrefying sores. ***The appearance of this plague after the enforcement of Sunday laws, buying and selling restrictions, death penalties legalised etc. will confirm that it the contest is over. Anyone who has not made their decision to receive God's seal by then will have missed out for eternity.***

The second plague verse 3, falls upon the sea, and it turns into blood, the third plague, verse 4, also the rivers and fountains (sources/springs) turn into blood; why? The bible says because they have shed the blood of the saints, so the Lord gives them blood to drink. You wanted blood? Well here it is in great quantities. Imagine the oceans turning into blood, no creature can survive in that, neither can any ships sail in it. Therefore, there will be an immediate cessation of the import and export trade, no more oil supplies etc., no food supplies from foreign shores, the beginnings of the greatest famine ever experienced, yet still more is to come. The very rivers turn into blood, just like during the time of the Pharaohs of Egypt, but this time all around the world. Imagine picking up a glass of water and it turns to blood before your very eyes. You may be saying to yourself, no way, this has never happened before, things will always be as they have been. Look around, are things as they used to be? We just need to learn to trust the word of God that if He says it will happen, then it will happen.

The fourth plague verses 8-9, is poured out on the sun, and men are scorched with great heat. Notice how our modern-day scientists are insisting that the "Ozone layer" is being depleted, allowing "Ultra-Violet rays" to penetrate the atmosphere, which could result an increase in skin diseases? There is a massive media drive trying to convince humanity that we are the ones causing global warming or climate change through carbon emissions etc.? Here again Satan knows the scriptures better than these scientists, and knows his time is short, so he deceives them into believing that mankind can do something about the impending doom that looms on the horizon, instead of preparing themselves for the coming of our Lord and Saviour Jesus Christ.

Under this 4th plague, it is possible that the Ozone layer could collapse completely allowing the sun's rays to strike the planet directly, however, what is certain, is that the Lord will allow the sun to scorch men with great heat, but they will not repent of their sins. According to Isaiah 24: 4 to 5 as we read in an earlier part of this book, "the earth is mourning and fading away" because humanity has broken the everlasting covenant. Dear readers it is not your car exhaust or airplanes etc., that is causing 'global warming' or 'climate change' it is the breaking of God's law in all its aspects, the refusal to acknowledge Him as our creator and His Lordship in our lives. He made the planet, it belongs to Him so why do we continue to refuse to acknowledge Him as the giver of life and therefore worthy of honour, glory and respect to the lifestyles He wants us to live by? Because we are choosing Satan as our king, the very one that is causing the diseases, the disasters and everything else alien to life, and because God gives us the freedom of choice, then we are experiencing the results of our choices, but God will bring it to a conclusion eventually because He cannot allow the type of life we on planet earth are experiencing to continue forever, make sense?

In the fifth plague verses 10 to 11, the Lord will pour darkness on the seat of the beast and his whole kingdom will be covered in darkness, and they will gnaw their tongues because of pain and their sores etc., and they will blaspheme the name of God, and not repent of their deeds. So the seat of the beast, Rome, will be covered with darkness and the false church located there, will be exposed for all its lies and hypocrisy. Not even Satan himself, who dwells there, will be able to do anything to undo what the Lord has done. They will be in total darkness, exposing the reality of all the spiritual darkness that has emanated from the Throne of Rome ever since she became set up as the 'Christian'? Church. I must point out to that the verses also state "his kingdom" therefore this indicates that wherever Catholicism rules there will be darkness.

During the sixth plague verses 12 to 16, Satan will succeed, yet again, in deceiving the whole world into believing that they can defeat the cause of God, therefore suggesting that it will be Satan's final attempt at destroying God's people before Jesus' second Advent.

The seventh plague, verses 17 to 21, describes the shaking of the planet to its very foundations, and the announcement from heaven that "It is done." This earthquake, or rather planet quake, will be so terrible that the mountains will not be found, and every island will disappear, and there will be the most violent hailstorm ever known to man. Hailstones the weight of a talent, which is approximately 57lbs or 26kgs in modern terms, will crash to earth from heaven. The storms that will generate such hailstones must be proportionate to the hailstones, extremely violent and unimaginable by any stretch of the imagination. Whatever could possibly be left standing, which is doubtful after so violent an earthquake, - the prophet Isaiah in chapter 24 verse 20 described the earth as "reeling to and fro like a drunkard", will be pulverised by such massive hailstones. To give an inkling of what such a hailstorm could be like we will quote an eye-witness account of a hailstorm which occurred, the weight of the hailstones approximately one pound (.45kg) in weight. True, they cannot be compared with a 57lb (25.85kg) hailstone, just like you would not expect a 100 ton express train to stop in the same distance as a 1 or 1.5 ton car or better still the damage either vehicle would cause travelling at 100 mph (161 kmh), on impacting a building, or other structure.

"We had got perhaps a mile and a half (2.4km) on our way, when a cloud rising in the west gave indications of an approaching rain. In a few minutes we discovered something falling from the heavens with a heavy splash, and of a whitish appearance. I could not conceive what it was, but observing some gulls near, I supposed it to be them darting for fish, but soon after discovered that they were large balls of ice falling. Immediately we heard a sound like rumbling thunder, or ten thousand carriages rolling furiously over the pavement. The whole Bosphorus was in a foam, as though heaven's artillery had been discharged upon us and our frail machine.

Our fate seemed inevitable," our umbrellas were raised to protect us, but the lumps of ice stripped them into ribbons. We fortunately had a bullock's hide in the boat, under which we crawled, and saved ourselves from further injury. One man of the three oarsmen had his hand literally smashed; another was much injured in the shoulder; Mr. H. Received a severe blow in the leg; my right hand was somewhat disabled, and all more or less injured.... It was the most awful and terrific scene that I have ever witnessed, and God forbid that I should be ever exposed to such another! Balls of ice as large as my two fists fell into the boat, some of them came with such violence as certainly to have broken an arm or a leg had they struck us in those parts. One of them struck the blade of an oar, and split it. The scene lasted maybe five minutes; but it was five minutes of the most awful feeling that I ever experienced. When it passed over, we found the surrounding hills covered with masses of ice, I cannot call it hail, the trees were stripped of their leaves and limbs and everything looking desolate....

The scene was awful beyond all description. I have witnessed repeated earthquakes; the lightning has played, as it were, about my head; and wind roared, and the waves have at one moment thrown me to the sky, and next have sunk me into the deep abyss. I have been in action, and have seen death and destruction around me in every shape of horror; but I never before had the feeling of awe which seized upon me on this occasion, and still haunts, and I fear will ever haunt me.... My porter, the boldest of my family, who had ventured an instant from the door, had been knocked down by a hailstone, and had they not dragged him in by the heels, would have been battered to death. ... Two boatmen were killed in the upper part of the village, and I have heard of broken bones in abundance. .... Imagine to yourself, however, the heavens suddenly frozen over, and as suddenly broken to pieces in irregular masses, of from half a pound to a pound weight, and precipitated to the earth." Hailstorm on the Bosphorus, by David Porter. Constantinople and its environs, vol;1;pp.44-47.

Would you wish to suffer the consequences of the above by the wrong choices, or receive the rewards of the faithful as detailed below?

"And I saw as it were a sea of glass mingled with fire: and them that had gotten victory over the beast, and over his image, and over his mark, and over the number of his name, stand on the sea of glass, having the harps of God. And they sing the song of Moses the servant of God, and the song of the Lamb, saying, great and marvellous are thy works, Lord God Almighty; just and true are thy ways, thou king of saints." Revelation 15:2-3.

"And I saw a new heaven and a new earth: for the first heaven and the first earth were passed away; and there was no more sea. And I John saw the Holy City New Jerusalem, coming down from God out of heaven, prepared as a bride adorned for her husband. And I heard a great voice out of heaven saying, behold, the tabernacle of God is with men, and He will dwell with them, and they shall be His people, and God himself shall be with them, and be their God. And God shall wipe away all tears from their eyes: and there shall be no more death, neither sorrow, nor crying, neither shall there be no more pain: for the former things are passed away. And He that sat on the throne said, behold, I make all things new. And He said unto me, write: for these words are true and faithful. And he said unto me, it is done. I am alpha and omega, the beginning and the end.... He that overcometh shall inherit all things; and I will be his God, and he shall be my son." Revelation 21:1-7.

Notice how these verses of scripture are so plain and simple. There are no longer any mysteries to be unravelled, their meanings are plain. So it will be found with all the following verses, for those who have overcome the beast, need no longer to search any mysteries, as these verses speak of the rewards the Lord has made available to every single member of the human race if we want it.

"And he carried me away in the spirit to a great and high mountain, and shewed me that great city, the Holy Jerusalem, descending out of heaven from God." Verse 11,

"And he shewed me a pure river of water of life, clear as crystal, proceeding out of the throne of God and of the Lamb. In the midst of the street of it, and on either side of the river was there the tree of life, which bare twelve

manner of fruits, and yielded her fruits every month:..."
Revelation 22: 1-2

Dear readers imagine a tree that has different fruits every month that provides whatever your body needs for you to live forever. Awesome, can't describe that.

"And he said unto me, these sayings are faithful and true: and the Lord God of the holy prophets sent his angel to shew unto his servants the things which must shortly be done. Behold, I come quickly: blessed is he that keepeth the sayings of the prophecy of this book. And, behold, I come quickly; and my reward is with me, to give every man according as his work shall be. I am Alpha and Omega, the beginning and the end, the first and the last." Ibid vs. 6, 7, 12-13.

"Eye hath not seen, nor ear heard, neither have entered into the heart of man, the things which God hath prepared for them that love him." 1st Corinthians 2:9.

"Let not your heart be troubled: ye believe in God, believe also in me. In my father's house are many mansions: if it were not so, I would have told you. I go to prepare a place for you, and if I go and prepare a place for you, I will come again, and receive you unto myself; that where I am, there ye may be also." John 14:1-3.

We cannot even begin to imagine the grandeur of Jesus' plans for our future.

"A fear of making the future inheritance seem too material has led many to spiritualise away the very truths which lead us to look upon it as our home. Christ assured his disciples that he went to prepare mansions for them in his Father's house. Those who accept the teachings of God's word will not be wholly ignorant concerning the heavenly abode... Human language is inadequate to describe the reward of the righteous. It will be known only to those who behold it. No finite mind can comprehend the glory of the Paradise of God. In the Bible the inheritance of the saved is called "A Country."

Hebrews 11:14-16, There the heavenly shepherd leads his flock to fountains of living waters. There are ever-flowing streams, clear as crystal, and beside them waving trees cast their shadows upon the paths prepared for the ransomed of the Lord. There the wide-spreading plains swell into hills of beauty, and the mountains of God rear their lofty summits. On those peaceful plains, beside those living streams, God's people, so long pilgrims and wanderers, shall find a home.

"My people shall dwell in a peaceful habitation, and in sure dwellings, and in quiet resting places." "Violence shall no more be heard in thy land, wasting nor destruction within thy borders; but thou shalt call thy walls salvation, and thy gates praise." "They shall build houses, and inhabit them: and they shall plant vineyards and eat the fruit of them. They shall not build and another inhabit, they shall not plant and another eat: Mine elect shall long enjoy the work of their hands." Isaiah 32:18, 60:18. 65:21-22.

Pain cannot exist in the atmosphere of heaven. There will be no more tears, no funeral trains, no badges of mourning. "There shall be no more death, neither sorrow, nor crying: ... for the former things are passed away." "The inhabitant shall not say I am sick; the people that dwell therein shall be forgiven their iniquity." Revelation 21:4, Isaiah 33:24.

In the city of God "there shall be no night." None will need or desire repose. There will be no weariness in doing the will of God and offering praise to his name. We shall ever feel the freshness of the morning and shall ever be far from its close. "And they need no candle, neither light of the sun; for the Lord giveth them light." Revelation 22:5. The light of the sun will be superseded by a radiance which is not painfully dazzling, yet which immeasurably surpasses the brightness of our noontide. The glory of God and the Lamb floods the Holy City with unfading light.

The redeemed walk in the sunless glory of perpetual day. "Now we see through a glass darkly." 1 Corinthians 13:12. There the redeemed shall know, even as also they are known. The loves and sympathies which God himself has planted in the soul shall there find truest and sweetest exercise. The pure communion with holy beings, the harmonious social life with the blessed angels and with the faithful ones of all ages who have washed their robes and made them white in the blood of the Lamb, the sacred ties that bind them together "the whole family in heaven and earth" Ephesians 3:15, these help to constitute the happiness of the redeemed.

There, immortal minds will contemplate with never-failing delight the wonders of creative power, the mysteries of redeeming love. There will be no cruel, deceiving foe to tempt to forgetfulness of God. Every faculty will be developed, every capacity increased. The acquirement of knowledge will not weary the mind or exhaust the energies. There the grandest enterprises may be carried forward, the loftiest aspirations reached, the highest ambitions realised; and still there will arise new heights to surmount, new wonders to admire, new truths to comprehend, fresh objects to call forth the powers of mind and soul and body.

All the treasures of the universe will be opened to the study of God's redeemed. Unfettered by mortality, they wing their tireless flights to worlds afar – worlds that thrilled with sorrow at the spectacle of human woe and rang with songs of gladness at the tidings of a ransomed soul. With unutterable delight the children of earth enter into the joy and the wisdom of unfallen beings. They share the treasures of knowledge and understanding gained through ages upon ages in contemplation of God's handiwork. With undimmed vision they gaze upon the glory of creation – suns and stars and systems, all in their appointed order circling the throne of Deity, upon all things, from the least to the greatest, the creator's name is written; and in all are the riches of his power displayed.

And the years of eternity, as they roll, will bring richer and still more glorious revelations of God and of Christ. As knowledge is progressive, so will love, reverence, and happiness increase. The more men learn of God, the greater will be their admiration of his character. As Jesus opens before them the riches of redemption and the amazing achievements in the great controversy with Satan, the hearts of the ransomed' thrill with more fervent devotion, and with more rapturous joy they sweep the harps of Gold; and ten thousand times ten thousand and thousands of thousands of voices unite to swell the mighty chorus of praise.

"And every creature which is in heaven, and on the earth and under the earth, and such as are in the sea, and all that are in them, heard I saying. Blessing, and honor, and glory, and power, be unto him that sitteth upon the throne, and unto the Lamb for ever and ever." Revelation 5:13.

The great controversy is ended. Sin and sinners are no more. The entire universe is clean. One pulse of harmony and gladness beats through the vast creation. From him who created all, flow life and light and gladness, throughout the realms of illimitable space. From the minutest atom, to the greatest world, all things, animate and inanimate, in their unshadowed beauty and perfect joy, declare that God is love." Great Controversy pp 674-8.

Far into the future, one thousand years after the Second Advent, when the New Jerusalem, built of transparent gold and all types of precious stones descends to earth, it will descend to the same location as the current Jerusalem. The mount of Olives will split in four directions to receive it; Zechariah 14:4. This event triggers the final and ultimate end of sin.

"And I saw an angel come down from heaven, having the key of the bottomless pit and a great chain in his hand.
And he laid hold on the dragon, that old serpent, which is the Devil, and Satan, and bound him a thousand years,
And cast him into the bottomless pit, and shut him up, and set a seal upon him, that he should deceive the nations no more, till the thousand years should be fulfilled: and after that he must be loosed a little season.
And I saw thrones, and they sat upon them, and judgment was given unto them: and [I saw] the souls of them that were beheaded for the witness of Jesus, and for the word of God, and which had not worshipped the beast, neither his image, neither had received [his] mark upon their foreheads, or in their hands; and they lived and reigned with Christ a thousand years.
But the rest of the dead lived not again until the thousand years were finished. This [is] the first resurrection.
Blessed and holy [is] he that hath part in the first resurrection: on such the second death hath no power, but they shall be priests of God and of Christ, and shall reign with him a thousand years.

And when the thousand years are expired, Satan shall be loosed out of his prison,

And shall go out to deceive the nations which are in the four quarters of the earth, Gog and Magog, to gather them together to battle: the number of whom [is] as the sand of the sea.
And they went up on the breadth of the earth, and compassed the camp of the saints about, and the beloved city: and fire came down from God out of heaven, and devoured them." Revelation 20:1-9.

The "MYSTERY OF INIQUITY" will be finally vanquished. The following verses confirm that the Mystery of God through Jesus existed from the beginning of and before the creation of this planet. Satan believed he could win, but what is the truth of the matter?

"Now to him that is of power to stablish you according to my gospel, and the preaching of Jesus Christ, according to the revelation of the mystery, which was kept secret since the world began.
But now is made manifest, and by the scriptures of the prophets, according to the commandment of the everlasting God, made known to all nations for the obedience of faith:" Romans 16:25-26.

The gospel of Christ and His kingdom is made manifest.
"See what [is] the fellowship of the mystery, which from the beginning of the world hath been hid in God, who created all things by Jesus Christ:
To the intent that now unto the principalities and powers in heavenly [places] might be known by the church the manifold wisdom of God, According to the eternal purpose which he purposed in Christ Jesus our Lord:"
Ephesians 3:10-11.

"In hope of eternal life, which God, that cannot lie, promised before the world began;" Titus 1:2.

Absolutely amazing dear readers. God the Father, the Son and the Holy Ghost were all involved in this plan just in case our planet fell into trouble because of the arch-deceiver.

One final confirmation of Satan being the father of the mystery of iniquity. How he got to that point is indeed a mystery because he was the most beautiful creature that God made. Unlike us humans being made out of dust, he was made from all types of precious stones. Let's read from Ezekiel 28: 12-13 & 15.

"Son of man, take up a lamentation upon the king of Tyrus, and say unto him, Thus saith the Lord GOD; Thou sealest up the sum, full of wisdom, and perfect in beauty.
Thou hast been in Eden the garden of God; every precious stone [was] thy covering, the sardius, topaz, and the diamond, the beryl, the onyx, and the jasper, the sapphire, the emerald, and the carbuncle, and gold: the workmanship of thy tabrets and of thy pipes was prepared in thee in the day that thou wast created.
Thou [wast] perfect in thy ways from the day that thou wast created, till iniquity was found in thee."

These verses confirm that 'Iniquity' began with Satan. He is the author of the MYSTERY OF INIQUITY.

In the final analysis, contrary to what many denominations or religious persuasions or their leaders may try to convince you into believing, or that there are many ways to heaven, or that we all serve the same God, but in different ways? I submit to you, with the information researched in this work, that that is not the case; and that there is only one way to obtain salvation, by following God's precepts as set out in the Decalogue. "I am the way, the truth and the life" is vindicated. The scriptures also make it plain that the Lord recognises that there are honest souls in other 'Christian' movements, including Judaism and Islam, but that they must come into Jesus' "One fold."

Satan has set up the "MYSTERY RELIGION" that still exists today in the form of the Catholic Church that actually from her own lips and words claims to be the "mother of all churches of the city and of the world" All other churches that follow her adulterated day and systems of worship are by default her daughters. Remember the scriptures declare in Revelation 13:3, "…..and all the world wondered after the beast". The Catholic Church has so influenced the world with its false Sabbath that over 99% of all businesses have their busiest days on the Saturday, God's original Seventh Day Sabbath. The business owners or their customers are highly likely to be unaware that they are breaking the commandment that directly confirms that our living God is their creator and this is replicated amongst all faith or non-faith groups.

"And other sheep I have, which are not of this fold: them also I must bring, and they shall hear my voice; and there shall be one fold, and one shepherd." John 10:16.

"Jesus saith unto him, I am the way, the truth, and the life: no man cometh unto the Father, but by me." John 14:6.

There is no record that Mohammed gave his life to save anybody, or any other popular spiritual icon, yet there is ample records that Jesus did.

So therefore, I submit to you, that the idea of many ways to obtain salvation can be only from the arch-deceiver himself. He does not care in what way you are deceived, as long as you are. He has devices, theories and ideas for all

509

classes, from the most highly educated and sophisticated to the illiterate. What might appeal to the lower classes may not appeal to the upper classes, therefore he adapts his deceptions to suit. The answer could be cleverly simple, if you love God follow 'all' His commandments, as that is the only sure way of finding your way through the maze of deceptions.

I trust that you have examined this work with humility of spirit and sincere prayers, and that it has gone some way to answering some or most of your questions.

There are only two outcomes at the end, follow Satan through any one of his deceptions, from pagan religions, new-age, humanist, evolutionist, atheistic or other philosophies or choose to follow Jesus Christ, the Only way, THE I AM, that gave His life on the cross. That manifested Himself as a human being to save us.

Quoting from Joshua 24:15 "And if it seem evil unto you to serve the LORD, choose you this day whom ye will serve; whether the gods which your fathers served that [were] on the other side of the flood, or the gods of the Amorites, in whose land ye dwell: but as for me and my house, we will serve the LORD."

And from the lips of Elijah as quoted in 1 Kings 18:21 "And Elijah came unto all the people, and said, How long halt ye between two opinions? If the LORD [be] God, follow him: but if Baal, [then] follow him….."

"Jesus saith unto him, I am the way, the truth, and the life: no man cometh unto the Father, but by me." John 14:6.

How important were we in the creation scenario?

"All heaven took a deep and joyful interest in the creation of the world and of man. Human beings were a new and distinct order." —RH Feb. 11, 1902.

"Next to the angelic beings, the human family, formed in the image of God, are the noblest of His created works." — RH Dec. 3, 1908

"God created man for His own glory that after test and trial the human family might become one with the heavenly family. It was God's purpose to repopulate heaven with the human family." 1BC 1082

"The vacancies made in heaven by the fall of Satan and his angels will be filled by the redeemed of the Lord." —RH May 29, 1900

Awesome isn't it, a far cry from having descended from apes. Have any and can any of the proponents of evolution show us a photo of their grandparent or great grand-parent that resembles an ape? If you were to ask that question of them you would probably get slapped in the face. Evolution is another deception of the enemy to rob us of our inheritance. Don't fall for it.

I close this book with these final quotes from Revelation.
"Blessed are they that do His commandments that they may have right to the tree of life, and may enter in through the gates into the city. He which testifieth these things saith. Surely I come quickly. Amen. Even so, come. Lord Jesus. The grace of our Lord Jesus Christ be with you all. Amen." Revelation 22:14, 20-21.

The New Jerusalem is an awesome City built of transparent gold and all types of precious stones. I most definitely would like to live in that city and be able to explore the entire universe over the billions and trillions of years of eternity with the God of eternity, where there is no more sickness and no more death. Wouldn't you? This will be a life that no human on earth can imagine.

"And he carried me away in the spirit to a great and high mountain, and showed me that great city, the holy Jerusalem, descending out of heaven from God,
Having the glory of God: and her light [was] like unto a stone most precious, even like a jasper stone, clear as crystal;
And had a wall great and high, [and] had twelve gates, and at the gates twelve angels, and names written thereon, which are [the names] of the twelve tribes of the children of Israel:

On the east three gates; on the north three gates; on the south three gates; and on the west three gates.
And the wall of the city had twelve foundations, and in them the names of the twelve apostles of the Lamb.
And he that talked with me had a golden reed to measure the city, and the gates thereof, and the wall thereof.
And the city lieth foursquare, and the length is as large as the breadth: and he measured the city with the reed, twelve thousand furlongs. The length and the breadth and the height of it are equal.
And he measured the wall thereof, an hundred [and] forty [and] four cubits, [according to] the measure of a man, that is, of the angel.
And the building of the wall of it was [of] jasper: and the city [was] pure gold, like unto clear glass.
And the foundations of the wall of the city [were] garnished with all manner of precious stones. The first foundation [was] jasper; the second, sapphire; the third, a chalcedony; the fourth, an emerald;

The fifth, sardonyx; the sixth, sardius; the seventh, chrysolyte; the eighth, beryl; the ninth, a topaz; the tenth, a chrysoprasus; the eleventh, a jacinth; the twelfth, an amethyst.

And the twelve gates [were] twelve pearls: every several gate was of one pearl: and the street of the city [was] pure gold, as it were transparent glass.

And I saw no temple therein: for the Lord God Almighty and the Lamb are the temple of it.

And the city had no need of the sun, neither of the moon, to shine in it: for the glory of God did lighten it, and the Lamb [is] the light thereof." Revelation 21:10-23.

Matthew 25:31 states "When the Son of man shall come in his glory, and all the holy angels with him..."

How many angels? We don't know exactly, but here is an indication.

"And I beheld, and I heard the voice of many angels round about the throne and the beasts and the elders: and the number of them was ten thousand times ten thousand, and thousands of thousands;" Revelation 5:11

Let us put that into perspective and use the lowest denominator of thousands. 10,000 x 10,000 x 1,000 x 1,000 equals 100,000,000,000,000. Twelve zeros after the first comma is 1 trillion. In this example we have 100 trillion. What would it be if we calculated 10,000 x 10,000 x 2,000 x 2,000, (because John does not tell us how many 1,000's to calculate) - the latter sum would come to 400,000,000,000,000 which is 400 trillion.

Can you imagine the scene – 100 trillion angels? 4300 trillion angels? - All the angels joining Jesus on that journey to gather His saints? Heaven will be emptied. What an awesome sight to see. Greater than any movie ever made. The biggest event ever in space. Can you imagine the light and awesome, mind-boggling energy being emitted?

Can you imagine cemeteries all over the world with graves breaking open as the righteous dead are raised and along with the living saints all rising up to meet Jesus as he appears from the east?

No person alive will ever be able to avoid witnessing this event, question is which group would you want to be in, those resurrecting to meet Jesus in the air and those that never died rising to meet Jesus in the air or those who have their feet firmly planted on the earth watching the drama unfold? The whole planet will be shaking with all that awesome power approaching. I know which group I want to be in. Do you?

This shaking of the planet reminds me of the verses from the prophet Isaiah. 24:17 – 20.

"Fear, and the pit, and the snare, [are] upon thee, O inhabitant of the earth.
 And it shall come to pass, [that] he who fleeth from the noise of the fear shall fall into the pit; and he that cometh up out of the midst of the pit shall be taken in the snare: for the windows from on high are open, and the foundations of the earth do shake.
The earth is utterly broken down, the earth is clean dissolved, the earth is moved exceedingly.

The earth shall reel to and fro like a drunkard, and shall be removed like a cottage; and the transgression thereof shall be heavy upon it; and it shall fall, and not rise again."

I leave it to your imagination of what this quake event could possibly be like. Is there any building that we can construct that will be able to resist a planet-wide earthquake, one so violent that the planet is swaying, one so violent that John in Revelation 6:14 also witnessed this massive quake and describing it "…the heaven departed as a scroll when it is rolled together; and every mountain and island were moved out of their places" Even the very heavens quaking?

Mount Everest? Mount Fuji? Mount Kilimanjaro? Mount Cook? Ben Nevis? Mount St. Helens? The Cairngorms? The Matterhorn? The Himalayas? A small sample of huge mountains that will move out of their places? What about entire Island Countries?

How many countries are Islands? United Kingdom? Ireland? New Zealand? The Caribbean and Pacific Island nations? Indonesia? New Guinea? Hawaii? New Caledonia? The list goes on.

Remember the Nepal quake in 2015 that experts say moved the City of Kathmandu 10 feet southwards? A planet wide quake will move mountains and islands as John described.
Are we beginning to witness warnings of this impending global quake? Check out the following news report:

'Ghost' earthquake ripples around the world - November 30, 2018 13:10:20
"A mysterious ripple of seismic waves has travelled thousands of kilometres across the globe, tripping sensors throughout Africa, Canada, New Zealand, and Hawaii, seemingly without being felt by a single person.

Key Points:

- Seismic waves beginning off the coast of Mozambique triggered sensors in Kenya, Chile, New Zealand and Canada

- The tremors lasted more than 20 minutes

- The earthquake went unnoticed until was picked up by an earthquake enthusiast online

The tremors started just off the shores of Mayotte, a French archipelago in the Indian Ocean between Madagascar and Africa, and would have flown under the radar if not for an earthquake enthusiast in New Zealand who had been tuned in to the US Geological Survey's real-time seismogram displays online.

They posted images of the readings to Twitter, prompting researches around the world to try to deduce where these bizarre waves came from.

Unlike traditional earthquakes, which produce a jolt of various high frequency waves, the readings from the Mayotte tremor picked up consistent low frequency waves that lasted more than 20 minutes. It was as though the planet rang like a bell.

Online theorists suggest covert nuclear tests, sea monsters, or a meteorite as the cause of the tremor, but Goran Ekstrom, a seismologist at Columbia University, told National Geographic the explanation was likely straight-forward.

"I don't think I've seen anything like it [but] it doesn't mean that, in the end, the cause of them is that exotic," he said.

Professor Ekstrom suggests that the seismic event actually did begin with an earthquake. He thinks it passed by surreptitiously because it was a slow earthquake.

Slow earthquakes are quieter than traditional quakes because they come from a gradual release of stress that can stretch over a significant period of time.

"The same deformation happens, but it doesn't happen as a jolt," Professor Ekstrom said.

Since May this year, Mayotte has been subjected to what is known as an 'earthquake swarm'; a cluster of hundreds of seismic events over a period of days or weeks, but the activity has significantly lessened in recent months.

Analysis by the French Geological Survey suggests the strange waves may indicate a mass movement of magma beneath the earth's crust, such as a chamber collapse.

Rhythmic motion, like sloshing of the molten rock, or a pressure wave ricocheting through the magma body have the potential to resonate in a similar way to the Mayotte readings.

The Democratic Republic of Congo was the site of a similar event in 2002, where a similar slow earthquake and low-frequency waves were linked with a magma chamber collapsing below the Nyiragongo volcano."

We have come full circle from Genesis 1, "In the beginning God created the heavens and the earth….formed man of the dust of the ground…"He planted the tree of life in the garden and we come through to the tree of life again and those who do His commandments will have access to that tree again.

Notice the "tree of the knowledge of good and evil" is no longer in the picture because sin and its instigator will be no more and there will not be the need of a tree to test the loyalty of the human race any longer. Hallelujah!! Amen!!

The fires of destruction were not meant for us humans. The devil and his angels do not want any humans to inherit the universe they forfeited. God needs to remove the curse of sin from His universe forever.

From the lips of Jesus Himself. "Then shall he say also unto them on the left hand, Depart from me, ye cursed, into everlasting fire, prepared for the devil and his angels:" Matthew 25:41.

You will not find any other records of a religious leader that died to redeem humans. You will not find any other being that had hundreds of prophecies fulfilled in detail about His coming, His life, death, resurrection and final victory in anyone but Jesus. Not Mohammad, Baha'u'llah, Confucius, Buddha etc. because they were mere mortals like us, hence unable to make a way for us. The only being that could take on Satan and win was our omnipotent creator God that transformed Himself and took on the form of humans to save us.

To repeat one of the quotes found at the beginning of this book "When you have eliminated the impossible, whatever remains, however improbable, must be the truth."

What other organisation is there on earth that pretends to be Christ's Church that fits the biblical prophecies that can be traced through history into our modern times that has assimilated and is perpetuating the MYSTERY OF INIQUITY? It is none other than the Roman Catholic Church. No matter the amount of legislation that will come about to force the inhabitants of earth to follow her dogmas and system of worship, she will still remain the whore of Revelation until God removes her and the master of the MYSTERY OF INIQUITY, Satan. No matter how many hundreds of millions of members she has, this does not constitute evidence of truth. No matter how many truths she incorporates with her lies, she is still the whore of revelation because once you put a drop of poison in a drink or a meal, the whole of it becomes poison. Come out of her and her daughter churches so that you can avoid receiving her plagues but instead receive the inheritance that God has made available to all. Choose you today who you will serve.

My question to you as you have come to the end of this book *(apart from the appendices)* and that you now have an understanding and the truth of what has been and is going on in our world, what are you going to do about it? Will you keep this knowledge to yourself or are you going to employ your best efforts to share this information with as many as possible? It's quite simple, let your friends and family know where they can get their own copy. If they are in a country where they cannot get a copy, acquire more copies and send to them. For ebooks, send them the link. Organise small home study groups to discuss amongst yourselves and get this knowledge in your heads because the time will come when you will no longer be able to have access to any form of media to be able to share, be it electronic or printed.

"And this is life eternal, that they might know thee the only true God, and Jesus Christ, whom thou hast sent." John 17:3.

We conclude with a few verses on the Mystery of Godliness because in choosing Christ you have chosen eternal life, the original plan for our existence. Don't miss out on it.

"These things write I unto thee, hoping to come unto thee shortly: But if I tarry long, that thou mayest know how thou oughtest to behave thyself in the house of God, which is the church of the living God, the pillar and ground of the truth. And without controversy great is the mystery of godliness: God was manifest in the flesh, justified in the Spirit, seen of angels, preached unto the Gentiles, believed on in the world, received up into glory." 1 Timothy 3:14-16

May our good Lord bless you as you prepare for what is coming to this world with rapid and blinding force.

Appendices

Appendix 1 - Secular history records of Jesus' redeeming visit to earth.

Tacitus, Roman historian, writing in about 115 AD

…Nero fastened the guilt and inflicted the most exquisite tortures on a class hated for their abominations, called Christians [or Chrestians] by the populace. Christus, from whom the name had its origin, suffered the extreme penalty during the reign of Tiberius at the hands of one of our procurators, Pontius Pilatus, and a most mischievous superstition, thus checked for the moment, again broke out not only in Judaea, the first source of the evil, but even in Rome,… Tacitus, *Annals* 15.44, translated by Church and Brodribb. *auctor nominis eius Christus Tiberio imperitante per procuratorem Pontium Pilatum supplicio adfectus erat* Tacitus, *Annales* 15.44

Gaius Suetonius Tranquillus (c. 69–140) wrote the following in his *Lives of the Twelve Caesars* about riots which broke out in the Jewish community in Rome under the emperor Claudius:

"As the Jews were making constant disturbances at the instigation of Chrestus, he (Claudius) expelled them from Rome".

And found a certain Jew named Aquila, born in Pontus, lately come from Italy, with his wife Priscilla; (because that Claudius had commanded all Jews to depart from Rome:) Acts 18:2

Phlegon was a historian who lived in the first century. There are two books credited to his name: *Chronicles and* *the Olympiads. Little is known about Phlegon but he made reference to Christ. The first two quotes are unique to Origen and the last quote below is recorded by Origen and Philopon.*

Written A. D. 80 — "Now Phlegon, in the thirteenth or fourteenth book, I think, of his Chronicles, not only ascribed to Jesus a knowledge of future events . . . but also testified that the result corresponded to His predictions."

Origen Against Celsus

"And with regard to the eclipse in the time of Tiberius Caesar, in whose reign Jesus appears to have been crucified, and the great earthquakes which then took place . . ."

"Phlegon mentioned the eclipse which took place during the crucifixion of the Lord Jesus and no other (eclipse); it is clear that he did not know from his sources about any (similar) eclipse in previous times . . . and this is shown by the historical account of Tiberius Caesar." *De. opif. mund. II21*

Thallus (circa A.D. 52) wrote a history about the middle east from the time of the Trojan War to his own time. The work has been lost and the only record we have of his writings is through Julius Africanus (A.D. 221). Below Julius Africanus refers to Christ's crucifixion and the darkness that covered the earth prior to his death.

Written A. D. 80 — "This darkness Thallus, in the third book of his History, calls, as it appears to me without reason, an eclipse of the sun. For the Hebrews celebrate the passover on the 14th day according to the moon, and the passion of our Savior falls on the day before the passover;

but an eclipse of the sun takes place only when the moon comes under the sun. And it cannot happen at any other time but in the interval between the first day of the new moon and the last of the old, that is, at their junction: how then should an eclipse occur when the moon is almost diametrically opposite the sun?

Essentially Thallus is making an emphatic statement that there was no lunar eclipse and that the darkness has no other explanation of being 'supernatural'

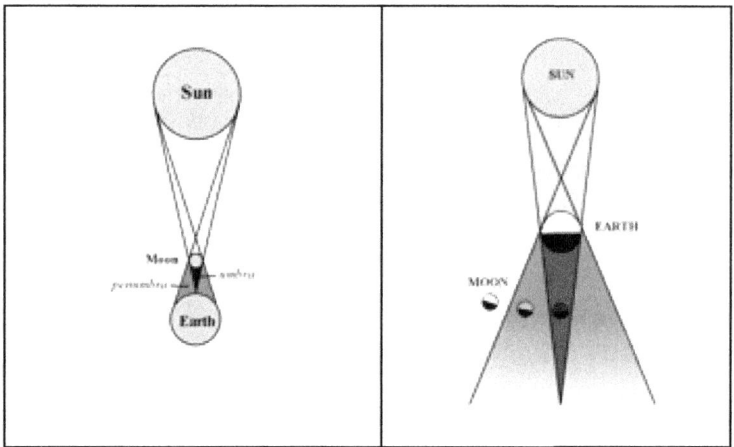

The darkness these secular historians are referring too are as per the following biblical accounts:

"Now from the sixth hour there was darkness over all the land unto the ninth hour. And about the ninth hour Jesus cried with a loud voice, saying, Eli, Eli, lama sabachthani? that is to say, My God, my God, why hast thou forsaken me?" Matthew 27:45-46. Mark 15: 33-34

"And it was about the sixth hour, and there was a darkness over all the earth until the ninth hour." Luke 23:44

Hadrian, Imperator Caesar Trainus, (AD 76-138), was considered a man of culture and the arts. It appears he preferred peace rather than war. The following quote comes from a letter sent to Minucius Fundanus, proconsul of Asia, about how to treat Christians.

Written A. D. 76 – 136 — "I do not wish, therefore, that the matter should be ignored without examination, so that these men may not be harassed, nor an opportunity given for malicious proceedings to be offered to informers. If, therefore, the provincials can clearly show their charges against these Christians, so as to answer before the tribunal, let them pursue this course only, but not just petitions, and mere outcries against Christians. For it is more fitting, if any one brings an accusation, that you should examine it."

Emperor Trajan (AD 53 - 117), Imperator Caesar Divi Nervae Filius Nerva Traianus, was one of the most famous Roman emperors of all time. His reputation as a successful military strategist is demonstrated by his military exploits, which expanded the Roman boundaries to the Persian Gulf. The quote below is a reply to Pliny, who had asked for directions in how to treat the Christians.

"The method you have used, my dear Pliny, in investigating the cases of those who are accused of being Christians is extremely proper. No search should be made for these people; when they are accused and found to be guilty they must be punished; with the restriction, however, that when the individual denies he is a Christian, and gives proof that he is not (that is, by adoring our gods) he shall be pardoned on the ground of repentance, even though he may have formerly incurred suspicion. Documents without the accuser's signature must not be admitted in evidence against anyone, since this introduces a very dangerous precedent, and is by no means consistent with the spirit of the age." *Pliny letters X, 97.*

Gaius Plinius Caecilius Secundus (AD 61-112), or Pliny the Younger, was the governor of Bithynia (AD 112) and a Roman senator. He wrote to emperor Trajan asking for guidance on how he should treat the Christians in his province. Written A. D. 112

"Christians were "meeting on a certain fixed day before it was light, when they sang in alternate verse a hymn to Christ as to a god, and bound themselves to a solemn oath, not to do wicked deeds, never commit fraud, theft, adultery, not to lie nor to deny a trust. . ."

Epistles X96

Flavius Josephus (AD 37-97), was born into a priestly Jewish family. He was a Pharisee and a historian for the Roman empire. He wrote several famous works: *"Antiquities of the Jews" and the "Wars of the Jews." Historians say Josephus was not a Christian.*

Now, there was about this time Jesus, a wise man, if it be lawful to call him a man. For he was a doer of surprising feats - a teacher of such men as receive the truth with pleasure. He drew over to him both many of the Jews and many of the Gentiles. He was [the] Christ; and when Pilate, at the suggestion of the principal men amongst us, had condemned him to the cross, those that loved him at the first did not forsake him, for he appeared to them alive again the third day, as the divine prophets had foretold these and ten thousand other wonderful things concerning him; and the tribe of Christians, so named from him, are not extinct to this day." *Antiquities of the Jews 18.3.3.*

Lucian, a second century Romano-Syrian satirist, who wrote in Greek, wrote:

"The Christians, you know, worship a man to this day — the distinguished personage who introduced their novel rites, and was crucified on that account... You see, these misguided creatures start with the general conviction that they are immortal for all time, which explains the contempt of death and voluntary self-devotion which are so common among them; and then it was impressed on them by their original lawgiver that they are all brothers, from the moment that they are converted, and deny the gods of Greece, and worship the crucified sage, and live after his laws". Lucian, *The Death of Peregrine*, 11-13 in *The Works of Lucian of Samosata*, translated by H. W. Fowler (Oxford: Clarendon, 1949) vol. 4

Pontius Pilate (1 BC - circa AD 37) was the fifth Roman procurator of Judea (AD 26 - 36), under Emperor Tiberius, who sentenced Jesus to death by crucifixion. The quotes below refer to the *Acts of Pontius Pilate, a document now missing. Its existence is strongly supported by Epiphanius (Heresies 50.1), Justin Martyr (First Apology) and Tertullian (Apology).*

"At His coming the lame will leap as a deer, and the stammering tongue will clearly speak: the blind will see, and the lepers will be healed; and the dead will rise, and walk.' And that He did those things, you can learn from the Acts of Pontius Pilate." *First Apology 48.*

"They pierced my hands and my feet,' was used in reference to the nails of the cross which were driven into His hands and feet.   And. . . they cast lots for His clothes, and after they crucified Him distributed it among them. And that these things did happen, you can ascertain from the Acts of Pontius Pilate.' *First Apology 35.*

Curse of the Rabbis
Daniel 9

Rabbis after the time of Christ have pronounced a curse on anyone who would attempt to calculate the dates of this chapter. - Talmud Sanhedrin 97b, Soncino ed., p. 659.

Sage said: "May the curse of heaven fall upon those who calculate the date of the advent of the Messiah, and thus create political and social unrest among the people." Sanhedrin, 97b.
Louis Newman and Samuel Spitz, *The Talmudic anthology: tales and teachings of the rabbis* (Behrman House, 1945): 277. ISBN 0874413036, 9780874413038

Appendix 2 – The legal precedences given to the See of Rome

THE CODE OF OUR LORD
THE MOST SACRED EMPEROR JUSTINIAN.
SECOND EDITION.
BOOK 1.
TITLE 1.

CONCERNING THE MOST EXALTED TRINITY AND THE
CATHOLIC FAITH AND PROVIDING THAT NO ONE
SHALL DARE TO PUBLICLY OPPOSE THEM.

1. The Emperors Gratian, Valentinian, and Theodosius to the people of the City of Constantinople.

We desire that all peoples subject to Our benign Empire shall live under the same religion that the Divine Peter, the Apostle, gave to the Romans, and which the said religion declares was introduced by himself, and which it is well known that the Pontiff Damascus, and Peter, Bishop of Alexandria, a man of apostolic sanctity, embraced; that is to say, in accordance with the rules of apostolic discipline and the evangelical doctrine, we should believe that the Father, Son, and Holy Spirit constitute a single Deity, endowed with equal majesty, and united in the Holy Trinity.

We order all those who follow this law to assume the name of Catholic Christians, and considering others as demented and insane, We order that they shall bear the infamy of heresy; and when the Divine vengeance which they merit has been appeased, they shall afterwards be punished in accordance with Our resentment, which we have acquired from the judgment of Heaven.   Dated at Thessalonica, on the third of the Kalends of March, during the Consulate of Gratian, Consul for the fifth time, and Theodosius.

2. The Same Emperors to Eutropius, Praetorian Prefect.

Let no place be afforded to heretics for the conduct of their ceremonies, and let no occasion be offered for them to display the insanity of their obstinate minds. Let all persons know that if any privilege has been fraudulently obtained by means of any rescript whatsoever, by persons of this kind, it will not be valid. Let all bodies of heretics be prevented from holding unlawful assemblies, and let the name of the only and the greatest God be celebrated everywhere, and let the observance of the Nicene Creed, recently transmitted to Our ancestors, and firmly established by the testimony and practice of Divine Religion, always remain secure.

Moreover, he who is an adherent of the Nicene Faith, and a true believer in the Catholic religion, should be understood to be one [pg. 10] who believes that Almighty God and Christ, the son of God, are one person, God of God, Light of Light; and let no one, by rejection, dishonor the Holy Spirit, whom we expect, and have received from the Supreme Parent of all things, in whom the sentiment of a pure and undefiled faith flourishes, as well as the belief in the undivided substance of a Holy Trinity, which true believers indicate by the Greek word amounsioV. These things, indeed do not require further proof, and should be respected.

Let those who do not accept those doctrines cease to apply the name of true religion to their fraudulent belief; and let them be branded with their open crimes, and, having been removed from the threshold of all churches, be utterly

529

excluded from them, as We forbid all heretics to hold unlawful assemblies within cities. If, however, any seditious outbreak should be attempted, We order them to be driven outside the the walls of the City, with relentless violence, and We direct that all Catholic Churches, throughout the entire world, shall be placed under the control of the orthodox bishops who have embraced the Nicene Creed.

Given at Constantinople, on the fourth of the ides of January, under the Consulate of Flavius Eucharius and Flavius Syagrius.

3. The Emperor Martian to Palladius, Praetorian Prefect.

No one, whether he belongs to the clergy, the army, or to any other condition of men, shall, with a view to causing a tumult and giving occasion to treachery, attempt to discuss the Christian religion publicly in the presence of an assembled and listening crowd; for he commits an injury against the most reverend Synod who publicly contradicts what has once been decided and properly established; as those matters relative to the Christian faith have been settled by the priests who met at Chalcedony by Our order, and are known to be in conformity with the apostolic explanations and conclusions of the three hundred and eight Holy Fathers assembled in Nicea, and the hundred and fifty who met in this Imperial City; for the violators of this law shall not go unpunished, because they not only oppose the true faith, but they also profane its venerated mysteries by engaging in contests of this kind with Jews and Pagans. Therefore, if any person who has ventured to publicly discuss religious matters is a member of the clergy, he shall be removed from his order; if he is a member of the army, he shall be degraded; and any others who are guilty of this offence, who are freemen, shall be banished from this most Sacred City, and shall be subjected to the punishment prescribed by law according to the power of the court; and if they are slaves, they shall undergo severest penalty.

Given at Constantinople, on the eighth of the Ides of February, under the consulship of Patricius.

4. John, Bishop of the City of Rome, to his most Illustrious and Merciful Son Justinian.

Among the conspicuous reasons for praising your wisdom and gentleness, Most Christian of Emperors, and one which radiates light [pg. 11]as a star, is the fact that through love of the Faith, and actuated by zeal for charity, you, learned in ecclesiastical discipline, have preserved reverence for the See of Rome, and have subjected all things to its authority, and have given it unity. The following precept was communicated to its founder, that is to say, the first of the Apostles, by the mouth of the Lord, namely: "Feed my lambs."

This See is indeed the head of all churches, as the rules of the Fathers and the decrees of the Emperors assert, and the words of your most reverend piety testify. It is therefore claimed that what the Scriptures state, namely, "By Me Kings reign, and the Powers dispense justice;" will be accomplished in you. For there is nothing which shines with a more brilliant lustre than genuine faith when displayed by a prince, since there is nothing which prevents destruction as true religion does, for as both of them have reference to the Author of Life and Light, they disperse darkness and prevent apostasy. Wherefore, Most Glorious of Princes, the Divine Power is implored by the prayers of all to preserve your piety in this ardor for the Faith, in this devotion of your mind, and in this zeal for true religion, without failure, during your entire existence. For we believe that this is for the benefit of the Holy Churches, as it was written, "The king rules with his lips," and again,

"The heart of the King is in the hand of God, and it will incline to whatever side God wishes"; that is to say, that He may confirm your empire, and maintain your kingdoms for the peace of the Church and the unity of religion; guard their authority, and preserve him in that sublime tranquillity which is so grateful to him; and no small change is granted by the Divine Power through whose agency a divided church is not afflicted by any griefs or subject to any reproaches. For it is written, "A just king, who is upon his throne, has no reason to apprehend any misfortune."

We have received with all due respect the evidences of your serenity, through Hypatius and Demetrius, most holy men, my brothers and fellow-bishops, from whose statements we have learned that you have promulgated an Edict addressed to your faithful people, and dictated by your love of the Faith, for the purpose of overthrowing the designs of heretics, which is in accordance with the evangelical tenets, and which we have confirmed by our authority with the consent of our brethren and fellow bishops, for the reason that it is in conformity with the apostolic doctrine.

The following is the text of the letter of the Emperor Justinian, Victorious, Pious, Happy, Renowned, Triumphant always, Augustus to John, Patriarch, and most Holy Archbishop of the fair City of Rome:

With honor to the Apostolic See, and to your Holiness, which is, and always has been remembered in Our prayers, both now and formerly, and honoring your happiness, as is proper in the case of one who is considered as a father, We hasten to bring to the knowledge of Your Holiness everything relating to the condition of the Church, as We have always had the greatest desire to preserve the unity of your Apostolic See, and the condition of the Holy Churches of God, as they [pg. 12] exist at the present time, that they may remain without disturbance or opposition. Therefore, We have exerted Ourselves to unite all the priests of the East and subject them to the See of Your Holiness, and hence the questions which have at present arisen, although they are manifest and free from doubt, and according to the doctrines of your Apostolic See, are constantly firmly observed and preached by all priests, We have still considered it necessary that they should be brought to the attention of Your Holiness. For we do not suffer anything which has reference to the state of the Church, even though what causes difficulty may be clear and free from doubt, to be discussed without being brought to the notice of Your Holiness, because you are the head of all the Holy Churches, for We shall exert Ourselves in every way (as has already been stated), to increase the honor and authority of your See. [pg. 125]

One Hundred and Thirty-First New Constitution.
[Novella 131 was issued in 545 A.D.]

The Emperor Justinian to Peter, Most Glorious Imperial Praetorian Prefect.

PREFACE.

We enact the present law with reference to ecclesiastical rules and privileges and other subjects in which holy churches and religious establishments are intrusted.
Chapter I.

Concerning Four Holy Councils.

Therefore We order that the sacred, ecclesiastical rules which were adopted and confirmed by the four Holy Councils, that is to say, that of the three hundred and eighteen bishops held at Nicea, that of the one hundred and fifty bishops held at Constantinople, the first one of Ephesus, where Nestorius was condemned, and the one assembled at Chalcedon, where Eutyches and Nestorius were anathematized, shall be considered as laws. We accept the dogmas of these four Councils as sacred writings, and observe their rules as legally effective.

Chapter II.

Concerning the Precedence of Partriarchs.

Hence, in accordance with the provisions of these Councils, We order that the Most Holy Pope of ancient Rome shall hold the first rank of all the Pontiffs, but the Most Blessed Archbishop of Constantinople, or New Rome, shall occupy the second place after the Holy Apostolic See of ancient Rome, which shall take precedence over all other sees.

Source: Corpus Juris Civilis (The Civil Law, the Code of Justinian), by S.P. Scott, A.M., published by the Central Trust Company, Cincinnati, copyright 1932, Volume 12 [of 17], pages 9-12, 125.

Appendix 3 - 1929 Mussolini Concordat with the Vatican, "healing the deadly wound" inflicted in 1798 and admitted to in 1870.

Heal Wound Of Many Years

Cardinal Gasparri

Premier Mussolini

Lindy Lands in Belize to Pick Air Line Field

Seven-Hour Flight Brings Colonel to Honduras City on Return Trip

VATICAN AGAIN AT PEACE WITH ITALY AFTER LONG QUARREL

Cardinal Leaves Sick Bed to Participate; Warmly Greets Premier

Chimes of St. John Lateran Peal as Signatories Wield Gold Quill Pen

ROME, Feb. 11 (Æ)—The Roman question tonight was a thing of the past and the Vatican was at peace with Italy. The formal accomplishment of this today was the exchange of signatures in the historic Palace of St. John Lateran by two noteworthy plenipotentiaries. Cardinal Gasparri for Pope Pius XI and Premier Mussolini for King Victor Emmanuel III.

In affixing the autographs to the memorable document, healing the wound which has festered since 1870, extreme cordiality was displayed on both sides. The Cardinal Secretary of State warmly welcomed the Premier to the old papal residence, while Mussolini showed particular attention to the venerable prelate by bidding him sit while the text of the accord was read.

Gasparri Leaves Sick Bed to Sign Document

Cardinal Gasparri left his bed, where he had been confined by grip since Saturday and braved the chilly and sunless weather in order that he might attend the ceremony which was the crowning act of his entire diplomatic career. Premier Mussolini did all he could to soften the rigors of the physical ordeal.

Pope Sees Settlement Between 'Father and Son'

Just as the signatories were wielding the gold quill pen the chimes of St. John Lateran pealed out as if for Christmas midnight and a throng of theological students grouped in the courtyard below broke into the strains of a te deum. "We thank thee, oh God, make safe thy people, oh Lord! and bless thy heirs and rule over them and extol them forever."

To this the Fascist blackshirt militia, personal bodyguard of the Premier, responding with a rousing "Eja, Eja, Alala!" for the Pope, the Premier and the King.

The Pope today in speaking to (Continued on Page 2, Col. 4)

Historic Scene in the Lateran Palace

By Rev. JOHN J. CONSIDINE.

There could be no more fitting scene for the great event, for it was from this Palace that Pope after Pope sent forth missionaries to carry the message of the Gospel to the uttermost ends of the earth. And the peace that has been made between the Holy See and Italy is not a peace for Italy, nor for any one nation or continent. It is meant for all the nations of the world, and it has been made by a Pope whose great desire is to unite all the nations under one banner—the banner of Christ the King.

THE TABLE OF THE SIGNATURES.

WAS IN MISSIONARY EXHIBITION.

It is noon on Monday, the fateful February 11, and we are standing by the obelisk at the north door of the Mother of the

GRAPHIC WORD PICTURE OF GREAT EVENT.

SIGNIFICANCE OF THE POPE'S SELECTION.

The following article, which depicts the scene at the signing of the pact between the Holy See and Italy points the significance of the fact that, whereas the Holy Father might have chosen the Vatican as the place for the signing of the Concordat whereby his Kingship has at last been acknowledged by Italy, he selected for the history-making ceremony the Lateran Palace of the Missions.

Their meeting was to have been a secret guarded for the inner circle, but the story, like so many of its kind, leaked, and a crowd, tense with excitement, is here to witness the passage of these two men whose pens will heal a wound of 59 years. I do not deny it—I am in a tremble at

few were reconnoitring, since the Museum doorkeeper said there had been but 129 visitors up to 5 o'clock. However, there in the Hall was Mr. Curtnoll, of the Associated Press, getting "color." He was nothing short of enthusiastic over the fact that he had discovered that the table upon which

ings, gifts of the Syro-Malabar Catholics. From the Upper Nile, in the heart of Africa, is more ivory, this time a carved elephant mounted with silver, a gift from Bishop Biermans, of the Mill Hill Missioners, London.

From Choco, in Colombia, South America, is a collection of ornaments in precious metals, once possessions of the Indians, and a large emblem moulded from pre-Colombian gold found near Bogota. From Alaska, then, in North America, is a chaplet of rosary beads carved from bone by the natives, and sent to the Pope by Jesuit missioners through General Nobile after his first visit to the Pope.

Europe is represented by a silver model of Castle Xavier, home of the apostle without peer, St. Francis Xavier of Navarre, a glory of Spain.

UNDER ONE BANNER.

Premier Mussolini sits with Cardinal Gasparri in these surroundings to-day, and takes the first step in swearing the good

THE LATERAN PALACE.

Churches of the world, St. John's. We have watched first Cardinal Gasparri and then Premier Mussolini drive into the Lateran Palace, and they are now sealing the accord between the Holy See and Italy.

the pregnant greatness of the moment, for my mind is dwelling not only in the piazza, or on the scene behind the Palace windows. My thoughts are shooting like the shuttle of a loom out from Rome to the four corners of the globe, weaving a fabric of the reverberations which this freeing of the Pope will awaken in every country where a Catholic heart throbs.

A MISSIONARY ATMOSPHERE.

There are newspaper men near me. A Frenchman is saying to himself: "This will make a good story to-night in Paris"; an Englishman; "This gets the first column in London this evening." A German visions Berlin and Munich; an American, sure, he sees his "stuff" in headlines from New York to San Francisco.

But I stop at no country in particular; it is the world-wide significance behind the event which is counting with me. More, it is the world-wide significance which Pope Pius XI. has made the conscious effort to put behind the event which grips me. Because, whether my companions the pressmen are going to take note of the fact or not, Pope Pius XI. has gone out of his way to give the signing of the accord between the Holy See and Italy a missionary atmosphere.

There were really no grave reasons why the document could not have been signed at the Vatican. Instead, the Holy Father decided that historic Hall of the Popes at the Lateran Mission Museum should once again see history, that the background of the signing of peace with the country in which the supernatural centre of the Church is found should be an institution organised to make clear that Catholicity is above all flags, all nations, labours for every people on earth.

THE HALL OF THE POPES.

Yesterday afternoon (Sunday) I anticipated the meeting of to-day by a visit to this Hall of the Popes, now the Hall of Conferences, of the Museum. Relatively

the signing was to take place was from the Philippine Islands.

A visitor to the Vatican Mission Exposition in 1925 would have noticed that the massive structure, made of a single piece of wood over six yards long and two yards wide, was the same that stood in the Hall of Oceania at the Exposition, a gift of Jesuit missionaries to the Pope. About this table this same Church and State are listening to a final reading of the accord and then the signatures.

The hall in which the table stands is spacious and richly decorated. The Lateran Palace, recall, was the home of the Popes for a thousand years, from 314 to 1305, and from it were sent out the messengers who brought the Faith to many of countries of Europe. It still retains in good condition its ornately-decorated walls.

FROM EVERY LAND ON EARTH.

The floor, paved in marble, is uncumbered with furniture, except for this now historic table and another large one at the opposite end of the hall, also constructed of a single cross-section of a tropic giant of the Philippine forests. At either end of the hall is a bust of a Pope—one of Sixtus V., builder of the Palace; the other, near the table of signatures, representing Pius XI., founder, in 1926, of the Lateran Mission Museum, to which 24 halls of the Palace are now dedicated.

About the walls, then, in finely-constructed glass cases are symbols of the Catholic Church on the five Continents, gifts to the Holy Father from Europe, Asia, Africa, North America, South America—not many, but a selection of the choicest among the thousands which fill the Museum.

WHERE EAST AND WEST MEET.

From China is a collection of ancient coins, one of the most complete in the world, numbering 6688 pieces in all, the oldest of which date from 1122 B.C. From India are ivory tusks, with lace-like carv-

will of Italy toward the Prince of Good Will, the leader of the Catholic millions of those five Continents.

The newsmen here in the Piazza will not mention it to the Parisians, Londoners, or New Yorkers, but this peace is not made alone for Italy, for Europe, for America. It is made by a Pope passionately devoted to uniting all men the earth over under one banner; a Pope from whom Asia, Africa, Oceania receive every whit the same concern as the Western world.

As I wait here I can see the Catholics of Peking, of Tokyo, of the Fiji Islands, of the East Indies, of Madras, of Uganda, of the banks of the Congo, of the White Man's Grave on the far African West Coast rejoicing that this peace has been signed in the Lateran, now their Palace, in Rome.

MUSSOLINI AND GASPARRI RATIFY LATERAN TREATY

LONG CHURCH-STATE STRIFE IN ITALY ENDED; POPE RELEASED FROM VOLUNTARY IMPRISONMENT.

Vatican City, June 7—(Æ)—All Rome resounded to the pealing of joyous church bells today as Premier Mussolini and Cardinal Gasparri solemnly exchanged ratifications of the historic lateran treaty bringing to an end the long strife between church and state in Italy.

Brief Ceremony

There were no speeches and the ceremony was brief and simple. One of its most striking and sympolical moments was when the great bronze doors opening out upon the colonnade of St. Peter's square which had remained half shut for 59 years were once more opened wide.

Premier Mussolini entered the vatican—for the first time in his life—shortly before eleven o'clock. He was dressed in his uniform as a minister instead of the usual cutaway which he wore when he signed the treaty on Feb. 11. The crowd gave him a hearty handclapping interspersed with cheers and then rushed across St. Peter's square to see the opening of the bronze doors which was to symbolize the coming to an end of the voluntary imprisonment of the pontiff.

Blesses King, Il Duce

At the conclusion of the signing Cardinal Gasparri, papal secretary of state, read a letter from the pope in which he said that his first act would be to send a telegram of benediction to King Victor Emmanuel blessing him and his consort and all the members of the royal family and bestowing a special benediction upon "Chevalier Mussolini."

The premier spent three-quarters of an hour within the vatican. He was accompanied by members of his cabinet.

State Sincere Wish

Premier Mussolini and Cardinal Gasparri composed a "proces verbal" in which they stated their "reciprocally loyal and sincere wish to observe the letter and spirit of the lateran accords."

The proces recognize: the pope's sovereignity and the status of Catholicism as the state religion in Italy.

Cardinal Gasparri signed this and then Premier Mussolini, after which they talked together for fifteen minutes.

$93,000,000 Check

Finance Minister Mosconi then gave the Cardinal a check on the bank of Italy for 750,000,000 lire (about $93,000,000) representing the first payment of the financial convention arranged at the time that the treaty was drawn.

Cardinal Gasparri and Benito Mussolini (seated) after exchanging treaty ratifications in the Hall of Congregations, the Vatican, June 7th, 1929.

Appendix 4 – The first attempt by US legislators to enact a National Sunday Law

"THOSE WHO OPPOSE ... MUST ABIDE THE CONSEQUENCES"

Church leaders demanded that the Government use Federal troops to keep Chicago's Columbian Exposition closed on Sundays.

Delegates to the 1887 National Reform Association Convention stood tall and determined. Aroused by the oratory of their spokesman, David McAllister, they agreed with him that "those who oppose this work now will discover, when the religious amendment is made to the Constitution, that if they do not see fit to fall in with the majority, they must abide the consequences, or seek some more congenial clime."1

Just a century before, Ben Franklin had commented: "When a Religion is good, I conceive that it will support itself; and, when it cannot support itself, and God does not take care to support, so that its Professors are oblig'd to call for the help of the Civil Power, it is a sign, I apprehend, of its being a bad one."2

But a lot could happen in 100 years. Men can forget. Early In 1863, when the Civil War and the crisis of national survival were the overpowering issues of the day, representatives of eleven Protestant denominations met in Xenia, Ohio, to create a national Christian theocracy. The National Reform Association made no effort to conceal its avowed intent to destroy Jefferson's wall of separation between church and state.

[70] The association's constitution warned of "subtle and persevering attempts . . . to overthrow our Sabbath laws" and pledged itself "to promote needed reforms in the action of the government touching the Sabbath" and "to secure such an amendment to the Constitution of the United States as will declare the nation's allegiance to Jesus Christ and its acceptance of the moral laws of the Christian religion, and so indicate that this is a Christian nation, and place all the Christian laws, institutions, and usages of our government on an undeniably legal basis in the fundamental laws of the land."3

But Lincoln and his Congress appeared to be more concerned with finding a means to penetrate the Confederate defense in Virginia. Pressure from the "reformers" continued, however, and a Reconstruction Congress finally formulated a response to the petitions. The House Committee on the Judiciary reported it "Inexpedient to legislate upon the subject," since the fathers of the republic had considered the matter and laid the foundation of a government which "was to be the home of the oppressed of all nations of the earth, whether Christian or pagan."

The committee pointed out that the founders of our nation had reasoned "with great unanimity that it was inexpedient to put anything into the Constitution or frame of government which might be construed to be a reference to any religious creed or doctrine."4

When, in 1892, Congress heard demands to attach a Sunday closing rider to the bill appropriating funds to the Columbian Exposition, New York Senator Hiscock counseled, "If I had charge of this amendment in the interest of the Columbian Exposition, I would write the provision for the closure in any form that the religious sentiment of the country demands."5

Connecticut Senator Hawley dared his associates to put in writing a denial that the United States was a Christian nation. "Word it, if you dare; advocate it, if you dare. How many who voted for it would ever come back here again? None, I hope."6

A Chicago newspaper reported the reaction of a House committee member on the World's Fair to the clamor for the Sunday-closing rider. [71] He allegedly admitted, "The reason we shall vote for it is, I will confess to you, a fear that, unless we do so, the church folks will get together and knife us at the polls next; and – well, you know we all want to come back, and we can't afford to take any risks."7

New Hampshire's Senator Blair sponsored a "Lord's Day" measure "To Promote Its Observance as a Day of Religious Worship," a measure vigorously promoted by the National Reform Association, the Women's Christian Temperance Union, the American Sabbath Union, and other organizations.

In addition to proposing a ban on "secular work, labor, or business" the bill sought to restrain interstate commerce, transportation of the mails, military musters and drills, as well as " transportation . . . by land or water in such way as to interfere with or disturb the people in the enjoyment of the first day of the week. . . . or its observance as a day of religious worship."8 It also condemned "any play, game, or amusement, or recreation" that could disturb others.

The hearings on the proposal before the Senate Committee on Education and Labor produced a long line of clergy testimonials urging passage. On the afternoon of December 13, 1888, a spirited exchange between Senator Blair and Alonzo T. Jones took place. Jones, a professor of history at the Seventh-day Adventist Battle Creek College in Michigan, took the offensive against the bill:

It is the religious observance of the day that its promoters, from one end of the land to the other, have in view. In the convention, now in session in this city, working in behalf of this bill, only yesterday Dr. Crafts said: "Taking religion out of the day takes the rest out."

In the "Boston Monday Lectures," 1887, Joseph Cook, lecturing on the subject of Sunday laws, said: "The experience of centuries shows, however, that you will in vain endeavor to preserve Sunday as a day of rest, unless you preserve it as a day of worship. [72] Unless Sabbath observance be founded upon religious reasons, you will not long maintain it at a high standard on the basis of economic and physiological and political considerations only."

And in the Illinois State Sunday convention held in Elgin, November 8, 1887, Dr. W. W. Everts declared Sunday to be "the test of all religion."9

The Elgin convention had pronounced:

That we look with shame and sorrow on the non-observance of the Sabbath by many Christian people, in that custom prevails with them purchasing Sabbath newspapers, engaging in and patronizing Sabbath business and travel, and in many instances giving themselves to pleasure and self-indulgence, setting aside by neglect and indifference the great duties and privileges which God's day brings them.

Resolved, that we give our votes and support to those candidates or political officers who will pledge themselves to vote for the enactment and enforcing of statutes in favor of the civil Sabbath.10

The Blair bill died in committee. Later, the Senator stripped the bill of the more obvious religious implications and on December 9, 1889, introduced another Federal Sunday-closing measure. Again it failed to gain adequate support and expired.

Sunday-law proponents learned from these skirmishes. They learned that the stronger the religious rationale advanced for creating the establishment, the stronger were

545

the constitutional arguments available to opponents. Consequently the reformers made an effort to cultivate the support of labor on the basis that a Federal blue law would serve a public-welfare purpose and promote the interests of the laboring man.

The industrial revolution, they argued, had worked hardships on the dignity and economic independence of the individual. Exorbitant profits were reaped at the expense of inadequate working conditions and wages. The working man deserved better. Sunday-law proponents sought to exploit this need by linking their cause to public welfare and the individual.

[73] When W. C. P. Breckinridge of Kentucky offered a "Bill to Prevent Persons from Being Forced to Labor on Sunday," it was channelled to a subcommittee of the House Committee on the District of Columbia for study. Sharp contrasts of opinion were aired in open hearings on February 18, 1890. The cast of characters mirrored the earlier hearings on the Blair bill. Ministerial proponents W. F. Crafts, J. H. Elliott, and George Elliott were joined by representatives of the W.C.T.U. Alonzo T. Jones, J. O. Corliss, and W. H. McKee, representing the Seventh-day Adventist Church, and a representative of the District Knights of Labor opposed the bill.

"No one is being forced to labor on Sunday in the District of Columbia," Jones reported. "Sunday legislation is, in reality, not in behalf of the laboring man at all. It is only a pretense to cover the real purpose – to enforce by law the religious observance of the day."11

In view of efforts to enlist labor support for the Sunday-law movement, the testimony of Millard F. Hobbs, chief officer of the District Knights of Labor, was significant. Although

546

he acknowledged the diversity of opinion relative to the Breckinridge bill within his organization, he stated that "the Knights of Labor, as a whole, have refused to have anything to do with it." Every Knight, he said, was in favor of a day of rest, some of two days, but because of the "religious side of the question," they opposed the bill. "What benefits the Knights of Labor wish to obtain, we think, can be better secured by our own efforts through our own organization than by the efforts of others, through the church."12

The subcommittee listened, and the bill was never brought to a vote. But Congress was not to escape easily the pressure for Federal action for enforced Sunday closing. When a rider was attached to the bill appropriating funds to the 1893 Columbian Exposition in Chicago, a flurry of Congressional debate ensued. In order to obtain Federal funds, the bill stipulated, the fair had to close each Sunday.

[74] The American Sabbath Union maintained that this measure will honor God and preserve the faith of the nation. . . . The nation's faith in God and His laws will be put to the test by the action of its Congress on this subject." The Wisconsin Sunday Rest Association urged that Sunday opening "would tend to break down the Christianity of our country." In October, 1891, a convention of Massachusetts Protestants went on record favoring the Sunday closing of the fair out of "respect to the religious convictions of the millions of Christian people in this great nation who believe that the Sabbath is one of the chief bulwarks of Christianity." 13

Congressmen felt severe pressure to support the rider. Comments in the Congressional Record as well as off-the-cuff remarks revealed concern for voter reaction. Remarked Senator Hawley, "Everybody knows what the foundation

547

is. It is founded in religious belief."14 Senator Peffer observed, "We are engaged in a theological discussion concerning the observance of the first day of the week."15

After days of spirited debate and revision, Sunday-closing advocates scored a victory as President Harrison, on August 5, 1892, signed the measure into law.

Citizens who earlier had not bothered to join in a petition protesting "against the Congress of the United States committing the United States Government to a union of religion and state, in the passage of any bill or resolution to close the World's Columbian Exposition on Sunday," suddenly reacted. Moves to open the fair on Sunday were initiated in Chicago, backed by the city council, the mayor, the press, and the management of the fair. Ironically, they gave religious reasons in support of Sunday opening. The Tribune talked loftily of religious services at the fair which would make "Sunday at the World's Fair . . . one of the grandest recognitions of the Sabbath known to modern history."16

[75] Religious leaders threatened boycott if the fair opened on Sunday. One excited group telegraphed the President, urging him to "suppress Chicago nullification with Jacksonian firmness and to guard the gates next Sabbath with troops if necessary."17 Another church organization demanded, in a wire to the attorney general, to know why Federal troops could not be "used, if necessary, to maintain inviolate the national authority, and keep the fair closed on the Lord's day."18

A Western newspaper editor found it contradictory to "appeal to the President to enforce closing, if need be, by military force" in order to show the world "'that we are a Christian nation."19

Sentiment for Sunday opening was given another opportunity for Congressional exposure following the introduction of a joint resolution in December, 1892, which would have left "the matter of Sunday observance entirely within the power of the regularly constituted authorities of the World's Columbian Exposition."

Samuel Gompers was the voice of the American Federation of Labor at Congressional hearings that followed. He deplored the Sunday closing of the Philadelphia Centennial Exhibition in 1876, which prevented him and thousands of others from attending: "I deny the right of any man or number of men to speak in the name of the wage earners of America, and to say that they favor the closing of the World's Fair on Sunday."20

Another labor representative blamed the Protestant evangelical churches for the Sunday closing and accused them of assuming to be guardians of the economic and moral affairs of the working people. He branded this conduct as willfully and ignorantly fraudulent and repudiated the right "of these churches or their representatives to speak or act for us in this matter."21

Susan B. Anthony spoke for an open fair. She recalled when Sunday streetcars were banned in Philadelphia, the struggle to open the Philadelphia Art Gallery and New York's Central Park on Sunday, and the "big, long fight before there was any music allowed in the park on Sunday." [76] She classed the Sunday closing of the fair as a "tyranny that should not be practiced by the Congress of the United States."22

Predicting that the resolution would die a natural death, the Chicago Herald of January 13, 1893, disclosed that the publicity given the issue "brought down upon Congress an avalanche of protests and appeals, from religious people and church organizations all over the country." The newspaper observed that organized opposition from churches and their ministers made some committee members timid to express their convictions by vote, since those demanding Sunday closing could lose their tempers, and at the next election, make trouble for those who vote against them."

Senator Quay of Pennsylvania had, the previous July, laid before the Senate suggested wording for "the closing of the exposition on the Sabbath day." "Congress will not reverse its action," because if it did, he reasoned, "it could have no other meaning than that the United States, the greatest and most prosperous nation on this earth, had declared officially through its chosen representatives in favor of desecrating the Sabbath and thus breaking one of the commandments."23 Two weeks later, after the hearings, Quay insisted the Senate would kill the reversal even if it got through the House. "The people of Chicago may as well give up this fight. They can't win it."24

Quay was right. Congress did not reverse itself. However, through a series of intricate legal manoeuvres the fair found a way to open its gates in a limited way on Sunday, and then repented almost immediately when Sunday attendance declined. Still, Congress had capitulated to religious pressure in 1892 and had given its authority to religious establishment. Although Senator Quay's "Sabbath day" nomenclature was amended out in the final form of the measure, the original intent and spirit could not be masked.

[77] While Congress had acted to close the gates of a world's fair on Sunday, it had simultaneously opened doors to a flood of demands for future sessions of the Federal

legislature to give legal recognition to religious practices. During the next half century Congress considered almost a hundred measures designed to honor Sunday.

Thanks to the clerical lobbyists of the American Sabbath Union, the $5,000,000 appropriation to the Louisiana Purchase Exposition (Saint Louis, 1904) carried the condition that fair directors "close the gates to visitors on Sunday."25 In 1906, the American Sabbath Union chalked up "another grand victory for the Sabbath cause" by persuading Congress to condition its appropriation to the 1907 Jamestown Exposition on the assurance that "the grounds of the exposition shall be closed on Sundays."26

When Alabama Congressman Heflin sent to the Sixtieth Congress in 1907 a bill to prohibit certain types of work in the District of Columbia "on the Sabbath day," a host of religiously oriented proposals followed in its wake. The flurry of pressure was so intense that the General Conference of Seventh-day Adventists through its president, A. G. Daniells, and its secretary, W. A. Spicer, sent "A Memorial to Congress" on January 29, 1908, reminding the legislators of the "wise builders of state" who had created a separation of church and state, and urging them "not to enact any religious legislation of any kind."27

In 1912, the Federal Government did agree to eliminate Sunday delivery of all but special-delivery mail in "post offices of the first and second classes"; but it has yet to capitulate to demands for a national Sunday law.

REFERENCES

1. Dr. David McAllister, in National Reform Convention at Lakeside,

Ohio, August, 1887. In American State Papers, Third Revised Edition
(Washington, D.C.: Review and Herald Publishing Association, 1943), page 234.

2. Benjamin Franklin, Letter to Dr. Price, October 9, 1780, Writings of
Benjamin Franklin, Albert Henry Smyth, ed. (New York: The Macmillan Company, 1906), Vol. 8, p. 154.

3. "Constitution of the National Reform Association." In American State Papers, pages 235, 236.

4. House Reports, Vol. 1, 43d Congress, Ist Session, Report No. 143. In American State Papers, page 237.

5. Congressional Record, July 13, 1892, page 6755. In American State Papers, page 280.

6. Congressional Record, July 13, 1892, page 6759.

7. Chicago Daily Post, April 9, 1892. In American State Papers, page 280.

8. Senate Bill No. 2983 (1888). In Ibid., pp. 243, 244.

9. Alonzo T. Jones, "The National Sunday Law," American Sentinel, 1892.

10. Ibid., p. 117.

11. "Arguments on the Breckinridge Sunday Bill," The Sentinel Library, No. 29, pages 28-30.

12. American Sentinel, February 27, 1890. In American State Papers, pages 276,277.

13. "Arguments on the Breckinridge Sunday Bill," Op. cit., pp. 23-24.

14. Congressional Record, July 12, 1892. In American State Papers, page 279.

15. Ibid.

16. Chicago Tribune, December 3, 1892.

17. Chicago Herald, May 19, 1893. In American State Papers, page 280.

18. Ibid. (May 16).

19. Webster City Graphic-Herald, quoted in the Des Moines Leader, June 1, 1893. In American State Papers, page 281.

20. Alonzo T. Jones, Sunday Closing of the World's Fair (International Religious Liberty Association, 1893), pages 118, 119.

21. Ibid., p. 31.

22. Ibid., p. 122.

23. Pittsburgh Leader, January 2, 1893.

24. Chicago Herald, January 19, 1893.

25. American State Papers, page 246.

26. Ibid, p. 282.

27. Congressional Record, January 29, 1908, Vol. 12, part 2, pp. 1264, 1265.

Dateline Sunday, Chapter 7.

Appendix 5 – Sunday Law hidden in Laudato Si

I will only highlight clause 237 where Sunday is hidden. Take note how far down the encyclical it is located. Why is this? Many arguments need to presented before the real reason for the encyclical can be made known. Don't be fooled by its language about the Sabbath etc, we have already established the truth in this regard where the papacy is concerned and there is no such thing as "the Jewish Sabbath" if the reference is to the 7th Day Sabbath then it is our eternal Father's Sabbath, it was never given only to the Jews, it was given to mankind before the Jews existed. The Jews were chosen to bring it back to all the nations.

ENCYCLICAL LETTER
LAUDATO SI'
OF THE HOLY FATHER
FRANCIS
ON CARE FOR OUR COMMON HOME

"237. On Sunday, our participation in the Eucharist has special importance. Sunday, like the Jewish Sabbath, is meant to be a day which heals our relationships with God, with ourselves, with others and with the world. Sunday is the day of the Resurrection, the "first day" of the new creation, whose first fruits are the Lord's risen humanity, the pledge of the final transfiguration of all created reality. It also proclaims "man's eternal rest in God".[168] In this way, Christian spirituality incorporates the value of relaxation and festivity. We tend to demean contemplative rest as something unproductive and unnecessary, but this is to do away with the very thing which is most important about work: its meaning. We are called to include in our work a dimension of receptivity and gratuity, which is quite different from mere inactivity. Rather, it is another way of working, which forms part of our very essence. It protects human action from becoming empty activism; it also prevents that unfettered greed and sense of isolation which make us seek personal gain to the detriment of all else. The law of weekly rest forbade work on the seventh day, "so that your ox and your donkey may have rest, and the son of your maidservant, and the stranger, may be refreshed" (Ex 23:12). Rest opens our eyes to the larger picture and gives us renewed sensitivity to the rights of others. And so the day of rest, centred on the Eucharist, sheds it light on the whole week, and motivates us to greater concern for nature and the poor."

Appendix 6 – State within a state

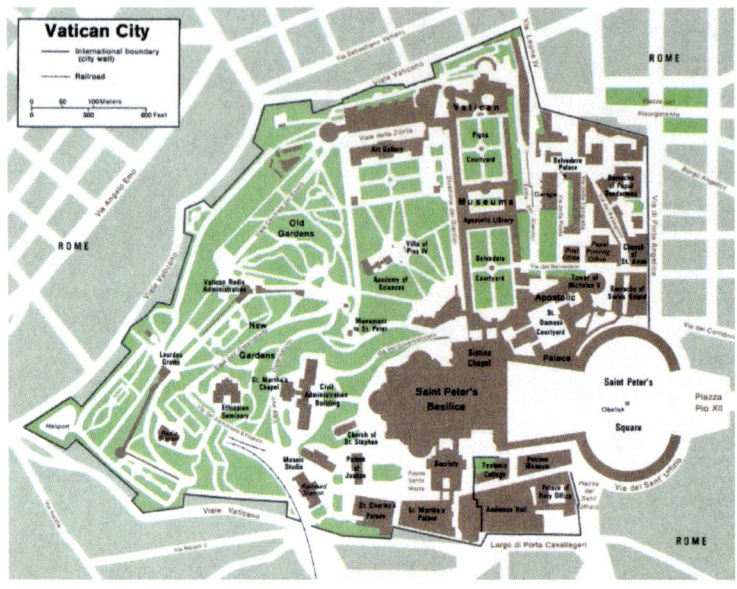

Appendix 7 – Evidence of the first global climate change event.

We are not conducting an extensive study of climate change in this appendix. There is ample information available elsewhere for the reader's research, I am seeking to whet your appetite to read and study more. There are books like "The Genesis flood" by Henry M Morris and John C Whitcomb, that explores the archealogical evidence of the catastrophic global flood that wiped humanity *(except Noah's 8)* and billions of creatures off the face of the earth and drastically altered the original eco-system that was perfectly designed for all forms of life and subsequently the original climate to what we have today.

There are other evidences such as tropical plant and tropical coral remains in both of the poles, of animals found in permafrost with vegetation in their mouths. Those creatures would have been frozen instantly. Recently dinosaurs have been unearthed with viable blood cells, how could it be that they were millions of years old as described by evolutionists.

We will quote a small amount of information from the following website, https://creation.com/startling-evidence-for-noahs-flood

Startling evidence for Noah's Flood

Footprints and sand 'dunes' in a Grand Canyon sandstone!
by Andrew A. Snelling and Steven A. Austin

"There is no sight on earth which matches Grand Canyon. There are other canyons, other mountains and other rivers, but this Canyon excels all in scenic grandeur. Can any visitor, upon viewing Grand Canyon, grasp and appreciate the spectacle spread before him? The ornate sculpture work and the wealth of color are like no other landscape. They suggest an alien world. The scale is too outrageous. The sheer size and majesty engulf the intruder, surpassing his ability to take it in."1

Anyone who has stood on the rim and looked down into Grand Canyon would readily echo these words as one's breath is taken away with the sheer magnitude of the spectacle. The Canyon stretches for 446 km (277 miles) through northern Arizona, attains a depth of more than 1.6 km (1 mile), and ranges from 6.4 km (4 miles) to 29 km (18 miles) in width. In the walls of the Canyon can be seen flat-lying rock layers that were once sand, mud or lime. Now hardened, they look like pages of a giant book as they stretch uniformly right through the Canyon and underneath the plateau country to the north and south and deeper to the east.

Figure 1. A panoramic view of the Grand Canyon from the South Rim at Yavapai Point. The Coconino Sandstone is

the thick buff-coloured layer close to the top of the canyon walls. Compare with Figure 2

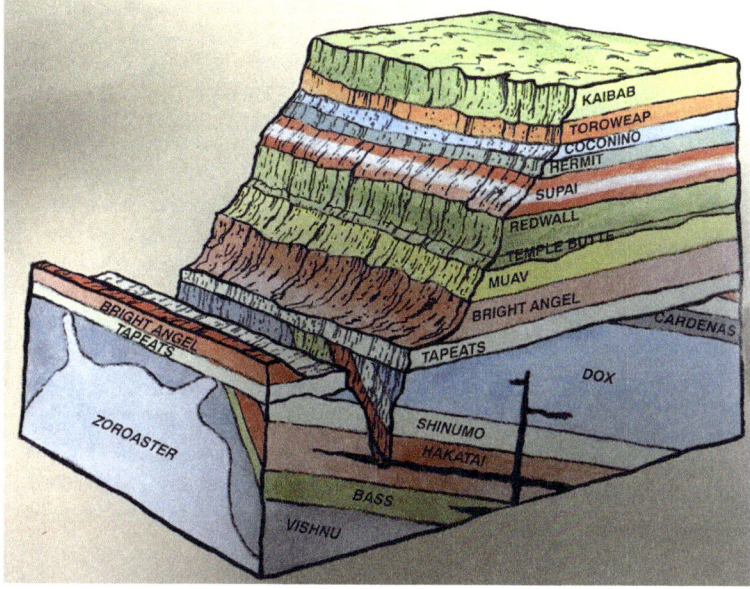

Figure 2. Grand Canyon in cross-section showing the names given to the different rock units by geologists.

The Coconino Sandstone

To begin to comprehend the awesome scale of these rock layers, we can choose any one for detailed examination. Perhaps the easiest of these rock layers to spot, since it readily catches the eye, is a thick, pale buff coloured to almost white sandstone near the top of the Canyon walls. Geologists have given the different rock layers names, and this one is called the Coconino Sandstone (see Figures 1 and 2). It is estimated to have an average thickness of 96 m (315 ft) and, with equivalent sandstones to the east, covers an area of about 519,000 sq km (200,000 sq miles).2 That is an area more than twice the size of the Australian State of Victoria, or almost twice the area of the US State of

Colorado! Thus the volume of this sandstone is conservatively estimated at 41,700 cu km (10,000 cu miles). That's a lot of sand!

What do these rock layers in Grand Canyon mean? What do they tell us about the earth's past? For example, how did all the sand in this Coconino Sandstone layer and its equivalents get to where it is today?

Figure 3. Cross beds (inclined sub-layering) within the Coconino Sandstone, as seen on the Bright Angel Trail in the Grand Canyon.

To answer these questions geologists study the features within rock layers like the Coconino Sandstone, and even the sand grains themselves. An easily noticed feature of the Coconino Sandstone is the distinct cross layers of sand within it called cross beds (see Figure 3).

For many years evolutionary geologists have interpreted these cross beds by comparing them with currently forming sand deposits — the sand dunes in deserts which are dominated by sand grains made up of the mineral quartz, and which have inclined internal sand beds. Thus it has been proposed that the Coconino Sandstone accumulated over thousands and thousands of years in an immense windy desert by migrating sand dunes, the cross beds forming on the down-wind sides of the dunes as sand was deposited there.

The Coconino Sandstone is also noted for the large number of fossilized footprints, usually in sequences called trackways. These appear to have been made by four-footed vertebrates moving across the original sand surfaces..."

Numerous scientists that held to evolution have had to reject it and accept intelligent design when they have conducted honest evaluations of the archaeologic records. It's your turn to continue your evaluations.

Appendix 8 – Key Issues with ONS Vaccination Mortality Report

For the full article from research gate, copy and paste the following into your browser.

https://www.researchgate.net/publication/356756711_Latest_statistics_on_England_mortality_data_suggest_systematic_mis-categorisation_of_vaccine_status_and_uncertain_effectiveness_of_Covid-19_vaccination

I have only included the introduction here:

"Latest statistics on England mortality data suggest systematic mis-categorisation of vaccine status and uncertain effectiveness of Covid-19 vaccination

Martin Neil1, Norman Fenton1 Joel Smalley2, Clare Craig2, Joshua Guetzkow3, Scott McLachlan1, Jonathan Engler2 and Jessica Rose4

3 December 2021

1 School of Electronic and Electrical Engineering and Computer Science, Queen Mary, University of London, UK
2 Independent researcher, UK
3 Hebrew University Jerusalem, Israel
4 Institute of Pure and Applied Knowledge, Public Health Policy Initiative, USA

Abstract

The risk/benefit of Covid vaccines is arguably most accurately measured by an all-cause mortality rate comparison of vaccinated against unvaccinated, since it not only avoids most confounders relating to case definition but also fulfils the WHO/CDC definition of "vaccine effectiveness" for mortality. We examine the latest UK ONS vaccine mortality surveillance report which provides the necessary information to monitor this crucial comparison over time. At first glance the ONS data suggest that, in each of the older age groups, all-cause mortality is lower in the vaccinated than the unvaccinated. Despite this apparent evidence to support vaccine effectiveness - at least for the older age groups - on closer inspection of this data, this conclusion is cast into doubt because of a range of fundamental inconsistencies and anomalies in the data. Whatever the explanations for the observed data, it is clear that it is both unreliable and misleading. While socio-demographical and behavioural differences between vaccinated and unvaccinated have been proposed as possible explanations, there is no evidence to support any of these. By Occam's razor we believe the most likely explanations are systemic miscategorisation of deaths between the different categories of unvaccinated and vaccinated; delayed or non-reporting of vaccinations; systemic underestimation of the proportion of unvaccinated; and/or incorrect population selection for Covid deaths.

1. Introduction

Our recent articles [1, 2] have argued that the simplest and most objective way to assess the overall risk/benefit of Covid-19 vaccines is to compare all-cause mortality rates of the unvaccinated against the vaccinated in each separate age-group. For such an assessment we need accurate periodic data on both age-categorized deaths and the number of vaccinated/unvaccinated people in each age group for that period.

Any systemic errors or biases can lead to conclusions that are inversions of the real situation. For example, simply reporting deaths one week late when a vaccine programme is rolled out will (with statistical certainty) lead to any vaccine, even a placebo, seemingly reducing mortality. The same statistical illusion will happen if any death of a person occurring in the same week as the person is vaccinated is treated as an unvaccinated, rather than vaccinated, death [16].

The UK Government (through its various relevant agencies) has been better than most countries in providing detailed data on Covid cases and deaths indexed by vaccine status. However, in [1] we highlighted the absence of relevant age-categorized mortality data for England, and major inconsistencies in the data provided by different agencies. Of most concern are the very different estimates provided by UKHSA (United Kingdom Health Security Agency) and the ONS (Office for National Statistics) of the number of vaccinated and unvaccinated people. The reports from UKHSA use estimates from the NIMS (National Immunisation Management Service) database [10], while the estimates from the ONS are based on 2011 census respondents and patients registered with a GP in 2019. Hence the ONS England 'population' (which therefore includes only people aged at least 10) is only approximately 39 million, compared to the approximately 49 million listed in NIMS. While our focus is on mortality by vaccination status, accurate periodic estimates for the proportion of people vaccinated are also crucial for determining vaccine effectiveness, since this is simply a comparison between the 'cases', hospitalisations and deaths per 100K vaccinated and unvaccinated.

An indication of just how critical this is illustrated by the latest UKHSA report [3] which showed that, in each age group above 29, the Covid case rate was higher among the vaccinated than the unvaccinated.

Figure 1: Covid-19 case rates based on UKHSA data in [3] and reproduced from [5]

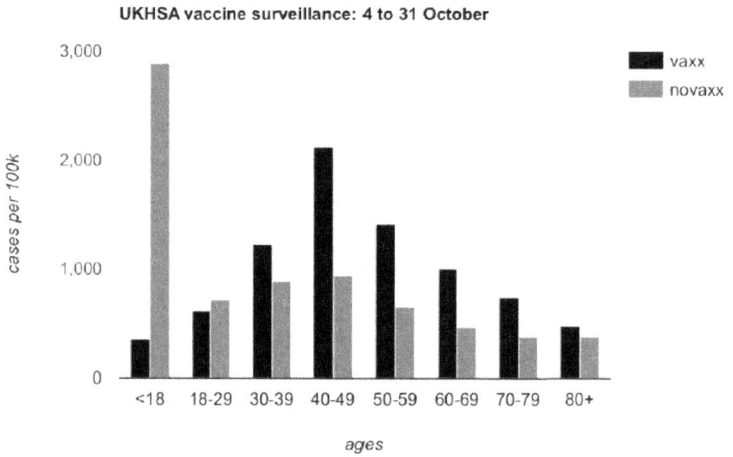

Figure 1: Covid-19 case rates based on UKHSA data in [3] and reproduced from [5]

The UKHSA report caused a flurry of indignation, and prominent scientists, such as Professor Sir David Spiegelhalter, claimed that the data was 'feeding conspiracy theorists worldwide' [4] and subsequently led to the UK statistics regulator stepping in and chastising the UKHSA for using inappropriate population denominators [5]. An article describing the fallout from this can be found in [6].

The justification for these criticisms (which were aimed at both UKHSA and any others simply reporting the UKHSA data) was that NIMS were double counting some vaccinated people, and hence the NIMS population estimates for the number of people vaccinated were therefore too high. They claimed that the ONS data 'fixed' this bias and hence properly adjusted the results. However, as we pointed out in [1], while the NIMS data may indeed overestimate the number of vaccinated, it is likely that it also underestimates the number of unvaccinated (a much more difficult number to estimate than those vaccinated).

One key question at that time was: how accurate is the estimate of the proportion of the population that is unvaccinated? In [1] we argued that the ONS data was underestimating the proportion unvaccinated; hence, ONS reported mortality rates (and by implication also effectiveness rates) were too high for the unvaccinated and too low for the vaccinated. Since then, the latest ONS Vaccine Effectiveness Surveillance Report for England has been released, on the 1st of November, and provides us with further evidence [7].

In what follows we attempt to analyse this latest 'age stratified' ONS report and other relevant sources of data on mortality to examine patterns of mortality and any connection this might have with vaccination.

In section 2 we examine the all-cause mortality rates in this ONS data. Section 3 then compares vaccinated and unvaccinated non-covid mortality. Section 4 looks at the correlation between the vaccine roll out and non-covid mortality, discussing curious oddities in the data that may be explainable by mis-categorisation of vaccine status at death. In section 5 we look to explain this and correct for this mis-categorisation. Section 6 focuses on covid mortality and looks at the relationship between vaccination and infection and hypothesises that the data is better explained by a temporal offset correction model that takes this into account. Further oddities in the population and death data are revealed in Section 6 and finally Section 7 discusses caveats in the analysis and draws conclusions."

Printed in Great Britain
by Amazon